A COLORADO HISTORY

THIRD EDITION
by
CARL UBBELOHDE
MAXINE BENSON
DUANE A. SMITH

PRUETT PUBLISHING CO.
BOULDER, COLORADO

Preface

Six years ago, when the first edition of this book was published, the Preface began with the statement: "This book is designed for reading, not for reference. It is intended to provide a modern introduction to the general history of Colorado for students and other readers, rather than to argue fine points of scholarship with specialists in local antiquities or legends, or to serve as a detailed, statistical reference work about the Centennial State." In preparing this edition for publication, we have continued that purpose, at the same time attempting to correct errors and redress imbalances that critics called to attention.

The first and most obvious alteration has been the change of authorship. The first edition appeared under the single name of Carl Ubbelohde; this edition has been jointly prepared by Ubbelohde (now Professor of History at Case Western Reserve University) and Maxine Benson (Colorado State Historian and Editor of *The Colorado Magazine*) and Duane A. Smith (Professor of History at Fort Lewis College). Together we have attempted to present a short history emphasizing the political and economic development of Colorado, without ignoring social and religious and educational activities in the Centennial State.

We have reduced in some measure the history of the pre-Territorial period and have expanded the chapters relating more recent events. Conscious of the need to describe the history of the state by observing all sections and regions of Colorado, we also have recognized the central role of the city of Denver—the political, economic and population center of the state. We have provided additional maps and illustrations, and an annotated list of published books and articles (arranged by chapters) to aid interested readers and curious students in finding their way to additional information and interpretations.

In replacing the footnotes of the first edition with the scaled-down "back notes" of this edition, it has been necessary to delete (except when directly quotes) all references to unpublished studies, particularly the many masters theses and doctoral dissertations that comprise a significant and useful source of knowledge about Colorado. Like all those who labor in the field of local history, we are indebted to the unnamed authors of those unpublished studies.

Our work has been greatly assisted by generous friends. In the first edition, particular acknowledgments were directed to Maurice Frink, former Director of the State Historical Society of Colorado, for reading and editing the manuscript; to Harry Kelsey, then State Historian and Editor of *The Colorado Magazine*, for permission to quote materials; to the University of Colorado Press, for similar privileges; and to Fred Pruett, an understanding publisher. In addition to those persons, and others named in the Preface to the first edition, we wish to express our gratitude to Tona Johnston, Elizabeth Opal, Alice Levine, and Ted Shields.

Carl Ubbelohde
Cleveland, Ohio
Maxine Benson
Washington, D.C.
Duane A. Smith
November, 1971   Durango, Colorado

Contents

1

A Prehistoric Prelude:
The Dwellers in the Cliffs

High above the valley floor stands the flat tableland. In later years the Spaniards called the river the Rio de los Mancos—the River of the Cripples; they termed the tableland Mesa Verde. Still later, Americans drew perpendicular lines and the tableland fell within the northeastern segment. It became part of Colorado. But that was centuries after the original mesa dwellers had vanished from the land.

The modern tourist, driving from Durango to Cortez on U. S. 160, sees the mesa looming large to the left, rising some 2,000 feet straight up from the floor of the valley. Twenty miles wide, it slopes backward from the startling promontory fifteen miles to the south. This flat tableland is cruelly severed by rugged canyons cut by eroding river water. On the mesa, and in its canyon walls, stands evidence of a civilization that had died long before any white man had climbed to the top of the tableland. No real knowledge or tradition passed from the cliff dwellers to their successors on the mesa; there is no historical link between the two civilizations. But man is always curious about his progenitors, and in the remnants of the cliff dwellers modern man finds much to ponder in casting up accounts of his own civilization.

Sometime in the unrecorded past, according to educated guesses, Oriental man found his way to Occidental America, crossing the Bering Strait and pushing down through the continents. The exact date of that migration may never be known. Perhaps 15,000, perhaps 20,000 or more years ago, Asiatic man found himself in the New World. Nomadic, depending upon wild animals and natural foods for sustenance, the American Indian battled the elements and the terrain for his very existence. Some of these Indians slowly changed their nomadic life and became an agricultural people, with fixed abodes and, in time, the additional refinements possible to those who forsake the hunt for the home.

The arrival of home-seeking Indians in the Mesa Verde region probably coincided with the beginning of the Christian Era in the Old World. From that time on, for the next thirteen centuries, they occupied the area. These Indian farmers passed through four more-or-less defined periods of advancement until, before they left the mesa, they could boast of a complex civilization.

The first time period, called the Basket Maker Period, extended from approximately the year 1 to 450 A.D. As long as the Indians retained their undomiciled lives, they left little evidence for the archeologist to use in reconstructing the patterns of their society. With the advent of fixed abodes arose the opportunity for the accumulation of artifacts that could later be unearthed and studied; long unused tools, household utensils, and weapons give us a picture of these Indians. Thus the earliest mesa dwellers of whom we have knowledge date from the era when they shed their nomadic habits and began to take up farming.

These short, black-haired, brown-skinned hunters learned the techniques of cultivating corn and squash, beginning the march from wanderers to stay-at-homes, with new leisure to develop arts and crafts. Of course that march was slow. Most of these early people probably never lived in houses, but sought shelter when it was needed in natural caves. Nor did they know how to make pottery. Their name, "Basket Makers," comes from their substitute for pottery— skillfully constructed, often decorated baskets. They designed baskets as containers for food and supplies; they wove baskets so tightly they could hold water or, by means of heated stones dropped into them could be used for cooking food.

Without houses, without pottery, the Basket Makers were handi-capped in comparison with later mesa dwellers. Probably their most serious deficiency was the lack of a good weapon. The bow and arrow had not yet made its appearance, and the first Basket Makers used instead the atlatl. This arm-extender or spear-thrower was a flattened, slender stick used to extend the reach of the arm and provide greater thrust in throwing a dart or a spear. It was neither accurate nor efficient as a weapon, leaving much to be desired for both hunting and warfare.

While the warm summer months on the mesa provided a climate in which clothing was not needed, the winter weather was severe enough to make clothes essential for comfort. The Basket Makers depended upon animal skins and woven fur strips fashioned into robes for protection against the cold. They wove sandals from yucca fibers. The only other article of clothing was a string apron worn at times by the women. Obviously, the Basket Makers limited their wardrobes to essentials. On the other hand, they were fond of jewelry and trinkets, and fashioned shells, bones, seeds, and stones into ornaments for their necks and ears. The great quantities of this jewelry found in the graves of the Basket Makers suggest that it played a large role in the lives of the Indians.

The Basket Makers' implements and tools ranged from wooden planting sticks to knives and scrapers, pipes and whistles. They used a *metate* or grinding stone to make flour of their corn. Their children were cradled in flexible reed "boards" with soft padding under the head, allowing the infants' skulls to develop naturally without abnormal flattening.

What elements of religion these Basket Makers professed and practiced is not easily deduced. They buried tools and jewelry with the dead, perhaps for the use of the departed in an afterlife. Burials were usually made in floors of caves or crevices in rocks; often more than one Basket Maker was placed in the same grave.

Such was the Indians' culture at the end of the first developmental period. They had made tremendous strides from their old nomadic life, conquering the secrets of planting and cultivating, harvesting and storing crops. Now modifications of those improvements slowly began to appear. The culture evolved into something so different from what it had been that a new term is needed to describe it.

The term "Modified Basket Maker Period" identifies the second developmental era, from 450 to 750 A.D. The changes were not simultaneous, but gradually three new elements made the Basket Makers' lives more complex, more modern than what they had known. To the amazing improvements their ancestors had perfected, the Modified Basket Makers added pottery, houses, and the bow and arrow.

The clay pottery that replaced the baskets probably was an invention borrowed from other tribes, rather than indigenously developed. Even so, the mesa Indians learned the new art slowly. Their first clumsy vessels were constructed of pure clay; they had little strength and less beauty. But they gradually added refinements: straw mixed with the clay, sand added for temper, rude kilns replaced sun baking. The pots provided a startling change from the basket days. New foods were added to the diet, and new methods of water storage eased the struggle for existence against the hazards of nature.

For housing the Modified Basket Makers developed the pithouse. They dug a hole, several feet deep and from ten to twenty feet in diameter. Then, using logs as a framework for the portion above the ground, they covered the framework with interwoven reeds and grass and placed a layer of earth over this "lath" to form combination sidewalls and roof. A small opening in the center of the roof provided both a smokehole for the firepit and an entrance used with a ladder. A ventilating tunnel furnished air for the fire in the pit. The Indians built some of their pithouses—probably the early ones—in caves, but gradually they abandoned those inaccessible sites for more expansive locations on the top of the mesa and in the valley floors. The new sites were relatively unprotected and suggest that the Modified Basket Makers lived without particular fear of their neighbors.

During these same years the bow and arrow replaced the atlatl. The mesa Indians probably borrowed the bow and arrow, like pottery, from other tribes. With characteristics peculiarly attractive to the game hunter, the new weapon offered greater accuracy at longer ranges than the atlatl.

Pottery, pithouses, and the bow and arrow were the radical advances of the era, but there were others. Beans were brought into the area as a new crop, and previously unknown varieties of corn appeared. The Indians domesticated the turkey, probably not for meat but certainly for the string-cloth fashioned from feathers to be woven into robes.

Then about 750 A.D. another demarcation line was crossed, leading into the Developmental Pueblo Period, which lasted until 1100 A.D. The word *pueblo* (Spanish for village or town) designates a most significant change during the eighth and following centuries. The Basket Makers had constructed most of their pithouses as single family structures. They had grouped their dwellings into villages, and some ruins indicate long rows of flat-roofed houses. Now, in the Developmental Pueblo Period, the Indians experimented with more complex multiple units, with walls of various materials, suggesting a pragmatic approach to an ancient housing problem. The Indians erected these new apartment houses all over the top of Mesa Verde. Ruins of similar structures exist in an extended area of the Four Corners region, into Utah, Arizona, and New Mexico. Population expansion seems obvious, while the unprotected nature of the mesa top dwellings suggests a period of tribal peace.

The first pueblos were rather crudely constructed of posts and adobe. By the end of the period, however, adobe had given way to masonry, increasingly well set. Some walls were now two stories high. And the kiva (a Hopi word used by archeologists to describe the rooms that resemble the modern Pueblo ceremonial chamber) now began to resemble the standard Mesa Verde kiva. Circular, subterranean, some twelve to fourteen feet in diameter, seven or eight feet deep, with walls of dressed stone, the kiva was located in front of the living rooms. Masonry pillars supported the roof of logs and adobe. Like the earlier pithouses, the kiva's only door was a small opening in the center of the roof, which also served as a smokehole. A vertical shaft brought air for the ceremonial fire on the floor. The *sipapu*, or small opening into the ground, symbolic entrance to the underworld or Mother Earth, indicates religious purposes for the kiva, although it probably was used for recreation as well. The resemblance between these kivas and the modern Pueblo ceremonial chambers affords an important clue to possible relationships between the prehistoric mesa Indians and modern Pueblo tribes.

Thus the Developmental society moved in architecture from the pithouse to the pueblo; from relatively crude to quite advanced construction. And there were other changes. The dull, natural hues of the pottery were abandoned for clear white, which showed designs more advantageously. Flat metates, as contrasted with the earlier trough-shaped stones, provided improvement in grinding corn.

The most novel change was the introduction of the wooden cradle board replacing the Basket Makers' pliable, pillowed reed-and-grass cradle. When archeologists unearth Pueblo skeletons they find the skulls deformed, with an exaggerated flattening of the back. For a time scholars believed that the Basket Makers and the Pueblos were two distinct, unrelated groups because of this radical difference in head shapes. More recently, with added study of physical characteristics, many authorities have come to believe that the skull differences resulted largely from the new type of cradle board. The hard, wooden board of the Pueblos was probably borrowed from some other group and became a popular fad.

The last two centuries of life on the mesa saw the climax of the long advance from simple agriculture to a complex culture—the Classic Pueblo Period of 1100 to 1300 A.D. During these two hundred years the Pueblos achieved their finest architecture. They carefully cut and laid up masonry walls; they plastered and decorated some of those walls with designs. Their villages became larger, containing many rooms; some rose to heights of three and four floors. The ruins of Far View House provide an interesting example. Here the Indians built an integrated complex of living and storage rooms, kivas, a walled court, and a tower.

Farming also reached new heights. Most crops were cultivated on the mesa top, but some small, terrace-like patches at the heads of the canyons were also used. In the floors of the canyons, the Pueblo people constructed dams for water storage—the earliest irrigation works in Colorado. Corn, beans, squash, and gourds were the main crops. For some items the Indians probably were dependent on trading expeditions outside the region, perhaps to the south. Cotton probably was not grown in any quantity on the Mesa Verde, so the presence of woven cotton cloth among the ruins suggests trade with other Indians. Salt, seashells, and turquoise also were acquired through trade.

This commerce with other people is one of the fascinating imponderables of these mysterious people. Just one old bill-of-lading would tell us much about them. But the Pueblo people never developed a system of writing. And that was only one of their limitations. They had no horses or livestock. They never developed the wheel. They used no metals.

Despite these limitations, the Classic Pueblo Period was a time of greatness. Some archeologists also believe it was a period of regimentation, with previously developed patterns used over and over again. The kivas became highly standardized, suggesting more rigid ceremonial practices. There also appears to have been a drawing together of the population and possibly a decline in total numbers. The pueblo dwellings became much larger, and tall round towers were built. Since the towers were usually connected by an underground tunnel with the kivas, they may have been used in ceremonials. But their strategic location, and possible use as watch towers, also suggests the need for vigilant defense.

And then the most startling innovation of all began. The Indians deserted the mesa top and built their pueblos in the caves in the walls of the canyons. Many families were involved in this descent to the caves; estimates of 600 to 800 separate cliff dwellings demonstrate the magnitude of the migration. Paradoxically, it was here, within the confined caves, that the pueblo builders produced their architectural masterpieces: Spruce Tree House, Square Tower House, and, most marvelous of all, the Cliff Palace.

Cliff Palace, Mesa Verde National Park.

Cliff Palace contained more than 200 one-room houses, forming a city in itself. It was built in terraces, rising three and four stories in places, with twenty-three kivas and housing adequate for more than 400 persons. The quality of the masonry construction and the interior plastering and painting of the walls in red and white represent refinements beyond anything known before.

Again the suggestion seems obvious: defensible sites for homes had become a necessity. Certainly the cliff dwellings in the almost inaccessible canyon walls provided an uncommon measure of security. Apparently some great danger, not present earlier, had come to threaten the mesa dwellers. But who or what that danger might have been can only be guessed at. Raids by nomadic tribes might have provided the impetus necessary to drive the farming Indians from the mesa into the caves of the canyons.

Whatever caused the concentration, it marked the beginning of the end of the Pueblo people in the Mesa Verde area. For a few more generations the cliff dwellers lived in their apartment houses in the caves. Then, at the end of the thirteenth century, they withdrew. They probably drifted southward; at least, tribal traditions of the Tewa, Hopi, and Zuni Indians tell of earlier migrations from the north.

The fact that the last quarter of the century—the years from 1272 to 1299—were years of extended drought may partly explain the withdrawal. These farming Indians, dependent upon their agriculture, probably sought other lands. But pressure upon the Pueblo people had earlier forced them into the caves, and there is no indication that they ever returned to the free and open days of mesa-top living. Perhaps the combination of the loss of security and the long drought made the once hospitable region no longer attractive to the cliff dwellers.

By the beginning of the fourteenth century the pueblos had become ghost towns. With their human inhabitants gone, the sophisticated structures suffered the usual ravages of wind and rain and began to decay and crumble. Before the processes of ruin had entirely erased the traces of these people, modern man stumbled into the area. In time he would act to preserve what remained as a monument to a civilization that had vanished—a prehistoric civilization of Colorado.

2

A Spanish Borderland

About two centuries after the cliff dwellers left Mesa Verde one of the great divides of human history was crossed. In 1492 three small vessels flying the Spanish flag and commanded by Christopher Columbus made their landfall in the Caribbean Sea. The Old World and the New World had met, and a new era had begun.

The frontiers of the Western Hemisphere now beckoned the leading nations of western Europe. Exploration, exploitation, and colonization became the great international games. The prizes—power, prestige, glorification of God through conversion of the heathen, and riches of gold and silver for royal treasuries—were enticing lures. For more than three centuries the game continued as the continents of America became pawns of the kings of Europe.

The Spanish nation was clearly in the lead during the sixteenth century. The Court of Madrid had financed Columbus and, with the help of the Papacy, it gained a demarcation between its lands and those of its then most dangerous rival, neighboring Portugal. Spain hurried preparations for additional voyages of discovery and conquest.

From her original toehold in the Caribbean islands, Spain pushed her fledgling empire in all directions. By 1521 Hernando Cortéz had reduced Mexico to a Spanish province, starting the flow of riches from the gold and silver mines there eastward across the Atlantic. Reaching out in search of further riches and souls for conversion, the conquerors continued their march.

Gold was the great lure that led all onward; beyond the horizon might be a second Mexico. The expedition led by Don Pánfilo de Narváez from Florida westward in 1528 was perhaps typical of many.

In some ways, however, it was unusual. Only four men escaped death from a shipwreck on the shores of the Texas gulf coast. One of the survivors was Cabeza de Vaca, the treasurer of the expedition. With his three comrades, he wandered the wilds of the interior regions of present-day Texas for six years. When these four "ghosts of the past" finally found their way to Mexico, they brought with them hair-raising tales of their exploits and rumors about seven cities of great wealth, situated somewhere to the north.

The rumors were similar to a European legend of seven bishops who had built seven cities on an island called Antillia in the Atlantic Ocean. That similarity should have made de Vaca's stories suspect, but in a new day of new worlds anything could be believed. To test the tale Antonio de Mendoza, the viceroy of New Spain, proposed a small scouting expedition to explore the northern frontier. He commissioned a Franciscan, Fray Marcos de Niza, to conduct the test. Estevan, an Arab Moor who had been with de Vaca, accompanied the friar. In 1539 Marcos and Estevan hurried northward from Mexico. They crossed the barren wastes of Sonora and eventually arrived in the Zuni country of what is now western New Mexico. Marcos sent Estevan on ahead; he never saw him again, for the Zuni put the Moor to death. The friar, learning of Estevan's fate, dared not go directly to the pueblo. But he climbed a ridge overlooking the buildings, viewing them from a distance. He seems to have assumed that he had found the fabulous Seven Cities.

Marcos hurried back to Mexico with his report corroborating de Vaca's rumor. The viceroy had now decided to mount a full scale expedition. He selected his personal friend, thirty-year-old Don Francisco Vásquez de Coronado, to lead the great enterprise. Together they gathered a remarkably strong force to search for the Seven Cities, now called "Cibola." Young Spanish noblemen eagerly volunteered for adventure and a chance at the gold. Some 200 horsemen, 70 foot soldiers, and almost 1,000 Indians joined the command. Livestock were driven along as a self-propelled food supply. The assembled expedition made a magnificent display as it rendezvoused at Compostella on the Pacific side of New Spain in the spring of 1540.

Once the march began the glamor and the splendor wilted fast. Northward from Compostella the caravan moved through desert country, finally reaching Hawikúh, the first of the Zuni pueblos. Cibola turned out to be no towering city of gold but only an unimposing village of Indian farmers. Fray Marcos' examination had been too hasty; his reports appeared fraudulent.

From Zuni, Coronado turned his forces eastward. Passing the Sky City of Acoma Pueblo, they travelled to the villages in the upper Rio Grande Valley. They spent the winter (1540-1541) near present-day Albuquerque. There they heard reports that the gold they were seeking was somewhere northeastward, at "Gran Quivira." The Pueblo Indians probably hoped to lure the Spanish away from their villages with these rumors. When spring came, Coronado set out to discover Quivira. He and his men journeyed into the Texas Panhandle and then turned north into the Arkansas River Valley in what is now Kansas. There they discovered that the villages of the Wichita Indians were even less imposing, even less like Cibola, than the pueblos of New Mexico.

Coronado turned his forces back again to the Rio Grande Valley, where they spent another winter. When warm weather returned they retraced their long pathway to Mexico. So ended the Coronado expedition—without silver or gold.

Of course, knowledge of the country had been gained and later colonizers could profit from that. And substantial foundations had been added to Spain's claim to the northern regions. But prospecting had turned sour. For decades thereafter, the Spaniards diverted their eyes from the north. More than a half-century passed before interest in the Rio Grande Valley revived.

When Spain again looked toward pueblo-land, it was for a different reason. England's bold sea dog, Francis Drake, had sailed his *Golden Hind* into the Pacific; Spain was certain he had found the Northwest Passage. To secure its claims against rival England, Spain decided to settle its northern frontier. In 1598, Juan de Oñate started for the valley of the pueblos, under contract from the Crown, with 130 soldier-settler families, a band of Franciscan friars, some 270 Indian and Negro slaves, and 7,000 head of stock. The "kingdom and provinces of New Mexico" was born that year. By 1609 Spain had founded the Royal City of Santa Fe, for many years to be the capital of the northern outpost of the empire, 1,500 miles from the seat of the vice-royalty at Mexico City.

Cross and Crown played dual roles in New Mexico as they had earlier in New Spain. The missionary friars were as eager to save the souls of Pueblo Indians as soldiers were to stretch the boundaries of the empire. Together priest and captain established an uneasy ascendancy over the Pueblo tribes as far north as Taos. The Spanish tried to protect the Pueblo people against the nomadic, marauding tribes of the plains. In the seventeenth century, the Apaches and their kinsmen the Navajos kept up a perpetual pressure on the fringes of the New Mexican outpost.

The far-spread Apache family, an Athapascan tribe of unexact origins, was divided into many subgroups. Together they encircled the pueblo region. Not all of the Indians were unfriendly; those roaming the regions to the northeast—called by the Spaniards the Palomas, Quartelejos, Carlaneas, and Jicarillas—tended to keep the peace. On the other hand, the Faraon Apaches on the east and the Gila Apaches and Navajos on the west seemed to be constant trouble-makers.

Farther north, in the mountains whose streams fed the Rio Grande, lived the then-friendly Utes. These Indians probably were originally from the northwest, for they were allied in language with the Shoshoni family. They never practiced agriculture, living instead by the spoil of their hunts and wars. The Utes were the most permanent residents of the Colorado region. They were in possession of the mountain passes at the time of the earliest Spanish penetration and would remain there far into the future.

It was not easy for Spain to devise a consistent policy toward the nomadic tribes. The friars attempted to spread the Gospel among them, but the lack of fixed abodes and the war-like tendencies of most of the tribes made conversions difficult. White settlers and their pueblo converts traded with the plains hunters, especially at the Taos fairs where the Indians exchanged deerskins, buffalo hides, and captive slaves for knives, horses, beads, and trinkets. But when marauders endangered the mission villages, warfare was necessary. And when runaway slaves from the pueblos sought sanctuary among the nomads, the Spaniards used force, if necessary, to win them back.

Gradually, through punitive expeditions against Indians and journeys to retrieve fugitives, the Spaniards pushed northward from Santa Fe, acquainting themselves with the area of present-day Colorado. Although it may not have been the first such expedition, sometime in the years between 1664 and 1680 Juan de Archuleta led a search party north from Taos to find and recapture Pueblo Indians who had escaped to a place called "El Quartelejo." The exact location of "El Quartelejo" has never been determined, but it was probably in southeastern Colorado, fifty or sixty miles east of the present city of Pueblo. From Archuleta's expedition, the Spaniards learned about the valley of the Arkansas River, known to them as the Nepesta or Nepestle River.

Toward the end of the seventeenth century, Spanish control of New Mexico was almost extinguished. In 1680 the Pueblos revolted against the European masters. The white colonists who escaped being killed fled southward to the Franciscan mission near El Paso where they remained for twelve years, waiting for a day of return. In 1692, under the leadership of Don Diego de Vargas, Spain re-established supremacy over the pueblo villages.

During these same years significant changes occurred in the regions north of Santa Fe. The Comanches, an offshoot of the Shoshoni tribe of Wyoming, moved their customary hunting grounds south to escape the pressures of the Sioux. Their linguistic kinsmen, the Utes, joined them in wars against the Apaches in the Arkansas River Valley. With the coming of the Comanches, the Utes, who had formerly been at peace with the Spaniards, turned hostile. They joined their new friends in attacks on the Pueblos as well as on the Apaches.

Added to the difficulties of Pueblo revolts and the hostile Comanches and Utes was the seemingly greater danger of imperial France. Following La Salle's trip down the Mississippi River in 1682, French traders and explorers travelled up the rivers that fed the Father of Waters. France soon claimed the drainage basins of the many tributaries to the west, stretching all the way to the crest of the Rocky Mountains. As French traders advanced up the Red and Arkansas rivers from Louisiana, their trade with the plains Indians in arms and horses flourished.

Pueblo revolts, Comanche and Ute raids, and French aggression each played a part in opening the northern regions to the Spaniards. The return to Santa Fe in 1692 under Vargas did not immediately end Pueblo efforts to rid themselves of their Spanish masters. In 1696 revolt flared again. The Picuris Pueblos fled northeastward to El Quartelejo. In 1706 Juan de Ulibarri, in command of 40 troops and 100 Indian allies, marched out to bring them back. Ulibarri traversed the region from Taos to the site of the present city of Pueblo and then turned east to Quartelejo. Here, in a formal ceremony, he claimed the area for his Spanish sovereign, Philip V. Spain, of course, had claimed it all along, but the French threats seemed to make a formal ceremony necessary. Ulibarri named the settlement Santo Domingo and titled the region San Luis. Then, having retrieved the fugitive Indians, he returned with them to Santa Fe.

Ulibarri also brought unwelcome news to the officials in Santa Fe. French traders had successfully penetrated the western plains. The Quartelejo Apaches reported frequent raids on their people by the powerful Pawnee tribe from the Platte River region to the north. The

Pawnee were friends of the French; French arms and tools captured in skirmishes were exhibited to prove it.

Similar disquieting evidence was uncovered thirteen years later, in 1719. Don Antonio Valverde, the governor of New Mexico, set forth that year on an extensive expedition to punish the Utes and Comanches. Valverde led his men through the country of friendly Jicarilla Apaches in northeastern New Mexico to the headwaters of the Purgatoire River (then the Rio de las Animas Perdidas en Purgatorio—the River of the Souls Lost in Purgatory), to the Arkansas River, and then east to the vicinity of present-day Las Animas. Here they were met by Quartelejo Apaches who substantiated the rumors of French activity and impressed upon them the problems they faced from raiding Comanches, Utes, and Pawnees.

The viceroyalty at Mexico City seemed to fear the French menace much more than the dangers of hostile Indians. A Council of War in January, 1720, ordered Governor Valverde to conduct reconnaissance against the intruding French. In response, Valverde sent an expedition led by Don Pedro de Villasur northeast to seek out the French. Villasur followed the now traditional route to El Quartelejo and from there continued north until he reached the Platte River. He then turned his force to follow the Platte downstream. Some distance from a Pawnee village, somewhere near the forks of the Platte, the hostile Pawnees, armed with French weapons, ambushed Villasur's party. The blow to the Spanish was crushing; the Pawnees killed thirty-two of the forty-two soldiers, including the leader, Villasur. Those fortunate enough to escape alive staggered back to New Mexico with the unwelcome news of the defeat.

The authorities at Mexico City now urged the establishment of a presidio or military garrison at El Quartelejo as a buffer against the French. The New Mexican officials, however, argued against it. They claimed the location was too distant and too exposed to be safe, and proposed the site called La Jicarilla, closer to the New Mexican settlements, as an alternative. In the end, no outpost was established at all. Rather, the Spanish invited the friendly Apaches to resettle in the Taos valley.

Actually, the French intrusion was temporarily halted. The Comanches had no desire to allow their Apache enemies to receive French arms and had created a buffer zone through which French traders did not pass. But farther north the French investigated other routes. Etienne Veniard de Bourgmont, in 1724, moved as far west as present central Kansas, presumably searching for a trade route from the Mississippi Valley to Santa Fe. And after him, in 1739, such a route actually was opened by two French brothers, Pierre and Paul Mallet, who travelled from Kaskaskia, in Illinois, up to the Missouri and Platte rivers and then southward to the Arkansas River. From there an Indian guide led them to Santa Fe. An embryonic trade route now connected the French and Spanish New World settlements.

Mid-eighteenth century witnessed remarkable changes on the northern New Mexican frontier. The Comanches had driven the northern Apaches from their homelands. Some of the Apaches sought sanctuary near the pueblos in the Rio Grande Valley. Others fled farther south. With French arms readily available, Comanche raids on the New Mexican settlements increased.

In addition, the Ute-Comanche alliance came to an end. The reasons for the separation of the former friends are unclear, but the effect for the Spanish was beneficial. Now the Utes made peace at Taos and, in a "diplomatic revolution," joined the Apaches and Spanish in their wars against the Comanches.

Also, the rivalry between France and Spain began to abate. In Europe, Spain and France were now allied in wars against Great Britain. This, of itself, did not bring a sudden end to their rivalry in America. Spain still viewed French control of Louisiana with sufferance and continued her determined policy of keeping the French from extending their province farther toward the southwest. But in 1762, France ceded to Spain all of Louisiana west of the Mississippi River. The northern frontier was again Spanish land and would remain so for the next forty years.

Spain's interest now shifted to the regions northwest of Santa Fe. Three years after the cession of Louisiana, in 1765, Don Juan Maria de Rivera led an exploring party from Santa Fe along the San Juan Mountains to the Gunnison River in search of precious metals. Rivera's party returned with ore samples, although they were not rich enough to generate great excitement. Even so, other prospectors probably followed Rivera into the La Plata region. At least, by the next decade the principal rivers there were designated by Spanish names.

New dangers now began to appear in the Far West, where Russia and Great Britain were threatening Spain's Pacific coast claims. The authorities of New Spain began to consider the feasibility of an overland route to connect the California settlements with those of the Rio Grande valley and northern Mexico. This consideration led to what some historians have called the greatest Spanish exploring adventure in the Southwest.

In 1776, year of independence for some far-off British colonies along the Atlantic coast, two Spanish priests started northwestward from Santa Fe. Fathers Francisco Domínguez and Silvestre Escalante, with eight other men (several of whom had been with Rivera earlier and thus knew something of the country they now traversed), worked their way along the San Juan Mountains to the Dolores River. From there the expedition travelled to the Gunnison and then north to the White River. Turning west, they headed toward the Great Salt Lake. The heavy snows and winter storms forced them to return to Santa Fe without reaching California, but the two Franciscan friars had led the first white expedition through some of the most treacherous terrain in all North America.

Meanwhile, the constant chastisement of hostile Indians continued. Since the Comanches were particularly troublesome and dangerous, the Spanish believed that crushing them would have excellent effects in dealing later with other tribes. In 1779 Governor Don Juan Bautista de Anza, with some 573 men, later to be joined by Apache and Ute allies, travelled northward from Santa Fe into the San Luis Valley. They crossed Poncha Pass and a segment of South Park. Instead of Comanches they found only a large herd of grazing buffalo. But, climbing the Front Range, they dropped down onto the eastern foothills. Here were the Comanches, led by Cuerno Verde— Greenhorn—their great chief. Anza's men delivered a resounding defeat to the Indians. Cuerno Verde, his eldest son, and some of his most renowned warriors died from wounds inflicted at the final encounter on Greenhorn Creek near the base of Greenhorn Mountain.

The Comanches were ready to make peace with the Spaniards, but an obstacle stood in the way. The friendly Utes, now sworn enemies of the Comanches, feared the effect such a peace might have on their own relations with the Spanish. Consequently, the first step was to bring the Utes and Comanches into friendship again. This Governor Anza accomplished in 1786, after which peace with the Comanches was possible. After suitable ceremonies the Comanches agreed to treaty terms with the Spanish, promising to give up their nomadic life and settle in villages after the manner of the Pueblos. Spain agreed to help them in the transition. Governor Anza selected a site in the Arkansas Valley, probably near the present city of Pueblo. There he sent laborers and supplies to build houses, seeds for planting fields, sheep, and cattle.

The Spanish called the intended settlement San Carlos. Begun in 1787, it failed early. The first year a Comanche woman died at the village. This the Indians considered a divine sign of the disapproval of their gods. They hurried away and the Spanish could not lure them back. So ended the first and last attempt by the Spanish to settle a village within the boundaries of present-day Colorado.

From Coronado in 1540 to short-lived San Carlos in 1787, Spain failed to push her settlements north of Santa Fe. To the east she colonized in Texas; on the Pacific coast her missions in California flourished. But the stretches north of New Mexico were never settled. In her search for precious metals, Spain failed to uncover the riches of the Rocky Mountains. The "northern mystery" remained from her, almost untouched. Utes and Comanches retained their hunting grounds, unspoiled by adobe pueblo, mission, or presidio. In the coming century, other men would dig the gold and silver the Spanish sought, but failed to find, in the northern borderland.

3

Exploring Louisiana

With the closing of the eighteenth century, European domination of North America neared an end. On the Atlantic seaboard, thirteen British colonies waged a war for independence and established a new republic. The United States of America stood as a model for other colonies to use as a pattern for revolution and independence.

Europe was soon rocked by the wars of the French Revolution and the Napoleonic struggles that followed. Out of those upheavals came a large severance of territory from the empire called New Spain. In 1800 Napoleon Bonaparte secured for France her old colony of Louisiana, giving to Spain in return a kingdom in Italy. At the time of this retrocession, France agreed that she would neither sell nor trade Louisiana to any other country.

But Napoleon's dreams of a revived French empire in North America vanished with his failure to control Hispaniola in the Caribbean. He offered Louisiana to the United States, and the young republic quickly grabbed the bargain. In 1803, in the most advantageous real estate transaction in its history, the United States doubled its size. Through the purchase, the eastern stretches of the former Spanish frontier became the territory of the United States.

The American people could not fully appreciate the bargain they had made, for the land beyond the Mississippi River was almost completely unknown to them. But official expeditions, financed by the federal government, soon started westward to gather information about the new territories. The famed Lewis and Clark expedition, planned before the territory was purchased, traversed the northern regions to the Pacific coast. And at the time that Lewis and Clark headed homeward, another exploring expedition was dispatched toward the southwest, led by a young lieutenant of the United States Army, Zebulon Montgomery Pike.

Lieutenant Pike was born in New Jersey in 1779. He had entered the army at an early age and had risen to the rank of lieutenant by 1805. In that year the army gave him his first opportunity at exploring. He headed an investigation of the upper Mississippi basin, visiting trading posts and taking official possession of the area for the United States.

The next year, on July 15, 1806, twenty-seven-year-old Pike set out from Fort Belle Fontaine, above St. Louis, on his southwestern expedition. Most of the twenty-two men with him were veterans from the Mississippi expedition. Their instructions were to return a party of Osage Indians who had been captured by the Potawatomis to their native villages; to arrive, if possible, at some "understanding" with the Comanches; to observe the geography, natural history, and topography; and to collect mineral and botanical specimens. When they reached the Arkansas River they were to split into two groups. Some of the men would descend the river to its mouth; the others would follow the river to its source, locate the headwaters of the Red River, and then descend that stream.

Pike's group travelled by boat to the Osage Indian villages near the present boundary between Kansas and Missouri. There they obtained horses and crossed the prairies to the Republican River where they met the old allies of the French, the Pawnees. An expedition of some 600 mounted Spanish troops from Santa Fe, led by Lieutenant Don Facundo Malgares, had recently visited the Pawnees. In some way the New Mexican officials had heard of Pike's expedition and had sent Lieutenant Malgares to find him.

The Spaniards appeared formidable to the Pawnees, especially compared with the small American force. The Indians advised Pike to turn east and forget about exploring, explaining that they had promised the Spanish they would warn Americans against advancing further west. Although somewhat apprehensive that the Pawnees might try to detain him, Pike determined to move on to the Arkansas River.

At the Big Bend of that river, Pike divided his party as directed. Six men descended the river in canoes while Pike led the rest of the company upstream. In mid-November they sighted the Rocky Mountains, giving "with one accord ... three *cheers* to the *Mexican Mountains*." By the end of the month they had reached the present site of Pueblo where they built a breastwork of logs for defense against hostile Indians or Spaniards.

North of the breastwork was a high peak that Pike had earlier described as a "small blue cloud" when he first saw it from the prairies. He now decided to try to reach its summit. Two and one-half days of climbing brought Pike and his companions near the top of Mount Miller (or possibly Blue Mountain), from which they could see the high peak they had set out to climb, still miles away. Pike decided that "no human being could have ascended to its pinical [sic]" in the condition he and his men were in; they wore only light cotton overalls. Snow lay waist-deep on the ground. So Pike failed to reach the summit, but he was the first American to describe the mountain and men who came after him called it Pike's Peak.

Moving west from the breastwork, the explorers camped one night near the present site of Florence; the next night found them at the mouth of the Royal Gorge. Pike believed he was now near the headwaters of the Arkansas, convinced that the narrow canyon indicated the main body of the river was below and not above him. He detoured to the north, moved into South Park—the Bayou Salado of the Spanish—and examined the regions of the upper Arkansas, mistaking the river for the Red.

It was now late in December. Supplies were running low. For two days before Christmas the men were practically without food. Then they found buffalo to celebrate the holiday, deep in the ranges of the Rockies.

By the fifth of January they had followed the Arkansas downstream through its gorge, discovering to their intense disappointment that they were back again where they had started. They had not found the Red River; their condition grew more and more desperate. Their horses were unfit for riding and their supplies were almost entirely expended. Pike built a blockhouse and left two men there; still determined to find the Red River, he led the rest of his company southward.

They encountered incredible hardships. But despite frozen feet and near starvation, they crossed the Sangre de Cristo range into the San Luis Valley. When they reached the Conejos River, Pike and his men built a fort of cottonwood logs. There the Stars and Stripes fluttered for the first time in the breezes of the San Luis Valley.

Pike thought he was on the Red River; actually, the Conejos is a tributary of the Rio Grande. Since they were west of the Rio Grande, the Americans were interlopers on presumed Spanish soil. In February scouts from New Mexico found them and invited them to go to Santa Fe. Although politely phrased, the request was obviously a command, not a casual suggestion. Knowing well enough that he had not force to fight the Spanish, Pike agreed to go.

In Santa Fe, Governor Alencaster confiscated Pike's papers and interrogated him at length. The governor seemed convinced that the Americans were spies and decided to send them to Chihuahua, 550 miles to the south. Alencaster assigned Lieutenant Malgares the duty of escorting Pike's party on most of the long journey. So the Spanish officer who had ridden out to intercept Pike on the Kansas plains the year before now guarded the American prisoners.

At Chihuahua, Governor Salcedo, after examining both the men and their papers, decided to keep the papers and send the men home. Again under guard, Pike and his companions were marched to the Louisiana-Texas border, where in July, 1807, the Spanish released them.

Pike had been promoted to captain during the expedition and other promotions followed. During the War of 1812, the thirty-four-year-old Pike, then a brigadier general, was fatally wounded leading the American attack on York (Toronto), Canada.

In some respects, Pike's expedition proved disappointing; he failed to find the source of the Arkansas and Red rivers. But he gathered valuable information about the geography and natural resources of the Southwest. Even though the Spanish confiscated many of his papers, Pike published his observations and impressions of what he had done and seen. His report, printed in 1810, was eagerly read in the United States. Europeans seemed no less interested as editions of Pike's journal appeared in England, France, Germany, and Holland. Zebulon Montgomery Pike was the first American—the first writer in English—to describe the mountain of his name and other such landmarks as South Park, the Royal Gorge, the Sangre de Cristo Mountains, and the San Luis Valley. Add to that his descriptions of the Spanish borderlands, from Taos to Chihuahua, and it is understandable why an expansive America delighted in his report.

When Pike made his exploratory journey into the Southwest, a definitive boundary had not been negotiated to divide American Louisiana from the provinces of New Spain. At the time of the purchase, Talleyrand, the French Foreign Minister, is reported to have answered questions by the Americans about the limits of Louisiana: "You have made a noble bargain and I presume you will make the best of it." "Making the best of it" was exactly what the Americans proceeded to do. The northern boundary was established in negotiations with Great Britain in 1818 at the forty-ninth parallel, from the Lake of the Woods on the east to the Stony (Rocky) Mountains on the west. The following year John Quincy Adams, the American Secretary of State, negotiated a treaty with Spain delineating the southern and western boundaries. The two nations agreed on a line drawn westward along the Red River, north on the one hundredth meridian, west again on the Arkansas River, north from its source to the forty-second parallel, and from there straight west to the Pacific Ocean. Everything north and east of the line was American; everything south and west was Spanish.

In the area now definitely established as United States territory lived Indians who were not consulted about their preference of white man's rule. The boundary line was drawn and agreed to at Washington and Madrid without regard for the actual inhabitants of the region. Yet while white men argued the fine points of their dividing line, the Indians were engaged in determining their own possession of the region.

The high country of the Central Rockies was still in the hands of the Utes. White men could come and white men could go, but the Utes still held their hunting grounds in the parks and valleys of the high mountains. The Ute tribe was composed of seven bands: the Weeminuche, Mouache, and Capote (Southern Utes) living in the southwestern corner of future Colorado; the Tabeguache or Uncompaghre band in the central Western Slope area; and the Grand River, Yampa and Uintah bands, who formed the Northern Utes. The tribe was now well equipped with horses, bought or stolen from the New Mexican settlements or captured in war or from wild herds. The horses eased the nomadic life of the Utes and increased the effectiveness of their warriors in battle.

The Utes kept a watchful eye on the plains to the east, where another transition in tribal occupancy was developing. In much the same fashion as the Comanches had moved south, pushing the Apaches from the Eastern Slope, new tribes from the north now were filling up the land between the Arkansas and Platte rivers. Among the newcomers were the Kiowas, drifting south from the headwaters of the Yellowstone and Missouri rivers. In time the Kiowas became friends of the Comanches and joined them in their hunting grounds, south of the Arkansas River.

At about the same time, or possibly a little later, two other new tribes took up a roving residence on the Eastern Slope plains. Both of these tribes were from the great Algonquian linguistic stock of the northeast: the Arapahoes and the Cheyennes. The Arapahoes originally had come from the Great Lakes region. Pressure, presumably by the Sioux (beyond which undoubtedly was similar pressure from advancing white men), caused the Arapahoes to move south and west. As they took up temporary hunting grounds in the Black Hills, they were joined by their linguistic kinsmen, the Cheyennes.

White men first encountered the Cheyenne tribe in the middle of the eighteenth century in northern Minnesota. When they left the upper Mississippi Valley, like the Arapahoes, they turned from a somewhat sedentary people to nomads on the plains. Moving first to the Missouri River, they found homes near the junction of that waterway and the Cheyenne River. From there, with the pressure of the Sioux still upon them, they wandered into the Black Hills and friendship with the Arapahoes.

Together the two tribes then moved along the eastern base of the Rockies, forcing the Kiowas to join the Comanches south of the Arkansas River. Perhaps by 1815, that river divided the tribes as an uneasy, unstable boundary. Sometime around the year 1840, the Arapahoes and Cheyennes would effect a peace settlement with the Kiowas and Comanches. Meanwhile, the undying friendship and alliance between the Arapahoes and the Cheyennes continued. The relationship begun in the Black Hills would remain even after the Cheyenne tribe had divided into two groups, with a southern segment clustered in the reaches of the Arkansas River and a northern group living in the area of the North Platte and Yellowstone headwaters.

These, then, were the tribes of the Rocky Mountain frontier at the time Spain and the United States arranged their international boundary: the Utes in the mountains, the Cheyennes and Arapahoes on the plains from the Arkansas to the Platte rivers, and the Kiowas and Comanches south of the Arkansas River. Toward the east, the Pawnee tribe chased buffalo in the Republican River area; in the North Platte region, the Sioux sometimes hunted in the outskirts of the Cheyenne and Arapahoe lands.

All of these tribes were nomadic, except the Pawnee who built earth lodges. The others lived in tepees or lodges made of buffalo skins stretched over a framework of light poles, making abodes easy to dismantle and transport. The Indians' basic diet was buffalo meat, but they also enjoyed meals of antelope, deer, rabbit, and dog. Buffalo and deer skins (often elaborately decorated) provided clothing. The bow and arrow gave the tribes an excellent weapon for both hunt and war. With portable lodges, horses for transportation, and a buffalo culture that made use of every item of the shaggy beast, the plains Indians wandered as game and weather directed. Although their areas of hunting and "home" were more or less well delineated, the tribes did not live completely isolated from each other. The plains Indians sometimes sought pines for lodge poles in the mountains; when buffalo became scarce in the mountain parks, the Utes would descend to the plains for some killing. Between the Arapahoe and Cheyenne tribes on the plains and the Utes in the mountains hostility was ever present.

One of the first reports that the Arapahoes and Cheyennes had come to live in the Eastern Slope area was brought back to the eastern states in 1820 by the members of the Long Expedition to the mountains. For thirteen years after the return of Pike and his men, the western region had received scant attention from official Washington. Other events had commanded attention—the continuing maritime problems with Great Britain and France; the actual war with Great Britain; the settlement of the Indian problems in the Old Northwest and in the Florida region; the expansion of population, industry, and agriculture in the burst of prosperity immediately following the war.

Then, with the settlement of the boundaries of Louisiana, official attention again was directed toward the West. Initial plans for a new reconnaissance of the western reaches were much more ambitious and extensive than the blueprint for Pike's journey had been. The "Yellowstone Expedition," as the public liked to call the new survey, envisioned a force of men moving up the Missouri River, searching the area for scientific information and establishing a federal fort at the Mandan Indian villages or at the mouth of the Yellowstone River. The fort would keep the Indians peaceful, negate the influence of British traders, and open a route to Oregon and, perhaps, even to China beyond. The army commissioned Colonel Henry Atkinson to lead the military phase of the expedition; Major Stephen H. Long was put in charge of the scientific phase.

Stephen H. Long, like his fellow-officer Pike, was eastern-born, a native of New Hampshire, a graduate of Dartmouth College. He had taught school and, on entering the Army Engineer Corps, had become a mathematics instructor at West Point. His exploring career started in 1817 when he was sent to investigate the Wisconsin and Fox rivers, tributaries of the upper Mississippi. He had also been commissioned to select sites for defensive forts in Arkansas and Minnesota.

The proposed fort at the Mandan villages was part of this general pattern of fortifications. It would help to hold the Indians in check, open the way for fur traders, and clear an eventual path for actual settlers. In July 1819, the much-heralded Yellowstone Expedition got

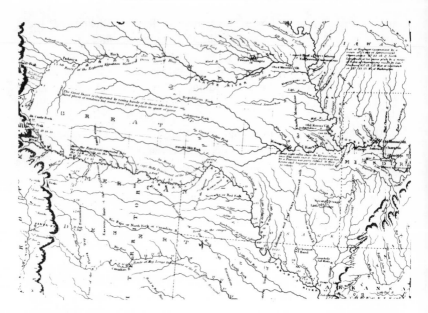

Long Expedition, showing Front Range area. (State Historical Society of Colorado)

underway. A steamboat, with bow decorations in the form of a dragon spitting smoke, designed to awe the Indians, started up the Missouri River. It progressed no further than Council Bluffs and there, as autumn descended, the expedition halted, largely because of the difficulties of steamboating on the shallow Missouri. The men built Fort Atkinson for winter quarters, and there an unfortunate outbreak of scurvy in the garrison resulted in many deaths. A curious American public, expecting significant reports from the expedition, was severely disappointed. Congress began to withdraw its support from the scheme.

Despite the trouble, however, the army did decide to conduct a different sort of expedition. Major Long, after a winter in the East, was sent back to Council Bluffs with directions to conduct a short, quick trip out to the western mountains to search for the source of the Platte River. He was to return by way of the Arkansas and Red rivers. Thus, while the federal government wrote off the military phase as a failure, it allowed the scientific phase something of a second chance.

Major Long organized an exploring party of nineteen men, including topographers, a map maker, a zoologist, a physician-botanist-geologist, a naturalist, and a landscape painter. The men were mounted on horses and, since the summer weather favored rapid travel, they made extraordinarily good time crossing the prairies. By the end of June, 1820, they were in view of the Rockies. Riding up the Platte Valley they viewed the mountain that later trappers and traders would call "Long's Peak," mistaking it at first for Pike's "great peak." The party continued past the present sites of Greeley and Denver, celebrating the Fourth of July in the river valley where "imagination only" had "travelled before . . . where civilization never existed—and yet . . . within the limits" of the United States. Each man got a gill of whiskey from the rations to celebrate the day.

Long guided his men over the divide separating the Platte and Arkansas valleys, following Monument Creek to the site of present-day Colorado Springs. Here Edwin James, the young scientist who would later write the history of the expedition, decided to try to climb Pike's Peak. With six companions, he started out early one morning. Four of the men remained at the base of the mountain to make measurements; they would miscalculate the height of the peak by 3,000 feet because they assumed they were much lower in elevation themselves than they really were. Dr. James and two of the men, each equipped with a blanket, a few pounds of buffalo meat, and a pound of corn meal, climbed from noon on, camping that night on the mountain side. The next morning they started upward again and by mid-afternoon they had reached the summit. They were the first white men on record to climb America's most famous mountain, and James was the first botanist in North America to collect specimens of the brilliant alpine flora above timberline. Major Long, in honor of their feat, labelled the mountain "James' Peak" in his reports. To the public, however, the mountain still belonged to Pike.

From the peak, Long's party continued southward to the Arkansas River. They examined the valley westward to the Royal Gorge and then moved downstream for a distance. Following plans, Long now split the men into two parties. Each group was to make its way back east to Fort Smith by a different route. Captain John R. Bell, with eleven men, descended the Arkansas River, while Major Long and the rest of the party turned south to search for the Red River. They crossed the Purgatory and the Cimarron, and came to a large river they assumed to be the Red. On this stream they turned eastward, only to discover after a time that the river emptied into the Arkansas and that they had been on the Canadian, not the Red River.

By the middle of September the two groups again were together at

Fort Smith, both having travelled downstream on the same river. The expedition had accomplished nothing as far as determining the sources of the Platte, Arkansas, or Red rivers. When compared with Pike's earlier journey, which had actually pierced the ranges of the Rockies, the Long exploration looks like a summer's outing in the mountains. Long and his men seem to have acted more like soldiers, less like explorers; they performed perfunctorily, without particular enterprise or imagination. They did collect quantities of important information about the Indian tribes of the plains and scientific information about the flora and fauna of the regions they traversed. But they had failed to identify the river heads they were commissioned to find, and the source of that elusive stream, the Red River of the South, was still unmapped.

Major Long later made other exploratory trips to the regions of Minnesota and the Red River of the North. Later still he became a railroad engineer, surveying part of the original route of the Baltimore and Ohio Railroad, inventing a new type of railroad bridge, writing the first textbook on railroading published in the United States. He died in 1864.

From the time of his western expedition until long after his death, the effects of the reports from his trip to the mountains would live on. Those reports had been particularly discouraging about the country east of the Rocky Mountains. Long labelled the region the "Great American Desert" on his maps, and his reports expanded on Pike's earlier pessimistic predictions that the "vast plains ... may become in time equally celebrated as the sandy desarts [sic] of Africa; for I saw in my route, in various places, tracts of many leagues, where the wind had thrown up the sand, in all the fanciful forms of the ocean's rolling wave, and on which not a speck of vegetable matter existed."

Major Long's reports claimed the whole region to be "uninhabitable by a people depending on agriculture" for a livelihood; the area would much better "remain the unmolested haunt of the native hunter, the bison, and the jackall." The concept of the Great American Desert proved long lived: for generations, maps in school texts continued the label and description, and American children grew up believing the high plains did indeed resemble the sandy Sahara.

Almost two decades of exploring by official expeditions had accomplished little more than slight scratchings on the surface of the Louisiana Purchase. A few of the rivers had been charted, but many more remained unmapped. Most of the plains and the mountains had yet to yield their secret resources. When white men fully explored the area, it would be men other than officers in the United States Army who led the way. It was left to the "Mountain Men," following the beaver trails, to become the true explorers of the Rocky Mountain frontier.

4

The Fur Frontier

Major Long's Great American Desert looked to some of his countrymen like a gift from the gods. An inhospitable desert frontier would ensure the purity of republican America against dangerous contacts with Old World monarchical institutions. What better defense against Spanish intrigues could there be than a wide buffer zone separating the United States and Spanish New Mexico? But to other Americans the desert was a challenge. In land miles, Santa Fe was only half as far from the Missouri River as it was from the Mexican capital. All trade goods had to be brought into New Mexico from the south, across hundreds of miles of difficult terrain. But if the western prairies could be crossed, and Santa Fe reached from the American river towns, a splendid commerce might be built, bridging the international boundary.

The idea was not new; the French had pursued the same scheme in the eighteenth century. Now, as then, obstacles stood in the way. Not the least of these was the age-old Spanish hostility toward alien interference in their imperial trade. But if Spanish rule in Mexico should end, that obstacle might be removed.

When the news of the abortive Hidalgo Revolt reached the United States in 1812, a group of nine or ten men, including Robert McKnight, James Baird, and Samuel Chambers, started overland from the Missouri Valley with trade goods for New Mexico. They expected a friendly welcome and large profits in a province no longer a part of the Spanish Empire. But by the time they reached Santa Fe the revolt had been crushed. Instead of welcoming the Americans, the New Mexican officials imprisoned them in the *calabozos*. There they spent almost a decade. The unlucky prairie traders were not released until the Iturbide revolution brought actual independence to Mexico in 1821.

Once the ties of empire had been broken, Mexican officials were indeed willing to expand their sources of supply. William Becknell was one of the first to discover the change in policy. Becknell was a merchant in the town of Franklin, Missouri. In September, 1821, with some twenty men, he travelled along the Arkansas River, and crossed Raton Pass into New Mexico. By the end of January, 1822, he was back in Franklin, reportedly emptying moneybags of big silver dollars on the streets and spreading the good word that the Mexicans wanted American trade. Becknell hurried to return with more goods. This time he used three wagons on a new route that cut across the Cimarron Desert. In so doing he justly earned his nickname, "The Father of the Santa Fe Trade," for he demonstrated that wagons could be used to cross the prairies. His route became the main trail of the westering merchants.

Trailing down to Santa Fe gradually became a more-or-less organized enterprise. The trail started at Independence, Missouri, a town connected by river boats with St. Louis, the emporium of all western trade. From Independence, the wagoners crossed well-watered prairies 150 miles to the tall timbers of Council Grove. There they halted and organized "trains" for defense against the Indian interference they could expect along the rest of the route. The men elected a captain of the caravan who was charged with maintaining order and defense. Leaving Council Grove, the wagon trains lumbered southwest to the Arkansas River, through arid plains infested with Pawnee and Comanche robbers. At the Arkansas River, the route divided. The main approach crossed the Cimarron Desert, the most frightful stretch of the journey. For fifty miles not a single water hole could be found. Kiowa and Comanche marauders roamed the area. Once across the desert, this main trail led directly southwest into Santa Fe.

The alternate route from the Arkansas crossing continued upstream along the river. This was the "Mountain Branch" of the trail, leading to the vicinity of present-day La Junta and then cutting off across Raton Pass into Taos or Santa Fe.

The wagon men found prairie travel slow and full of danger. The distance covered each day was determined as much by water courses and springs as by the speed of the oxen or mules pulling the wagons. At best the men could anticipate fifteen miles a day. And along most of the route defenses could never be relaxed. Raiding Indians lay in wait, more than willing to fight for a chance at the merchandise in the wagons. But despite the hardships and dangers the trade was lucrative—and romantic. For Anglo-Americans raised on a puritan morality, exotic Santa Fe offered girls who danced fandangoes, smoked cigarettes, and openly flirted "in the Latin manner."

Romance aside, Santa Fe was also a place where hard cash—gold and silver—could be won in exchange for goods from the States. The caravaners brought assortments of hardware and dry goods, especially brightly colored textiles. They leisurely bartered these American goods for furs, skins, gold, and silver. The profits of the trade varied greatly from year to year, for the whim of the provincial governor seemed to determine the customs duties. He might vary the tax on wagons from $10 to $750. Under such circumstances, bribery became a fine art and smuggling seemed a necessity.

The wagon traders took the gold and silver back to the Missouri River towns to pay off their creditors or to purchase new merchandise for the next season. The furs and skins—mostly beaver pelts and buffalo robes—could be sent for sale to St. Louis where they brought handsome profits. Santa Fe became a gathering place for furs from a wide area, including the mountain regions to the north.

The fur trappers and traders were another group of men who refused to be intimidated by the Great American Desert. Beaver fur was one of the most precious commodities on the continent. Nature had given it to man for the taking. The beaver pelt provided a high-priced product in a small package: a single pelt sold in eastern markets for six to eight dollars, yet it was small and light enough in weight to be brought out of the interior regions where the trapping took place.

Trapping and trading for furs in the Rocky Mountains had begun even before the Santa Fe Trail was opened. When the Spanish dragoons escorted Pike to Santa Fe in 1807, he found there a James Purcell who had been trading with the Indians on the South Platte and in South Park. And Manuel Lisa, whose Missouri Fur Company had earlier penetrated the beaver lands of the upper Missouri River Valley, sent men south along the mountains to trade with the Indians in 1810 and the following year dispatched a party to the Arkansas Valley.

Ezekiel Williams, one of the leaders of that party, had taken nineteen trappers to the headwaters of both the Arkansas and South Platte rivers. Trapping and trading as they went, the men met a variety of fates. Some wandered south to Santa Fe; some were killed by Indians. Williams and two companions were captured by the

Arapahoes. After two years, Williams escaped and made his way back to Missouri. The next year he went west to the mountains again, this time with a party of trappers led by Joseph Philibert. He found the furs that he had cached on his earlier venture; these and the harvest of pelts gathered by the rest of the party were brought back to the States.

The situation looked promising for fur-gathering in the mountains. Two St. Louis merchants, Auguste Chouteau and Julius de Munn, bought out Joseph Philibert and went west with forty-five trappers in 1815. But after two successful seasons, the company was captured by the Spaniards despite earlier encouragement the Americans had received from New Mexican officials. In Santa Fe, the trappers were tried by court martial. They were set free but their furs and trade goods, worth an estimated $30,000, were confiscated. That acted like a brake on others who had intended to follow Chouteau and de Munn to the Southwest for furs. But, as in the case of the trade on the Santa Fe Trail, once the Mexicans had achieved their independence they reversed the policy toward American traders.

One of the first outfits to discover the changed attitude at Santa Fe was the Glenn-Fowler Company. Hugh Glenn and Jacob Fowler, with eighteen men, left Fort Smith, Arkansas, in September of 1821 on an expedition to the Arkansas River Valley. Early the following year they built a "House nine loggs High" on the future site of Pueblo. From there they trapped and traded in the surrounding area and sent expeditions to Taos and Santa Fe. Their success was soon duplicated by others.

The techniques of the fur business of the central Rockies varied. Some white men gathered furs themselves; others remained traders, dependent on Indian and white trappers to bring in the pelts and exchange them for such trade goods as flour, cloth, tobacco, and trinkets. Although proscribed by federal licensing regulations, whiskey was often a commodity in this commerce.

However the trade was conducted, it was cannibalistic in nature. The trappers were always consuming their source of supply, and they continually had to move farther into the interior. There were advantages from this constant movement: if the traders contacted Indians who had not been well educated in the business, they could expect to pay lower prices for the beaver pelts, and, like the Spaniards searching for gold and silver, they always dreamed of the bonanza beaver pond, just over the horizon.

Taos, New Mexico, provided all that was needed as a base of

SHS fur trade diorama. (State Historical Society of Colorado)

operations for the trappers of the Arkansas and San Luis valleys, and most of the Western Slope area as well. Here men could dispose of their furs to the merchants of the Santa Fe trade. Here, where New Mexican officials were less numerous than in Santa Fe, the fur men might hope to evade trapping and trading regulations. Here too they could find relaxation with a species of liquor dubbed "Taos Lightning" and other questionable comforts of a frontier adobe village.

The trappers and traders were a conglomerate lot: French-Canadians who brought with them extensive knowledge of fur gathering, Mexicans who moved north to try their hand at the game, Americans who wandered up the river courses into the mountains. Nationality faded as the fur men adopted as common garb the utilitarian fringed-buckskin suit. Uneducated but wise to the ways of rivers and trails, this "reckless breed of men" needed little capital to embark in the enterprise. A rifle, some traps, and a horse or two provided the minimum investment for fur gathering. It was a lonesome, often perilous, always difficult life. But when the season ended with a goodly crop of pelts, the trapper could return to Taos and home.

Taos provided a center for the individual trappers of the southern and Western Slope streams. Farther north, the fur merchants inaugurated another type of operation. With the great Missouri River complex as a natural highway, the northern area had attracted the attention of large fur companies even before Lewis and Clark reported the region excellent for trapping. The trading companies working the area were merciless in their competition for furs; each tried to monopolize the choicest trapping lands and squeeze its competitors from the region.

Operating out of the Pacific Northwest was the far-flung British-owned Hudson's Bay Company, with its base at Astoria (later Fort Vancouver) and a regional post at Fort Hall in present Idaho. John Jacob Astor's American Fur Company settled the headquarters of its Western Department at St. Louis and operated out of Fort Union at the mouth of the Yellowstone River. Groups of trappers led by Nathaniel J. Wyeth and Captain B. L. E. Bonneville increased the competition. But the man who introduced the most novel feature of the trade was General William Ashley.

Ashley's initial enterprises in the upper Missouri basin were unspectacular, despite the later luster of the names of some of his employees: Jim Bridger, Thomas Fitzpatrick, Jedediah Smith, Louis Vasquez. What brought Ashley fame and fortune was a new technique of pelt gathering. Instead of depending on the trappers to come to a permanent trading post, Ashley devised the most romantic feature of the fur frontier—the summer rendezvous. This "fair in the wilderness" convened in ever-changing locations. Pierre's Hole in eastern Idaho might be chosen for the rendezvous one year; Cache Valley on Bear River north of the Great Salt Lake, or Brown's Hole on the Green River, might be chosen the following season.

The site was known in advance by the Mountain Men and company brigades, and when the agents arrived with wagons of trade goods, trappers from all over the Rockies appeared for the event. The rendezvous was more than a trading experience. It offered the otherwise solitary trappers gaiety, gambling, contests of skill, whiskey to drink and Indian maidens to woo—a combination bazaar, carnival, and reckless spree.

For the fur merchant, the rendezvous held other attractions. Since no permanent trading post was involved, Indian fears of encroachment on their hunting lands were reduced. The traders could move the site from season to season, to take advantage of the best trapping conditions. And, since the pelts were all gathered at one time, the merchant could arrange more easily for their transportation out of the mountains to the markets in the East.

The rendezvous brought instant success in the form of a personal fortune to General Ashley. In 1825 he sold the business to three of his ablest employees—Jedediah Smith, David E. Jackson, and William Sublette. They managed the enterprise for four years and then sold it to a larger group of Mountain Men (Thomas Fitzpatrick, James Bridger, Milton Sublette, Henry Fraeb, and Baptiste Gervais), organized as the Rocky Mountain Fur Company. It took that company three seasons to pay off the debt and it operated one year after that—a year full of competition from the acquisitive American Fur Company, a better financed organization with superior marketing facilities. In 1834, the Rocky Mountain Fur Company gave up the struggle, selling its assets to the American Fur Company.

The rendezvous system attracted attention, but some traders preferred to use permanent trading posts. On the Gunnison River, near the present site of Delta, Antoine Robidoux built Fort Uncompahgre (sometimes known as Fort Robidoux). Robidoux had found his way into the Green River country in the mid-1820s. By 1833 he had a score or more men trapping for him in the valleys of the Western Slope and had built a reputation for himself as the "kingpin" trader of the region. In Brown's Hole, in the extreme northwestern corner of present Colorado, Fort Davy Crockett provided a base for beaver trappers. This post was short-lived and so restricted in attractions that the Mountain Men called it Fort Misery.

The building of forts and trading posts on the Eastern Slope was delayed until after the best years of beaver trapping. During the decade from 1830 to 1840 both the supply and the price of beaver skins declined. The animals became scarcer and the fashions in Paris and London changed as the silk top hat replaced the beaver hat. Pelts dropped in price until they brought little more than one dollar each. Many traders then turned from beaver pelts to buffalo robes, and permanent posts became more necessary.

White men did not hunt the buffalo during these years. They left the work to the Indians. The division of labor in the tribes dictated that the males conduct the hunt while their squaws stretched and dried the robes. A buffalo robe could be bought for three or four dollars, unless it was a "silk" robe—fine-haired, of slightly lighter color—and then the price might be double that amount.

The robe merchant kept his trading goods at a post to which the Indians could bring their robes—a simpler process than bartering on the prairies. The robes were bulky and needed protected storage. The trading posts along the Eastern Slope answered those needs. From them the robes could be shipped on wagon caravans along the Santa Fe Trail to the south or the new Oregon Trail to the north.

The activities of Bent, St. Vrain and Company dominated the buffalo robe trade in the region for years. The four Bent brothers—Charles, William, Robert, and George—had followed the western trade to Santa Fe from their home in St. Louis. Their partnership with Ceran St. Vrain proved to be extremely successful. Bent's Fort—or William's Fort, as the company termed it—was built in 1833 on the north (American) bank of the Arkansas River, between present-day La Junta and Las Animas. The location was excellent: the post could be utilized by the Indian robe hunters of the prairies and by the remaining fur trappers in the mountains. At the same time, the fort sat astride the Mountain Branch of the Santa Fe Trail.

The Bents constructed their fort of thick adobe, with walls fifteen feet high and towers at two corners. A gateway in one of the walls provided the entrance to the *placita*. Inside the walls low-roofed warehouses, living rooms, kitchen, and storage sheds were backed up against the outside walls. There was a corral for horses at the rear of the fort. And, on the river bank, an adobe ice house provided facilities for keeping meat as well as the necessary ingredient for iced drinks during the hot summer weather.

For almost two decades the company and its fort on the Arkansas dominated the robe trade of the valley and extended regions beyond. The fort was also a welcome haven for travellers on the Santa Fe Trail and provided a quasi-military base in the midst of the Arapahoe and Cheyenne Indians. Colonel Henry Dodge counselled there with the plains Indians in 1835 during a summer march with his First Dragoon companies of United States troops. More usual visitors were the veteran Mountain Men. A group of them was usually in attendance at the fort—men like Thomas Fitzpatrick and Jim Bridger, Dick Wootton and Jim Beckwourth, Kit Carson and Jim Baker.

Bent's Fort dominated but did not control the territory. Farther upstream on the Arkansas River, John Gantt and Jefferson Blackwell built a trading post in 1832. It proved to be as short-lived as a similar structure Maurice Le Doux built near the site of present-day Florence. When the trade in buffalo robes replaced the commerce in beaver pelts, the South Platte Valley to the north became dotted with adobe trading posts.

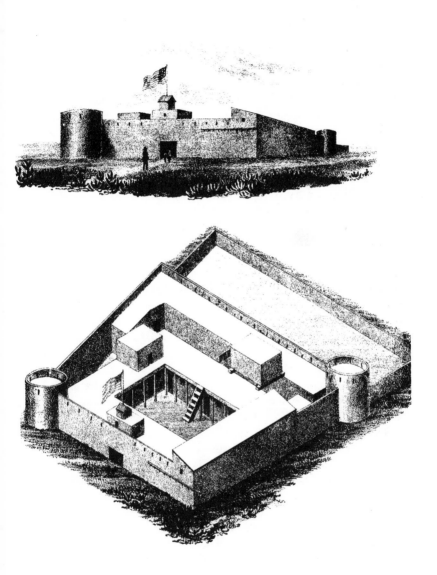

Bent's Fort, as it appeared in the 1840s. (State Historical Society of Colorado)

The first of these valley forts was operated by two experienced Mountain Men, Louis Vasquez and Andrew Sublette. In the autumn of 1835, these partners located their Fort Vasquez on the river near the present town of Platteville. For a few years they seem to have conducted a brisk business. However, in 1840 or 1841, Vasquez and Sublette sold their facilities to another partnership, which soon became bankrupt and quit the post in 1842.

A second trading post was erected in the valley shortly after the building of Fort Vasquez. Lancaster P. Lupton, a West Point graduate who came west with the Dodge excursion in 1835, was intrigued with trading possibilities in the area and resigned his army commission to return west and build Fort Lupton in 1836. For nine years he conducted trade with the Indians. When trade slackened, he tried his hand at planting crops and grazing livestock near his fort.

Two other Mountain Men, Henry Fraeb and Peter A. Sarpy, financed in part by the Western Department of the American Fur Company, constructed Fort Jackson in 1837 near present-day Ione. Like the beaver trade, the robe commerce was competitive. Sarpy once informed his partner: "My object is to do all the harm possible to the opposition and yet without harming ourselves."[1] Such competition often introduced liquor into the trading, with ruinous effect on both Indians and the honest traders.

The potential threats of Forts Lupton and Jackson stirred Bent, St. Vrain and Company to build a post farther north on the Platte, about six miles northwest of the present town of Platteville. This "branch" enterprise they called Fort Lookout, later changing the name to Fort George and finally to Fort St. Vrain. The company also moved to buy out Fort Jackson from Fraeb and Sarpy in 1838; however, they probably never used the post since it was only ten miles from their own Fort St. Vrain.

By 1840, the best days of the trade were ended. The beaver trade was gone; the buffalo trade could not support so many trading posts. In time all of the forts were deserted. Yet despite their failure to mature into permanent settlements, certain advances had been made. The valleys and passes of the mountain ranges were now known to the Mountain Men who later would guide "official" explorers through them. The Indian tribes had been met and traded with, and some of their strengths and weaknesses had been discovered. The legend of the Great American Desert had been banished from the minds of at least a few men. All these things would seem more significant later, when men came in greater numbers to invade the Rocky Mountain frontier.

The Frontier in Transition

The decline of the fur and robe trade in the Rocky Mountain region ushered in an era of transition. For two decades trappers and traders had tramped the trails and passes until most of the area had been seen, although little of it had been mapped. But except for the trading posts along the Arkansas and Platte rivers, nothing resembling permanent settlements had yet taken root. The arid plains were uninviting to agriculturalists and the Indian trade could support a limited population at best. Both Mexican and American governments may have looked upon the region as a desirable buffer zone, desolate and inhospitable enough to keep their citizens apart.

By 1840, however, many Americans were no longer interested in isolation from Mexico's northern provinces. Expansion was in the air. The Texans' successful revolt against Mexican rule had projected the question of annexation of that province into domestic politics. Beyond Texas was California, increasingly desirable to the people of an expanding United States. North of California was the Oregon country, still in dispute between its joint landlords, Great Britain and the United States.

The long Oregon Trail, leading up the Platte River, across South Pass, along the Green and Snake rivers, with a final plunge from Fort Boise to the valley of the Columbia, provided the entrance to the rich agricultural paradise of the Pacific Northwest. The trail to Oregon was not only long; some of the stretches, particularly the mountain crossings, taxed the immigrants' strength and determination. As the number of travellers to Oregon increased, western expansionists demanded surveys of the trail to find better crossings of the Divide and to locate sites for military posts to protect the travellers. This was to be done at government expense in the public interest. No man was more insistent that the government hurry such aid—to help the frontier-seeking farmer and to ensure American title to the Oregon country—than a senator from Missouri, Thomas Hart Benton.

Benton, the acknowledged spokesman for the trans-Mississippi West, sponsored a $30,000 federal appropriation for preliminary mapping of the major trails over the mountains in 1842. Perhaps it was not surprising that the man chosen to lead the surveying party was Benton's son-in-law, twenty-nine-year-old John Charles Frémont.

Frémont was born in Savannah, Georgia, in 1813. In true Horatio Alger fashion he had overcome the obstacles of illegitimate birth, the early death of his father, and extreme poverty as a youth. Educated at Charleston College, he taught mathematics in the Navy and assisted in surveys for the United States Topographical Corps. His patron, Joel Poinsett, secured a commission as second lieutenant for him in the corps in 1838. For three years Frémont worked on surveys between the Missouri River and the northern frontier. Then, in 1841, he provided social Washington with a choice scandal by eloping with Jessie Benton, the daughter of the Missouri senator. Family peace restored, the Senator managed to secure the assignment of surveying the Oregon Trail for his handsome son-in-law.

The expedition was to be a modest affair. With twenty-eight men, Frémont was to survey the country between the Missouri River and South Pass. This most easily travelled segment of the trail ran through country already familiar to many Mountain Men. But from the surveys accurate maps would result, sites for military posts could be suggested, and—best of all to an expansion-minded West—the virtues of the Oregon country would be advertised at a time when the joint British-American occupation annoyed disciples of Manifest Destiny.

Lieutenant Frémont was fortunate in employing Kit Carson as his guide, for few men knew more about the trails and passes of the West. Carson had been born in Kentucky in 1809, but had grown up in frontier Missouri. In his teens he had joined a Bent, St. Vrain and Company wagon train on a journey to Santa Fe. For almost a decade he had trapped and traded out of Taos, seeking employment as a hunter at Bent's Fort when the fur trade declined. He had come back to civilization in 1842, but found it far from satisfying and was pleased to join Frémont in the expedition along the Oregon Trail.

The Fremont party travelled up the Platte River to Fort St. Vrain.

From there the young leader headed for the American Fur Company post at Fort Laramie and then through the valley of the Sweetwater to South Pass. After a short excursion into the Wind River Mountains, Frémont and his men completed their relatively uneventful trip by journeying eastward to home. The expedition lasted only three and one-half months. Frémont spent the winter in Washington, D.C., preparing a report of his journey to serve as a trail guide for future immigrants. He also began to prepare for a longer trip he would make when the weather cleared in the mountains.

In the spring of 1843, Frémont returned to the Rockies. From Fort St. Vrain, he and his guides, Kit Carson and Thomas Fitzpatrick, searched the front ranges for a useful pass over the Divide. In this search, Frémont was disappointed, as others had been before him and many would be later. Splitting his party, Frémont then sent Fitzpatrick with some of the men on to Fort Laramie with the supplies. Carson and Frémont led the rest of the men up the sixty-mile canyon of the Cache la Poudre River, up and along the eastern base of the Medicine Bow Range, until they struck the Oregon Trail.

Moving westward, the survey explored the basin of Great Salt Lake and swung up into the valley of the Columbia, reaching Fort Vancouver. Then, instead of moving down the trail to home, Frémont took his men south and west, crossing the Sierra Nevada Mountains in a difficult climb (mid-winter, 1844), and settled down for rest and refitting near Sutter's Fort in the Sacramento Valley in California.

On his way home, Frémont traversed the central Rockies, from Brown's Hole on the Green River, through North, Middle, and South parks, and on through Bent's Fort. If he had been looking only for a suitable wagon route he had found one somewhat shorter than any surveyed earlier, although still impracticable for heavy vehicles. But by this time, Frémont probably had other objectives in mind. American interest in California was surging; knowledge of the passes leading into the province soon might become valuable military information.

In fact, the country was about to elect James K. Polk to the presidency on a platform featuring expansion in the Northwest and the Southwest. Frémont's father-in-law was now the chairman of the Senate Military Committee, and the young surveyor had no difficulty gaining War Department approval for a third expedition. The actual objectives of this third trip to the West are unclear. Frémont had with him some sixty men—a large number for a surveying party. Probably both Benton and Frémont believed that by the time the expedition reached California the United States and Mexico would be at war. The scouts and scientists then could be converted into a small fighting corps to help wrest California from the Mexicans.

Frémont travelled the Santa Fe Trail to Bent's Fort. Again the trusted Carson served as guide, helping to move the expedition up the Arkansas River, over the Continental Divide at modern-day Fremont Pass, northwestward to the White River, across the Great Basin and the Sierras, and into the Sacramento Valley. There Frémont would find for himself and his men a place in the history of the Mexican War.

In the year of Frémont's third expedition (1845), Colonel Stephen Watts Kearny led a military reconnaissance from Fort Leavenworth to Fort Laramie, then to South Pass, back to Fort Laramie, south to Bent's Fort, and from there again to Leavenworth. His objectives included gathering information about the region, protecting travellers on the Oregon and Santa Fe trails, and persuading the Indian tribes to be peaceful, by demonstrating the military might of the army and by holding councils with them.

With officers like Frémont and Kearny, and fur traders and travellers crisscrossing the central Rockies, sooner or later someone was going to settle down and start raising vegetables on some river bank. In time it happened. As the fur trade waned and trappers found the old trail life less profitable, some of them forsook the roving life to attempt a little farming. When that happened, several short-lived, semi-agricultural settlements were begun.

One of the first was called El Pueblo, also known as Milk Fort, because the inhabitants kept some goats at the place. It was located about five miles above Bent's Fort on the Arkansas River. Visitors described its inhabitants as Mexican and American Mountain Men, weary from their lives of trapping, who settled there to grow small crops of foodstuffs which they sold to trading posts in the region. It was soon abandoned.

Other men settled "the Pueblo" or "Fort Pueblo" at the confluence of Fountain Creek and the Arkansas River, in 1842 or earlier. Frémont visited this village in 1843, noting in his journal that the residents were "mountaineers" and their wives came from "the valley of Taos." They farmed a little and conducted a "desultory" trade with the Indians. Three years later the historian Francis Parkman stopped at the place during his western travels and commented on its primitive construction—"nothing more than a large square enclosure, surrounded by a wall of mud, miserably cracked and dilapidated."[1]

In 1846 some forty-three Mormons, trekking westward on t Oregon Trail, learned at Fort Laramie that they were ahead of rath than behind the main group of emigrants. Discovering that the rest or the party would winter near Council Bluffs, this small group moved southward to winter near Fort Pueblo. They were joined there by soldiers from the "Mormon Battalion" who had enlisted in the United States Army during the Mexican War and now, sick or disabled, were sent to the Arkansas Valley to recuperate. In the spring of 1847 the Mormons continued their journey to the valley of the Great Salt Lake.

There were other settlements—one at the mouth of Hardscrabble Creek on the Arkansas, another on the Greenhorn, and the Bent-Hatcher farm on the Purgatoire. All these were deserted by the time of the Gold Rush: the settlers were victims of isolation, discouraging poverty, and perhaps Indian attacks.

Although agricultural settlements did not flourish, title to the area was worth contesting. In 1836, when the Texans revolted from Mexican rule, the defeated Mexican general, Santa Anna, promised the Rio Grande as the southern and western boundary for Texas. He soon claimed that the promise had been given under duress and refused to honor it. Thus both Mexico and Texas claimed the land between the Arkansas and the Rio Grande. During its nine years as an independent nation, the Lone Star Republic sent out two military expeditions to make good its claim. Both failed, and Mexico continued to hold the disputed lands.

The Texas threats, coupled with certain signs of interest in the Texas claims by the United States, led Mexico to consider filling up the region with settlers. Early in the years after 1840, Mexico granted lands north of Santa Fe in the areas south of the Arkansas Valley and in the San Luis Valley. Two grants in the San Luis Valley, the Tierra Amarilla and the Conejos grants, had originally been given in the previous decade. Now the Conejos Grant was reaffirmed, and others were made. Carlos Beaubien and Guadalupe Miranda successfully petitioned for the later-named "Maxwell Grant"—more than 1,500,000 acres, stretching northeastward from Taos. To the north of the Maxwell Grant, reaching as far as the Arkansas River and encompassing almost 4,000,000 acres of land was the Las Animas Grant. It was given to Cornelio Vigil and Ceran St. Vrain. Bordering these grants on the west were the Sangre de Cristo Grant, extending westward to the Rio Grande, given to Luis Lee and Narciso Beaubien in 1843, and the smaller Nolan Grant, south of the Arkansas River,

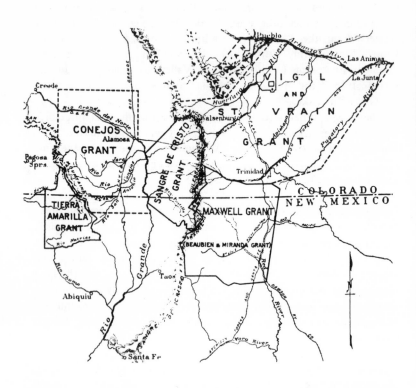

Mexican land grants in Colorado. (State Historical Society of Colorado)

received by Gervacio Nolan in 1843.

Mexico expected the recipients of these grants to colonize settlers on them. In this way, her claims to the area would be secured against Texan and American threats. But the grants were made too late and the attempts of the owners to settle them were too feeble. Before the policy served its purpose, the United States had annexed the Texas Republic (March, 1845) and had made the Texas claims to the Rio Grande boundary her own. The long anticipated war between the United States and Mexico began in May, 1846. Before that summer ended, the land grants and much larger stretches of Mexico's domain would be taken from her.

In June, 1846, the American "Army of the West," commanded by Colonel Stephen W. Kearny, moved southwestward from Fort Leavenworth. After a month's march, 1,700 troops and the massive supply train reached Bent's Fort on the Arkansas River. From there, after rest and reorganization, the army started for its first objective—Santa Fe.

There was no Mexican resistance, as more than one traveller on the trail had predicted. On August 18 the American flag was raised over the Royal City. Kearny remained in Santa Fe for a month. Then, after appointing Charles Bent the governor of the province, the recently-promoted General Kearny started for California. The conquest of New Mexico turned out to be less than completely bloodless. The following winter (1847) an uprising in New Mexico was crushed by the American forces in a battle at Taos Pueblo; but not before Charles Bent and others had lost their lives.

In February, 1848, the Mexican War ended with the Treaty of Guadalupe Hidalgo. Mexico ceded to the United States the entire southwestern region, from Texas to the Pacific Ocean, from the Rio Grande to the forty-second parallel. All of what was to become Colorado was now within the domain of the United States.

With the Mexican War ended, many Americans turned their attention to an idea frequently discussed before the fighting began: a transcontinental railroad to ease transportation to the Oregon country (American now, to the forty-ninth parallel, by virtue of a settlement with Great Britain in 1846) and to California. The war had demonstrated dramatically the difficulties of the long overland route and the longer sea voyage, either around Cape Horn or by way of the Isthmus. Most Americans assumed that the federal government would pay all or part of the costs for such a railroad. But there was little agreement as to the best route for the road. Every town in the Missouri and Mississippi valleys viewed itself as a likely eastern terminus of the railroad.

St. Louis, in particular, was interested in the project. In 1848 businessmen from that city hired John C. Frémont to find a suitable railroad route from St. Louis to the Pacific. Frémont had reached California at the end of his third expedition; he and his men aided in the American occupation of the province. He had become involved in a struggle there between Commodore Stockton and General Kearny, and, after a much-publicized court martial, Frémont resigned his army commission. Now, under the St. Louis auspices, he conducted his fourth, near-fatal expedition to the West.

With thirty-three men he travelled the familiar path to Bent's Fort and Fort Pueblo. He had hoped to engage Kit Carson as guide, but Carson was not available. Another veteran Mountain Man, "Parson" Bill Williams, agreed to take the assignment. There were warnings of disaster from the veterans of the mountains and the forts, but Frémont was undisturbed by prophecies of doom. He was determined to make the journey in wintertime in order to prove completely the practicability of the railroad route.

The crossing of the Sangre de Cristo mountains was accomplished despite the winter weather. Frémont moved his men across the San Luis Valley and, heading into the San Juan Mountains, attempted to cross the Continental Divide in the upper Rio Grande Valley. The snowdrifts deepened and the temperatures slid downward as the men climbed toward 12,000-foot elevations. They never crossed the Divide; the expedition bogged down completely in the extreme winter weather. The only hope for escape was rescue from the south, so Frémont sent four men to New Mexico. When sixteen days passed without word from them, he took four others and started south, leaving the rest of the party to follow as best they could. On his way down, Frémont found three of the four men he had sent out earlier; the fourth man had died. Pushing on into Taos on horses procured from Indians, Frémont started a relief party to rescue what remained of his group.

Most of his equipment was lost; all the mules were gone. Eleven of the thirty-three men perished in the winter wilderness. No other party exploring the Central Rockies paid such a price for failure. Historians still argue about who was to blame for the debacle. Frémont's admirers claim that Bill Williams was an unreliable guide, unfamiliar with the passes out of the San Luis Valley. Others insist that Frémont disregarded the advice of his hired scout and alone was responsible for electing the difficult crossing.

Frémont's failure to find a suitable railroad route for the businessmen of St. Louis by no means ended the planning for a transcontinental line. In fact, the discovery of gold in California now emphasized the need anew. But the northern and southern sectional interests so bitterly contended the advantages of their own sections that no single route could be agreed upon. In 1853 Congress appropriated $150,000 for four separate surveys of possible routes to the Pacific. One of these would study the land between the thirty-eighth and thirty-ninth parallel.

Captain John Gunnison of the Topographical Corps was assigned this survey through the central Rockies. His command was rather extensive—thirty members of the scientific team and a military escort of thirty dragoons commanded by two officers. Using eighteen six-mule wagons, in addition to an instrument wagon and an ambulance, they hoped that the route could be thoroughly tested.

Gunnison's surveying party moved up the Santa Fe Trail, over La Veta Pass, into the San Luis Valley. Gunnison's way out of this mountain park was a distinct improvement over Frémont's attempted route five years earlier. The survey climbed up and over Cochetopa Pass and then down to the Gunnison River to the Grand (Colorado) River, for a distance following Escalante's route of three-quarters of a century earlier. The way was far from smooth; chopping trees and moving rocks to get the wagons through was hard work. In fact, Gunnison and his men concluded that the elevations they had traversed were so rugged that a railroad could be operated only after extensive, expensive tunneling.

When they reached the Grand River, the party turned to the west. In the Utah desert, Paiute Indians fell upon the party, murdering Captain Gunnison and seven of his men and mutilating their bodies. Lieutenant E. J. Beckwith, the second-in-command, led the way into Salt Lake City and the party returned from there to the States the following year.

When it was announced that John Gunnison would lead his survey into areas that Frémont had already traversed, the "Pathfinder of the West" was in Europe. Frémont now returned to the United States. With the help of his father-in-law, he financed his fifth and last expedition—a rival survey to Gunnison's. He followed almost exactly the route that Gunnison had marked; he contributed almost nothing to the general information about the area. He did, however, complete his survey during the winter months, thus demonstrating the feasibility of an all-weather route through the mountains.

The surveys for the Pacific railroad were completed by 1854, but the strife between North and South would delay the project for more than a decade. By the year 1854 the whole sectional issue was about to explode again. Four years earlier the forces of compromise had put together agreements designed to dispose of the thorny question of the status of slavery in the new lands acquired from Mexico. The creation of Utah and New Mexico territories as part of the Compromise of 1850 left an unorganized expanse of federal domain lying east of the Rockies. In 1854 that territory was divided at the fortieth parallel into the Kansas and Nebraska territories. Thus, from 1850 to

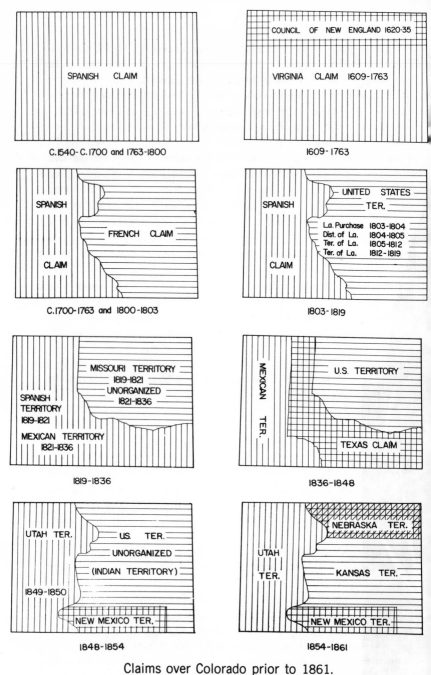

Claims over Colorado prior to 1861.

(Courtesy of Colorado, Hafen & Hafen, Old West Publishing Company)

1854, future Colorado was politically divided into three parts: Utah Territory in the west, New Mexico Territory in the south, and the unorganized part of the Louisiana Purchase in the east, north of the Arkansas River. After 1854, the area of future Colorado was divided among four territories—Utah, New Mexico, Kansas, and Nebraska. Probably none of this was of great interest to the American public at the time, for Kansas Territory had become the commanding focal point of the West. North and South soon pounced upon the newly-created territory in a bloody curtain-raiser to the drama called the Civil War.

Yet the years were not without significance for the future Colorado region. In the areas east of the mountains, the plains Indians increasingly threatened traffic on the Oregon and Santa Fe trails. Earlier, in 1846, the federal government had created the Upper Platte and Arkansas Indian Agency and appointed Thomas Fitzpatrick as agent. Fitzpatrick, known in the West as "Broken Hand," was an excellent choice for the position. He represented the best of the traditions of the veterans of the mountains, including specific knowledge of the regional tribes. He centered his activities as agent at Bent, St. Vrain and Company's fort on the Arkansas River. Here he met the Cheyennes and Arapahoes in council in August, 1847. Two years after that, Bent's Fort was no more. Tradition relates that William Bent, disgusted at the federal government's refusal to agree to his purchase price, moved out his supplies and blew up the place. Bent then moved down the river, constructing a new, much less imposing Fort Bent which the army eventually took over in 1860, renaming it Fort Wise.

Actually Bent's old fort had been quite far south for the agency's activities. The American Fur Company's post at Fort Laramie proved a more central location and, after the federal government bought it in 1849, the Indian agents used it in their work. Fort Laramie is particularly memorable as the site of the great plains Indian council of 1851. September was set for the largest gathering of the tribes ever held in the West. More than 10,000 Indians were there, some tribes "en masse" and others represented by delegations. Not all the tribes were friends, but they did not mar the occasion with war. Cheyenne, Arapahoe, Snake, Sioux, Assiniboin, Gros Ventres, Aricara, and Crow listened and replied solemnly to the harangues of Superintendent David Mitchell, head of the Central Superintendency at St. Louis, and Agent Fitzpatrick. Between the speeches and the pipe smoking there was time for military maneuvers, dances, and dog feasts during the fifteen-day session.

In the treaty that resulted the plains tribes agreed to live in peace and to hunt within tribal boundaries marked off for them. The Cheyennes and Arapahoes were assigned the area north of the Arkansas River and east of the mountains. The Indians agreed to allow white men to move through their tribal lands and to build forts for the protection of travellers on the overland trails. In return, the agents promised to bring out and distribute $50,000 worth of trade goods annually for the next fifteen years. (Congress reduced the trade goods provision to $15,000 when the treaty was ratified.) The terms agreed upon, the agents then distributed presents from twenty-seven bulging wagons. Along with a treaty made with the Comanches, Apaches, and Kiowas at Fort Atkinson two years later, the Fort Laramie Treaty awaited the test of time that alone would determine its effectiveness.

While government agents treatied with the plains Indians, it also was necessary to direct attention to the Utes in the mountain parks. In fact, even more serious work was needed there where the first permanent white settlements within present Colorado were developing. The Treaty of Guadalupe Hidalgo that ended the Mexican War stipulated that all private property rights in the areas ceded to the United States would be respected. In this way the federal government became an interested party in the extensive land grants the Mexican government had made earlier in the Arkansas and San Luis valleys. It fell to the surveyor general of New Mexico Territory to investigate and report on the validity and extent of the land grants. Congress might then accept, modify, or reject the surveyor's findings. And, in time, the federal courts were also involved, when conflicting claims resulted in litigation. Some of the claims were rather quickly disposed of: the Sangre de Cristo, the Maxwell, and the Tierra Amarilla grants were confirmed in full. Congress reduced the Nolan and Vigil and St. Vrain grants. The Conejos claim remained in litigation for decades and finally was rejected by the courts.

Although these lands had been granted to encourage settlement on Mexico's northern frontier, none of them contained a single village when the Mexican War ended. Three years after the peace treaty, in 1851, the first permanent white settlement in Colorado was planted: San Luis on the Culebra River. In the next few years, it was followed by San Pedro, San Acacio, and Guadalupe. The settlers, moving north from New Mexico, brought with them experience in irrigating arid lands and soon had dug ditches to water their fields of wheat, corn, and beans. Their cattle and sheep grazed in the San Luis Valley. The settlers also reproduced their familiar adobe-constructed homes and by 1858, at Conejos, had erected Our Lady of Guadalupe Church—the first church structure within the boundaries of the future state of Colorado.

Life in the valley was slow-paced and always difficult. The Indians helped to make it so. During the war the army had sent units from Santa Fe, commanded by Major William Gilpin, to check hostile tribes in the north and west. The objective was tranquility, and efforts were made to persuade the Utes to remain peaceful. By 1849 success was reaped in the first formal treaty concluded between the United States and the Utes. The Indians agreed to stop their warfare and to settle on agricultural lands.

But the peace was not kept. When hunting became difficult for lack of game, the sheep and cattle of the settlers proved too desirable for the Utes to ignore. In 1852, in an effort to check the Indian raids, the United States built Fort Massachusetts to the north of the villages. Located on Ute Creek, at the foot of Mount Blanca, the fort housed a small garrison of soldiers and provided headquarters for the Indian agents. The fort alone, however, did not awe the Indians. Difficulties continued and an organized campaign against the Utes and Jicarilla Apaches seemed necessary.

In 1854 minor conflicts between whites and Indians reached a climax in the episode known as the Fort Pueblo Massacre. On Christmas Day, a celebration at the fort turned into a bloody fight in which fifteen white men were killed and a woman and two boys were carried away by the Indians. General John Garland, commanding at Fort Union, New Mexico, decided to march against the tribes. He added volunteers to his regular troops and sent them north to Fort Massachusetts. An encounter with a war party in the Saguache Valley in March, 1855, resulted only in the flight of the outnumbered tribesmen. But the following month Colonel Thomas Fauntleroy surprised a group of Indians across Poncha Pass. His men killed forty warriors and captured their supplies at the low cost of two wounded soldiers. Through the summer, minor fighting continued, but by autumn the Indians were ready for peace-making.

Near Abiquiu on the Chama River, New Mexico Governor David Merriweather and Agent Kit Carson concluded a treaty with the Mouache Utes and another with the Jicarilla Apaches. The United States Senate never ratified the treaties, probably because the lands to be reserved for the tribes were thought to encompass lands already settled on by whites. But, even without ratification, the treaties did improve the relationship between the settlers and the Indians for some years.

That relationship may have been helped by the relocation of Fort Massachusetts. Critics had earlier pointed out that the army post was too distant from the villages to protect the settlers. In 1858 the army moved the post six miles to the south where, although nearer the village, it still commanded the approach from the east over the Sangre de Cristo Mountains. The post was now renamed Fort Garland. For almost three decades garrisons there would provide security for the San Luis settlers.

As the decade of the 1850s drew to a close, the Rocky Mountain frontier was a fairly quiet place. The Laramie and Atkinson treaties provided a measure of safety for travellers on the overland routes to Oregon and California. The treaties with the Utes and Jicarilla Apaches, and the garrison at Fort Garland, had stabilized the San Luis frontier and protected the little agricultural villages in the valley. Except for those villagers and a few trappers and traders who remained to work the remnants of the fur frontier, the region was devoid of white population. With the main trails to the West running north and south of the mountain barrier, and the agricultural frontier still located back on the Missouri River line, it would have been safe to wager that many years would pass before many people would come to make their homes and their fortunes in the Rocky Mountain frontier.

6

Gold Rush

The high mountains had kept their secret well. No Spaniard ever found the key that would unlock the gold and silver treasures of the Rocky Mountains. Juan Rivera had travelled northward in 1765, looking for the precious metals. He had returned to Santa Fe with ore samples, but evidently the Spanish did not see in them the token of an El Dorado. As later trappers, traders, and explorers crossed and recrossed the mountain trails and passes, they sometimes found small quantities of gold in the stream beds. James Purcell, an American whom Zebulon Montgomery Pike met in New Mexico in 1807, told the explorer about finding gold in the northern ranges, but the inclusion of the story in Pike's report created no great interest. William Gilpin, traveller with Frémont and campaigner against the Indians, recounted tales of gold in the Rockies, but no one paid much attention to him, either. Then, in 1848-1849, the nation reeled under the excitement of the gold discoveries in the recently-won province of California. After that, anything could be believed. The way was opened for El Dorados everywhere and anywhere. Some of the Forty-niners made their way to California by cross-country routes, over the Great American Desert and the Rocky Mountains. A few of them stopped to prospect along the way, particularly those who had panned for gold in the Georgia fields earlier. They found "color" on a few of the tributaries of the South Platte River, but not enough to detain them on their trek to California. However, some of those miners, after returning from the California camps, remembered the streams of the central Rockies.

One such man was William Green Russell of Georgia. He had accumulated considerable mining experience, both in his home state and in the California fields. After his return to Georgia, he decided to organize a prospecting party to survey the Rocky Mountains seriously. His brothers Oliver and Levi shared his hopes and dreams of a mining empire in the mountains. William was related by marriage to the Cherokee Indians, and much of the planning was based on correspondence with Cherokees in present-day Oklahoma, some of whom had actually found gold in the foothills of the Rockies on their way to California. The prospecting enterprise would be composed partly of Georgians and partly of Cherokees from the Indian nation.

In February, 1858, the three Russell brothers, with six companions, set out from Georgia for the West. On the Arkansas River they met the Cherokees as planned, and as they moved along the Santa Fe Trail other fortune-seekers joined them. Eventually the party would number 104 persons. When they reached Bent's Fort, they turned northwest and by May 23 were at the site where Cherry Creek flows into the South Platte River. There they stopped, got out their pans and gear, and started prospecting the river beds. Neither on Cherry Creek nor on Ralston Creek nor on any of the other streams rushing from the mountains did they find anything promising in the bottoms of their pans. For twenty days they kept at their work. Then some of the men decided to forego the further pleasure of standing in stream beds, washing out gravel with ice-cold water, and returned home.

The Russell brothers and ten other men stayed on, and during the first days of July, 1858, they found "good diggings" at the mouth of Dry Creek. They panned out several hundred dollars worth of gold dust before they exhausted the small pocket. The quantity was insignificant, but it was, perhaps, the most important discovery ever made within the region, for from this meager showing the great Pike's Peak gold rush developed.

The Russell group now was convinced of the ultimate success of their venture. They spread out along the ranges, seeking to duplicate their discovery on Dry Creek. While they were gone from the site of their first find, others joined them in the quest for gold. An entirely distinct and separate group of men had come west from Kansas Territory because of a rather unlikely story that an Indian named Fall Leaf had brought back from the mountains the previous year.

In 1857 the army had sent Colonel Edwin V. Sumner and a troop of soldiers to the Cheyenne country to chastise the Indians for raiding traffic on the Platte River trail. Fall Leaf, a Delaware Indian from the reservation near Lawrence, in Kansas, had been one of the guides on that expedition. When he came back to the Territory, Fall Leaf had with him a "bunch of gold nuggets tied up in a rag." He claimed that, while he was in the mountains, he had bent over a stream to take a drink of water and saw the nuggets lying on the rocks. John Easter, a butcher in Lawrence, heard Fall Leaf's story and decided that such an indication of gold warranted a prospecting expedition. When the weather cleared in the spring, Easter had his group ready to move west but by then Fall Leaf had decided not to go along. He was determined to stay in Kansas; even promises of provisions for his family did not persuade him to guide the group to his magic stream. Perhaps he considered the party too small for safe travel across the danger-infested prairies; some say he was unable to go because of injuries from a drunken brawl; most likely he was afraid he would not be able to find the same stream again.

The anxious would-be argonauts were in a quandary, but they finally decided to go ahead with their plans. As they moved along the Santa Fe Trail they were joined by others until, like the Russells before them, their numbers were considerably increased. As they came up the Arkansas Valley they strained their eyes for the first sight of the famous landmark, Pike's Peak. Heading in that direction, they did their first actual prospecting in the shadow of the mountain. They found no gold there, nor were they any more successful in South Park. Finally they decided to go over the ranges into the San Luis Valley and dig near Fort Garland. Then they heard the news that the Russells had found gold on Cherry Creek and, quickly changing plans, they hastened toward the north.

When the Russell group returned to Cherry Creek from their prospecting tour, they found the men from Lawrence, as well as some Indian traders who had joined them, delighted at the unusual prospect of companionship. And there, within a few weeks, gold seekers from the East began to arrive, explaining that the news was abroad in the land that there was gold at Pike's Peak. It had happened that, in July, while the Russells were enjoying their first success at Dry Creek, John Cantrell and other mountain traders from Fort Laramie had visited them. These veterans of the Rockies had stayed a few days, digging in the sands a little themselves. Then they had gone eastward over the plains to Kansas City for the winter. From them the first news confirming the rumors of Pike's Peak gold discoveries reached the rest of the world.

Men acquainted with prairie winters realized that the time for safe

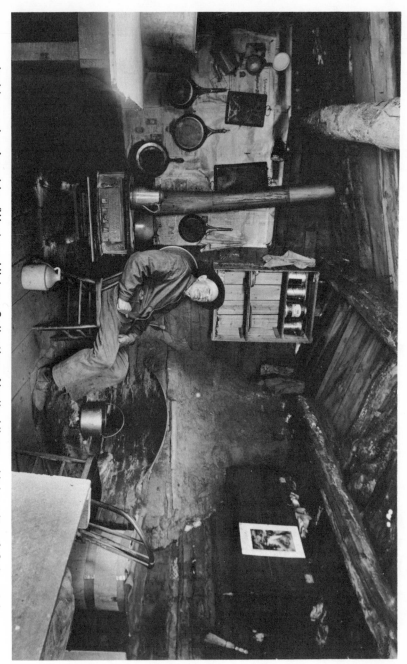

Inside a miner's cabin. (Western History Collection, Norlin Library, University of Colorado)

travel to the diggings had already passed, but there were some who decided to risk the chance of early snows and blizzards in order to reach the gold fields ahead of the others. Most of these Fifty-eighters headed for the mouth of Cherry Creek where the Russell discovery had been reported. They found there the remnants of both the parties, fixing up winter quarters, talking about the panning for gold they would do in the spring, and already engaged in manufacturing "cities."

The Lawrence party had been disappointed to find, on their arrival at Cherry Creek, that the Russells' gold pocket had already been cleaned out. But they decided they could capitalize on the situation anyway. They staked out a town—Montana City—a little to the north of Dry Creek. This venture died an early death, for the promoters soon recognized the superior advantages of another site and organized a second town—St. Charles—on the east side of Cherry Creek. Then, leaving one man to defend their embryo metropolis, the Lawrence group hurried back to Kansas Territory. There, during the winter, they would attempt to gain a charter for their town from the territorial legislature, and advertise and promote their undertaking.

The St. Charles Town Company was strictly a business venture, with closed stock, requiring settlers to buy shares in the organization. Many of the gold seekers saw little necessity for purchasing cabin sites when so much land was available, free for the taking. Yet the advantages of organization for the protection of property and person could not be completely ignored. As the numbers on Cherry Creek increased, late in October, a public meeting was called and a new town company was established in rivalry to the St. Charles venture. On the opposite (west) side of Cherry Creek, the new Auraria Town Company, named after a town in the gold region of Georgia, staked out its site and advertised free entry to all settlers.

This was the situation when, in mid-November, General William NORTON Larimer led a group of men from Leavenworth, Lecompton, and WELTON Oskaloosa into the area. The General, his son Will, and their friend GROUP Dick Whitsitt were also experienced town promoters and, in addition, they had joined forces with a group of men from Lecompton commanded by "Colonel" Ed Wynkoop. These Lecompton men carried with them actual commissions as officers of Arapahoe County, signed by the governor of Kansas Territory. Arapahoe County included in its boundaries all of Kansas Territory west of the 103rd meridian. The territorial legislature had created it on paper in 1855, but it had never actually been organized. Many of Larimer's

group, including these officials of Arapahoe County, seem to have
come to the diggings mainly for the purpose of town-promotion and
office-holding; gold mining was something they were content to leave
to others.

Larimer and his allies surveyed the scene and decided to acquire
the St. Charles site on the theory that it had been abandoned. The
one St. Charles man who had been left to guard the property later
charged that the Larimer group won his consent to "jumping the
claim" by serving him whiskey until he was inebriated. However
gained, Larimer and his men were now in control of the real estate.
With a hopeful eye toward the east, they renamed the town Denver
City, after the governor of Kansas Territory, General James W.
Denver.

Cherry Creek provided a boundary between Auraria and Denver
City, separating the rival communities. But the promoters of those
towns were not alone in their pretensions; other settlements with
hopes for future greatness were soon initiated in the Pike's Peak
region. North of the Cherry Creek settlements, gold seekers from
Nebraska City camped at the Red Rocks near the mouth of Boulder
Canyon to begin Boulder City. Further north, on the Cache la
Poudre, fur trader Antoine Janise styled a cluster of cabins Colona,
later named La Porte. West of Denver City and Auraria, in the valley
of Clear Creek, Arapahoe City and Golden Gate were platted in the
last weeks of 1858. And to the south, at the mouth of Fountain
Creek, near the ruins of old Fort Pueblo, gold seekers laid out the
town of Fountain City. Others staked the site of El Paso near Pike's
Peak.

During the fall and winter the men in the new towns built their
cabins and talked about their plans for prospecting when warm
weather returned and the hills could be scoured for gold. The basis
for their hopes was weak enough—only small pockets of gold dust
like the one the Russells had found on Dry Creek in July. But those
men who reached the area in the fall of 1858 at least could take
comfort in the fact that they had completed the trip across the plains
and would have a decided advantage over the argonauts who were
certain to crowd the region when warm weather arrived.

In the valley of the Missouri River, self-appointed experts on the
Pike's Peak diggings were already at work promoting the spring rush.
D. C. Oakes, who had been in California during the rush days there,
had come out to the Pike's Peak country with a group from Iowa.
After a quick look-around he had gone back to Pacific City, Iowa,

and there he published a guide book to the region. Oakes' creation was only one of many such "bestsellers" that flooded the country during the winter of 1859. In their enthusiasm, the authors of these Pike's Peak guide books often allowed themselves to be carried from reality into a golden, glistening dream world. They boldly announced that the gold was as common in the Pike's Peak region as the waters of the mountain streams or the sands along their banks. Intentionally or not, they led their readers to believe that the most useful equipment to carry to the diggings was containers to hold the gold nuggets picked up like pebbles from the stream beds. Small wonder that these literary products found ready readers.

Another group of men, almost as quick to take advantage of the news from Pike's Peak, were the merchants and tradesmen in the towns along the Missouri River. Times were difficult for these men: the Panic of 1857 had plunged the country into a deep depression and the Midwest had been particularly hard hit. Many merchants believed that their salvation had appeared in the guise of the gold news, for if large numbers of argonauts could be enticed into equipping themselves at their particular establishments, the depression might be rocketed into prosperity. None of the towns in the valley was backward or hesitant to claim itself the best, the logical, the only good outfitting point for prospecting parties about to cross the prairies. Kansas City, Leavenworth, Atchison, Omaha, even St. Louis—each proclaimed itself the natural gateway to the Pike's Peak gold fields.

The cities situated on the already proven trails westward were in the best position to make good those claims. Towns astride the Oregon Trail (Platte River route) to the north, or the Santa Fe Trail (Arkansas River route) to the south, had an advantage over the others. Of all the crossings, the Platte River route probably was the most heavily travelled. But between the two well-established trails, two alternative routes came into prominence. Both the Smoky Hill Trail and the Republican River route had sponsors claiming them the most direct, the shortest, or the safest for travel.

As the winter of 1859 came to a close, the valley towns braced themselves for the anticipated horde of gold seekers. They were not disappointed. Their own advertising, coupled with that of the guide book publishers, had churned up enormous interest in the mines. But these alone could not have created the tremendous excitement, based as it was on so flimsy a foundation as the small quantity of gold actually uncovered. The same economic conditions that had whipped the merchants in the valley towns to such labors for provisioning also motivated many a gold seeker. Times were hard, cash was scarce, jobs were almost nonexistent. Many men who would never have left their homesteads in prosperous times decided to find their own panacea for the depression in the Pike's Peak gold fields. Men who would certainly have been intimidated by the long journey to a far place like California, blithely began the shorter, but still hazardous, trip to the Rocky Mountains.

No census taker stood and counted the argonauts who left the States for the gold fields that spring of 1859. Historians have estimated that number at somewhere around 100,000 persons. Perhaps one-half that many actually reached the Rocky Mountains; the rest either changed their minds along the way or, unfortunately, met their deaths on the trails. Of the 50,000 who may have reached the diggings, probably one-half or more became discouraged at the hard work and small returns, and started homeward after only a few days or weeks at Cherry Creek. Those who did not join the "Go Backs" stayed to dig and wash and search for gold; many stayed to plant towns, open stores, provide services, and make their living "mining the miners."

Some of the Fifty-niners crossed the prairies on horseback. Others travelled by mule train. Probably most of them rode in wagons pulled by oxen, reportedly the best animal for the trip across the plains. Some of the emigrants who lacked the money to procure better transportation tramped westward on foot, with packs on their backs, even though the attempt to cross the prairies this way was described by contemporaries as "madness—suicide—murder." A few of the gold seekers pushed wheelbarrows and handcarts. One dreamer tried a fantastic device: a Wind Wagon, with wheels underneath and sails above for the winds to propel. This prairie ship was scheduled to "sail" between Westport and the Pike's Peak camps on a twelve-day, round-trip routine. The ship and its passengers would travel over 100 miles each day. Unfortunately, the romantic contraption came to anchor in a gulch not far from its port of clearance.

However the trip to the gold fields was made, it was an arduous undertaking. Seven hundred miles or more, the trails ran westward, "crossing countless unbridged water courses, always steep-banked and often miry, and at times so swollen by rains as to be utterly impassable by wagons. Part of this distance . . . [was] a desert, yielding grass, wood, and water only at intervals of several miles, and then very scantily . . . To cross it with teams in midsummer, when the water courses ... [were] mainly dry, and the grass eaten up ... [was] possible only to those who ... [knew] where to look for grass and water."[1]

There had been doubters of the story of Pike's Peak gold all through the late summer and fall of 1858—men who would have applauded Mark Twain's definition of a mine as a "hole in the ground owned by a liar." There were enough "humbug" criers to keep the uncertainty alive all winter. The editor of the *Chicago Press and Tribune* was such a critic. He cautioned his readers that "more cherries will be found at home than at Cherry Creek, and we believe there is more gold to be dug out of every Illinois farm than the owners will ever produce by quitting the home diggings for those on the headwaters of the Arkansas and Platte."[2]

He had a point. If all the gold at Pike's Peak turned out to be only small deposits of gold dust like those found by the Russells and their immediate followers, mass disappointment was in the cards for thousands of men. Such a cruel fate would have brought horrible repercussions and a disastrous situation for the optimistic townmakers already at work on their plans. For a time it appeared that the cynical critics were right; that gold in paying quantity did not exist at Pike's Peak. As many of the early arrivals became discouraged, the contingents of "Go Backs" seemed to equal the westbound travellers on the trails. The chants of discontent threatened to swell into a chorus of "humbug."

Luckily for the future of the place, a few men had kept searching during the winter months for the likely looking gulches. And before the spring of 1859 was very old, good news greeted the newcomers. Three independent discoveries of more than ordinary gold sites established beyond doubt the existence of Pike's Peak gold. Each of the finds was adventure in itself; together they provided the opening wedge into three gold camps that would dominate the region for some time.

George A. Jackson was a man of considerable mining experience, not unlike William Green Russell. He had been in California from 1853 to 1857, and in those years had gained a practical education in prospecting for gold. In January, 1859, he went hunting in the hills above Arapahoe City with some companions. Leaving them, he pushed his way alone up Clear Creek Canyon. Near the place where Chicago Creek joins Clear Creek, in the severest of difficulties, he made his find. Thawing the hard, frozen ground by building fires, and melting snow in a tin cup to wash the debris, Jackson panned out about a half ounce of gold. He wore out his belt knife with the digging and he realized that he must wait until spring to exploit his discovery. He marked the spot and recorded in his diary: "Feel good tonight." Back in Arapahoe City he related his discovery only to Tom Golden, a man whose mouth was "as tight as a No. 4 Beaver trap" and who could be trusted to keep the secret.[3]

A second streak of luck occurred the same month of January, 1859. Six men from the settlement at the mouth of Boulder Canyon decided to try their fortunes at prospecting during an interval of warm winter weather. They found gold, in quantity, at the foot of Gold Hill.

Finally, in April, John H. Gregory, from Georgia, who had been panning on the north fork of Clear Creek, not too far distant from the Jackson discovery, retrieved gold that told his experienced eye that somewhere nearby a rich lode of gold in rock must have decomposed enough to allow nuggets to wash into the stream bed. He was certain he found the site of a paying lode mine, but a spring snow storm ended his prospecting, and he returned to the settlements, keeping his secret to himself.

By that time the Boulder Canyon news was common property. Soon Jackson would meet with some argonauts from Chicago and together they would organize the Chicago Mining Company to exploit the Clear Creek placer. Then Gregory fell in with a group of Indiana gold seekers, led by Wilkes Defrees. In return for a grubstake, Gregory led them to his promising site and there, on May 6, the first lode mine was uncovered. Now the news spread everywhere: three rich finds, exciting enough to empty the valley towns of their population as everyone rushed to the gulches to claim an early share of the diggings.

Denver, Auraria, and Boulder—and the other valley settlements—might be convinced, but there were still some doubters back East crying "humbug." In fact, so much controversy raged that three journalists from well-established newspapers decided to investigate the claims and report the honest facts to their readers. Henry Villard of the *Cincinnati Commercial*, Albert D. Richardson of the Boston *Journal*, and the national favorite, editor Horace Greeley of the New York *Tribune*, surveyed the scene in June. Rumor still reports that the mine Greeley washed gold from was salted, but perhaps this was unnecessary. All three of the journalists seem to have caught something of the contagion of the place, and although their report cautioned against unwarranted enthusiasm, their generally favorable verdict undoubtedly helped to swell the tide of argonauts in the summer of 1859.

Certainly the Pike's Peak region experienced a phenomenal metamorphosis during those months. The area of greatest attraction was the region surrounding the original Gregory claim in Gregory Gulch. The Russell brothers, with a company of newly recruited Georgia prospectors and equipment enough to engage in full-scale mining, opened up placers in Russell Gulch, about two miles from Gregory's lode. In no time the valley claimed several towns—Black Hawk, Gregory Point, Mountain City, Central City, Nevadaville—all strung out up the steep incline.

Not everyone was satisfied with conditions at those camps. Some preferred Idaho, the leading town in the vicinity of Jackson's find. Others crossed the mountain passes into South Park, initiating such pick-and-shovel camps as Tarryall, Hamilton, Fairplay, and Buckskin Joe. By late summer, the prospectors had reached the Blue River, on the other side of the Divide.

When the snows of winter fell, the Pike's Peak area was a far different place than it had been twelve months before. Mountain camps had drained population from the valley towns, although many miners probably climbed down from the high hills to spend the winter in the supply towns. Denver and Auraria no longer rested easy in their claims as the central points for supplying the mines to the west, for in June, 1859, W. A. H. Loveland, and others, had opened the town called Golden City. And along the mountain base, others had platted settlements like Canon City and Colorado City. Obviously, a new day had dawned in the Rocky Mountain frontier.

Miners and Merchants

When William Green Russell's party of gold seekers dug their first gold dust from the bed of Dry Creek, they found exactly the type of gold for which they had been looking. They had come to the Rocky Mountains to prospect for "free" gold. Gold in its free form exists in a variety of shapes: nuggets, scale, shot, wire, grains, flour, dust. It is usually found in stream beds or along the banks of creeks in sites called placers. The man who worked the placer mine was, in many ways, the trail blazer for all other mining activities. Taking gold out of the gravel of a stream bed is the simplest operation of mining. The gold needs no smelting or refining; it is not bulky and can be transported easily from frontier areas.

Every experienced prospector knew that gold in such a placer could well indicate proximity to another type of free gold deposit—a lode. Lodes are free gold in rock formation. The vein or streak of ore in the rock, usually quartz, might run for great distances into the earth, requiring more complex procedures for removing it from the surrounding rock, moving it to the surface, and separating the free gold from its matte of quartz or other rock.

Early gold mining in the central Rockies was either placer or lode mining, and almost every method used in the extraction processes had been known in California during the rush days there. Many of the techniques, in fact, had their origins much earlier, for they were part of the European knowledge of mining, transferred to the New World through the Spanish experience in Mexico and California. Many of those who came to Pike's Peak had participated in the California rush and they introduced their accumulation of mining wisdom into the new fields. Through them, newcomers and amateurs mastered the arts.

Placer mining was the simplest of all mining operations for the process of extraction involved only the separation of the free gold from the dirt, mud, or gravel with which it was mixed. In working a placer, the miner relied on his pan for washing the debris. Although many kinds of household utensils—from washpans to saucepans to frying pans—temporarily filled the requirement, a well designed mining pan was made of sheet iron, with sloping sides and, perhaps, a copper bottom. The miner filled the pan with debris and water and, holding it just below the surface of the stream, dissolved the dirt and washed out the pebbles by agitating the pan. Since gold is a heavy metal, it sank to the bottom of the pan where it could be recovered with forceps or, more efficiently, by using mercury. The gold and the mercury formed an amalgam. By heating this amalgam, the miner could drive off the mercury, condense it, and use it again. The free gold remained as a residue.

Panning for gold was hard work. An experienced man could work his way through only one-half cubic yard of dirt a day. To speed up the washing process "mass production" methods were introduced into the gulches almost from the beginning. The implements used—the rocker, the long tom, the sluice-box—all were variations on the gold pan theme. They all provided a means of agitating the debris, either by movement, in the case of the rocker, or by rushing water through a trough, as in the long tom and the sluice-box. All of these devices were designed to wash the dirt and gravel in a more rapid fashion than a single miner could accomplish with his pan. Two men operating a rocker, one carrying the dirt and the other rocking, could clean out three to five cubic yards of dirt a day. But these methods were of value only for washing the coarser debris. All of them necessitated a final panning of the residue to garner the fine gold.

These processes required a constant use of water. Without that precious liquid no pan, no rocker, no sluice could be operated. Thus the mining season sometimes was limited to the warmer months of the year when the water in the creeks and streams was not frozen. And if the water was not immediately accessible to the gulch it had to be brought by ditches from the nearest source—or the dirt had to be dragged to the water. It was much easier to move water through ditches than to move the dirt to the streams, so the water channels were begun very early. Ditch digging in the mountains was also hard work. Some of the ditches had to carry water ten or twelve miles through rugged mountain terrain.

More ornate water works sometimes were constructed for the

placer mines. Boom dams were used in some locations where the flow of the stream was not large enough to operate a sluice. Here the water was collected behind a dam, and when enough had been gathered, the accumulated flow was let loose with a velocity great enough to wash the debris. Hydraulic mining was even more complex. In this process the water was dammed at elevations higher than the gulch. When a large quantity had been accumulated, the water was shot through hoses and nozzles, with pressure great enough to wash the gold-bearing gravel down stream banks or gulch walls.

Placer or gulch mining was "poor man's mining," for an individual could embark upon a career with a gold pan at very little expense. But placer mining was also likely to be rather limited in its returns. The big strikes were lode finds, and then considerably more labor and equipment were required to redeem the precious metal. Near the surface the fissure might have weathered and the rocks decomposed enough for easy extraction. But the vein of ore soon lured the lode miner deeper into the earth. Shafts and tunnels would have to be dug to follow the vein. When pick-and-shovel work no longer loosened the pay-rock, the miner drilled holes to fill with powder and blasted the rock to bits. When the shaft had been dug quite deep, whims and windlasses were used to raise the ore to the surface. Deeper holes could be worked better with horizontal tunnels. The miners then could remove the ore much easier and the tunnel also provided a drain for water that collected at the bottom of the shaft.

After the ore was worked loose from the rock and brought to the surface, the gold still had to be recovered from the quartz surrounding it. This required crushing. The early pulverizing implements were primitive, crude stone mortars, and Spanish *arrastres*. The arrastre consisted of two large rocks, the bottom one flat and the top one attached to a pole so that oxen or other animals could revolve it. The rock was pulverized between the two stone surfaces. After crushing, the gold still had to be separated from the debris by washing in pans. The arrastre was a slow, cumbersome mill. If the ore was high-grade, and returned a proportionately large quantity of gold in each ton of ore, the men operating it made reasonable profits from their labor. But for most ores, what was needed was a more rapid crushing method—an instrument capable of pulverizing more ore at less cost. That need was answered by the early introduction of stamp mills.

A stamp (or quartz) mill, in its elementary form, consists of heavy weights which are raised by mechanical means and then dropped on the ore. The first stamp mills in the Pike's Peak area were operated with water or horse power; when steam engines were introduced the efficiency of the mills increased remarkably. In 1859 only one stamp mill was in operation, near Nevada City. By the following season, however, more than 150 mills had been brought across the prairies and set up in the gulches. Ball mills were also used. These were iron spheres, into which the ore was placed, along with hard metal pellets. The sphere revolved on a shaft; the force of the hard pellets flying against the ore pulverized the rock. However crushed, the ore needed washing and treatment with mercury; thus water was as much a necessity for operation of the mills as it was for placer mining. Some men dug wells in order to obtain clean water to use in milling, rather than depend on muddy stream water. Obviously, mills were considerably more expensive than simple gold panning, but lode mining could more than pay the expense of freighting the machinery from the States, setting it up, and keeping it in repair for operation.

Both the mining and the reduction of lode ores was a more complex procedure than that of placer mining, and the costs involved in time, capital, and labor were far greater. But in both lode and placer mining, the men who came to the fields with some money, or at least some provisions, were the most fortunate of the argonauts. They could prospect for a time on their own capital, hoping to strike it rich before their reserves ran out. Those who had nothing were compelled to work as common laborers for others. They might expect to make from one to three dollars a day in addition to their board. If they were frugal, they might accumulate enough money to start prospecting for themselves.

While it is probable that almost every man who came to the Pike's Peak gold fields in the early rush, at one time or another, tried his hand with the mining pan, there were many who found the work too hard, the returns too meager. Others came with no intention of mining for a daily occupation. Some men had decided even before they crossed the plains that their own particular trade or talent would be in demand in the gold towns. The necessity of providing goods, supplies, and services for the men in the diggings gave many a chance to make a living—and a few to make fortunes—from the miners' trade.

It has been estimated that the mining frontier required a population at least five times more numerous than the number of men actually working the mines. So, the infinite variety of small business establishments that characterized any American town of mid-nineteenth century were soon duplicated in the supply towns at the base of the mountains and, to a lesser extent, in the mining camps themselves. Blacksmiths, bakers and saloon keepers, butchers, hotel and boarding house proprietors, druggists, liverers, and dance hall managers, bankers, barbers, and retailers of general merchandise, jewelers, gunsmiths, and brewers—and scores of other tradesmen opened their shops on either side of the wide, dirt main streets of the towns.

Meat was usually the only commodity, except for wood, that the miners in the mountains provided for themselves. Even then, some of the gold seekers preferred to spend their waking hours digging and washing, rather than hunting wild animals or chopping down trees. A few fresh vegetables were grown in the area. Within the first full season, the summer of 1859, some enterprising, perhaps disappointed gold seekers turned to onions and radishes instead of the glittering metal and began to irrigate small plots of ground in the valley of the South Platte River. Some corn was available from Charley Autobees'—and other—pioneer farms in the Huerfano Valley south of the diggings. But almost every other item of supply needed by the miners had to be brought into the camps from hundreds of miles away.

In no time at all a feud broke out over who was dependent upon whom in the supply business. The miners complained that they were held at the mercy of the merchants in the valley towns for the goods they needed; that they were forced to pay discriminately high prices. The retailers and suppliers, on the other hand, insisted that they were making extremely small profits, despite the high prices. They pointed out that the great cost and radical fluctuations in prices were beyond their control; that they were dependent on an irregular and frightfully expensive transportation system for the goods carried across the prairies. The merchants tried to obtain their supplies from all directions: east from the Missouri Valley towns, south from New Mexican villages, west from the Mormon settlements in Utah. But regardless of the sources, prices were always high, partly because the demand for goods remained greater than the supply. The situation was bad enough during the summer months, but in winter, when blizzards and bad weather increased the difficulties of transportation, prices went even higher.

Clashes between miners and merchants were inevitable, not only because of the prices charged for goods by the merchants, but also because the tradesmen in town set the price for much of the miners'

gold. Whatever barter took place during the early months of the gold
rush soon gave way to a new standard circulating medium—gold dust.
It was acknowledged a difficult medium to use. A pinch between
thumb and forefinger was supposed to represent twenty-five cents;
larger amounts were determined by using a scale. The dust was
elusive stuff, sticking to scales, pouches, and hands. One pioneer
woman later recalled that, in the post office, "once a week we would
sweep the office floor and wash the sweepings and get quite a little
gold dust."[1] Moreover, the dust could be easily mixed with brass
filings and other baser metals by amateur counterfeiters. In order to
convert the dust to coins, it had to be shipped to the federal mint at
Philadelphia, or to one of the branch mints (San Francisco, New
Orleans, Charlotte, N.C., or Dahlonega, Ga.). Costs of transportation
on such precious cargoes were high, and fear of losses was always
great, for renegades on the prairies might rob the stages. In addition,
the delays in transactions between the Pike's Peak country and the
eastern cities were frustrating, for they increased the difficulties of
completing business transactions.

Clark, Gruber and Company, a Leavenworth banking house that
had opened branch operations in Denver City, was one of the six
banks in the town in 1860. After obtaining dies and machinery in the
East, Clark, Gruber and Company began to cast $10 gold pieces in
July, 1860. Private mints were not then illegal in the United States,
but to make certain that its coins would be favorably received, this
banking house used a little more gold in each coin than the federal
coins contained. In time the company would also fabricate $2.50, $5
and $20 pieces, continuing their operations until the federal govern-
ment bought their mint in 1863. (It was assumed that the United
States would continue minting operations. Actually, the establishment
became an assay office only, until 1906 when the Denver Mint was
established. Clark, Gruber and Company, reorganized in 1865,
became the First National Bank of Denver.) Two other private mints
were in operation in the Pike's Peak country for a time, and some
men experimented with scrip—or shinplasters—which were printed
paper notes of small denomination. In these ways the problems of
gold dust currency were partly overcome.

All this was helpful for the merchants and tradesmen in the valley
towns, but the miners coming in to buy supplies had gold dust—not
Clark, Gruber coins—in their jeans pockets. The price of gold
remained in contention between miners and tradesmen. In the spring
of 1861 the Central City merchants joined to establish a schedule of

prices they would allow for gold, including such classifications as Clear Creek gold priced at $7 an ounce, Russell Gulch gold at $6 an ounce, the best average quality of retorted gold at $15 an ounce, and common, badly retorted, or dirty gold at $12 an ounce. The Central City traders sent their schedule of prices to a newly formed Chamber of Commerce in Denver. That group added to the list and then attempted to make it effective among its members. In practical terms, the new prices meant reduced prices for some of the gold that was traded in Central City or Denver. Howls of protest went up from miners and mill owners, adding to the already smoldering hostility between mountain gulches and valley towns. That hostility had earlier been expressed by a speaker at a mass meeting of miners in Gregory Diggings: ". . . the valleys were dependent upon the mountains but the mountains were not dependent upon Denver and Auraria. If we can purchase our goods at the same prices in Golden City, and they will receive our gold at the usual price, we had better patronize them, or if we should send a train of thirty or forty wagons to the States through Denver and Auraria, to supply our wants, they may be soon convinced as to whether the mountains were dependent upon the valleys." The Russell District miners put the case more bluntly: "Merchants furnishing us goods have no right whatever after making their profit on their goods to speculate upon our dust."[2]

While a certain sympathy goes out to the miners in their problems, the tradesmen also had difficulties of impressive dimensions in trying to bring supplies into the Pike's Peak region. The barrier of the Rocky Mountains deflected the main overland routes to the north (Oregon Trail) and south (Santa Fe Trail). At the same time, the mining districts were some 600 miles from the sources of supply on the Missouri River. Most freighters used teams of oxen to pull the heavy merchandise wagons over the prairies. The beasts travelled very slowly; water and feed were scarce on the plains; attacks by Indians, robberies by renegades, and bad weather all added hazards to the commerce.

Moving supplies from the valley towns like Denver or Boulder or Golden City up the grades to the diggings was also difficult. There were no roads into the mountains worthy of the name until toll companies began to construct them after 1860. When they were finished, these roads added toll costs to the already high charges of freighting, even though many of the roads were so poorly designed and constructed that they were little better than trails. Each new season of mining brought added demands for extension of the roads for each new season saw the opening of new gold camps, farther from the supply towns. These new camps also offered inducements for further town building: California Gulch, for example, with its rich placers at the headwaters of the Arkansas River, provided the impetus for the creation of Pueblo in July, 1860, near the earlier settlement called Fountain City.

As for passenger travel to the gold frontier, Russell, Majors and Waddell of St. Joseph, Missouri, had a decided advantage over rival staging companies when the rush began, for they were already operating in the region. The federal government had recently granted them a contract to haul supplies to army units in Utah Territory. These men now created the Leavenworth and Pike's Peak Express Company to provide daily coach service between Kansas and the Cherry Creek settlements. With some forty coaches, each capable of carrying eight passengers, the Leavenworth and Pike's Peak Company charged a fare of $100 to $125 for a one-way trip, including meals. The journey across the plains took about twelve days at the beginning, but when the company substituted the South Platte route for the Republican River trail, it cut the time to about one week.

The coaches travelled continuously, day and night. Short stops were made along the way at stage or relay stations that would be distinctive features of prairie travel until the lines no longer operated. The stations always provided a source of amusement to foreign visitors. A French traveller described them: "At the relay stations you will find waiting a hand basin and a pitcher of water, with soap and a towel that turns endlessly around a roller. You will find mirrors, combs, and brushes, and even tooth brushes, all fastened by a long string, so that everyone may help himself and no one will carry them off. You might laugh in Paris at these democratic customs; here they are accepted by all and are even welcome, except perhaps the tooth brush, which is regarded with a suspicious eye."[3]

Despite its original advantage over competitors, the Leavenworth and Pike's Peak Express was a short-lived company. In 1860 it was reorganized as the Central Overland, California and Pike's Peak Express Company—a name so long that the initials COC & PP (Clean Out of Cash and Poor Pay) were inevitably substituted. This was the organization that ran the romantic but also short-lived Pony Express across western America. The Pony Express used a relay station at Julesburg, but never provided direct service to the Cherry Creek towns. Then, in 1861, the COC & PP sold out to Ben Holladay's Overland Mail and Express Company. Five years later, Holladay's line was taken over by the rival Wells, Fargo & Company.

At the beginning, the private stage companies carried letters, for high fees, to and from the mining camps. The Pike's Peakers, however, wanted direct, daily mail service and in March, 1861, when Congress offered a million dollar subsidy to the company that would undertake a daily transcontinental mail, with Denver and Salt Lake City serviced either by the main line or by extension routes, Denver stirred itself to convince everyone of its claims for a location on the direct east-west route. What was needed was a usable pass through the mountains west of the city. Captain Edward L. Berthoud, hired to seek out such a pass, and his guide, Jim Bridger, found the crossing known today as Berthoud Pass. But despite the discoverers' enthusiasm, further investigation revealed that the grade up Clear Creek Canyon would be difficult, while the high pass with its winter snows would require extensive tunnelling for all-weather operations. Another decade and more would pass before the first wagon road would be built over Berthoud Pass.

So the daily mail service used the Oregon Trail, with the gold camps serviced by a tri-weekly branch from Julesburg. But in 1862, when Indian raids disrupted traffic on the main trail, the mail company did send its stages down the South Platte route to Denver and then north on the old Cherokee Trail. In this way, the Cherry Creek towns achieved their desire of a daily mail service that tied them to the rest of the country. Shortly after that, in 1863, a branch telegraph line crossed the sage hills from Julesburg to Denver, and in time other extensions would connect Central City and Pueblo to the main telegraph circuit. Thus the problems of communication were lessened considerably. Transportation difficulties, however, were not as easily ended. It was 1870 before the iron horse chugged along its rails into Denver, to bring the benefits and the problems of railroading to the Pike's Peak country.

8

Culture Comes to the Gold Towns

The glorious Fourth of July in the election year of 1860 seemed like a good time for the fledgling communities of the Pike's Peak area to celebrate. In Denver an appointed committee of civic leaders worked out the arrangements for the patriotic occasion. A thirty-two gun salute greeted the sun rising over the eastern plains on the morning of the holiday to usher in the festivities. A parade through the main streets provided the first exciting attraction. Participating groups included the ladies of the Temple of Liberty, the Freemasons, the Odd Fellows, the Sons of Malta, the Pioneer Club, the Sabbath schools, and the Turners. Such a list of organizations alone was enough to dispel any doubts about the civilization of the town that was less than two years old. Then, in traditional style, the orators reminded the Pike's Peakers of the glorious heritage of the Republic. The horse races at Reynolds Course, some three miles below Denver, probably provided the high point of the day. When another thirty-two gun salute marked the sunset, the citizens knew that, although separated by miles of prairie land from the rest of the nation, and still unacknowledged by the federal government, Denver had cele-brated the Fourth of July in fitting fashion.[1]

There was need for only one celebration in the Cherry Creek towns that year, for Denver City and Auraria had merged their interests and buried their antagonisms several months earlier. On the moonlit night of April 5, on the wooden bridge spanning Cherry Creek, the town fathers of the rival communities had celebrated the union of their enterprises. Competition was a luxury these men could no longer afford. Up the canyon of Clear Creek the men of Golden City were proving dangerous rivals. And to the north and the south other competitors threatened. The time had come to join hands. So the town of Auraria had died, and the combined city called Denver had been born.

It was to Denver that most of the newcomers from the States headed. Here the stage lines and the freight routes from the east converged; here was the major supply center for the mountains to the west; here a ferry operated across the Platte River until bridges were built. From the very beginning, the confluence of Cherry Creek with the South Platte River acted like a magnet in drawing the immigrants to it. Despite the lack of trees and the somewhat barren aspects of the infant town, it was a welcome sight to the traveller, weary from the long and tiring stage ride across the plains. Miners deserting the high hills during the winter months found it equally attractive. Every year the place grew more civilized. What might be lacking one year was more than compensated for by the grandiose hopes and prophesies of what was to come the next.

The amazement at the speed with which Denver took on the aspects of an older, more established town was not confined to the local "boosters." Aliens to the region reacted with almost as much pride in the accomplishments. Travellers constantly registered surprise at what they termed Denver's "solid progress" despite all the discouraging circumstances of isolation, lack of authorized government, Indian scares, and the fluctuating prophesies about the future of the mining camps.

What was true of Denver was true to only a lesser degree of other towns in the valleys and in the mining districts. On the Upper Arkansas in California Gulch in July, 1860, for example, Webster D. Anthony found a log cabin store which boasted "the first Glass windows" in the settlement of Sacramento City, a thriving town where "only a few weeks ago not a house was seen."[2] And in that same month, a visitor to New Tarryall in South Park wrote: "How long since this town was built? Two months. How many houses does it contain at present? About two hundred. What is the name of this principal street? Broadway."[3]

The weather vanes of society were infinite in variety, but one of the most obvious was the type of building that lined the streets of the towns. Construction seemed to follow a similar pattern of growth in all the centers. The rude log cabins and tents of the first years were replaced by frame houses and shop buildings as soon as a saw mill had been brought into the area to afford the luxury of siding and boards. After frame buildings with shingled roofs came brick structures. The final step was the creation of stone and masonry buildings. In the early years, frame buildings dominated the frontier towns. If buildings were used for public purposes, fashion dictated a false front, with a painted sign to advertise the shop or service.

The towns were generally laid out, as much as possible, on the approved rectangular grid. In the gulch towns in the mountains it was sometimes impossible to plan any cross streets, for the canyon walls were so close together there was room for only one long main street. Everywhere the streets were unlighted and unpaved, becoming dusty in summer and turning into quagmires throughout much of the rest of the year.

The pride of every community—valley or gulch— was the church building or buildings, once they had been erected. Nothing else seemed to indicate quite so surely the permanence of the town and its success in duplicating society back in the States. In the first years in the mining towns, the population was overwhelmingly male, for many men had come to the diggings planning to go home again as soon as they had found their gold or had exhausted their money. The town promoters realized that a stable, permanent population could not be assured until married men with families became residents. A church building, with tower or steeple, and perhaps even a bell, openly advertised that a town was a fit place for women and children to live.

The emotional response to a completed church on the frontier was intensified by the ever-present awareness of the region's isolation from the rest of the country. As one of the early settlers recalled: "When for the first time the old bell pealed out in clear tones its call to worship,—tones which were strange, indeed, to the ears of these isolated westerners—tears came to the eyes of more than one person whose soul was stirred by the memory of a little church back in the 'states.' "[4]

The earliest religious services in the gold fields were presided over by men who had been lay leaders in their congregations back home. By the spring of 1859 such temporary and spontaneous services began to be replaced with more regularly framed organizations. In April the Methodist Episcopal Church established its Pike's Peak and Cherry Creek Mission within the Kansas-Nebraska Conference, sending out the Reverend Messrs. W. H. Goode and Jacob Adriance as missionaries to organize congregations. By August they had established what later became the Trinity Church in Denver. The desire of the town builders to further such activity is apparent from the offer of both Auraria and Denver town companies to present free building sites to the congregation that would erect the first house of worship. The Methodists were followed on the scene by the Episcopalians, led by the Reverend Mr. H. J. Kehler, who established the Church of St. Johns in the Wilderness in Denver in 1860. Presbyterian services were also conducted in Denver that summer and a small Jewish society established the Temple Emanuel congregation the same year. The Baptists and Congregationalists followed shortly thereafter.

In the spring of 1860, Catholic Bishop John B. Miege travelled from Leavenworth, in Kansas, to Denver. Viewing the new settlements as too remote from his home cathedral for supervision, he recommended transferring the area to the jurisdiction of the bishop at Santa Fe. Thus Bishop J. B. Lamay at the New Mexican capital then sent his Vicarate Apostolic, Father Joseph P. Machebeuf, with Father J. B. Raverdy, to Denver in October, 1860. These priests managed, through hard labors, to finish a church building in time for celebration of the mass on Christmas Day, 1860.

All these early religious establishments were of mission nature, and provided a real test to the trained clergy who staffed them. The congregations in the settlements like Denver and Central City needed organization; buildings demanded financing and construction; small settlements, particularly in the mining gulches, needed ministering, too. Itinerant preaching was more the rule than the exception, as clergy of many faiths carried the gospel to miners in isolated gold camps. Most of the clergymen found affairs to their liking and proceeded to make their work a testament to their faith. Sometimes their first impressions were less than they had expected: when the Reverend Mr. William Crawford of the American Home Missionary Society arrived in Denver in 1863, he was tempted, he said, when preaching ". . . to give out the hymn of Watts: 'Lord, what a wretched land is this, which yields us no supply, no cheering fruits, no wholesome trees, no streams of living joy.' " Yet, said Crawford, ". . . some of the Denverites think they have found the best spot on earth. Poor, deluded mortals."[5] But, whatever their first thoughts, the clergymen generally spared neither themselves nor their followers in their mission activities.

The companion civilizers of the churches were the schools. Although the initial population of the Pike's Peak gold towns tended to be predominantly male, it was not long before families who had settled in the region recognized the need for instruction for their children. By October, 1859, Denver could boast its first classroom.

This was a private establishment, headed by "Professor" O. J. Goldrick. The schoolmaster had come to Denver like a fugitive from the theatre—his contemporaries recalled later his arrival "as a bullwacker, driving his ox team, yet dressed in broadcloth suit, 'stovepipe' hat, and kid gloves"—a schoolmaster who, tradition boasts, cursed his oxen in learned Latin! Irish-born, with reputed study both at the University of Dublin and Columbia College in New York, Goldrick had taught school and worked for book publishers in Cincinnati before coming to the gold country. His Union-Day School cost each pupil $3.00 a month. On the first day thirteen children appeared in the classroom—"2 Indians, 2 Mexican, the rest white and from Missouri."[6]

Following Goldrick's example, other schools were soon in operation. Some of these, like the first, were privately operated, although they probably were poor paying propositions since even the earliest of the "professors" found it necessary to become a casual newspaper correspondent to augment his income as schoolmaster. Catholic and Episcopalian congregations sponsored other schools. By 1860, classes were being conducted also at Mount Vernon and Golden and at Boulder, where a frame building was erected especially for the purpose—Colorado's first schoolhouse. Earlier schools had used rented quarters. Before the establishment of public schools, the private schools filled the void at the beginning and their contribution as a civilizing factor on the mining frontier was significant. The Pike's Peak gold camps were much more comfortable places to which a man might bring his family once educational facilities, no matter how limited, were available for his children.

Since the mere mention of schools was likely to dispel doubts about life in the wilderness West in the minds of potential immigrants, the newspapers and town promoters early saw the excellent advertising potential of such institutions. Perhaps for that reason, great excitement was generated over the possibilities of an institution of higher education. By May, 1863, plans had been drawn and the Denver Seminary was begun, largely under the auspices of the Methodist Church, although its founders attempted to keep it from becoming too closely identified with any one denomination. They changed the name the following year to the Colorado Seminary and soon had managed the construction of a building and had secured a charter. Thus the institution that would later become the University of Denver was a going concern, almost before the public school movement was initiated.

Schools and universities were not the only institutions used by the publicists to attract attention to the area. Realizing that unless the instability of the mining population could be overcome by attracting more permanent residents than the "here today—gone tomorrow" prospectors, the early newspapers of the Pike's Peak region all succumbed to varying degrees of "boosterism." More sane in his approach than some, yet still unwilling ever to sell his adopted city short, William N. Byers and his *Rocky Mountain News* established an early ascendency over the rest of the news sheets in the gold towns. Byers, a one-time surveyor, left his home in Omaha, Nebraska, in March, 1859, in the vanguard of the argonauts moving west. With Dr. George Monell and Thomas Gibson, he set out across the prairies for the diggings with a printing press and supplies for a newspaper in his wagon. On April 23 the infant *News* was born, beating out by minutes John Merrick's *Cherry Creek Pioneer* as the first Pike's Peak newspaper.

The competition proved brief, for Merrick sold his *Pioneer* to Thomas Gibson after he had run the first issue, taking his grubstake to the hills to finance some prospecting. Gibson would stay with the weekly *News* until the spring of 1860 when he started the daily *Rocky Mountain Herald*. Such competition forced Byers to convert the *News* to a daily too. And soon the area was full of rival enterprises: the *Register* at Gregory Gulch, the *Western Mountaineer* at Golden City, the Black Hawk *Journal*, the *Gold Reporter* at Mountain City, the *Boulder Valley News*. Some of these newspapers were short-lived ventures, but no self-respecting community in either valley or gulch could afford to ignore the possibilities of enticing an editor and a press to set up shop. As soon as a town was started, its founders and merchants needed a newspaper to demonstrate the success of their venture and to advertise the "city's" advantages to the rest of the world. As the editor of the Canon City *Times* pointed out, "a city is as much indebted to its public journal for its progress and'prosperity as to its avenues of trade."[7]

By 1867 five daily, eight weekly, and two monthly papers bore Colorado imprints. In the pages of those newspapers are the telling indications of the society they served. Here the professional men—the lawyers, the doctors, the dentists—advertised their services. From the newspaper columns another aspect of the steady transition from wilderness to civilization can be traced, as associations of men with common interests are recorded. For example, by June of 1860, enough physicians had arrived in the Cherry Creek area to create the

Jefferson Medical Society. Although short-lived, it lasted long enough to adopt a code of ethics and a uniform fee of $3.00 a visit. A city hospital had also been organized by that year.[8]

Nor were the professional people the only ones who saw potential advantages from collective action. In the summer of 1863 the carpenters in Denver organized an association, through which they adopted a minimum wage resolution calling for payment of four dollars a day for their work.[9] And the typesetters in Denver had organized Typographical Union No. 49 even earlier.[10]

Social, rather than economic forces, motivated the organization of other groups. Lodges and clubs seemed as easy to transport westward as stamp mills or flour barrels. The Masons, the Templars, the Odd Fellows, the Turners—and many other organizations—were soon well established in Denver, Central City, and many of the other towns. By 1866 Denver assumed it was aged enough to rate a Pioneer's Association which, in exclusive fashion, restricted its membership to 1858-1859 immigrants—the pioneers of a mere seven or eight years earlier.

Much of the recreation of the pioneers was more casual, less formal, than that provided by the clubs and lodges in the towns. Nature had created a splendid playground for the settlers, with trout streams, wild animals, and scenic wonders everywhere. The central Rockies had seen big hunts before the gold rush. In 1855 Irish Baronet Sir St. George Gore, with numerous retainers, dogs, horses, and wagons, had hunted through North, Middle, and South Parks, with the reported killing of several thousand buffalo, forty grizzly bears, and unnumbered antelope and deer. Now, with growing enthusiasm, this sportsmen's paradise was openly advertised as the finest on the continent, and excursions from the valley towns as well as from the States—and even the Old World—racked up hunting records which often indicate something more like slaughter than sport.

Along with trout and grizzly bears, the mountains also provided hot springs which were quickly converted into sites for health seekers, furthering an infant Colorado industry called tourism. For example, only a few years after the opening of the gold fields, the soda springs near Idaho Springs were in use as a water cure and bathing establishment.

In the towns, sporting events were a conspicuous and exciting part of life. Wrestling and boxing matches were natural accompaniments to the predominantly male society of the early years; a wrestling match highlighted the first Christmas celebration at Cherry Creek. Horse racing was another favorite, perhaps the most widely enjoyed of all recreational occasions. Participants and spectators alike found the races, and the wagering on them, exciting avenues of escape from the drudgery and routine of frontier life. Guns, blankets, horses, gold dust, town lots, mining claims—and for the Indians, even wives—could be and were wagered on the races.

And when the race was over, the place to retire and talk about it, or to plan the next event, was the town saloon. These poor men's social clubs played so conspicuous a part of the main-street life of western towns that, a century later, the image is still vivid. These liquor-dispensing establishments might vary greatly, but they often were operated as adjuncts to gambling halls, billiard parlors, or bawdy houses. Tradition accords them a prominent place in the town life, and no stories are more often repeated than the incongruous tales of early religious services conducted in the bar room, with gambling tables quieted long enough to allow the "parson" his chance to preach.

Although it spoils the picture of the frontier as a place that was always wild, and always rough, and always wide-open, truth intrudes the qualification that temperance sentiment also was a positive force in most of the towns. Restrictions to regulate saloons appeared almost as soon as the saloons themselves. Some mining districts contented themselves by declaring that "all Gambling houses and Drinking saloons that are open for the carrying on of their business on Sunday be considered . . . a nuisance."[11] Others went further; the miners of Nevada District, for example, resolved "that there shall be no Bawdy Houses Grog shops or Gamboling Saloons within the Limits of this District."[12]

More refined, but still well patronized features of town life were the music halls and theatres. Offerings might be limited in the early years, but to sweat-stained miners or tired tradesmen, seeking diversion from their laboring hours, the quality was less important than the opportunity for relaxation. Entertainers found appreciative, applauding patrons, eager to view their offerings. And the gap between musical variety shows and genuine drama was quickly bridged. Home talent soon gave way to travelling companies of players who crossed the plains to bring culture in the form of dramatic productions to the miners.

With theatres and saloons, schools and churches, the towns advanced. Sometimes, however, the pattern of progress was rather rudely jolted. On the wintry morning of April 19, 1863, a fire burned out of control in Denver, and before the volunteer fire companies managed to stop its advance, the flames had destroyed the heart of the city. The seventy buildings and estimated $197,200 worth of supplies and goods consumed by the fire were a serious loss. But costly and discouraging though it might be, the city bounced back with enthusiasm as it contemplated the new construction that would replace the old, congratulating itself that the new buildings would be largely of brick and stone, instead of wood—"that fragile and combustible material" that identified the buildings of a pioneer town.[13]

The Denver fire of 1863 was bad enough, but the next year the town suffered another and worse disaster. On the night of May 20, 1864, the waters of Cherry Creek rose and a "wall of water" swept down the valley, carrying with it the Methodist Church, the *Rocky Mountain News* office (which Editor Byers had diplomatically placed between the once-rival towns of Denver City and Auraria), the City Hall and all the records stored there. Eleven lives were lost in the flood. The lesson could hardly be ignored, and a healthy respect for the character of the mountain streams was learned. But again, instead of grieving over the losses, the young town plunged forward with renewed determination.

With such enthusiasm and such energy the towns of the Pike's Peak region were built. Within little more than a decade of their births they seemed no longer strange, primitive objects to be considered pretentious in all their claims to greatness. The Englishman James Thomson summed it up neatly when he described his impressions of Central City in 1872: "We have churches, chapels, schools, and a new large hotel, in which a very polite dancing party assembled the other evening. . . . We have a theatre, in which we now and then have actors. The rough old days with their perils and excitements, are quite over; the 'City' is civilised enough to be dull and commonplace, while not yet civilised enough to be sociable and pleasant."[14] The birthing times were over. The Pike's Peak towns had entered their awkward adolescence.

9

Legal Beginnings

"Pike's Peak or Bust" read the signs on the canvas wagon coverings. The "Pike's Peak country" was the closest thing to a name the new diggings had. Actually, most of the area of the earliest gold strikes was legally a part of the Territory of Kansas. Since 1854, the fortieth parallel had separated that territory from Nebraska Territory to the north. South of the Arkansas River the New Mexican officials ruled, while the Western Slope was within the boundaries of the Utah Territory. These were the political boundaries. However, much of the land had been expressly reserved by treaty for various Indian tribes. Thus the Pike's Peak argonauts moved onto lands belonging to Indians, lands hundreds of miles away from the capitals of the four federal territories. Too distant for effective control from any one of them, the gold seekers were left to provide their own devices for law and order in the diggings.

If the immigrants settled in the valley towns they found themselves provided with a type of organization formed mainly for purposes of town-booming and lot-selling. Although basically economic in motivation, at least the leaders of the town companies were interested in protecting their property and the property of their clients. In these towns instruments known as "people's courts" functioned as temporary mass meetings to try, and often execute, criminals who had attempted to interject lawlessness into the community. It was government self-manufactured, completely indigenous, and in many respects, highly democratic.

The miners in the gulches and hills followed the example of the town promoters and similarly created their own governmental agencies. They called their creations "mining districts," for which they established officers and procedures that became highly effective for governing. The mining districts tended to be more formal in organization than the people's courts, for the miners wrote constitutions providing names, boundaries, and officers for their districts. They also regulated the size and method of claim proving, and established procedures for settling disputes. The officers were few in number: a president; a recorder or secretary to enter the claims in the record books; a constable or sheriff to serve writs and summonses. Since no miner cared to lose unnecessary time at work on his mine, the officers were elected for short terms. They were not paid salaries, but, rather, were allowed stipulated fees for their work. For example, the recorder in some districts collected one dollar for each claim entered on the district records, and corresponding amounts for other official duties.

By far the most important function of the district officers was to see that the claim system worked properly. Actually, all claims were of doubtful legality since the Indians still held title to much of the land. But, acting on the assumption that the federal government would soon extinguish the Indian claims, the settlers proceeded to arrange a system of their own, based on the pre-emption laws. These federal statutes provided that actual settlers on land of the public domain would have the first chance to purchase their holdings when, and if, the land was surveyed and offered for sale at the public land office.

There were many types of claims arranged, each designed for a particular purpose or to suit certain conditions. The mountain, lode, or quartz claim gave the right to work a lode or vein of ore. While the dimensions of all claims varied from district to district, and from time to time, the usual size of the lode claim was 100 feet in length and 50 feet in width. In most districts, prospectors could pre-empt no more than one claim on any one lode. Gulch or placer claims usually were measured 100 feet up and down the gulch, from bank to bank. Since water was an integral part of all mining operations, water claims were instituted, measured in feet up and down the streams. More extensive water rights were necessary for operating stamp or lumber mills, and these were usually designated as mill site claims, with the size determined by the amount of water required for a suitable dam or to keep a mill wheel operating. Not as common, but still of use, were timber claims for cutting trees in areas other than the mineral claims of the miner. And there were other variations: patch claims for diggings in placers outside stream beds or gulches; tunnel claims for digging into lode shafts; cabin claims and ranch claims.

Claims were perfected by the discoverer staking off each end of the site and marking on the stakes the name of his claim and his own name. The discoverer then had ten days, not counting Sundays, to record his claim and was given the right to one additional claim on the lode or gulch as an incentive reward for his discovery. Once he had recorded his claim, others could locate on the lode, in numbered sequence in either direction from the original claim. No one under sixteen years of age could hold a claim, and all claims (except that of the discoverer) had to be improved or worked on. Satisfactory improving usually was accomplished by working one day in every ten until ten days of work had been completed. If the claim was not improved, it was declared vacant and could then be reclaimed by someone else.

These requirements were devised to be more than mere formalities. The codes were arranged to answer the need for protection of the miners' property and when disputes arose they were settled according to methods prescribed in the written codes. Although procedures varied from district to district, the method of deciding disputes in Gregory Diggings was probably typical. A miner claiming a grievance concerning his claim called on the recorder of the district. That officer then selected nine disinterested miners, and the parties to the controversy alternately struck names from the list until three remained. This panel of three arbitrators decided the case at once. If the miner did not agree with their decision, the recorder called a general meeting of all miners in the district who, by majority vote, could sustain or overrule the panel's decision. If the original verdict was upheld, then a party refusing to obey the verdict could no longer hold a mining claim in the district. Like most legal codes, that of Gregory Diggings underwent frequent changes, and the procedures of trial were refined in a pragmatic fashion. In time, the appeal stage was modified so that a jury of twelve men reviewed cases on appeal from the decision of the arbitration panel.

The process of creating and functioning under legal codes for claims was repeated in the several hundred mining districts organized in the Pike's Peak country in the first years of the gold rush. The governments were indigenously established, with no authority other than the "sovereignty" of the individual miners who agreed to place themselves under the districts' control. But such procedures were by no means unique to the Colorado mountains; they had been native to the American climate since the Mayflower Compact of 1620. More directly related to the Pike's Peak experiences were the mining districts formed during the California gold rush a decade earlier. The California districts had borrowed freely from Spanish customs and laws and the hybrid results from the mixture of parentage worked well in the Rocky Mountains, despite some disappointments. One attempt, in the spring of 1860, to confederate several of the districts in order to establish uniform codes of laws proved abortive. However, even without success in this endeavor, the mining districts more than proved their worth during the years that preceded the organization of Colorado Territory in 1861.

What worked for the miners in the mountains also worked for the agricultural settlers in the valleys. There claim clubs came into existence to secure for squatters their particular tracts of land against both latecomers and speculators. Here again, the techniques were borrowed from earlier frontiers, where claim clubbing had developed in agricultural regions like Wisconsin and Iowa. Perhaps a typical club of this kind was the El Paso Claim Club, organized in August, 1859. The club operated under a written constitution with elected officers, including a panel of arbitrators to settle disputes concerning the validity of claims on some eighty square miles (51,200 acres) of land in the valleys of Fountain, Monument, and Camp creeks. This land had not been surveyed by the federal authorities, so it was necessary to describe the claims of the members in terms of natural features like streams and trees. The Indian title to the land had not been extinguished and the major purpose of the club was to provide collective security to the settlers until such time as the federal government cleared the Indian titles, surveyed the land, and was ready to sell it at public auction. Although not nearly so numerous as the mining districts, one or more claim clubs were organized in each of the river valleys of the Eastern Slope and one club protected properties across the front ranges in Middle Park in 1860.

The town companies, designed principally to secure likely sites for speculation and profit, and the mining districts and claim clubs, whose main purpose was to secure and hold valuable land claims, all provided rudimentary government for the settlers within their boundaries. They were all extra-legal, but, particularly in their early months, they served their purpose well. They protected personal and property rights until more legitimate governments were established, and they punished offenders in quick and simple procedures. Persons accused of wrongdoing were tried before assembled citizens; once the verdict was pronounced, the guilty man was usually punished immediately, for the pioneer miner or tradesman had neither time nor money to maintain prison facilities. Whipping, banishment, hanging—depending on the seriousness of the crime—were usual punishments. The process of justice was simple, perhaps democratic, certainly speedy, and it might even have been fair. The most obvious defects were the lack of appeal from the decisions of the courts and the haste with which cases might be disposed of.

Common offenders against the public peace were horse thieves, perhaps the most numerous criminals of western America. But competing with them for notoriety were highwaymen, petty thieves, cheating gamblers—in fact, the usual host of depraved characters associated with a highly mobile, mining society. In the mineral districts and agricultural valleys, claim jumpers created problems. To punish them and other criminals, the elementary law worked quite well.

Volumes have been written about the lawlessness of the rip-roaring frontier and the Pike's Peak mining camps usually are not excepted from the general statements. Horace Greeley got into the act early by including in his western report the assertion that there were " . . . more brawls, more fights, more pistol-shots with criminal intent in this log city [Denver] of one hundred and fifty dwellings, not three-fourths completed nor two-thirds inhabited, nor one-third fit to be, than in any community of equal numbers on earth."[1] There is probably nothing more difficult than attempting to draw the definitive line describing the extent of crime and unruly life in the mining camps, but a good guess is that the Pike's Peak frontier was never quite as roaring as either Editor Greeley or later fiction writers have suggested.

Yet no matter how effectively the mining districts and the people's courts took care of local criminals, the yearning and striving for legitimate, recognized government in the Pike's Peak diggings was continuous from the very beginning. Not only was state-making and senator-electing something of an American passion; the Pike's Peakers fully understood the advantages to be gained from political controls recognized by the federal government, yet tailored to the needs of the mining frontier.

This explains why, in November, 1858, during the first autumn at the diggings, the relatively tiny population voted at Auraria to send a delegate to Washington, D.C., to try to gain territorial status for the region. At the same time, with seemingly equal enthusiasm and, if later memories were correct, with equal fraud on both sides of a "wet" vs. "dry" split in the population, the voters elected a representative for the Kansas Territorial Legislature. From this shotgun method, one or the other might result in legitimate recognition. A. J. Smith travelled east to Kansas and was seated in the legislature there. Hiram J. Graham, who had defeated the "wet" candidate William Clancy to become the congressional delegate, carried with him to Washington a petition requesting the creation of a new territory. When he arrived at the national capital he found others already at work on the scheme. A bill was introduced for the formation of the Pike's Peak region into Colona Territory, but it died at birth in the House of Representatives in January, 1859. Two other attempts that winter at congressional territory-making also proved unsuccessful.

With the arrival of the horde of immigrants in the spring rush of 1859, demands became insistent that if Congress was not going to act, then the argonauts themselves should establish an independent territorial—or state—government of their own. In April, at a meeting in "Uncle Dick" Wootton's store building in Auraria, delegates representing Fountain City, Eldorado, El Paso, Arapahoe, Auraria, and Denver City determined that a state was needed. The preferred name was Jefferson. A call went out for the election of delegates to a constitutional convention to be held in June. That convention, with fifty men representing thirteen different districts, convened as scheduled. But by June many immigrants were on their way home, disillusioned by their lack of success at gold mining. The number of "go backs" was great enough to raise the question again of whether a state or territory would best fit the needs of the communities.

Small wonder that the delegates were undecided; even today it is almost as easy to be surprised at their actions, for "note the dashing boldness of these resolute pioneers. Here was a convention representing less' than two thousand people, less than half of them fixed residents, before any great mines had been opened, or even discovered; before the capabilities of the soil were known; before an acre of land had been planted, and whilst every soul was in doubt whether or not there ever would be a basis for support of even a small population, taking measures without precedent, without authority of law, and without the slightest prospect of ratification, for the creation of an independent commonwealth."[2]

Unable to decide the question, the convention adjourned until August and then it nicely straddled the problem by drafting both a state constitution and a memorial to Congress requesting territorial status. The two propositions were presented to the people, who voted 2,007 for territorial status, 1,649 for statehood. It has been estimated that no more than one-fourth of the residents of the Pike's Peak area actually cast their ballots.

Nonetheless, acting on this indication of popular preference, a territory was manufactured in October, without any authority to do so by Congress. The voters then elected Robert W. Steele governor of their creation—Jefferson Territory. He was to be aided in his administrative chores by such other high potentates as a secretary, a treasurer, an auditor, an attorney-general, a chief justice, two associate justices, a supreme court clerk, a marshal, and a superintendent of public instruction.

The constitution of the new territory provided for a two-house legislature. Elections for legislators were held and a thirty-one day session convened in November, 1859. This Jefferson legislature enacted provisions for officers' salaries, a judicial system, the creation of counties, and the chartering of many kinds of corporations. But it was one thing to pass laws, and another to enforce them, particularly if they involved taxes. When the legislature levied a poll tax of one dollar on each resident, hundreds of miners in the hills pledged to resist the collection of any tax imposed on them by the territory. In so doing, they repudiated the government itself.

Nor were taxes the only problem. Some of the residents viewed the Jefferson government with jealous, suspicious eyes and continued to place their hopes in the Kansas territorial legislature. Actually, as its founders well knew, Jefferson Territory could only be a temporary make-shift. Congressional approval was imperative for success. Thus, all through the days of the Jefferson experiment, agents and influence were used to prompt congressional action. The times, however, were not conducive to success; the slavery debate between North and South, and the approaching presidential election of 1860, absorbed the time and energy of Congress and the politicians to the exclusion of most other matters. One thing, however, did emerge from these attempts—the name of "Colorado."

Jefferson was not a popular name for the future territory; some people argued that Washington should be the only president honored by such distinction since all presidents could not be equally treated, and others, of the new Republican Party, were opposed because Thomas Jefferson was too closely associated in memories with their rivals, the Democrats. Many alternative names were suggested— Yampa, Idahoe, Nemara, San Juan, Lula, Weapollao, Arapahoe,

Colorado, Tahosa, Lafayette, Columbus, Franklin—so many in fact, that as late as February, 1861, a miner informed his correspondent to direct his letters ". . . to Denver City with the name of this Territory, whatever Congress is pleased to call it."[3] But gradually the name "Colorado" gained in favor, and it was ultimately assigned to the region.

Meanwhile, the government of Jefferson Territory was growing more impotent each month, although it remained in nominal existence throughout the summer of 1860. The actual control of affairs in the area devolved into the hands of the local, popular agencies—the miners' districts, the claim clubs, the people's courts. Dissatisfaction with the state of affairs appears to have become rather widespread. One man complained: "We are neither in the Union or out of it. We are not sufficiently a territory to have laws, neither so far from it as to have the privilege of making our own laws with the power to enforce them. With what shameful neglect were we treated by that august body at Washington and also by the great father J[ames] B[uchanan]."[4]

Another resident expressed the grievance this way: "This Rocky Mountain Country with its two hundred thousand souls has received just about as much legislative aid at Washington as the Fe Gee Islanders. No mail service for the next twelve months that can be relied on; no extinguishment of the Indian title; no territorial organization, and, in fact, no sort of governmental recognition for the advancement of our interests here . . . so we are compelled to adopt the squatter sovereignty doctrine, making our own laws."[5]

This was the situation in the Pike's Peak area at the time the election of 1860 was fought out back in the States. The winner of that contest was the candidate of the young Republican Party, Abraham Lincoln. Southern members of the Congress, consistent with earlier warnings, now started to pack their bags and leave Washington. As they withdrew, Kansas Territory, which in its six years of existence had contributed more than its share to the events now transpiring, could be admitted as a free state to the Union. On January 29, 1861, Congress voted statehood for Kansas, with its present western boundary.

This meant that the new state's limits ended a long distance from the Pike's Peak gold camps, and the settlers in the mountains were in an even more disorganized status than before. But action to remedy the situation was soon forthcoming. A bill to create Colorado Territory was introduced into the Senate almost immediately after the creation of the state of Kansas. With fewer southern members to fear more free-soil votes, the bill passed the two houses. On February 28, 1861, the lame-duck president, James Buchanan, signed the "birth certificate" for the Territory of Colorado.

10

Warpaths Red and White

The infant territory called Colorado was brought into the world at the time its parent nation experienced the opening traumas of the greatest crisis in its history—the Civil War. Throughout the years of bloodshed that followed, from Fort Sumter in April, 1861, until Appomattox Court House in April, 1865, the convulsions of the war echoed within the territory, despite its relatively isolated geographic location. And before the end of the conflict had come, the territory would experience its own military problems, as the Indians of the Eastern Slope attempted to drive the white intruders from their hunting lands.

Argonauts who had come to the Colorado mines since the original discoveries of gold in 1858 represented a wide variety of "home" states in both the North and the South. It was, therefore, inevitable that some of the residents of the territory would reflect their native sections' "cause" when the Civil War began. Considering the emotional appeals of both sides, however, it is somewhat remarkable that so few demonstrative incidents occurred in Colorado. Southern sentiment appeared one morning in Denver, when the Confederate flag hung from a store front, but loyal Unionists disposed of it in a hurry. The Unionists, who comprised a majority of the settlers, limited their demonstrations to patriotic rallies, where they enthusiastically approved resolutions pledging support to the national government.[1]

There was a curious tone of restraint in these resolutions, however. The declarations of loyalty to the Union were followed by protestations of peaceful intentions and hopes for harmony among all of the territory's people, not only, as they put it, because the framers loved peace, but also in case they had "need of all for the common defense against the Indian tribes around" them. The exposed and isolated situation of the mining frontier demanded that sectional differences be submerged in the interest of defense against a more immediate danger that existed locally.

In one respect, at least, the Coloradans were fortunate, for the war did not begin until after the creation of the territory, and legitimate, relatively stable government soon was to be instituted in the region. It was also fortunate that President Lincoln selected an avowed Unionist as the first governor of the new territory; in fact, William Gilpin's appointment to that post was particularly the result of his demonstrated loyalty to the Union cause. His views on the sectional crisis thus coincided with those of the majority of the territory's residents, and his leadership helped insure the continued commitment of Colorado to the nation. Lincoln's choice was well received in the territory for another reason too. Gilpin was familiar with the territory he would govern, for he had explored with Frémont, campaigned in the area during the Mexican War, and was nationally known as a western enthusiast.

For most first governors of new territories in the nation's history, the tasks of instituting political agencies proved a full-time occupation. For Governor Gilpin, however, problems of defending the region against potential enemies—Indian or Confederate—relegated civil affairs to a subordinate position. After his arrival in the territory, in late May, 1861, Gilpin did set in motion the necessary procedures for operating the territorial government. In this work he was aided by his fellow officers who had also received presidential appointment to territorial positions: Lewis Ledyard Weld, the secretary of the territory; Benjamin F. Hall, S. Newton Pettis, and Charles L. Armor, the first justices of the supreme court; Copeland Townsend, the marshal. Gilpin himself appointed additional administrative officers, including an attorney-general and a surveyor-general.

While the executive and judicial officers were appointed, the legislative branch of the territorial government was to be elected by the residents, as was the territorial delegate who would represent Colorado's interests in the national congress. By September elections had been completed, the first territorial legislature convened in Denver, and Republican Hiram P. Bennet—nicknamed "Garden Seed" after the campaign because of his promises to send voters free vegetable seeds—was on his way to Washington as delegate from the territory.

There was much work for the legislature's nine-member Council (upper house) and thirteen-member House of Representatives (lower chamber) to do in their first session. Basic, foundation codes were needed for both civil and criminal law. These were put together, with considerable borrowing from the law books of Illinois and other established states. The legislature carved the territory into seventeen counties and created machinery for their government. And, of particular importance considering the times, the legislature enacted statutes creating the territorial militia.

The military defense of the gold regions, to this time, had been largely a federal concern. The settlers expected that the United States Army, from garrison forts in the region, would and could control any threats to their peaceful existence. And the army had garrisoned both Fort Garland in the San Luis Valley and Fort Lyon (Bent's New Fort, later Fort Wise, and now renamed again) on the Arkansas River. But what in easier times had appeared adequate defense suddenly seemed woefully insufficient, for several reasons.

For one thing, the army garrisons were physically separated from the concentration of the mining population, too far south to really protect the new towns. In addition, with the outbreak of the Civil War, it was doubtful if the army could pay much attention to the frontier areas when it was so fully engaged in the more serious warfare in the East. Finally, there were more threats to the peace than had ever appeared before—in fact, three different, hazardous possibilities arose. Southern sympathizers within the. territory might attempt to wrest the area from Union control and attach it to the Confederacy, although this was the most minor of the threats. However, an area known as Mace's Hole southwest of present Pueblo did become a hotbed of rebel activity, and an attempt was made to organize an effective Confederate regiment of men from such areas as California Gulch and Georgia Gulch. A second possible danger might come from the Confederacy itself, for the gold of Colorado would be a great prize for the South, perhaps worth an invasion of the mineral regions of the West. This, as events developed, proved no idle fear. Finally, the Indians, sensing the awkward state of the white defenses, might grow restless and start trouble—with the aid, some thought, of Confederate agents. This, too, became a very real problem for the territory in the months ahead.

All these fears and worries troubled Governor Gilpin, a veteran of western military campaigns and a determined Unionist. Gilpin realized that he could expect little immediate aid from the federal authorities. He decided, therefore, that since the dangers were too great to defer action, he would himself act and, if necessary, explain later. Gilpin appointed a military staff, started to raise a volunteer infantry regiment, and began to gather implements of warfare. No public money was available for such purposes, but the governor issued some $375,000 in drafts on the federal treasury, fully expecting them to be honored by the national government since they were to be used for the defense of the territory and the cause of the Union. And, in fact, Gilpin would later claim that before leaving Washington for Colorado he had received verbal authorization from Lincoln to issue such drafts on his own responsibility.

At first most of the Colorado merchants, tradesmen, and citizens were willing to go along with the governor's preparedness campaign. A few men voiced objections, but they soon gave way when the governor and his aides suggested that the alternative to the drafts was outright confiscation of needed supplies. Gradually, however, an undercurrent of uneasiness began to grow concerning the validity of the drafts. When news from Washington corroborated rumors that the federal treasury was unwilling to validate the drafts, the consternation in the territory was enormous. Gilpin found himself a most unpopular man among the Colorado people; where only a few months earlier he had been warmly welcomed as exactly the sort of man the territory needed, now some citizens circulated petitions requesting his removal. The fact that the Gilpin administration had awarded the territorial printing contract to the *Daily Colorado Republican* (thereby angering the powerful and vocal *Rocky Mountain News* Editor William N. Byers) did nothing to help Gilpin's position. Finally, beset on all sides, Gilpin decided to go to Washington to plead his case in person.

Meanwhile, whatever their legal status, the drafts had provided the funds necessary to organize and equip the First Regiment of Colorado Infantry, ten companies strong. In the summer of 1861 the regiment trained at newly-constructed Camp Weld, near Denver. By the end of the year, the volunteers were a relatively well-trained and equipped force, ready for action. And that action was soon forthcoming, for in the early winter of 1862, while Governor Gilpin was still in the East, the regiment was ordered south to join Colonel Edward R. S. Canby's Union forces in New Mexico. There one of Gilpin's worries had developed into an actual threat. General Henry H. Sibley was moving a Confederate army across the southwestern deserts, attempting to wrest the area from the Union.

By the time the Colorado volunteers reached New Mexico they

were greeted with the news that the Texan army under Sibley had already taken the city of Santa Fe and was preparing an attack on Fort Union. In March, at a place called Glorieta Pass, between Santa Fe and Fort Union, the Colorado regiment performed with considerable credit to itself and to the territory. The Union men, with the Coloradans playing conspicuous roles, routed Sibley's Texans in the engagements sometimes called the "Gettysburg of the West." That victory seemed to vindicate, for historians if not for contemporaries, the treasury drafts issued by the unpopular Colorado governor.

Unfortunately, the Union victory offered little immediate amelioration for the territory's financial problems. Gilpin's drafts had tied up most of the circulating currency and there was still no indication that the drafts ever would be validated. Eventually the federal treasury agreed to adjust the matter, upon presentation of itemized statements of claims by the holders of the drafts. But by that time Gilpin had been almost completely repudiated. If there had been no war, he probably would have been remembered as a very able first governor of Colorado. As it was, serious mistakes in judgment and attitude, including his assumption that all of his opponents were perforce rebels, contributed to his downfall. Effective in April, 1862, President Lincoln removed him from the governorship.

To replace him, Lincoln selected John Evans, a different sort of man. Both governors were staunch Union supporters, but where Gilpin's credentials for the office had centered in his previous experience and knowledge of the West and its problems, Evans' attractiveness was his proved ability as a successful organizer and entrepreneur in the Midwest. The new governor's first career had been in medicine, but he had added to his successes in that profession energetic and profitable enterprises in railroading and real estate. Combined with this was an aggressive interest in education. He had assurances already that his midwestern activities would not be forgotten, for his name was perpetuated in the city of Evanston, Illinois, hometown of Northwestern University which he had helped to found. He was, in addition, a friend of the President, and had early supported his political career.

When Governor Evans arrived in May to take personal control of the territory, he found that some of the earlier fears that had so concerned Governor Gilpin no longer were major problems. The Confederate thrust in New Mexico had been halted, and there had been no eruption of Southern sympathizers within the territory itself. Two minor diversions would occur—a small group of Confederate officers attempting to carry gold out of the territory and a brief raiding excursion by the guerrilla leader, James Reynolds, in the San Luis Valley—but these were disposed of very quickly. On the other hand, Gilpin's third fear—that of an Indian attack—had not ended, and before the Civil War came to an end, the Indian problem would bring bloodshed to the territory and an end to John Evans' governorship.

Evans' problems with the Indians, of course, had their roots in an earlier era. More than a decade earlier, at the Fort Laramie Treaty Council, in 1851, the Cheyennes and Arapahoes had agreed to accept the Eastern Slope stretches between the South Platte and Arkansas rivers as their designated hunting lands. Then gold was discovered, and the argonauts rushing to the Pike's Peak mines moved onto the reserved Indian lands, fully expecting that the federal government would extinguish the Indian claims and ratify the gold seekers' precipitate actions. The expectations, in time, became demands. In the autumn of 1860, before territorial government was assured Coloradans, federal agents opened negotiations with the two tribes, or parts of them, at a council on the Arkansas River.

At that council the whites seemed to have their way. The Arapahoes and Cheyennes agreed to surrender all their former hunting lands, except a triangular-shaped reservation between the Arkansas River and Sand Creek. This new reservation was to be surveyed and divided so that each tribal member received forty acres of land. The federal agents promised the tribes a $30,000 subsidy for fifteen years, a grist mill, a saw mill, and schools for the arid reservation. With this help, the Cheyennes and Arapahoes were to begin the difficult transition from nomads to peaceful farmers.

On paper, the Indian "problem" was settled—only it proved to be less simple than that. For one thing, difficulties arose from the administration of Indian affairs at both the national and local levels. Political considerations, rather than competence for the job, often were involved in the appointment of agents, with the Indian service in some cases becoming a convenient dumping ground for relatives or friends of high officials in need of employment. Once appointed, Indian agents sometimes used their positions for personal gain; for example, it was charged that during the early 1860s Upper Arkansas Agent Samuel Colley, whose son Dexter was a trader, contributed to the misappropriation of treaty goods intended for the Indians under his jurisdiction.

As for the Arapahoes and Cheyennes themselves, there were

neither fences around the Sand Creek Reservation nor soldiers at its boundaries to keep them on their lands. In addition, not all of the tribesmen were in sympathy with the promises made by their chiefs at the council. Some claimed, in fact, that they had not been represented at the sessions. Younger braves, in particular, seemed to grow less disciplined, more belligerent. As they talked about their problems around camp fires, the more aggressive warriors undoubtedly argued that the white man's actions had changed; where earlier fur trappers and traders had been as mobile as the tribesmen themselves, since the gold discoveries white men had acted in a different fashion. They settled in permanent villages, brought their women and children with them, and showed no signs of ever moving away. The Indians also were aware of the embarrassing divisions within the white men's ranks. The Civil War had brought a sudden reversal in the flow of immigrants; the mining camps and supply towns were becoming less populated and less protected. Perhaps the time had come to drive out the intruders and redeem the tribal hunting grounds.

While the Indians were contemplating such ideas, the relatively isolated and unprotected white settlers were also aware of changed conditions. Increasingly they faced the possibilities of a full-fledged Indian uprising. Their fears were composed of a variety of ingredients. For one thing, they could hardly ignore former Governor Gilpin's intense concern earlier. Now, in addition, disturbing news from the north reported the Sioux in Minnesota on the warpath in the summer of 1862, leaving a trail of bloody destruction and death. In this atmosphere of uneasy apprehension, rumors could be, and were, believed that the Confederacy intended to aid the Indians of the plains. When the tribesmen increased their attempts to purchase horses and firearms, the frontier communities interpreted it, as all frontier settlers always had, as a certain sign of belligerent intentions. Coloradans of Union sympathies had responded gallantly to Gilpin's call for soldiers to fight the Confederates earlier, and their New Mexican exploits had been warmly applauded in the territory. But that had been white man's warfare, against a "civilized" enemy. What all settlers—even those of self-proclaimed "neutral" disposition toward the Civil War—now faced was the possibility of a greater danger from "barbarians," psychologically a much more disturbing thought.

Following a not uncommon practice, John Evans had been appointed ex officio superintendent of Indian affairs as well as governor of the territory. The two positions were not really compatible, however, for as governor, Evans had to protect the citizens of the territory, while as superintendent of Indian affairs, he was responsible for the welfare of the Indians, who were not citizens. Moreover, while he was experienced in many areas, there was little in his background to equip him in dealing with the Indians. Nonetheless, John Evans was deeply immersed in the problem. One thing that could be done was to request the return of the volunteers from New Mexico. The First Regiment was brought back to the territory and scattered in small units to provide some protection to most parts of the region. But this was hardly sufficient to satisfy the settlers, and when the troops recruited in 1862 and 1863 were mustered into federal service, with the majority of them sent off to Kansas and Missouri, the gold towns found themselves literally drained of volunteers and still without adequate military protection against the Indians.

The alternative choices of action available to Evans were not promising. He could and did continue to plead with the federal authorities for army units to protect the frontier, and for authorization to recruit additional volunteer units within the territory for home defense. In the light of experience, however, he could hardly hope for quick and favorable action on his requests. So he was left with the alternative of stop-gap diplomacy with the tribes, attempting to hold council with the Indians and demonstrate with words rather than action the folly of their ways. The tribesmen, however, seemed disinterested in peace talks; their attitude was indicated by their complete indifference, in the fall of 1863, to the governor's invitation to meet for a treaty session on the eastern plains.

Until the spring of 1864, despite the tension that had been building in the white settlements for months, actual conflict with the Indians had been confined to rather isolated incidents of harassment of traffic on the overland trails and occasional, limited stock-running and horse-stealing from the ranchers. But when warm weather returned to the area in 1864, the tempo of affairs increased. The tribesmen became less guarded in their actions, raiding ranches closer to settled towns, striking more often and with more daring at the freighters' wagons and stages on the South Platte Trail. Then, on June 11, a turning-point of sorts was reached when the Indians, in a savage attack on a ranch about twenty-five miles southeast of Denver, killed Nathan Hungate, his wife, and their two daughters. When the scalped and mutilated bodies of the Hungate family were publicly displayed in Denver, the settlers braced themselves for a direct assault on the city, and at the same time they demanded immediate and complete revenge.

The governor, his advisers, and most of the military leaders, by this time, all seem to have concluded that a general campaign against the Indians was inevitable. But Evans, less impatient than some to end the affair, recognized that some Indians were still disposed to peace. So he formulated a policy designed to separate the hostile tribesmen from those who were friendly. On June 27 Evans issued a proclamation "To the Friendly Indians of the Plains," directing all Indians who wanted to demonstrate their friendship with the whites to gather at federal forts, where supplies and protection would be offered to all who came in. "The war on hostile Indians," he warned, "will be continued until they are all effectually subdued." Perhaps the choice offered to the Indians was not apparent to them; at least there was no response to the governor's invitation. And while the raids continued, the undeclared and still largely undefined hostilities brought ever more serious problems to the territory. Mail service was disrupted; shop keepers' inventories dwindled; prices increased dramatically as traffic on the overland trails ceased. More and more frequently whites now talked of an exemplary strike at the Indians—a total blow that would end the weary months of fear and rid eastern Colorado of Indians, once and for all time.

Finally, in August, Evans proclaimed to the white citizens that any resident who desired to fight hostile Indians could engage in such "private" warfare and keep the loot from his efforts. And, even more impressive, the Governor had at last secured authorization from the War Department to raise a regiment of soldiers, with enlistments valid for 100 days of service.

As for the Indians, whatever plans they might have had for a massive attack on the settlements did not mature. There is evidence that they had contemplated simultaneous strikes at the white villages in August; at least Elbridge Gerry, who lived in the South Platte Valley with the Indians, hurried to Denver to warn Evans of the possibility. But no such attack occurred.[2] Soon the cool nights of autumn told the Indians that the time for peace and provisions was at hand. Acting as though Governor Evans' earlier invitation had not expired, Indians began to appear at Fort Lyon, especially some Arapahoes who indicated that they were finished with their raiding. The Cheyenne Chief Black Kettle also indicated a desire to talk peace.

Major Edward W. Wynkoop, commanding officer at the fort, decided to escort seven chiefs to Denver for a parley with Governor Evans and his aides. It is at this point in affairs that events become highly confused, and subject to a variety of interpretations. Some historians believe that Evans was dismayed at Wynkoop's actions, for by this time peace was no longer his goal. According to this view, Evans feared embarrassment that might result from peaceful termination of affairs, because of his constant pleas for troops and general exaggeration of the Indian problem in his reports to federal authorities. Then, too, both Evans and Colonel John Chivington, at this time, were deeply involved in the political arena, especially in the abortive attempt to gain statehood for Colorado. Whatever the reasons, the council ended in a vague and inconclusive manner. Evans informed the chiefs that the "matter had been turned over to the military authorities with which alone they must deal." The army officers then suggested that the Indians' next move might be to their reserved lands. So there, on the Sand Creek Reservation, the Arapahoes and Cheyennes established their winter camp. Since they were now on their reservation—where they had not been for some time—and since they had been told to go there, they considered themselves at peace with and secure from their white neighbors.

The Indians might have considered the affairs settled, but the whites had other plans. At least some of the white leaders were now rigidly committed to a policy of tribal extermination, and they now had a military unit to begin the work. Evans' regiment of 100-day men were ready for service. What they lacked in discipline and equipment they more than made up in their eagerness for a campaign against the Indians. When the governor left the territory for a visit to the national capital, Colonel John Chivington, in command of the "Bloodless Third" Regiment, in Evans' absence, decided to strike the decisive blow. If his regiment were not used soon, the enlistments of his men would expire.

John Chivington, a Methodist clergyman, had attracted attention three years earlier when the First Colorado Regiment had been recruited, informing Governor Gilpin then that he preferred a "fighting to a praying" commission. He had been granted his request, and at the battles of Apache Canyon and Glorieta Pass, during the New Mexican campaign in 1862, had distinguished himself and his command. Now, with characteristic energy, he prepared to teach the Indians a lesson they would not forget and, according to his critics later, prepare the path for a political career for himself. He moved his men to Fort Lyon and, joined with other troops from there, he continued, by a forced all-night march, to Sand Creek. He took special care that no news of his approach reached the reservation. At sunrise, on November 29, 1864, he sent his regiment in attack against the Indian camp.

The accounts of the engagement at Sand Creek that November day make unpleasant reading. Colonel Chivington seemed to lose control of his men early in the day. Subject to slaughter, mutilation, and reckless savagery, braves, squaws and children alike felt the full force of white vengeance. George Bent, the half-Cheyenne son of William Bent who was in the camp at the time, described later what it was like. "The Indians all began running, but they did not seem to know what to do or where to turn. The women and children were screaming and wailing, the men running to the lodges for their arms and shouting advice and directions to one another."[3] No two observers or later-day experts have ever agreed on the total number of Indians in the camp when fighting began or the number of Indians killed. Chivington's own estimate, in boastful tone shortly after the engagement, placed the number of Indians surprised by the attack at almost 1,000, with half that number killed. Lower estimates suggest that something closer to a total of 500 Indians might have been sleeping in their lodges when the attack began, and that one-fifth of that number were killed. One thing alone seems uncontroverted: no prisoners were taken. Those Indians who did not manage to escape from the battlefield were killed by Chivington's men.

The Sand Creek engagement brought immediate and bitter repercussions, not only in the territory, but all the way to the national capital. An investigation by the Congressional Joint Committee on the Conduct of the (Civil) War ended its deliberations by condemning Chivington for having "deliberately planned and executed a foul and dastardly massacre which would have disgraced the veriest savage among those who were the victims of his cruelty." A military commission spent months in another investigation. An indication of the violent opinions concerning Sand Creek can be seen in the never-punished assassination of Captain Silas S. Soule, an outspoken critic and witness against his fellow-officer, Colonel Chivington.

The commander was not without supporters. Some of his friends insisted that the only reason for the flare-up of hostile reaction was that Governor Evans, and much of the Colorado bar, were then trying to force the removal of the territorial judicial officers, and that the judges had instigated the congressional investigation. Others claimed that the loudest opponents of Chivington were those who had lost trade goods in the attack and were bitter about their financial losses. Some whites insisted that the fresh scalps of settlers found in the camp were justification enough for the engagement. Many settlers, wearied by the months of incessant Indian troubles, and remembering the Hungates and others who had lost their lives in Indian attacks, unhesitatingly applauded the premise of quick, complete extermination of the tribes.

So the arguments ran. The Chivington supporters claimed the engagement was a true battle, and exactly what the Indians deserved. The critics termed it a massacre, unjustifiable under the circumstances. Regardless of the merits of the attack, the episode was a sad commentary on Colonel Chivington as a military leader. The same man who had proved so capable a field commander at Glorieta Pass badly botched the Sand Creek engagement. With troops in superior number, much better equipped, Chivington took the major part of a day to finish off the Indian camp.

Even more serious as a condemnation of the engagement was the fact that the attack accomplished nothing of merit, for the Indians now were stirred to revenge. Those who had escaped from the battlefield joined their brethren to make counter-offensives against the whites. In January, 1865, they sacked the station and stores of Old Julesburg in the northeastern corner of the territory. They returned to plunder Julesburg again in February, burning the place to the ground.

Seemingly the only satisfactory answer to eliminate difficulties between whites and Indians was that used by the federal government when it created reservations of land for the Indians and then used force to keep the Indians on those lands. For even this policy to work, the lands of the Indians needed to be segregated at some distance from the whites, and a military force was needed to keep the Indians on the reservation. For obviously the Sand Creek reserve had not answered the whites' demands for ridding the area of the tribes.

It was not until October, 1867, when the Medicine Lodge Creek Treaty was perfected, that the Cheyenne and Arapahoe tribes agreed to move to the Indian Territory. Even then, they were to be allowed hunting privileges off the reservation and, at times, they would revert to older habits of raiding travellers and settlers. By this time, however, the Civil War had ended in the East and veterans of the Union Army were now available for duty on the western plains. With their help later, short engagements within the eastern Colorado boundaries were quickly put down.

In September, 1868, an attack by some 1,000 tribesmen under Chief Roman Nose pinned down a party of fifty United States scouts from Fort Hays, in Kansas, on what later was named Beecher Island in the Arikaree Fork of the Republican River. The name honors Lieutenant Fred Beecher who was killed during the engagement. The siege lasted nine days, until units of the federal cavalry relieved the scouts. The following summer (1869) a band of Indian raiders was pursued by federal troops from Kansas into northeastern Colorado and attacked at Summit Springs, about six miles from present-day Atwood. The white soldiers killed fifty Indians, including Chief Tall Bull, and redeemed two white women who had been captured by the Indians in Kansas.

The Battle of Summit Springs was the final military engagement between whites and plains Indians in the eastern part of the territory. Indian problems were by no means ended for the settlers, for to the west, in the mountains, the Utes still retained hunting grounds, and the day would come when this "last frontier" would be demanded by white settlers. But for the immediate future, the plains of the Eastern Slope were cleared of the tribes, and the white settlers now could bring in their railroads and irrigation ditches, cow herds and windmills, without fear of their destruction by the Indians.

11

Smelters and Railroads

Any American frontier opened for settlement during the years of the Civil War had cause for disappointment in its economic progress. With the nation locked in bloody warfare to decide the question of its continued existence, most peaceful pursuits had to await an end to hostilities. So it was with Colorado. And even after the war ended, the remaining years of the decade were filled with exasperating problems in the territory. The Indian menace on the eastern plains constituted a major threat to domestic tranquility until the Cheyennes and Arapahoes had been removed. In some respects, an even greater possible disaster than Indian warfare unnerved Coloradans through much of the decade. Rumors circulated that the gold mines were running out. Colorado—epitome of the mining frontier—was threatened with the most formidable of possible economic dangers. The gold mines had summoned the population into the wilderness; around their continuing production men had linked their fortunes and their lives. Uneasy apprehension could so easily be converted into hysterical bankruptcy of the territory. It all depended on the good earth's treasures and what men could make of them.

For a time the idea that the gold-bearing ores were dwindling was unthinkable. This was especially true in the "Little Kingdom of Gilpin"—the county in which the most profitable mining properties were located and in which Central City, with its satellite towns, proudly proclaimed its importance, often taking precedence over the "Queen City of the Plains," Denver. In Gilpin County the original Gregory Lode had been uncovered; here the Russells, returning from Georgia in the spring of 1859, had found their rich placers. And it was here, in the winter of 1863-64, that the attention of eastern capitalists centered as Colorado mining stocks became a fad of investors.

Several elements contributed to the investment madness. A rise in the price of gold, nationally, played its part. So did the fluid capital available for investment in greater quantity than the country had ever known, the result of profits and profiteering during the Civil War. Colorado mining stocks happened to appear at a time when the demand for investment opportunities increased, and the consequences might have been predicted. As demands for shares of the golden harvest of the mines increased, the price for stocks climbed upward. The listing of nearly 200 Colorado mining companies' stocks on the New York and other eastern exchanges indicates the market for such securities. With such ready acceptance, it was probably inevitable that bad or worthless properties would be peddled along with the valuable and honest enterprises. It could not last, for in time some of the investors would find themselves without returns on their investments. When the bubble broke, as it did in April, 1864, it left behind a bad reputation for Colorado mines.

Aggravating the situation was the rumor about the exhaustion of the territory's mineral wealth. It was a fact—not merely a rumor—that the easy ores were vanishing. The precious metal from the simply worked lodes and placers of the early years had been extracted, and although many men kept faith in their conviction that the hills were still full of gold, there was little doubt but that some new methods of mining and reduction of ore were needed. The easy, early ores had been no great problem. The gold was largely free gold, chemically unassociated with other elements. Washing, or crushing and washing, with amalgamation with mercury, sufficed to redeem the gold. Now, however, the ores brought to the surface of the mine shafts contained gold mixed with other elements, no longer separable by mere mechanical procedures. The day of the chemist and the metallurgist was at hand. Unfortunately, before sanity returned to the mining camps, an "era of process manias" transpired.

In the circumstances, understandably, straws were clutched at, and any artist of deceit might make his fortune promising the new, the simplest, the least expensive, the only process that would bring about the alchemy necessary to divorce the gold from the natural allies with which it was found. When crushing in stamp mills no longer resulted in satisfactory separation of the ores (no more than one-fourth of the total gold in the ores reportedly was being recovered by the mills) many came to the conclusion that the ores must be roasted before the gold could be amalgamated. One invention for this purpose followed another; desulphurization, since many of the ores were identified as sulfides, became the abracadabra of the new alchemists. Speculators wasted thousands of dollars on sweeping claims of perfect successes put forward by deluded or deluding proprietors of patents.

This process mania, commencing in 1864 and continuing for almost four years, extensively damaged the reputation of the Colorado mines. Added to the delusion of the stock purchasers of the East who had too hastily succumbed to promotional literature concerning mining investments and consequently lost their capital, it might easily have ruined the future of the industry for a long time. About the only good aspect of it all was the fact that the frightening situation did not last longer than it did. What ended the process mania was the real success that Nathaniel P. Hill experienced when he opened his smelting operations at Black Hawk in 1868.

Nathaniel Hill, a professor of chemistry at Brown University in Providence, Rhode Island, had been sent to Colorado in 1864 by Boston capitalists· to investigate their recently purchased mining properties. Intrigued by the local problems of ore reduction, Hill set to work to solve the riddle of the gold ores. Travelling to Europe twice to investigate smelting processes there, he finally arranged shipments of sample Colorado ores to Swansea, in Wales, for experimentation. Those tests proved that the ore could be smelted into mattes with copper bases and, in 1867, Hill organized the Boston and Colorado Smelting Company. The next year the company began smelting operations at its plant at Black Hawk. The process involved crushing the ore, then reducing it by concentrating the gold ores on copper mattes (in technical terms: by using a calcining furnace and a small reverberatory). These plates then were shipped to Swansea refineries for final treatment. By 1873 the Boston and Colorado would complete its own separating works, making the expensive European shipments unnecessary. That left only the gold to be worked out. For a few years the concentrates were sent to Boston, but by 1875-76, the final process also would be introduced at the Hill plant.

Despite a multiplicity of problems—questions of proper purchase agreements with miners for their ores, costs of operation, and a general uncertainty of proper technical procedures at times—the Hill smelter was a success from the beginning. It made its originator a local hero as well as a wealthy man. The problem of the refractory

The Boston and Colorado Smelter, Black Hawk. (State Historical Society of Colorado)

Stack of silver bars smelted at Boston and Colorado Smelter. (State Historical Society of Colorado)

ores had now been overcome, and the Colorado gold mines had been rescued from disaster.

The solution to the ore problem brought a promising ending to a decade that had vacillated between the heights of success in 1859-60 and the depths of despair and defeat in the mid-sixties. Though mining in the sixties had been based on gold, another metal—silver—was gradually gaining significance. As early as August, 1859, stories of silver discoveries appeared, followed in the next few years by further reports, reflecting as much as anything else the general excitement over Nevada's Comstock. Silver had also been mined as a by-product in Gilpin County, but the first real mines were opened in 1864 near Georgetown. This camp, the first of Colorado's "silver queens," was the focus of interest that spilled over into the Snake River district across the Continental Divide into Summit County.

Despite excited hopes and high assay reports, silver mining languished due to the lack of an economical method of smelting. Lorenza Bowman, a Negro from Missouri with experience in the lead mines, helped develop a method which was successful on the surface ores. But the deeper ores were more complex and required more complicated procedures. Following the collapse of the gold speculation, it proved difficult to interest outside investors in an industry that promised only expensive and trial-and-error experimentation before dividends could be declared. At the end of the decade, Georgetown had smelters, although experiments were still being conducted to find a more practical method; major production was imminent. The more isolated Snake River mines stagnated, awaiting the success of their neighbor and a cheap, rapid means of transportation before they too would bask in the glory of a mining boom.

The 1870s ushered in Colorado's silver era. Before the decade ended discoveries would be made from Boulder County to Dolores County, on a southwest axis bisecting the state. Georgetown would be eclipsed as Leadville came into its own. The silver boom started in Boulder County with the discovery of the Caribou Mine in 1869, followed by a rush to the area the next year which produced the camp of the same name. Here was the excitement, speculation, and promise of wealth which would be repeated so many more times before the era ended. Caribou was isolated, nestled as it was near the Continental Divide, and the most northerly of Colorado's silver camps, but it nevertheless attracted national and international interest. Eventually, a Dutch company purchased the Caribou Mine for $3,000,000, only to lose it three years later in 1876 at a sheriff's sale. Mismanagement, low ore reserves, poor mining methods and misrepresentation, if not complete dishonesty, on the part of the seller, plagued the company from the beginning. The new owners were Jerome Chaffee and David Moffat, constituting a partnership that lasted into the 1880s and affected Colorado mining significantly.

Such diversification of mining activities was promising. An economy that rested exclusively on gold might crumble and die overnight, as the process problem had illustrated. But whether the ore was gold or silver—or even the products of the expanding agricultural settlements—one problem confronted everyone in Colorado. Transportation was still *the* major economic concern. Despite near-heroic efforts all through the territory's first decade, a solution would not be reached until 1870. Yet each year brought more need for change. It is estimated that more than 100,000,000 pounds of freight reached Colorado by wagon in 1865,[1] and even larger quantities were brought in each succeeding year.

There was little argument about the type of transportation needed: railroads, and only railroads, would bring a satisfactory transportation system to the territory. But the method by which railroads were to be lured to Colorado was not as readily agreed to. At first most of the dreaming was intimately associated with a larger American dream—a transcontinental railroad, spanning the prairies and mountains, tying the nation together with bands of iron rail.

Colorado, astride the nation, contemplated a railroad that would place her on the mainline to the Pacific. She should have remembered the negative reports resulting from John Gunnison's survey before the Civil War. But she did not, and when the sectional struggle between North and South, which had kept a solution to the road from consummation for almost a decade, erupted into actual warfare, the demands for a recognition of Colorado's claims were raised again. With southern congressmen no longer participating in national affairs, the North was free to proceed with its own favorite route. In 1862 Congress chartered the Union Pacific Railroad to build the eastern portion of the transcontinental line. All Colorado was elated at the prospect. Governor Evans, one of the 158 "commissioners" charged with the duty of organizing the railroad, on his first evening in Denver spoke of how it would benefit the community. Expectations soared that through his influence and that of others rails would come through the territory on the way to California.

Such optimism proved grossly ill-founded. Surveyors earlier had reported that a better crossing of the Continental Divide lay to the north. No Colorado pass, not even recently discovered Berthoud, could match the gentle grades of these northerly ones. Despite Evans' continued promotional efforts while governor and afterwards, Colorado would be disappointed.

The Civil War hastened the chartering of the railroad, but delayed its construction. Not until the summer of 1867 did the Union Pacific build its roadbed and lay its rails across the Wyoming prairie. Then came predictions and prophecies that Denver and her sister Colorado communities would soon fade away. Cheyenne, to the north, blessed with the transcontinental railroad, loomed as the likely prospect to become the regional metropolis; "Denver was too dead to bury." Prophets who voiced such sentiments, however, reckoned without full appreciation of Colorado's leaders. Determined to save their investments and their hopes for the future, Coloradans soon worked out plans for building connecting branches—feeder lines—from the Union Pacific tracks south into the territory.

The Colorado Central Railroad Company seemed the most logical to make the initial connection with the Union Pacific. Golden's William A. H. Loveland, promoter, politician, mine owner, and rival of Evans and his Denver followers, had organized the road with the help of Edward L. Berthoud and encouragement from the Union Pacific itself. The town of Golden expected to profit from becoming the southern terminus. Though smaller in population than Denver, Golden never hesitated to compete with its large neighbor. If it could claim no other advantage, it was closer to the Gilpin County mines. Initially, Denver supported Loveland's idea, until it became clear that Golden would be on the main line and only a branch would serve its rival. Denver and Arapahoe County, which had previously voted to float bond issues to aid in construction, now refused to approve the bonds, not wishing to boost Golden to economic superiority. Here the matter temporarily rested, while both groups sought other support.

While Loveland planned his Colorado Central, another possible railroad connection appeared in the east. The Union Pacific Eastern Division, soon to be renamed the Kansas Pacific, building westward from Kansas City, promised to move trains into Denver at an early date. As long as its government aid for financing held out, the Kansas Pacific set a rapid rate of construction. But by late 1867, construction funds were exhausted and the railhead in western Kansas, still miles short of Denver, could not be pushed forward without additional help. To make matters worse, there were rumors that the Kansas road was seriously interested in diverting its line to the Arkansas Valley, bypassing Denver altogether.

These were dark months for Denverites. Railroad prospects for their city dimmed considerably. The Union Pacific was miles to the north; the Colorado Central had chosen to build from Cheyenne to rival Golden; the Kansas Pacific was bogged down in western Kansas. Property values in Denver began to spiral downward and tradesmen began to desert the Mile-High City. Only determined resistance to this flight from the "sinking ship" could salvage the city's future. Those who chose to remain optimistically organized a Board of Trade and, with organizational help from Union Pacific and Kansas Pacific officials, immediately announced their plans for a "home town" railroad.

They called it the Denver Pacific, to be built as a branch line from Cheyenne to the territorial capital. Financing, as usual, proved the major obstacle, despite imaginative efforts of the Denver leaders to seek aid in every direction. The citizens were summoned to contribute—cash, pledges, material, or labor, as their circumstances allowed. Arapahoe County, freed now from its former promise to aid the Colorado Central, underwrote a bond issue to further the enterprise. But all these efforts were not enough. It became quite evident that if the road was to be finished, more help from the outside was necessary. Both the Union Pacific and the Kansas Pacific looked favorably on the venture, hoping to use the branch line to tap the mining resources of the territory. They were willing to give some aid. Congress agreed to a 900,000-acre land grant, although it meant a merging of the 100-mile line with the Kansas Pacific. Now the track laying could proceed. In June, 1870, the road from Denver to Cheyenne was completed in a traditional ceremony, including the driving of a silver spike presented by the city of Georgetown.

The Kansas Pacific also increased its federal land grants. With about 3,000,000 acres of new lands as aid, the road successfully marketed additional securities, and could resume construction. Its interests now tied directly to Denver's progress, the Kansas road forgot about the Arkansas Valley and determined to build as rapidly as possible to the capital city. When grading was started from Denver eastward toward the finished portion of the road, the crews working on the two ends of the line entered into a friendly competition. On the last day, the two crews recorded the remarkable feat of laying ten and one-fourth miles of track in ten hours' time.[2] In August,

1870, the first locomotive moved across the Kansas Pacific tracks into Denver. The Queen City now had two rail outlets to the rest of the nation.

That year, 1870, was also the year of birth for another railroad that was to become intimately identified with the territory and future state of Colorado. General William J. Palmer had been a director of the Kansas Pacific line; he had also supervised the construction of the Denver Pacific. He now began organizing a new road—the Denver and Rio Grande—designed to reach south to El Paso, Texas, and through connections there to form a link with Mexican railroads. Palmer's plan envisioned a north-south spine, with feeder roads west to the mining camps and east to the newly-settled agricultural communities in the valleys. This scheme was a radical departure from generally accepted principles of railroading. Most roads in the American West were laid out on an east-west axis. Moreover, the Denver and Rio Grande was to be built with narrow-gauge trackage, three feet wide instead of the growing American standard width of four feet, eight and one-half inches. The narrow roadbeds would allow greater flexibility in surmounting the difficulties of construction over high mountain passes, up steep canyon floors, and around difficult curves.

The narrow-gauge road would become, in time, convincingly adapted to the mountainous terrain of Colorado. In later decades, it would become the "standard" for the area, completely fulfilling the prophecies of utility and, at the same time, inspiring respectable laughter for its picturesque qualities: "It doubles in, it doubles out, leaving the traveller still in doubt whether the engine on the track is going on or coming back."[3]

Palmer planned and organized his road in 1870-71; actual construction got underway in the spring of 1871. By autumn of that year the road had built its narrow-gauge bed and laid its thirty-pound rails from Denver to the vicinity of Colorado City. There, through its subsidiary, the Colorado Springs Company, it laid out a new town— Colorado Springs—with full expectation that the choice location would make it a fashionable summer resort. The next year the Denver and Rio Grande constructed its line south along Fountain Creek until it reached a site across the Arkansas River from Pueblo. There another of its subsidiaries, the Central Colorado Improvement Company, established another new town—South Pueblo. By the end of the year 1872, the road had also reached the coal field area near Florence, again establishing its own townsite of Labran. Two years later the Rio Grande's locomotives steamed into Canon City.

By that time the capital city of Denver was in an enviable position. The Denver Pacific tracks north of Cheyenne gave it an outlet on the transcontinental; the Kansas Pacific rails tied it directly with Kansas City; the Denver and Rio Grande provided transportation to the southern part of the territory. Denver had clearly bested its rival, Golden, in the race for railroads. Loveland's Colorado Central had still not completed its connection with the Union Pacific. Unable to fulfill that promise, in 1870 the line did build tracks connecting Denver and Golden, to take advantage of the railheads that city now enjoyed. And the Colorado Central had continued laying its track up Clear Creek Canyon. By 1877 its trains were climbing to Black Hawk and, the following year, to the riches of the Gilpin County mines.

Loveland had dreams of continuing westward, over Berthoud Pass, using narrow-gauge if necessary. But no realistic engineer could advise such an undertaking. The pass reaches an altitude of 11,315 feet and the grades are much more precipitous than even the wildest professional imagination could envision climbing with rails. Loveland considered using cable-buckets for the highest altitudes, but his road never moved beyond Georgetown and the Central City districts. In other directions, in time, the road was more successful. Starting north from Golden, after much delay, it tapped the new village of Longmont in 1872, and five years later it reached Fort Collins and a junction with the Denver Pacific, four miles from that town.

While Loveland's Colorado Central never used its projected right-of-way across the Continental Divide, its plans blocked the original schemes of another Colorado railroad. Former Governor John Evans, inveterate railroad promoter, who had been a leading figure in the Denver Pacific road, helped organize the Denver, Georgetown and Utah Railroad Company, but found the way blocked by Loveland and a lack of financial assistance. Reorganized in 1872 as the Denver, South Park and Pacific, with Evans still the driving force, the company planned to build up South Platte Canyon and on into South Park, but the panic of 1873 made it extremely difficult to market the securities Evans had counted on for fund raising.

The depression did not prevent the line's reaching Morrison, a settlement organized by a townsite company with which Evans was associated, where shipping revenue from the local stone and lime quarries paid company expenses. Local acclaim was gained by hauling summer excursions of Sunday School children, earning it the nickname, "the Sunday School Line." Though he continued his efforts,

Evans was unable to find investors and experienced only frustration until 1876 when construction started. It stopped soon after, resulting in another reorganization. Finally, in 1877, construction was resumed and carried through to completion, spurred on by the Leadville silver bonanza. The Leadville rush brought prosperity to the road, and Evans found himself caught in the maelstrom of railroad-control struggles which hit the state late in the decade.

In the southeastern part of the territory, where the Denver and Rio Grande was extending its north-south road, other companies were planning extensions from the east. The Atchison, Topeka and Santa Fe Railroad, chartered in 1859, had begun to entertain transcontinental dreams. By 1873 it had built west as far as Granada in the Arkansas Valley, within the eastern boundary of the territory. There construction halted for two years in the wake of the financial panic. Both Pueblo and Bent counties were induced to come to its rescue with financial aid raised by bond issues and, with that help, the tracks were extended to La Junta by December, 1875. The following March the "Banana Line"—so-called because of its yellow coaches—had reached the city of Pueblo.

The Kansas Pacific road also revived its interest in the Arkansas Valley. At the town of Kit Carson, on its mainline through the Eastern Slope, the Kansas Pacific started building a branch southward to West Las Animas. By 1875 it also had reached La Junta. Within a few years, however, it became apparent that the area lacked sufficient resources to support the road, and the Kansas Pacific abandoned the division in 1878, removing the tracks from the right-of-way.

Meanwhile, south from Pueblo, the natural routes all led to Trinidad, near the historic Raton Pass crossing toward Santa Fe. Both the Atchison, Topeka and Santa Fe, from La Junta, and the Rio Grande, from South Pueblo, were building toward that town. In 1876 the Rio Grande reached El Moro, its company town five miles from Trinidad. The Santa Fe moved its tracks directly into town the next year. There, in the months that followed, the two railroads would compete for possession of the pass into New Mexico. The Rio Grande was also building toward Santa Fe by the alternate route across La Veta Pass and on into the San Luis Valley, reaching Fort Garland in 1877.

While the years from 1870 to 1880 saw Eastern Slope railroad construction in full swing, other parts of the territory were less fortunate. There wagon roads, or perhaps pack trails, provided the only available transportation. Berthoud Pass was not climbed by rails.

In fact, it was only after several abortive attempts that a wagon road was finally finished, and stages and freight wagons began to cross the Divide there in October, 1875. Eventually the state would buy the road from its owner and Berthoud became the first free crossing from the Eastern Slope.

As the railroads reached out to tap the wealth of the mining districts, both prospered, because cheap transportation was a key to the success of mining. Before the rails, however, there were trails and wagon roads to pioneer the routes. It was in this business that the Russian Jew, Otto Mears, small physically but a giant in energy, gained statewide fame. Mears frequently sold his rights-of-way to the railroad and eventually organized his own lines. With the rise of rail transportation came the development of major smelter centers, such as Denver, with access to ore, fuel, and labor markets. Here at last were the factors that produced important improvements in smelting, so long dominated by small establishments scattered in the mining districts. Colorado had impressively matured considering the rather slim prospects of 1870.

By the year 1880, with eastern Colorado served by a relatively extensive network of railroads, the transportation problems of the territory's first decade had ended. In their place, other problems had arisen. Much of the financing of the roads had come from outside the territory, and the control over those railroads remained in alien hands. Even a "home town" road like the Rio Grande would, in time, find itself engaged in a losing battle against outside financiers. Nor was this the only difficulty. The Rio Grande itself had angered many Coloradans. General Palmer had played a dangerous game of seeking community support for his railroad and, when approaching an established town, placing his trackage in one of his self-made company towns next door. Colorado City, neighboring the new Colorado Springs, or Pueblo, viewing South Pueblo across the Arkansas River, had reason to be unhappy with the railroad builders. Even Denver merchants, who had seemingly emerged victorious in their struggles to gain rail connections, would in time come to realize that the potential power of the roads was something to be carefully watched. But, whether viewed as curse or blessing, the railroads with all their features, good and bad, had come to stay.

12

Utopias in the Desert

Some Colorado communities owed their existence to gold fields; others to advantageous sites providing access to the mining gulches; some to the whims of the railroad engineers. But in the 1870s a new type of town building came to the territory—cooperative and semi-cooperative ventures in wilderness planting. Prompted by a series of hoped-for advantages, accompanied by some rather serious disadvantages, these colony towns of Colorado contributed a unique chapter to the history of settlement in the territory.

The colony plan of settlement, in many ways, was well adapted to conditions in Colorado. These settlements were designed as agricultural communities. As such, they would rely on irrigation for much of their farming and considerable advantage would accrue from constructing and operating irrigation ditches by cooperative, rather than individual effort. The feared loneliness of farm life on the western prairies, with the accompanying dangers of possible Indian attacks, might be mitigated by group settlement. Perhaps better prices could be gained for the land settled upon if a group, rather than individuals, negotiated the contracts to purchase the holdings.

There were, of course, corresponding disadvantages. Any person who partook of the colony's benefits would have to pay a price in loss of part of his individual freedom. The group's interests would take precedence over those of the single farmer. Management of the first class—intelligent, dedicated, diplomatic—was not particularly easy to enlist, as the failures of similar schemes in the East and Midwest had already demonstrated. There was also the possibility, if not the probability, that quarrels and friction would develop over the distribution of lots, farms, labor, and eventual profits.

WELTON DITCH on HUERFANO RIVER

But, balancing the advantages and disadvantages, enough men were swayed into believing the plans would work to bring into Colorado Territory a rather unusual number of attempted colonies. Most of these followed a similar pattern. They were usually organized in some eastern or midwestern city. Arrangements were concluded for the purchase of land and cooperative settlement with a railroad company, or a subsidiary land company organized to dispose of railroad lands. It was a nice meeting of interests, for the railroads not only had large stretches of federal land grants to sell but also recognized that until the land was taken up and agricultural products were available for freight, their lines could not hope to fully prosper. Thus the railroads were interested in the colony schemes and widely advertised the settlements. With their help the agricultural colonies provided the instrument by which the farming frontier suddenly leaped from a diagonal line cutting across central Kansas and eastern Nebraska to irrigable lands in the shadows of the Rocky Mountains.

There were differences in the various schemes of colonization, although generally they all endeavored to be known as "colonies." Some of the settlements were planned as completely cooperative ventures. Labor, capital, and profits were to be shared by the members. Others were semi-cooperatives, with certain details arranged by the leaders of the societies, at the same time allowing each individual member the right to exercise his own free choice in many decisions. And, finally, there were colonies which were not cooperative at all, except that they used the name "colony" to induce people into believing that they were designed on a cooperative scheme.

The first colony actually to take up lands within the territory was a thorough-going, full-fledged cooperative endeavor. Carl Wulsten had come to the United States from Prussia before the Civil War. He had served in the Union Army and had then settled in Chicago where he edited a German-language newspaper. In that fast-growing, rapidly industrializing city he saw around himself, and his fellow-Germans, nothing but misery and dirt. There seemed to be nothing in the future except continued long hours of back-breaking work in the city's factories. Prompted by a concept of communal living as a means to escape this plight, and envisioning an agricultural society somewhere in the Great American West where his fellow immigrants could again attain dignity and economic well-being, Wulsten organized the German Colonization Society in August, 1869.

The Society named a selection committee that came to the territory in November to choose a site for the future settlement.

They decided to locate in the Wet Mountain Valley. The Society petitioned Congress for a special grant of 40,000 acres of land, but when the request was refused, the leaders concluded to settle the colony anyway, depending on individual land claims for ownership. Back in Chicago, they helped their fellow colonists pack their belongings, and hurried to purchase tools and equipment they would need in their new homes. In mid-winter, 1870, the Society, numbering about 300 men, women, and children, with their household furniture, tools, implements, and livestock boarded a special train in Chicago. The train carried them to the end of the Kansas Pacific tracks, at Fort Wallace in Kansas. There they appealed to the United States Army for wagons to transport them the remainder ot their journey, and for troops to protect them against Indians. The federal authorities agreed to the requests, much to the amusement of many territorial residents who could not help but contrast these developments with their own, earlier experiences. They had come to the territory by their own devices, with little or no military protection against Indians who had really been a problem; now the government was furnishing an escort "to cover the march of these teutons along the peaceful cornfields of Pueblo and Fremont counties."[1]

In March, 1870, the colonists arrived on their lands in the Wet Mountain Valley. Under the leadership of their president, Carl Wulsten, they built their homes, plowed their lands, and planted their first crops. They named their town Colfax, in honor of the then vice-president of the United States. Capital, labor, and profits, if any, were to be pooled for five full years in a communistic arrangement. But, as had happened so often in other such ventures, dissensions began to erupt immediately within the group.

The difficulties were numerous and, in the end, proved insurmountable. There was no common religious or social principle to bind the members together. Wulsten was often tactless in treating members of the society; "hot-headed, arbitrary, and impracticable," he proved less than a perfect leader. His successor, James Judd, was even less able. The crops planted the first season did not mature satisfactorily because of the short growing season in the valley and an unusually early frost. There was considerable hostility to the group in some parts of southern Colorado, based partly on the "alien" character of the settlement, and partly on the rumors that the Republican administration in Washington was championing the settlement as the first of several groups designed to provide a Republican majority in otherwise normally Democratic areas of the territory.

Society members who were unhappy with the experiment for one reason or another began to withdraw from Colfax. When federal officials seized shingles and lumber that the colonists had cut and sawed without paying the "stumpage" tax for taking timber from the public domain, the end of the affair was hastened. Most of the settlers then moved to other territorial towns—to Pueblo, Canon City, or Denver. Those who remained in the valley divided the property and took up their individual claims on the government land. So ended the first chapter in Colorado colonization.

About the same time that Wulsten's group was selecting a committee to travel west to choose the location for settlement, Nathan C. Meeker, the agricultural editor of the New York *Tribune*, was touring the western territories. Meeker was an experienced hand at cooperative colonies. From 1844 to 1857 he had been a resident at the Trumbull Phalanx at Braceville, Ohio. By the time he returned from his western tour, Meeker was convinced that it would be possible to settle a cooperative community in Colorado. His publisher and editor, Horace Greeley, who had already seen something of the territory, endorsed the idea enthusiastically. Meeker called a public meeting for December 23, 1869, at Cooper Institute in New York City. There the Union Colony was born. Meeker, appropriately, was chosen president; a constitution was drafted; and memberships were offered for sale to temperance men of good character for a fee of $155.

The money raised by these fees was to be used to select and purchase the site for the colony. Each member would receive one town lot and a parcel of farming land in return for his investment. Meeker, Robert A. Cameron, the vice-president of the colony, and A. C. Fisk were appointed the selection committee. They viewed several sites in the territory and reportedly had almost decided on a stretch of land in South Park when William Byers persuaded them that the finest agricultural area of Colorado was centered in the South Platte Valley. He evidently convinced them, for they finally agreed to an excellent location near the confluence of the Cache la Poudre and the South Platte rivers. There they purchased a large block of land from the Denver Pacific Railroad (12,000 acres for $60,000), provisional title to an additional 60,000 acres, and a few private entries, to keep their colony cohesive—all of which would give them ample room to grow on. The colony also incorporated itself under territorial laws.

The Union colonists began to arrive on their lands in the spring of 1870. The town they established they named Greeley, although for the first months it wasn't much of a town. To supplement the usual tents and temporary shelters, the colonists purchased a large building in Cheyenne and moved it down the Denver Pacific Railroad to Greeley. They fitted it up as a lodging house and christened it the Hotel de Comfort. That first season they surveyed the plot and laid out the streets of their town; they planted trees; they opened a school for their children. And, perhaps most important of all, they dug their first irrigation ditch. Water was necessary if they were to harvest a crop the first season, and the ditch was a constant concern until they had turned water onto their fields.

All this was hard work, with small comfort for the present. But most of the colonists seemed willing to undergo the early hardships in expectation of better times to come. There were a few quitters who spread adverse reports, like the man who advised: "If you can't possibly stay where you are, *dont go to Greeley, Colorado Territory! That* is the last place on the face of this terrestrial ball that any human being should contemplate a removal to! Greeley, Colorado T., is a delusion, a snare—it is a fraud, a cheat, a swindle . . . ."[2]

And, since Horace Greeley himself, and his newspaper, were controversial, the political enemies of Greeley found much to scoff at in the new venture. When the great Horace arrived in town in October, 1870, his lecture to the colonists was variously reported in the territorial press. One editor laughed at the idea of Greeley being able to advise western settlers: "What Mr. G. knows about farming is not likely to be more valuable in this Territory than the experience of the old settlers."[3]

Either because of or in spite of Editor Greeley, the quitters and the scoffers were soon proved wrong. Sobriety, sense, or something led the colony to early prosperity. The economic base of the settlement was its agriculture. The irrigation system was added to each year, and from the waters spread over the fertile valley lands, the Greeley farmers harvested amazing crops. There was a problem of the wheat fields being trampled under by roaming cattle from surrounding ranches, but in time the Union colonists fenced their crops in, and their neighbors' cattle out, with a wire fence around the perimeter of their holdings. This $20,000 fence became a point of ridicule among outsiders, who referred to the colonists as "saints" and jested that the fence had been erected to separate the "Bible-loving inhabitants" of Greeley from the "barbarians" out in the open spaces. Another problem connected with the fence resulted from the refusal of the political authorities to allow the colony to put gates across the public roads. This necessitated stationing guards at the openings. But, despite criticism and difficulties, the fence secured the colonists' fields from destruction.

In the village of Greeley, diversification of the economy was attempted. A tanning plant for buffalo hides processed about a dozen robes a day, and for a time income ran as high as $2,000 a month. And the town also began to wear the mantle of a cultured society. A library, a lyceum, a farmers' club, and a dramatic association were organized. Theatricals—and dancing—were allowed by the "Saints" but intoxicating liquors were strictly forbidden, in accordance with the original terms of organization. By 1880, when the colony ended its corporate status at the expiration of its charter, it had firmly developed the foundations for the town of Greeley and its surrounding farm-lands to build on.

The rather spectacular success of the Union colonists made it inevitable that it would become the prototype of other such enterprises. Not all the imitators would enjoy the same success, but the Chicago-Colorado Colony, organized in the fall of 1870, came very close to matching it. In March, 1871, this Chicago group, with cooperation from the National Land Company (the agency handling land grants for the Denver Pacific and Kansas Pacific railroads) located their site on Middle St. Vrain Creek, naming their town Longmont. Lots and plots were distributed, irrigation ditches dug, and the place prospered. Part of its success was due to the intense desire of the settlers to "make good"; part resulted from the help of the colony's "fairy godmother," Mrs. Elizabeth Thompson of New York, who purchased memberships for poor settlers, and in other ways encouraged the undertaking. Then too, the location was excellent, the irrigation water from Left Hand and Boulder creeks, in addition to St. Vrain Creek, was more than adequate, and the management of the colony was intelligent and efficient.

South of Greeley, on the Denver Pacific Railroad, the remnant of a town called Evans furnished the site for another colony. Evans had originated when it served as a temporary terminal for the Denver Pacific Railroad, but once the road had finished construction to Denver, the place had all but died away. In 1871 a colony organized by the St. Louis-Western Company, launched in Illinois by a Reformed Presbyterian minister, the Reverend Mr. Andrew C. Todd, settled on the site. Evans was never to capture the sure success of Greeley, but it managed to stay alive and proved to be a thorn in the side of the Union Colony because it openly allowed grog houses and taverns within its limits—a temptation that sometimes lured colonists from Greeley.

There was almost magic in the name "colony" for a time in the territory. Promotional schemes that had little or nothing in common with the cooperative colonial endeavors took the name and used it, hoping thereby to attract more settlers to their lands. The Platte River Land Company, for example, "boomed" its settlement called Platteville as a "colony" although it had none of the true features of cooperation, and was strictly a speculation scheme to promote settlement on the land owned by the company. The Denver and Rio Grande Railway's subsidiary townsite and land companies also used the name "colony" in promoting Colorado Springs and South Pueblo. Although Robert A. Cameron, who helped General Palmer organize the townsite companies, had gained some of his experience in town planting in the Union Colony adventure, the railroad's towns, like Platteville, were ordinary speculative promotions.

None of the towns of the decade masquerading under the colony title carried its promotional campaign to greater extremes than David S. Green's Southwestern Colony town of Green City. On the South Platte River, some twenty-seven miles downstream from Greeley, Green located two sections of government land and then set out to sell more than 5,000 town lots to people in the southern and border states. Green City tradition insists that some of the advertising circulars distributed by the promoters pictured steamboats at a wharf, suggesting that Green City would become a major commercial center as well as the hub of a prosperous farming area. Some settlers did move into the embryo town, but many lots were purchased merely for speculation. On such shaky foundations, no town could succeed and Green City was soon nothing but a bad memory of misleading promotion.

Farther down the Platte River, another settlement was begun at this time that in no way proclaimed itself a "colony." Immigrants from Tennessee and Mississippi, dissatisfied with life in the southern states during the reconstruction days after the Civil War, began the town of Sterling in 1873-74, about three miles northeast of the town's present location. When it was rumored that the Union Pacific Railroad was planning a branch line from Julesburg to La Salle, Sterling residents decided to try to gain the location of a division point between Denver and Omaha. They offered the railroad a donation of eighty acres of land as an inducement to locate the shops in their town, and when the offer was accepted, the future of

Sterling was assured. The town then moved to its present location.

Westward, toward the mountains, Fort Collins came closer to satisfying the requirements of a true colony than many other new settlements. The site of Fort Collins had been a military reservation, named Camp Collins. Abandoned by the War Department as a federal post, the site was bought up by a town company which planned the new city of Fort Collins. Memberships were offered for sale to persons "of good moral character" in the Fort Collins Agricultural Colony. Settlers could purchase memberships for $50, $150, or $250, entitling them to city lots, farming land, or both. Homes and commercial buildings were under construction by 1873, and the town ditch for irrigation was dug that same year.

Toward the end of the decade (1870-1880), other colonization schemes were effected that differed from the earlier towns. These later colonies were more closely tied to religious groupings. For example, the Mormons established themselves in two separate colonies in the San Luis Valley before the end of the decade. Members of the Mormon church from Alabama, Georgia, and Tennessee founded Manassa, south of Alamosa, in 1878. Two years later fellow-religionists from Salt Lake City settled at the junction of the Conejos and Rio Grande rivers in a town they called Ephraim. The unhealthful marshes there prompted a move five years later to Sanford. Some anxiety over the plans of the Mormons resulted from these two small towns. Several southern Colorado newspaper editors engaged in virulent editorializing against this "invasion" of the valley; rumors predicted a plan of the Mormons to establish a belt of colonies, twenty-five miles apart, all the way from Utah through Colorado to Nebraska. Some feared that the Mormons "would hold the balance of power in the politics of Conejos County which would result in political ruin for that part of the State."[4]

Another colony of settlers arrived in Fremont County in 1882. Emanuel H. Saltiel, who owned silver mines at Cotopaxi, arranged through the Hebrew Immigrant Aid Society to settle sixteen families of Jewish immigrants from Russia and Poland on his lands. The experiment was not a particularly happy one. While the farming lands were supposed to be located in the Wet Mountain Valley, the colonists instead were given rather barren lands for which no water was available for irrigation because of prior appropriations. In the view of some critics, the interested sponsors of the project were more concerned with populating the town of Cotopaxi than in providing a new start in life for the refugees. When no satisfactory arrangements for aid could be negotiated with Saltiel, appeals were made to Jewish families in Denver for help. Finally the Hebrew Aid Society advised the immigrants to leave Cotopaxi, giving to each family $100 to help them settle in other places.

All these colonies—successful or not—were undoubtedly stimulated by the Board of Immigration that the territorial legislature created. Beginning its labors in 1872, the Board induced many persons to come to Colorado through its literature and promotional campaigns. As in other similar ventures, the claims of the Board were sometimes exaggerated; the emphasis was perhaps too often placed on the attractive features of the territory and too seldom on those characteristics of Colorado life that required patience and concerted effort to overcome. More serious, to some critics, was the failure of the Board to provide any help for immigrants after their arrival in the territory. "It is better to have no Board of Immigration at all," wrote one observer, "better not to waste time and money in advertising and entreating unless proper avenues are opened and the way cleared for such worthy people as may respond and are disposed to remain."[5] Some historians have suggested that the Board may indeed have ultimately accomplished more harm than good; but in the days of its operation, it played a vital, if controversial, role in furthering the great goal of peopling the territory.

13

Carpetbaggers' Kingdom

For fifteen years—from 1861 to 1876—Colorado was a colony of the United States. Most of the territorial officers, from governor to justices of the Supreme Court, were appointed by the national government, rather than elected by the people of the territory. Coloradans were allowed to select a delegate to the national Congress, but that officer's powers were limited; he could debate but he could not vote. The territory had no actual representation of its interests in national legislation. For this reason alone there were constant attempts to replace the territorial status with a state government. The desire for statehood was made doubly determined by the constantly shifting political scene in Washington. Each succeeding change in power there tended to be reflected in shifting office-holders appointed to territorial positions.

In many ways the story of territorial government and politics is a continuing chronicle of attempts to gain statehood for Colorado. The events were always played on two different and widely separated stages. In the territory itself, factions favored and factions opposed the anticipated conversion to "statedom" as they believed the change would benefit or harm their own interests. At the same time, political groupings in the national capital viewed statehood for Colorado favorably or unfavorably as a change in the status of the territory might be expected to bring good or ill fortune to them.

The presidential election year of 1864 marked the first major attempt to gain Colorado statehood. In that year, when the territory was a mere three-year-old, the Republican Party, hard-pressed by its lack of success on the battlefields of the Civil War, feared for its future in the political campaign. In addition to such precautions as converting the official name of the party to the Union Party, and nominating as Lincoln's running mate a War Democrat from a border state, Andrew Johnson, the party pushed three enabling acts through Congress. (An enabling act was permissive legislation, allowing a territory to frame a constitution and submit it to the voters for approval; if such approval was gained, the president of the United States then could proclaim statehood for the territory.)

Colorado, Nebraska, and Nevada territories were all given the chance to bring their expected Republican electoral votes to the polls that fall. Nine additional votes might insure the margin of victory for the party. Nevada accepted the offer and became a state. Nebraska refused. Coloradans found much in the offer that was appealing. The obvious advantages of change included the benefits of "home rule," the bolstering of local pride, a hoped-for influx of eastern capital to revive stagnated mining, and the advantages to be reaped from actual congressional representation. With two senators and a representative voting the territory's interests, "unfortunate" legislation like the Pacific railroad bill, or a proposed federal tax on mining, might be altered or enactment prevented. And, not least, unpopular territorial officials would no longer be able to hide behind the national patronage; "carpet bag" government would come to an end. All these motivations combined to build enthusiasm for statehood in the territory.

The enabling act required the summoning of a convention to draft a constitution for the proposed state. Haste was necessary, for the constitution would have to be written and approved by the voters in time for the President to proclaim statehood before election day if the votes from Colorado were to count in the presidential canvass. Independence Day that summer, 1864, found the delegates to the constitutional convention gathered at Golden to begin work. However, they soon adjourned to Denver, where facilities were less limited, and there they completed their deliberations.

From the beginning, men favoring statehood securely controlled the convention. The statehood men by and large were Republicans and Denver oriented, such as Governor John Evans, John Chivington, William Byers, and Central City's Henry Teller, who was just beginning a long and distinguished career in Colorado politics. The necessity for haste appears to have led these men into a serious procedural error. Blinded by their own enthusiasm for statehood, they underestimated a latent, largely unexpressed hostility to change and the role that personalities could play. In order to save time, they fashioned a slate of candidates for the new offices statehood would require; the voters then could ratify their choices at the same time they approved the constitution. They chose D. T. Towne for governor; Colonel John Chivington was to become the state's congressman. Modestly reserving their own names from the slate, Evans and Teller presumably anticipated allowing the state legislature to reward them with the two United States senatorships.

From this maneuver an immediate hostility to the whole statehood movement resulted. Many citizens became convinced that the Evans-Teller group was more concerned with offices than with the welfare of Colorado. Some men who had failed to secure places on the "ballot" moved over to lead the opposition to statehood. They soon discovered that there were other reasons for opposing the change. Many residents objected to the tax increases that would result when the federal government withdrew its subsidies for officers' salaries. Democrats saw no merit in hurrying three electoral votes for their opponents in the coming presidential race. Others were apprehensive about the extension of the federal conscription laws to Colorado, a change that would accompany the transition to statehood.

In addition, there was a bloc of anti-statehood votes in the southern counties. No particular political friendship had ever developed between the Spanish-American settlers predominant in those counties and the Anglo-American settlers who formed the majority of the residents in the northern region. Although conflicts between the groups were rare, it was only a few years later when a violent eruption occurred at Trinidad, on Christmas Day, 1867. A wrestling match mushroomed into a riot, which in turn became a four-day siege of a building where a supposed murderer of a Spanish-American and his friends took refuge. Cavalry from Fort Lyon and Fort Reynolds quelled the "Battle of Trinidad." The barriers of culture and language undoubtedly contributed to the latent hostility of the southern counties to political domination by the northern sections. Since the Democratic Party was favored by the majority of the southern residents, Republican-achieved statehood and probable control of offices promised nothing of special attraction for them.

The combination of all these various forces was sufficient to defeat the statehood movement by a decisive majority: 1,520 for to 4,676 against. It was difficult for those who claimed Colorado residents were interested in statehood to explain the vote. Once the ballots were counted and the constitution and candidates rejected, the congressional enabling legislation was technically dead. But, surprisingly, a new movement for statehood rose like a phoenix, and interestingly its leadership included men recently opposed to the scheme.

Among these men was Denver's urbane Jerome Chaffee, mining man and speculator, but above all politician—perhaps Colorado's consummate politician of that era. He and Teller came to dominate the Republican party, initially as rivals. The party was split into two factions, commonly referred to as the Denver and Golden crowds, each jealously guarding its own interests. The former had many of the territorial leaders—Evans, Chivington, Chaffee, and Byers—while the latter included Loveland and Teller, who switched sides after the 1864 debacle. For nearly a decade this split would have ramifications in various local issues.

With Chaffee's aid, a call was now issued for another constitutional convention, to meet in the spring of 1865. The assumption was that, if a constitution was drafted and accepted by the people, the national authorities would not refuse to admit Colorado to statehood on a mere technicality. But what the leaders failed to take into account was that Colorado's potential electoral votes were no longer needed. The election was over and the Republicans had weathered the crisis. Nonetheless, the statehood advocates continued in their plans. The voters ratified their constitution by a thin margin, although they rejected an accompanying proposal for Negro suffrage.

At this point it would have been wise to await word of presidential approval. But, instead, the statehood leaders sponsored an election for "state" officers. Three parties presented candidates: the Republicans, the Democrats, and a third group called the Sand Creek Vindication Party. The Republicans triumphed, capturing a majority of seats in the "state" legislature, electing the "governor" (William Gilpin, attempting another political career) and the "congressman," George Chilcott. When the unauthorized "state" legislature convened, it selected John Evans and Jerome Chaffee United States Senators.

The victory of the statehood faction and the Republicans in the "state" election proved short-lived, however, because the reaction in Washington was anything but favorable. Already lines were being drawn between the Radicals and President Andrew Johnson in the battle that would dominate the national political scene for the next few years. Johnson had no particular desire to increase the majority of Radical Republicans in Congress and, despite assurances from Colorado Republicans that they were loyal to his administration, he had reason to suspect they were wavering. Johnson refused to proclaim statehood on the grounds that no enabling legislation existed for the recently transpired activities, nor did he heed renewed pleas of the statehood men.

This action drove statehood advocates into the Radical camp in an attempt to persuade Congress to enact a new enabling bill. The narrow margin of victory, less than 200 votes, did nothing to help the statehood efforts. Even more damaging in the minds of the Radical leadership was the rejection of Negro suffrage when, just at this time, the leadership was showing increasing interest in guaranteeing votes for Negroes. A third factor that hurt the attempt was the aftermath of the Sand Creek Massacre, which rocked the territory, led to a Congressional investigation, and helped bring about the removal of Governor Evans.

Meanwhile, the territory continued to exist as a federal colony, governed by officials appointed in Washington. In the fall of 1865 Colorado received its third governor, Alexander Cummings of Philadelphia. Evans' removal from office had been considered for some time. His dismissal had been recommended by a committee formed to investigate the Sand Creek Massacre. Other motivating factors were a dispute about mining legislation, which brought some demand for a change, and the fact that Johnson probably wished to use his patronage privilege for his own ends.

Cummings, one of the most controversial men to hold the governor's office during the territorial era, has been called by a recent historian, "a hack politician, a spoilsman," and earned from his contemporaries the title, "His Turbulent Excellency." The petty quarrels that swarmed around him were generated partly by his adamant opposition to statehood. But his own personality—his stubbornness and unwillingness or inability to compromise on political matters—did little to win friends among influential Republicans in Colorado. He lasted only seventeen months in the office. In May, 1867, Johnson removed him and named A. Cameron Hunt as governor.

The pattern of patronage and politics continued to rule the appointment of territorial officials. One of the most distressing facts of territorial status, in the eyes of many Coloradans, was the practice of the dominant political party to look upon the western territories as convenient "dumping grounds" for office-seekers with claims for partisan preference. Territorial offices were particularly useful for "taking care" of defeated, lame-duck office-holders. The coming and going of the governors was bad enough; lesser offices seemed to many to be filled with even less desirable appointees.

In addition to officials appointed from Washington, there was also a considerable number of patronage positions to be filled locally. These led to a constant scurry and scramble among the leaders of the dominant party in the territory, for continued control of the party often rested on the ability of a group to successfully juggle the spoils of office. Some of the positions were desirable because they legitimately carried with them large fees. The clerkship of the supreme court, for example, reportedly was worth close to $4,000 a year, "the best office in the Territory."[1] Other posts presumably were desirable because they presented opportunities to engage in petty, and sometimes not so petty, graft. Besides appointive offices, the spoils of territorial politics also involved contracts for public printing, and other services as well. Here, too, controversy seemed the rule rather than the exception. Rival newspapers and printing establishments jostled for supremacy in the affection of the officers who awarded the contracts.

It would be inaccurate to blame the territorial status for all the shortcomings of Colorado's political life in these years. But many residents did believe that statehood would bring more responsible government. In the year 1866 such men were pleased by a brief resurgence of sentiment for statehood. Congressional leaders of the Republican Party, anticipating the need for additional supporters, passed a new enabling act for Colorado, with an eye on the off-year congressional elections that fall. President Andrew Johnson promptly vetoed the act on the grounds that the population in the territory was insufficient for statehood. Congress tried to override the veto, but failed. Since these same months saw the Radical Republican majority in Congress muster votes to override presidential vetoes in most other matters, including a statehood bill for Nebraska, it is apparent that the issue of Colorado statehood did not have undivided support in the dominant congressional group.

And in the territory, the fight had by no means ended either. With renewed efforts emanating from the statehood advocates, their antagonists girded for battle to defeat any move to elevate the territory's status. The Denver "ring," led by John Evans and Jerome Chaffee, worked diligently for admission to the Union. These men still controlled the unrecognized and non-functioning "state" administration of 1865, needing only national approval to become the government of Colorado.

Opposing them was the "Golden gang" led by Henry Teller, ready to take issue with the Denver Republicans on statehood or any other question. The split between the two groups was particularly focused on the commercial rivalry between the two towns, especially in their competition for railroads. The division of political spoils added another element to the rivalry. Then there was the controversy over the location of the territorial capital. The first legislature had been called to meet in Denver; during its session the members determined to convene in Colorado City for the second session. They had met there in 1862, but after a few days returned to Denver and its greater comforts. Golden then offered the use of a building and free firewood, and the legislature accepted the offer and moved to that city.

From then, until 1867, both Denver and Golden claimed the honor of being the capital, and the legislature shifted sessions from one town to the other. Territorial Secretary Samuel H. Elbert, growing weary from moving the legislative furniture back and forth, reportedly muttered that the "first railroad needed in Colorado was the most direct line between its two capitals."[2] Finally, in 1867, Denver was named the permanent seat of government.

While Evans, Chaffee, and the Denver Republicans won the capital, the fight over statehood continued. Whatever might be said about the merits of the argument, Teller and his anti-statehood group were winning many friends. Statehood was becoming less and less attractive to many Coloradans. In the spring of 1868, a last attempt was made to use the constitution and officers of the 1865 movement. The United States Senate Committee on Territories conducted hearings in Washington on the question—1868 was election year again! Evans and Chaffee submitted statements to the committee, emphasizing their estimates that population in Colorado was increasing rapidly and had reached a total between 75,000 and 100,000 people. In their view, the majority of these residents were eager to enjoy statehood.

Teller, speaking for the other side, denied the population increases, insisting that no more than 30,000 people then lived in the territory. (Two years later the federal census would count less than 40,000 residents, an increase of only 5,000 since 1860.) Teller was also confident that a referendum among the voters would demonstrate a majority in the territory opposed to statehood. In Washington, Teller spent time with Senator Roscoe Conkling of New York, and other influential senate members. He did his work well; it was soon apparent that a statehood bill could not pass Congress. Evans and Chaffee, in a final, desperate move, "resigned" their never-sanctioned offices, hoping to eliminate some of the opposition. But the noble act did little good. From 1868 until the approach of the presidential election of 1876, Colorado statehood was a dead issue. "Carpet bag" government might be unpleasant, and even corrupt, but the statehood advocates had small success railing against it for the next seven years.

Even without electoral votes from Colorado, the Republicans experienced no great difficulty electing their candidate, U. S. Grant, to the presidency in 1868. The new President soon moved to employ the patronage of territorial offices, and Colorado prepared to welcome its fifth governor—General Edward McCook. The new governor was no stranger to the territory. In 1859 he had joined the gold rush to Gregory Gulch and had practiced law for a brief time in Central City. Then, during the Civil War, he had attained the rank of major general in the Union Army. His career as Colorado governor was far from quiet. Determined to make the most of his powers, playing the customary game of spoils, McCook managed to alienate a large part of the Colorado political community during the next few years.

Not the least of his crimes against the commonwealth involved favoritism he showed his brother-in-law, James B. Thompson, whose insatiable appetite for public office led him to be the governor's private secretary, auditor of public accounts, and a special agent to the Utes (headquartered in Denver!). McCook, meanwhile, dabbled in land speculation, railroad projects, and cattle ranching. Together the two proceeded to use their offices to enhance their private welfare; for example, they made $22,000 net profit on a cattle transaction involving a sale to the Utes.

Anti-McCook sentiment brewed, especially in the Denver crowd. An investigation by David Moffat and Samuel Elbert uncovered some of the scandals, and Chaffee, now territorial delegate, presented the results in Washington. Petitions circulated demanding McCook's removal, and Grant eventually bowed to pressure, naming Evans' son-in-law, Samuel Elbert, governor. McCook did not surrender willingly and leveled some accusations and charges of corruption of his own. He convinced Grant of the justice of his case. The president, thereupon, in 1874 removed Elbert, who had been in office less than a year, and replaced him with McCook. The unpopular McCook had become a genuine liability to Colorado Republicans, who split into factions over this latest example of "carpetbaggism." This division allowed the Democratic Party, after a bitter campaign, to elect Thomas Patterson territorial delegate over Chaffee, who had led a valiant but losing battle against McCook's reappointment. This defeat was too much for the local Republicans, who feared what it portended for the future. They insisted that the governor must be removed, and the harassed Grant finally conceded to their demand. In three years three men had been appointed governor. How much longer, Coloradans wondered, would they be victims of Washington's capriciousness?

With McCook's second and final removal, a general overturn of territorial offices followed. To have all the men except one judge removed and replaced created "a great sensation for a small western territory, which attributed the President's action to the results of a game of poker between himself and Delegate Chaffee."[3] To some, the shambles of expiring regimes followed so closely upon each other that all was confusion. The "revolving-door" character of the Colorado governorship impressed many observers as peculiarly unfortunate. The editor of the Laramie (Wyoming) *Sentinel* prophetically stated: "We don't reckon there was ever a territory or state that required so many governors for home consumption as Colorado, and her future historians will likely go crazy in tracing out and recording them."[4]

The vacancy created by the second removal of McCook was filled by John L. Routt, the last of Colorado's territorial governors, destined to become Colorado's first state governor. Routt was a Kentuckian who had served as captain of an Illinois regiment during the Civil War. There is a tradition that General Grant noticed the officer's ability during the Vicksburg campaign. At any rate, after the war Routt was named second assistant postmaster. From that office, Grant assigned him to the Colorado governorship, in time for him to serve during the transition to statehood.

14

The Centennial State

The year 1876 promised to bring to the American people one of the most exciting presidential elections in the history of the Republic. Despite the poor showing of the Liberal Republicans and Democrats four years earlier, when they had tried to match Horace Greeley against U. S. Grant for the presidency, the Republican leaders were worried. Grant was no longer eligible to be a candidate under the restrictive two-term tradition. Reconstruction governments in only three of the southern states were supported by federal troops, and most of the southern electoral votes were probably lost to the opposition. In addition, the disclosures of scandals and corruption during the Grant administrations would give the Democrats a surplus of ammunition to use in the campaign.

So once again the Republicans in Washington looked favorably on aspiring western territories, feeling again the need for the security of additional electoral votes. The Republicans confidently translated Colorado statehood to read "three Republican electoral votes." In the initial stages it was necessary to keep the Democrats content by linking the measure for Colorado statehood with an enabling act for New Mexico Territory, which in all likelihood would favor the Democratic Party. On the last day of the session, March 3, 1875, Congress approved the Colorado legislation. The New Mexico bill failed.

Thus Colorado again was given a chance to enter the sisterhood of the Union. By this time the people of the territory should have been familiar with the procedures to be followed. A constitutional convention would be called. It would draft a basic charter for the new state which, when finished, would be presented to the people for ratification or rejection. If the electorate approved the document, it would be forwarded to Washington. Then the President would complete the process by proclaiming Colorado a state.

The territorial leaders proceeded to set in motion the necessary steps in this procedure. First they summoned the voters to elect thirty-nine delegates to the drafting convention that would meet in Denver's Odd Fellows Hall in December, 1875. The Republicans suggested a non-partisan canvass, because they had recently suffered the internal divisions brought on by Governor McCook. The Democrats, who had experienced their only political victories because of those divisions, refused. Nonetheless, the voters selected twenty-four Republicans and only fifteen Democrats as delegates. Actually, the partisan division was neither very important nor very apparent throughout proceedings of the convention. When divisions occurred, they resulted from other issues. Religious persuasions brought a cleavage between Roman Catholics and Protestants; the mining delegates sometimes differed with the delegates from the agricultural areas. As usual in American state constitutional conventions, the lawyers were the most numerous of the occupational groups represented. A total of fifteen members of the bar sat in the convention. The rest of the delegates were divided in occupation among miners, farmers, bankers, newspaper editors, and railroad men.

Much of what the convention did was routine work, rather easily agreed to by a large majority of the delegates. The convention had no control over some of the provisions of the constitution. For example, Congress had stipulated that the boundaries of the state would be identical with the boundaries of the territory. Other features of the charter were taken wholesale from the constitutions of states already in the Union. A bill of rights was included directly in the constitution, listing the traditional Anglo-American personal freedoms and privileges in considerable detail. These caused little debate, as did the basic plan to provide the traditional separation of the state government into three branches.

The executive branch was to be headed by an elected governor. Six additional officials would be elected to serve with him: a lieutenant governor, a secretary of state, an auditor, a treasurer, an attorney general, and a superintendent of public instruction.

The legislative branch was titled the General Assembly. It was to be a bicameral body, divided into a senate of twenty-six members and a house of representatives of forty-nine members. The representatives would be elected for two-year terms; the senators for four-year terms. By a specific clause of the document, the ratio between the two chambers (twenty-six to forty-nine), was to remain the same when any future apportionments were made.

The third branch, the judiciary, was to be headed by the state supreme court, originally composed of three members elected for nine-year terms. The justice with the least time remaining in his term would serve as the chief justice. An unusual provision of the judicial clauses empowered the state supreme court to render "advisory" opinions when requested. In addition to the supreme court, the constitution established district courts and a county court for each county.

Most of these provisions were fixed with a minimum of difficulty. But there were other sections of the constitution that were not so easily settled. The most difficult problem of all concerned the attempt to determine the limits of the state's authority to regulate economic activity. The year was 1876; in the Midwestern states "Granger" legislatures were at the peak of their power. Farmers and allied interests there, chafing under domination by railroad and storage companies, had used the previously social-minded Patrons of Husbandry, or Grange, organizations to elect their leaders to the state legislatures. In these chambers, the Grangers had successfully campaigned for regulatory legislation to limit fares and charges by railroads and terminal facilities. Granger sentiment had invaded some of the agrarian regions of Colorado, and now was apparent in the convention debates.

At the same time, however, Colorado had other, opposite interests. The new state was still a frontier community, without large domestic capital resources. The mines in the mountains and the farms on the plains cried alike for capital investments to bring them into high productivity. That capital had to come from the East and from Europe. A harsh, inflexible code restricting corporations would create an unfavorable climate to risk investors. Thus the problem was "how to protect the interests of the people without scaring away the capital that was so essential for the economic development of the region."[1]

In the end, the convention tried to walk a narrow line, avoiding both the extreme of rigid regulation on the one hand and the dangers of an unrestricted economy on the other. The delegates who feared the power of uncontrolled corporations were responsible for these provisions of the constitution: all incorporations were to be perfected under a general incorporation law, thus eliminating the hazards of private legislation; no irrevocable charters were to be granted; all out-of-state corporations were required to maintain an agent or a place of business within the new state; all railroads were to be considered "public carriers"; consolidation of parallel or competing railroad lines was forbidden, as were all unjust and unreasonable discriminations between individuals in their business with such corporations; the jurisdiction of the state courts was retained in case of consolidation of a state corporation with a foreign corporation, at least over that part of the corporate property within the limits of the state.

These restrictions and regulations placed the state a goodly distance from pure "laissez-faire." But, in comparison with the legislation that had issued from the Granger-dominated legislatures of the Midwest, it was a kind of "half-way" settlement. The constitution contained no provision for the establishment of a railroad or public utilities commission. There were no clauses specifying the right of the state, or its agencies, to determine maximum railroad or storage rates.

While this problem of economic regulation undoubtedly presented the delegates with their greatest challenge, the convention generated much more noise and heat in its debates over the Deity. Many delegates believed that the absence of specific reference to God in the federal constitution was a serious omission. In many states, such an acknowledgment of Divine Power had been included in the preamble to the constitution. Now the question of whether or not to include such a statement in the Colorado charter stirred considerable controversy. At length the convention decided to acknowledge a "profound reverence for the Supreme Ruler of the Universe."

Even more heated were the debates over the use of school funds. Congress, in the enabling legislation, had provided that two sections of land in each township were to be reserved for the use of the schools. Even if this land was sold eventually for only the minimum price, a windfall of $10,000,000 would result. Immediately the delegates divided on the question of apportioning the grant. Was it to be used only for publicly supported schools, or would it be more fair to include the parochial institutions in the apportionment? The question pitted Protestants against Roman Catholics in debate. In the final determination, the delegates adopted a clause specifying that "no state aid other than exemption from taxation for any sectarian institution" ever was to be provided.

A further problem that arose to delay the convention was the question of woman suffrage. In the centennial year of American independence, women's rights groups, local and national, deluged the delegates with petitions, suggesting the potential honor that Colorado might achieve by becoming the first state in the Union to declare political female independence. The drafters, however, decided to forego heroism. They made a slight nod to the ladies by allowing them the right to vote in school district elections. But for a voice in honest-to-goodness partisan contests, they would have to await the decision of the general (male) electorate on a promised proposal for an amendment. Two years later, the question was placed before the voters and they rejected it.

The woman suffrage question, like that of economic regulation, actually was compromised as far as possible by the delegates. They were motivated primarily by their fear of controversy; their timidity followed naturally from their desire to shun any issue capable of seriously dividing the electorate and crippling the chances for ratification. Only in the matter of disposing of the school funds did the delegates take a strong position when they wrote the clauses upholding the traditional separation of church and state, and here they undoubtedly calculated the dominant strength of the Protestants. As for the constitution as a whole, it was probably much too long as it was written. Too much detail had been included and matters that might well have been left to future legislatures were included in the basic charter.

After eighty-seven days of work, on March 14, 1876, the constitution-makers adjourned their convention. The members left Denver for their home counties, to work for ratification of their product. The electorate balloted on the first day of July that summer. By a resounding majority—15,443 to 4,062—the people of the territory accepted the constitution. All that remained was the arrival of good news from Washington.

President Grant did not keep the Coloradans waiting long. The national elections were fast approaching and Republican votes would be needed. On August 1, 1876, he issued the proclamation of statehood from the White House. Colorado responded with her three Republican electoral votes that fall, which proved fortunate for the party since this was the disputed election when Rutherford Hayes' victory over Samuel Tilden rested precariously on a one-vote margin. Locally the entire Republican ticket for state offices, headed by John Routt for governor, was elected, and the party also won the majority of seats in both houses of the new legislature. Their only defeat came in the selection of a representative to Congress. A squabble over scheduling the election led to a contested decision, finally settled by the national House of Representatives which gave the seat to Democrat Thomas Patterson. Republicans Henry Teller and Jerome Chaffee became the first senators from the new state.

Admittance to the Union proved an enthusiastic occasion for bolstering local pride. Not all Americans were as happy, however. A Pennsylvania editor growled: "Colorado consists of Denver, the Kansas Pacific Railway, and scenery. The mineral resources of Colorado exist in the imagination. The agricultural resources do not exist at all." And a New York newspaper was even more uncomplimentary: "There is something repulsive in the idea that a few handfuls of miners and reckless bushwackers should have the same representation in the Senate as Pennsylvania, Ohio, and New York."[2]

Easterners might sneer at the baby commonwealth, but to the citizens of the new state, such words were of small import. The East had traditionally been opposed to the "rising West" and Coloradans were not deflated in spirit by the critics beyond the Mississippi. The optimism of the decade from 1870 to 1880 was too entrenched to be driven away by mere words. Population alone refuted the pessimists. In 1870 the territory had counted only 40,000 souls. Ten years later that number had increased almost fivefold, to a total of 194,327. Denver, which had registered the grand increase of exactly 10 people (4,749 to 4,759) between 1860 and 1870, now contained the amazing total of 25,000 persons. In warm weather, there were even more people in the Queen City, for Denver was becoming a mecca for summer tourists. In 1878 the four main hotels in the city hosted some 25,000 visitors during the summer season.

Not all the visitors were pleased with what they saw. Many would probably have echoed the sentiments of Isabella Bird, who, in 1872, had described Denver: "I looked down where the great braggart city lay spread out, brown and treeless, upon a brown and treeless plain which seemed to nourish nothing but wormwood and Spanish bayonet."[3] But others found the place attractive, if not in itself, then at least as the gateway to the scenic wonders of the Rocky Mountains. The natural splendors of the peaks and valleys, widely advertised by railroads in their quest for passengers, became the objective of many visitors who came to look and to marvel. Men soon began to augment the natural scene with conveniences for these tourists. Although intended for more practical purposes, the "Georgetown Loop," built to cover the mile and a half from Georgetown to Silver Plume, would soon become a favorite tourist attraction. The thrill of seeing massive mountains while riding across the "Devil's

Gate Viaduct" was worth the price of the railroad fare.
The Royal Gorge enticed many others. Frank Fossett, in his guide
for travellers, assured those contemplating a trip to the canyon of the
Arkansas River that, as was the case with the Grand Canyon of the
Colorado, thousands had visited it, but harm had "befallen none, for
despite the seeming horror of the situation, the appalling depth and
rugged paths, the fascination of the danger gives birth to the greatest
caution."[4]

The hot mineral springs in the hills also beckoned tourists,
particularly the health-seekers. Colorado was now beginning to capitalize on its climate, proclaimed by many as ideal for the sufferer
from tuberculosis. Fossett was almost rhapsodical in his prose: "The
asthmatic forgets in the quiet of undisturbed slumber his nightly
suffocation; the victim of chronic bronchitis discovers a new lease of
life, and after the lapse of a very brief period he finds it hard to
realize that he has been so recently afflicted with a cough so
distressing, so violent, or so dangerous. The sufferer from malaria, in
that most obnoxious form called fever and ague, is glad to have
found a land where fever and ague never come."[5]

The "pitch" was directed to all the infirm, but in particular,
eastern and midwestern physicians had begun to advise tubercular
patients to seek relief in the Rocky Mountain region. They sometimes
suggested that their patients plan the trip westward in several stages,
making temporary stops at Kansas towns along the way to acclimate
the lungs to the changing altitude. Denver and Colorado Springs and
other towns beckoned the sick and the near dead—the tourists who
"ghostlike . . . glided through the corridors and shivered in the parlors
and at the dining tables. Waiters were seen on the staircases carrying
meals to the rooms of those who would never leave them again, and
the direful echoes of hollow coughs resounded through the halls."[6]

If the disease had progressed to its final stages, the invalid might
not only find no cure, but unfortunately meet an earlier death from
the change in altitude. But many were more fortunate, and added
years to their lives by rest, diet changes, and the climate of their new
surroundings. By the decade of 1880-1890, perhaps one-third of all
Colorado settlers could be classified as "health-seekers," an index to a
facet of Colorado's development that has never been fully considered
or described.

Infirm or not, visitors and tourists left their dollars in the
Centennial State. But what were looked upon as even more desirable
than tourists were genuine immigrants who came to stay. No effort

was spared to spread the word that the former frontier was now a
stable, permanent, culture-sprouting place. The advertisers had some
facts to prove it. Consider, for example, the matter of higher
education. Where less than thirty years before the Indians and the fur
men had bartered pelts there now stood no less than five institutions
of higher learning. In Denver, Colorado Seminary had become the
University of Denver. In 1867 the Seminary had been forced to close
its doors because of indebtedness. After twelve inactive years, the
college reopened for classes, in the fall of 1880, with a new name—the
University of Denver and Colorado Seminary.

In Boulder, after existing on paper for some years, the University
of Colorado was now a going concern. In 1877 its first class of
forty-four students arrived for instruction. No need, of course, to
dwell on the fact that President Joseph A. Sewell discovered that the
students were poorly prepared for collegiate courses, necessitating
emphasis on the preparatory school. Instead, concentrate on the fact
that the first class was "on its way," and that by 1883 seven
graduates would receive their diplomas.

The proud Coloradans could relate how the Congregationalists had
found General Palmer's new town of Colorado Springs ideally suited
to their plans for a college in the Rocky Mountains and how, in
1874, they chartered Colorado College. Or how the territorial legislature, in the same year, had appropriated $45,000 to begin a School
of Mines in the city of Golden on the campus of burned-out Jarvis
Hall, a boys' school the Episcopalians had operated there. Or how
Fort Collins promoted a college for itself, and succeeded in gaining
legislative approval for the establishment of the College of
Agriculture. A land-grant institution, organized in accordance with
the federal Morrill Act of 1862, the Agricultural College of Colorado
opened in 1879 for its first enrollment of nineteen students.

Such good works made excellent topics for the local promoters.
But, as it turned out, none of them could compare to a different sort
of magnet that soon enticed hordes of men to the new state. All the
colleges and social institutions in the West faded in comparison with
the attraction of quick and easy wealth. Gold had provided that
impetus in the beginning. Now a new metal came to take its place.
Suddenly, high and deep within the ranges of the Rockies, there was
Leadville—and silver there seemed to make all else dull and commonplace.

15

Carbonate Camps

The discovery of gold and the subsequent Pike's Peak rush spawned the first large white population to settle in Colorado. In the decade that followed, gold mining continued to be the heart of the territory's economy. Gilpin County and its camps dominated the mining scene; it would take most Coloradans a long time to think in terms of other metals. Men like William Byers or William Gilpin could soar into flights of oratory describing additional mineral possibilities, but even after miners in Clear Creek County had discovered silver, prospectors and investors would not divert their attention from gold. Despite the Caribou silver mines and news of discoveries in the San Juans, gold continued to hold center stage. Silver triumphed, nonetheless. With Leadville and the proudly proclaimed title, "The Silver State," Colorado emerged as the greatest mining state in the country, as some of the wild promises of 1859 came true with silver gouged out of hundreds of mines.

In the upper Arkansas River Valley, under the shadow of Mounts Massive and Elbert, prospectors of 1860 stumbled onto a rich gold placer. Optimistically named California Gulch, it became the mecca for one of the larger intra-territorial mining rushes. For a season, Oro City, which grew up along the gulch without much planning or encouragement, had been considered one of the most promising new camps. Then, as the placer gold was panned out, people drifted away to more promising diggings. For a decade the district and the camp stagnated, seemingly forgotten relics of earlier days.

The discovery of the Printer Boy Mine, a gold quartz lode, at the head of the gulch, briefly renewed interest in the area in the late 1860s. Oro City was relocated near the mine, but the flurry proved short-lived. With a population of 251 in 1870 and declining mining, Oro City offered few incentives to newcomers.

Appearances can be deceiving and this was an example. As early as 1873, the Oro City assay office reported silver in numerous ore samples and in November the *Rocky Mountain News* published the story of a meeting of "prominent" citizens to discuss the erection of reduction works for "our silver ores." (This belies the traditional story of William Stevens and Alvinus Wood discovering silver and purchasing all available claims.) The problems were similar to those that hindered Summit County: the nearest mills were too far away to allow anything but extremely high grade ore to be shipped, and the real worth of the mines had not been proven.

The base was laid in 1876 for the rush that would follow in the next three years. Prospecting increased; the *Engineering and Mining Journal* reported that $21,000 worth of silver had been mined in Lake County that year, Interest was being aroused. Oro City, however, was not destined to claim the glory of being the center of a bonanza silver district; this distinction went to the new camp of Leadville, a few miles to the northwest. There, in the summer and fall of 1877, discoveries were made eclipsing everything in California Gulch. Attention and population shifted from Oro City to Leadville.

Throughout the winter, excitement mounted. A rush to Leadville began in the spring of 1878, with the curious, the hopeful, the tenderfoot, and the experienced prospector mingling freely in the giddy atmosphere of the 10,000-foot elevation and a mercurial silver bonanza. In April the Little Pittsburg Mine was discovered on Fryer Hill, the most important of the early mining areas. It launched Horace Austin Warner Tabor on a career that eventually put him in the United States Senate and made him one of Colorado's best known legendary figures. Tabor, a veteran prospector and storekeeper in California Gulch, Buckskin Joe, and Oro City, had a change in luck when he grubstaked August Rische and George Hook, the men who discovered the fabulous Little Pittsburg. The Tabors rose from comfortable middle-class respectability as Oro City's leading citizens to millionaire status. For the next three years, it seemed Tabor could do no wrong in mining or in investments. Eventually, his financial plunging led to his downfall, but not before he rejected his faithful first wife Augusta to marry Elizabeth McCourt, better known as Baby Doe, creating one of the era's greatest social scandals.

Tabor, who moved to Leadville in the summer of 1877, had emerged as one of its leaders even before he had acquired his wealth.

He worked hard to promote the camp, helped organize municipal government, and had been elected the first mayor. Larger horizons opened for him as his wealth grew. The Republican Party tapped him for lieutenant governor in 1878, and his improved status brought him into contact with many of the state's noted miners and speculators, including Chaffee and Moffat. He speculated with abandon; for "pocket money" he purchased the Matchless Mine, which produced for nearly a decade to help support his other financial adventures.

Others found their fortunes almost as quickly. The hills of the district seemed to be stacked with silver. The first "boom" year of 1878 saw some $2,000,000 worth of the metal extracted; the count went up to over $9,000,000 the next year. In the decade between 1879 and 1889, more than $82,000,000 worth of silver was dug up, smelted down, and shipped from the Leadville region.

Founded in 1877 and incorporated in 1878, Leadville soon surpassed all Colorado communities but Denver in population, while Lake County, under this stimulus, grew from 500 to 24,000 persons by the time of the census of 1880. Nearly astride the Continental Divide, Leadville lived high and grew fast, its mining history almost eclipsed by its town-making efforts. In many ways, Leadville was a repetition of other "boom" towns, but here the spectacle of sudden growth was exaggerated. No other Colorado camp until Cripple Creek could compare with Leadville in numbers or wealth. All the ingredients of civilized life were wanting, and men and women were not hesitant about trying their hand at making dollars—one way or another—by meeting those demands. Butchers, smeltermen, milliners, prostitutes, grocers, barbers, boarding house operators, newspapermen, bankers, and saloon keepers—all of them catered to the needs of the new "Cloud City."

Profiteering seemed the rule, not the exception. Staple groceries sold for four times the Denver prices. A barrel of whiskey reportedly could be made to work a $1500 profit; hay sold for $200 a ton in winter. This sort of bizarre inflation came about largely because of the difficulties of freighting goods into the camp. Denver, Colorado Springs, Canon City, and Georgetown were the sites of the railheads, and all were at least seventy-five miles distant from Leadville. Some improvement came with the building of the "High Line" wagon road over Loveland Pass in 1879. Then Georgetown, terminal of the Colorado Central, was only sixty miles away and the trip, in good weather, could be made in one day with four-horse teams.

Even after the goods arrived in Leadville, "chaos prevailed in the

Leadville's Chesnut Street in 1879. (Denver Public Library Western Collection)

location and identification of freight, for it must be remembered that within a period of six months nearly sixty thousand persons were being added to the population. All had to be housed, clothed and fed, and every requirement had to be transported hundreds of miles over rough mountain roads. As the 'end of the track' advanced from week to week, machinery and merchandise of every conceivable description was piled upon the right of way in the uttermost confusion. Wagon freighters were unable to handle the enormous tonnage offered. Hundreds of loaded wagons arrived daily, and their cargoes dumped on confused heaps within twenty enormous warehouses, without attempt at sorting, classifying or indexing. Merchants with waiting storerooms and clamoring customers were frenzied by their inability to secure consignments after arrival."[1]

Under such conditions, travel and shipping rates were nothing but exorbitant. Passengers were charged ten cents a mile from Denver to the terminus of the Denver and South Park Railroad; freight rates ran as high as $29 a ton—more than for goods shipped by water from New York City to California around Cape Horn. Only the construction of a railroad directly into Leadville would ease the situation, and more than one road was already heading in that direction. Colorado railroaders, boasting of their more than 1,000 miles of operating trackage in the state in 1878, discovered that until Leadville was included in the network their profits would never reach full potential.

The Denver and Rio Grande had quickly sensed the importance of the Leadville traffic and had begun its plans. But before it could act it had to wage a highly competitive battle with the Atchison, Topeka and Santa Fe road. The Santa Fe and the Rio Grande found themselves potential rivals for two points: Raton Pass into New Mexico and the canyon of the Arkansas River, leading to Leadville. Early in 1878 the Santa Fe began construction across Raton Pass, thus presumably blocking the Rio Grande's chances of entering the New Mexican capital by the old trail route. Almost simultaneously, work crews of the two roads appeared in the Royal Gorge of the Arkansas, determined to secure the narrow defile leading to the new silver camp. Before much actual violence was committed by either side, the roads' attorneys had transferred the contest to the courts. During the litigation the Rio Grande experienced humiliating moments, including a lease to the Santa Fe, and unleasing, and finally, the interjection of new ownership in the person of financier Jay Gould. Gould, also owner of the Union Pacific and Kansas Pacific lines, achieved a place on the Rio Grande's Board of Directors shortly after his purchase of company stock. Not until February, 1880 was the complicated situation unravelled at a meeting in Boston between all interested parties.

According to the Boston "treaty," the Rio Grande agreed to give up its plans to build south over Raton Pass to El Paso, Texas, acknowledging the historic crossing as Santa Fe country. It also promised not to build eastward toward St. Louis, a move that Gould had threatened. The Santa Fe Railroad, in return, committed itself to withdrawal from the Leadville route and promised to forget its plans to build from Pueblo to Denver. The lucrative but long-delayed Leadville traffic would be carried over Rio grande tracks through the contested gorge, with that railraod paying the Santa Fe the cost of its work in the canyon and a bonus for the settlement. The east-bound freight carried by the Rio Grande would be delivered on a fifty-fifty basis to the Union Pacific and the Santa Fe.

Two years had passed while the contest between the roads tied up construction toward the silver camp. Now, with a settlement reached, the Rio Grande hastened to complete the line. Building up the valley, the railroad company continued its town-building habits by buying up homesteaders' lots and laying out the city of Salida (South Arkansas) on the way. Before the end of 1880, it had reached Leadville.

While waiting to complete that line, the Rio Grande had pushed the construction of its other branches, especially the extension over La Veta Pass into the San Luis Valley. On July 4, 1878, the railroad brought its first train into the new town of Alamosa. This extension grew in significance after the Raton Pass route to New Mexico was closed by the Santa Fe construction. If the Rio Grande was to reach the New Mexican capital, it must do so by building south from the San Luis Valley. In 1880 what came to be known as the "Chilli Line" connected Alamosa with Espanola, New Mexico. However, the Boston agreement prohibited construction for some time of the remaining forty-four miles to Santa Fe.

While the Royal Gorge "war" between the Rio Grande and the Santa Fe captivated the public's imagination, the Denver, South Park railroad also had designs on the Leadville traffic. By 1878 the South Park had completed its line from Denver through Platte Canyon to Bailey, and was in an advantageous position to carry Leadville freight to the end of its tracks, whence the freight was hauled by wagon into the silver camp. But then, for reasons still obscure, instead of heading from Bailey directly to Leadville, the South Park swung in an arc through the mountain park and reached Nathrop in 1880, on its way to the Gunnison area. At Nathrop it intersected the Rio Grande tracks. Through an arrangement with that company, the South Park sent its trains up the Arkansas Valley into Leadville. The days of the South Park's independence proved to be as limited as the Rio Grande's. The Union Pacific, dominated by Jay Gould, bought the road and immediately extended a line from Como over Boreas and Fremont passes to Leadville in 1884.

With control of the South Park, the Union Pacific was rapidly consolidating its hold over transportation in northeastern Colorado. The Colorado Central, Loveland's dream road, had fallen to Gould control in 1879, the year after the eastern financier had taken the Kansas Pacific into his hands. From the Colorado Central terminal at Georgetown, Gould envisioned an extension to Leadville, too. Under his auspices, the Georgetown, Leadville and San Juan railroad was organized and, in grandiose style, the famed Georgetown Loop was constructed, lifting trains the 638-foot step above Georgetown to Silver

Plume. A few miles west of there, at Graymont, construction abruptly halted.

For travellers on their way to Leadville, whether by Rio Grande coaches through the Royal Gorge, or the South Park over Fremont Pass, or via Georgetown and the horse-drawn stage, the trip must have been tiresome. People going to Leadville wanted to get there in a hurry. When they arrived, they might very well have been disappointed at their first sight of the place. The hillsides had been denuded; the pine forests were cut down to make charcoal for the smelters, since coal or coke was not available in quantity until the railroads reached Leadville.

In the first rush any type of construction was deemed appropriate; the startled visitor saw log cabins, false-fronted wooden stores, varied types of shacks, and even tents throughout the camp. These gradually gave way to brick and frame construction, though a lawn remained a rarity, while littering was common. Over all hung smoke from the smelters, the mine buildings, and the town. Mayor Tabor and the city fathers worked hard to provide a government with some controls, but the newness and tremendous growth worked against resolving sanitation, general nuisance, and criminal problems. The lack of a stable tax base hindered development of water works, street improvement, and the hiring of needed officials. The constant danger of fire spurred the formation of volunteer companies, which served until a regular fire department could be hired. Local mine owners, such as Tabor, furnished money for equipment and fancy uniforms.

A town did emerge, passing through the camp stage very quickly. It had been born to serve the needs of the mines and miners, and serve them it did. A business census in the spring of 1879 listed among its findings 31 restaurants, 17 barber shops, 51 groceries, 4 banks, and 120 saloons. Lots that had been worth less than $100 two years before were now selling for thousands, and rents jumped correspondingly. At night Leadville put its best face forward, the soft lights masking the bleakness of a jerry-built community. At dusk the variety houses, dance halls, theatres, gambling halls, and saloons awakened from their day-long slumber. All types of entertainment were available, from the foulest dive to the handsome Tabor Opera House, which opened in November, 1879. The red-light district claimed to be one of the country's best, a dubious distinction. Leadville had come of age as the silver queen of Colorado.

Though less noticeable because they were less spectacular, more significant developments contributed to the town's stability. The organization of numerous churches, the building of schools, and the growth of residential areas reflected the coming of families and the disappearance of the rough frontier trappings. Along with these came fraternal lodges and social clubs. Gas lights and telephones soon appeared in the business district and in some homes.

Above all else, Leadville was a sudden economic opportunity that created a frantic, feverish race to quick fortune. A variety of paths to the rainbow's end, other than mining, appeared. Two of the best lay in real estate speculation and the building of rental property. Many men ignored mining and concentrated on services and supplies, where a steady if not spectacular income awaited the fortunate ones. Freighting, until the railroad came, was lucrative and even afterward the wagons went from the tracks to the more isolated camps. Some men were content to labor in the mines, while others hired out only as a temporary expedient until they could find their own bonanzas.

The lucky prospectors and investors were really lucky. Tabor was not alone in his good fortune. Samuel Newhouse was one of those who prospered early; he would move from Leadville to become an important copper "king" and, in time, erect the famous Flatiron building in New York City. John L. Routt, of contemporary political fame, the Colorado governor, bought part interest in the Morning Star Mine which later sold for a million dollars and netted the then ex-governor a goodly fortune. Alva Adams, of future political fame, banked his money from the Blind Tour Mine.

The smelting men also prospered. By 1881 fourteen smelters and ore reduction plants were filling up the valleys with their evil-smelling fumes. Among the earliest of these was the Harrison works, opened in 1877, and the future Grant Smelting Company, dating from the following year. The Grant soon had seven furnaces in operation, treating 175 tons of ore each day, producing three carloads of base bullion every twenty-four hours. And it was at Leadville that the future "Smelter King," Meyer Guggenheim, reached his first successes in the Centennial State.

Meyer Guggenheim had come to the United States in 1847 from Switzerland, a poverty-cursed nineteen-year-old. From peddler in Pennsylvania to commission merchant during the Civil War, he courted and won financial success. In 1879, with R. B. Graham, he bought the A. Y. and Minnie properties in Leadville. They were reported to bring him profits of $1,000 a day; a decade later they would still be valued at some $14,000,000. Meyer sent his son Benjamin to Leadville to watch over the mining operations and it was through Benjamin that Edward R. Holden interested the senior Guggenheim in investing in his smelter at Denver.

As wood became scarcer as a smelting fuel, the operators began to use coking coals from Trinidad, more desirable than wood or charcoal although transportation costs kept the price extremely high. It was natural for smelter owners to try to locate their works in strategic centers. The Boston and Colorado had earlier discovered that by moving from Black Hawk to Argo, near Denver, they effected significant economies because of the added ease of securing coal. While much of the Leadville ore was reduced locally, both Denver and Golden also grew as smelting centers. The giant Grant Smelter in Denver began operations in 1878.

Immense amounts of labor were needed to work the smelters and the mines. Italians, Austrians, Croats, Serbs, Slovenes—the newly arrived immigrants from southeastern Europe provided the majority of the unskilled laborers for smelter furnaces and mine tunnels. As though to emphasize the difference that had come to mining operations since the days of the earlier rush to the gold camps, the Leadville mines were a mere three years old when they were rocked by the first major labor disturbance in the state's mining history. The individualistic days when mines were owned by the same men who worked them, and when those who classified as day laborers shifted for themselves, were now past. Mining properties had become corporate enterprises and laboring men had joined together into unions—in this case, the Miners' Co-operative Union, secretly chartered by the national Knights of Labor.

In late May, 1880, the Leadville mines were hit by a strike that started with a walkout by the laborers at the Chrysolite mine. For the next three weeks the town was gripped by the strike, which eventually so worried the "respectable" citizens, especially the owners, that pressure was brought to bear on Governor Pitkin to declare martial law and send in state troops. He did and his action broke the strike, but not before threats of violence were heard from both sides. Reasons for the strike mystified contemporaries; explanations ranged from a demand for higher wages to an owner-motivated movement to mask the failure of the Chrysolite.

The strike hurt Leadville, but less than other events of that same year—the failure of both the Little Pittsburg and the Chrysolite mines. The Little Pittsburg, which had brought Leadville into its bonanza era, collapsed in February amid charges of stock speculation, over-promotion, and mismanagement. Many unhappy eastern speculators were left holding stocks that dropped in price from over thirty dollars to five dollars per share by April. This did little to increase confidence in Leadville stocks, or in some of Colorado's well-known businessmen; Chaffee and Moffat, for example, were both involved. Just before the outbreak of the strike, rumors circulated that the Chrysolite was going the same route. Although it did not collapse immediately, it teetered on the brink of disaster and finally fell in late September. Chrysolite shares, which had soared to more than forty dollars, now plummeted to the three and four dollar range. Leadvillites took some solace in blaming eastern management and over-expectations, but Easterners were disenchanted and leery about further investment.

With these events the initial mining phase of Leadville's history came to an end. An era that had been born of excitement and nurtured by over-optimism was now closed. After the shocks of 1880 came a re-evaluation of methods and development and a more conservative mining approach. There was still plenty of ore to dig from the hills around Leadville, and prosperity continued in the 1880s. But never again would the district be considered ripe for easy wealth.

The Leadville crash resembled that which hit Gilpin County gold mines back in 1864. In both cases all mining stocks suffered and absurd inflation in values never returned. Another parallel between the Gilpin County gold mines and the Leadville silver camp developed. As the first mining gulches had filled up, sending crowded, excited prospectors scurrying over the surrounding areas to find other Eldorados, so a revived interest in mining at Leadville scattered prospectors far and wide over the state, into regions that had earlier been looked at and rejected as possible mining districts. In the immediate vicinity of Leadville, silver camps like Robinson and Kokomo and the Ten Mile district were opened very rapidly. Near the head of the Roaring Fork of the Colorado River, rich silver carbonates were uncovered. In 1880, Aspen came into being, soon to be elevated as seat of the newly created Pitkin County.

South and west of Leadville, only a few miles east of the boundary of the Ute Indian reservation, new life was injected into the area around Gunnison. In 1874 Sylvester Richardson, and others, had organized a town company with sixty $100 shares of stock and had laid out Gunnison. But it was the carbonate ores unearthed there after the Leadville strike that made it more than a straggling frontier townsite. Now, in a wide swath around the town, satellites sprang up, at St. Elmo and Tin Cup, Irwin and Gothic. Smelting operations in Gunnison were underway by 1882. South and east of there, in the Wet Mountain Valley, discovery of silver ores not far from the Rosita gold mines created Silver Cliff, founded in 1878.

As a sort of exclamation point to end the silver saga, in 1890 the mines at Creede were opened. This "last of the silver towns" created its own romantic history and even entered the realm of poetry in Cy Warman's words:

> It's day all day in the day-time,
> And there is no night in Creede.

Even though the new discoveries caught the public's attention and investors and the eternally hopeful flocked to Creede, it was not like it had been back in 1859 or at Leadville. It was easy to get to Creede—one could almost ride the railroad to the site—and settled communities were all around it, unlike the neighboring San Juan region back in the 1870s, which suffered for a decade because of its isolation. The pioneering phase passed quickly and so did Creede's moment of fame. The price of silver had fallen steadily and before long came the crisis of 1893, with the repeal of the Sherman Silver Purchase Act. Creede's production would never equal that of Leadville, but it was here that the curtain rang down for the last time on two decades of silver rushes.

Almost as feverish as the prospectors' race to new mining camps was the railroads' rivalry to follow them in. The Gunnison region is a good example. The South Park road had extended its line from Nathrop over Alpine Pass; the Denver and Rio Grande pushed a branch from Salida over Marshall Pass. Starting about the same time, the Rio Grande won the race when its trains arrived in Gunnison in late summer, 1881. It was this "branch" to Gunnison, soon extended to Grand Junction, that became the road's "mainline" for many years. North from Leadville, the Rio Grande built to Robinson and by March, 1882, to Red Cliff. The Colorado Midland and the Rio Grande both struck out for the ores of Aspen and again the Rio Grande won the contest, reaching that silver camp in 1887. The Midland arrived in Aspen the next year.

The railroads followed the passes and gorges that nature had carved through the mountain ranges, leading often to long and round-about routes. The airline distance from Denver to Leadville, for example, is 75 miles; the shortest railroad route covered 151 miles.

Aspen and Leadville are 30 miles apart by air; at one time it took 131 miles of railroad track to connect them. Yet twisting and tortuous though the transportation network might appear on the maps, without it the extension of Colorado's mining frontier would have been greatly delayed. Together, miners and railroaders were rapidly invading some of the last unoccupied wilderness in the nation.

16

Open Range Days

While men scrambled over the mountain slopes of central Colorado, seeking another Leadville, radical changes were also taking place on the plains east of the Continental Divide. The removal of the Cheyenne and Arapahoe Indians to reservations outside Colorado had created a huge expanse of unoccupied, unclaimed grassland. Within a short time a different kind of economic enterprise developed there, as this "open range" became dotted with cow herds, eating free and growing fat on the public domain.

Ever since the Spanish had penetrated the eastern Colorado prairies, a few cattle had lived on the plains, but those semi-wild beasts were too limited in number to be of great importance. It was not until the gold mines had been opened, and Anglo-Americans swarmed into the Colorado hills, that cattle raising on the region's open plains became a major enterprise. Then, for some three decades, it flourished, leaving when it died a legend unsurpassed—a major episode in the national folklore—and, its direct descendant, the modern ranch cattle industry of contemporary Colorado.

Tradition has long related that the origins of the range cattle industry are to be found in the tales of prospectors who brought oxen to the gold fields in 1859, and freighters who carried supplies westward from the Missouri River towns. The argonauts and wagonmen, so the story goes, sometimes turned their beasts loose on the plains after their arrival in Colorado. Instead of meeting early deaths, the oxen flourished on the native grasses, even during winter weather, thus educating men in the values of the prairie as cattle country. Why men who had seen buffalo survive on those same grasses should have been surprised to discover that domesticated cattle could live on them is something of a mystery. But, at any rate, some freighters and some prospectors came to realize that the cattle industry might offer more certain and greater economic returns than transportation or mining, and they inaugurated the cattle industry in the territory.

A situation that encouraged such decisions resulted partly from the effects of the Civil War. After the Union Army won control of the Mississippi River, most of the Confederate markets for cattle could not be reached by Texas ranchmen. It was unpatriotic to sell anything to Northerners, and the number of cattle in Texas multiplied in rapid fashion. As the supply increased, the price of beef in Texas dropped to absurd levels. Cattle sold so cheaply there that ranchmen could not afford to brand their stock. There were no buyers, even at prices as low as a dollar or two a head. At the same time, beef cattle were selling in the North at war-inflated prices of more than thirty dollars a head. As the Civil War drew to a close, an unusual opportunity appeared. If the Texas cattle could be herded or trailed northward to the railroads that were being constructed across the prairies, they could be shipped eastward by rail to profitable northern markets.

The great grasslands that stretched from the line of agricultural settlements in Kansas and Nebraska, on the east, to the foothills of the Rocky Mountains, on the west, thus became the scene of trail herds driven north to railroad terminals. At the railheads, the cattle were separated, with parts of the herds sent eastward by railroad to slaughter houses, and the remainder of the herds driven westward to ranges for fattening. In addition, other cattle were driven directly into Colorado from Texas. The territory's grasslands offered ideal conditions for fattening the beasts. Much of the natural prairie grass was either buffalo or grama grass—low-growing plants that could survive trampling, close grazing, and drought, and still proved nutritious fodder in cold weather when other grasses had lost their food value because of freezing.

Trailing cattle into Colorado began in 1859, when John C. Dawson brought the first reported herd from Texas to the Territory of Jefferson. But it was not until 1864-65 that stock were driven north in large herds. Then within a short time, several trails were developed leading into Colorado and the bonanza days of the open range were born. By 1870, when the first railroads reached Denver, trailing into Colorado and fattening cattle there became even more profitable than before, since transportation directly from the territory to eastern markets was more easily arranged.

A good cow trail provided certain necessary elements and avoided the most undesirable features. Water was essential, and rivers and ponds spaced not more than five or six miles apart made an otherwise satisfactory trail quite superior. At most, water holes and camp sites were needed at least fifteen miles from each other, for herds could not be moved much farther than that in one day. Yet rivers and water courses also had to be crossed on the drive north, with the least amount of hazard to the herd, so good fords were necessary. Farmers and their fences were avoided; rough, broken country and heavy timber were shunned whenever possible. The trails were constantly shifted to avoid Indian reservations, quarantine legislation, and homesteaders. Today it is difficult to trace the exact location of many of the once prominent cow roads. Some trails that originally were pushed through Kansas, by the middle of the 1880s led into eastern Colorado. The trails were known by name—Chisholm, Western, Lone Star. The two best known roads entering Colorado were the Dawson Trail, which came into the Arkansas Valley, and the Goodnight Trail, farther west, from New Mexico.

It would be difficult to decide whether gold prospecting or cattle trailing involved more economic risk. So many variables were involved in the cattle enterprise, each contributing to the eventual success or failure of a drive, that to list even a few of them indicates the tone of uncertainty that characterized the ventures. Branding expenses, herd size, number and training of men and horses, trail conditions, water courses, storms encountered, health or disease of cattle, the attitude of Indians, the frequency of stampedes—these and many other elements played a role in the final determination of profit or loss.

The cost of trailing from Texas to the high plains was estimated at about one dollar a head. The wages of the cowboys and the maintenance of equipment could both be covered by that sum. The feed along the trail was free—a gigantic government subsidy. Since cattle were worth more in Colorado than in Texas (in 1880, an average value of $14.50 a head compared with $9.30 a head) there was a workable margin of potential profit, even after trail costs had been calculated and paid.

The cattlemen prepared their herds for the drive by marking a "road brand"—a single letter or simple mark—on each beast. After sale, the new owners would brand the cattle again, with their own symbols. At first branding was a hit-or-miss affair, but in 1867, after the Colorado Stockgrowers Association was created, that organization's secretary recorded members' brands. Five years later, in 1872, a more formal system was effected when the territorial legislature enacted a "brand law," assigning each county a letter to be placed by the side of the owners' personal brands. The county clerks were charged with the responsibility of eliminating duplicate brands within their counties. After 1885 an even more centralized system was used, as all brands were then registered with the secretary of state. Lists or books of brands were printed, and proved useful in identifying cattle and apprehending rustlers.

The trail herds generally numbered between two and three thousand head of cattle. A larger herd was more likely to stampede; overhead expenses ran too high for smaller units. Perhaps the count on the herds crossing the Arkansas River at Trail City in southeastern Colorado from June 9 to July 20, 1886, was typical. Fifty-seven herds made the crossing between those dates; the largest numbered 3,300 head; the smallest contained 70 head of cattle. Yet despite the difficulty of handling large trail herds, cattlemen sometimes drove as many as five to seven thousand head at one time.

The ratio of men to cattle on the long drive differed from outfit to outfit. Sometimes two cowboys were hired for every three hundred head of cattle; others worked at a ratio of twelve or thirteen men to 3,000 beasts. Similarly there were differences in the number of horses provided for the drive. At least two per cowboy were needed, but the number ranged upward of six or seven per man. Most of the cattlemen started their herds north from Texas early in March. With good luck, this would bring the drive to an end in Colorado in late June or early July—time enough to allow the cattle to become acclimated to the region before winter.

During its early years the range cattle enterprise offered a relatively free and open economic opportunity to anyone. The cattle themselves were the only major investment. Everything else—water, feed, cowboys' wages—was either free or very inexpensive. Those men with ability, energy, and initiative who "got in on the ground floor" were able to build large herds and create from them magnificent fortunes. In relatively short time, these "Cattle Kings" became a dominant aspect of the open range. Greatest of them in Colorado was John Wesley Iliff. He had come to the Pike's Peak gold camps in 1859; two years later he began to invest in cattle. When the Union Pacific railroad reached the high plains north of Colorado, Iliff wrangled the contract to supply beef to the construction crews. By 1887 he owned some 15,000 acres of range, much of it fronting the water courses of the South Platte River, stretching from Greeley to Julesburg in the northeastern corner of the state.

There were others. John Wesley Prowers, a man who had worked for the Bents as a freighter on the Santa Fe Trail, in 1862 purchased cattle in Kansas to start his herd. He concentrated on short-horned Herefords, rather than Texas cattle. By 1881 he owned forty miles of river frontage on the Arkansas, giving him control of some 400,000 acres of range land, enough to graze herds of 10,000 cattle. James C. Jones was another Arkansas Valley "Beef Baron." Coming to Colorado in 1879, later than either Iliff or Prowers, Jones pre-empted range lands south of the Arkansas and gained control of enough land to graze some 15,000 head of cattle, all branded with the "JJ" brand.

During the years from 1870 to 1880 the individual Cattle Kings flourished, but their power was never absolute. There always were some restrictive aspects to the generally free and unregulated cattle enterprise. For example, the roundup developed into a systematized, collective activity. It became a necessary adjunct of range life because each cattleman's herds roamed freely with others. Twice a year the stockmen in a wide area herded the cattle to one location. In the spring new calves were branded with the owners' marks. The fall roundup was used to count the stock and separate the beasts destined for the slaughter houses.

In 1871 the Colorado stockmen reorganized their earlier association into a more efficient lobbying group. Partly as a result of its requests, the territorial legislature enacted a roundup law the next year, formalizing the procedures of the roundup. The commissioners of each county in the territory were authorized to set a time for both fall and spring roundups, and to appoint agents to take care of the mavericks—the motherless calves. (The mavericks were either distributed proportionately among the stockmen or sold.) The roundups were big affairs. In the spring of 1877 some 500 men, with 3,500 horses and 50 chuckwagons, started west from Holly in the Arkansas Valley Roundup. In time the county units proved too small for effective roundups and in 1879 the legislature divided the state into larger units called roundup districts. For each of the sixteen districts created, the governor designated inspectors to oversee the roundup events.

By the time the roundup district law was enacted, the cattle business was rapidly changing character, for investors at home and abroad had begun to see in western cattle—raising an attractive investment field. English and Scottish investors were particularly active in the creation of corporate ranching, forming investment companies and anticipating rapid, large returns on their capital. The most spectacular of these ventures, in many ways, was the Prairie Cattle Company, organized in 1881. It put together an expansive cattle empire, with a northern unit in Colorado, a central unit extending through New Mexico and Oklahoma, and a southern unit in Texas. In Colorado it purchased the "JJ" brand stock of James Jones, added other holdings to that, and soon gained control of a fifty-mile-wide strip from the Arkansas River to the southern boundary of the state. The earliest years were exceptionally prosperous for the company. At the first annual meeting of stockholders, it was announced that the returns equalled twenty-six per cent of the paid-up capital.

Ironically, almost simultaneously with the inception of corporate ranching, the years of trouble began. Many elements contributed to the collapse of the open range cattle empire. The "nesters" were a major cause of irritation and trouble to the stockmen. Under the agricultural homestead legislation of 1862, farmers were allowed to cut the public domain into small parcels and set up fences around their acres. Immediately the formula for countless Western stories and movies was born. The fencing actually was largely delayed until the perfection of the barbed-wire machine (1874) which allowed barbed-wire to be sold at a cost the homesteader could afford. But after the machine-produced wire was available, a farmer could fence a mile for about $100, and he began to enclose his homestead.

The cattlemen turned to fencing too, but with a difference. They had no particular claim to much of the public domain they used for grazing. At first they were not hindered in closing off the government acres, but in 1885 Congress enacted legislation forbidding fences on the public lands.

What the stockmen had hoped for these years was help, not hindrance from the federal government. At an earlier time the cattlemen had talked about the desirability of the government's withdrawing major parts of the arid plains from homesteading, restricting its use to livestock only. In the year of Colorado's statehood, the Interior Department had considered a suggestion that, from the 100th meridian to the Sierra Mountains, the homesteading laws be forgotten and the area reserved for ranchers. A response to the idea was included in President Rutherford Hayes' message to Congress the next year: "These lands are practically unsalable under

existing laws and the suggestion is worthy of consideration that a
system of leasehold tenure would make them a source of profit to
the United States, while at the same time legalizing the business of
cattle raising which at present is carried on upon them."[1]

The Colorado Stockgrowers Association also favored the idea. In
1878 that group petitioned Congress to set aside the plains region
which, it said, was unsuited for anything but "pastoral purposes"
because of its lack of rainfall and climate. Emphasizing distinctions
between "agricultural" and "pastoral" use of land, the stockmen
thought that 3,000-acre homesteads for ranching would be more
practicable than the smaller 160-acre farms then provided for agriculture. But the changes that eventually were made in the federal land
laws came long after the open range was gone.

Farming settlements continued to disrupt range activities, and in
1884, in St. Louis, cattlemen in convention there proposed the
establishment of a permanent cow trail, from the Red River of the
South to the Canadian border. This roadway would be set aside from
public lands, with private entries bought out in the places where they
interfered. The trail, from five to fifty miles wide, would be
completely fenced, with streams bridged and junctions with branch
trails and railroads provided. Although Congress never enacted the
necessary legislation, the concept alone demonstrates the changes that
had come to the cattle industry.

Cattlemen would continue to consider farmers as particularly
responsible for their problems, but the homesteaders' fences were not
the only element hastening the end of the open range. In the river
valleys, where irrigation was beginning to flourish, water ditches
created dangers and obstacles for driving cattle. And quarantine laws,
which the states began to erect at their boundaries, also checked the
movement of cattle across the range. Colorado enacted such a law in
the mid-eighties, forbidding the driving of cattle across the state lines
unless the herd had been held for ninety days or inspected and
certified as disease-free by a veterinarian.

Overstocking of the range also played a role in the collapse of the
cow bonanza. With the huge investment corporations competing for
profits, it was natural for each to try to make returns rapidly. As a
result, many more cattle than could possibly be supported on the
range were brought in and the predictable consequences were reaped,
especially in the years of poor weather, such as the winters of the
great blizzards of the late 1880s.

During the years of the open range's decline, the Colorado

cattlemen, particularly through their Stockgrowers Association, looked to the state legislature for help. This might take the form of
creating a favored position in law for the cattle interests, or to
regulate some phase of the range operations. Legislation of the first
sort, for example, fixed upon the railroads, rather than upon the
cattlemen, the responsibility for animals killed by trains. In 1886 a
total of 2,242 head of cattle were reported killed by railroads in
Colorado and compensation was sought. No matter how scrawny and
scrubby the critter, the owners always seemed to have lost prime
beef. The railroads came to understand that it was probably less
expensive to fence their rights-of-way than to compensate cattlemen
for dead beasts.

On the other hand, the cattlemen were also beginning to realize
that their own greed had contributed to their difficulties. Overstocking of the range, particularly with inferior cattle, had not been
in their best interests. So they also requested and received legislative
aid in regulating the number and quality of bulls on the open range,
and in quarantining to halt diseases among their herds.

In fighting one enemy, the cattlemen did not wait for legislative
aid; they usually managed to win with their own devices. That enemy
was the sheepman. In length of time, the sheep industry of Colorado
quite clearly held priority over the cattle industry. The early settlers
on the Mexican land grants in the southern part of the state had
grazed sheep on the lands around their villages before the gold rush.
These had been relatively poor-grade sheep, but after the coming of
the argonauts, both mutton and wool were in great demand in the
new Colorado communities and the sheep industry spread through
the San Luis and Arkansas valleys. In 1868 the Pueblo *Colorado
Chieftain* reported 195,000 sheep in Conejos and Costilla counties,
" ... Las Animas county has about 87,500 and Huerfano and Pueblo
Counties about 35,000, totalling 317,500 sheep for southern
Colorado."[2] Although these statistics were probably exaggerated,
they indicate that sheep herding was well established in southern
Colorado during the first decade of territorial government.

It was not until 1869 that fine-wooled Merinos were introduced
into Colorado, and the beginnings of improved breeding were made.
This marked the origins of the sheep industry in Weld County, soon
followed by a lesser industry in South Park. By 1886 the number of
sheep in the state was estimated at 2,000,000 head. In those early
years, in northern Colorado, the sheep were driven into grazing areas
by methods not unlike those of the long drives of cattle from Texas.

The story of the conflicts between sheepmen and cattlemen forms one of the less pleasant phases of the history of the open range. The cattlemen often resorted to brutality in attempts to force the sheepmen from the range, for the cattlemen believed that destruction of the grasses resulted from grazing sheep. Not only did the sheep crop the grass closely; there was an ancient belief among cattlemen that cows would not drink at water holes used by sheep and that cows would not graze where sheep had crossed because of offensive odors left by the oil glands in the hooves of the sheep. As the poet put it:

A sheep just oozes out a stink
That drives a cowman plumb to drink!
Its hoofs leave flavors on the grass
That even make the old cows pass . . .
Sheep ranges, cattle sure won't graze,
But—cowboys hate sheep anyways! [3]

That "hate" that existed "anyways" sometimes rested on an emotional antagonism between sheepmen and cattlemen, resting at least in part on ethnic differences between the two groups. Sheepmen sometimes were Spanish-speaking people; cattlemen were "Anglos." Some cattlemen looked on sheep tending as a degrading, unprogressive occupation.

The sheepmen, in law, might have had as much "right" to use the public domain for grazing as the cattlemen, but the test of control often was based on the ability to wrest or maintain possession of the range. An organization known as the Cattlegrowers Protective Association, with members in many Western Slope communities in Colorado, dedicated itself to keeping the cattle ranges free from sheep. The association's common name was the "Night Riders," which indicates its strategy in the contests. Often the cattlemen drew a dividing line, beyond which they warned sheepmen not to move their flocks. In the late 1880s and 1890s, Western Slope Colorado, especially the present northern counties of Routt, Moffat, Rio Blanco, and Garfield, was a scene of almost continuous warfare over the rangelands as cattlemen and sheepmen struggled to maintain or improve their control.

Nor did the fight end with the collapse of the open range. It continued into the era of cattle ranching—as opposed to cattle ranging—and on into the twentieth century with its leased government lands and reserved grazing areas.

17

Beyond the Continental Divide

The Continental Divide—separating the waters falling eastward and southward into the Gulf of Mexico from the waters falling westward to the Pacific Ocean—also separates Colorado into two major geographic areas. That portion of the state west of the Divide, irregular in shape and strangely varied in topography, is termed the Western Slope. Much of this part of Colorado was not opened for settlement until after 1880; not until after the mineral discoveries in the San Juan Mountains in the southwestern corner of the state were made, the Ute Indians removed from previously arranged reservations, and railroads built for transportation to the valleys and plateaus of this western region did settlers come in large numbers to reduce the last Colorado frontier.

The mineral discoveries and the Indian removals are so interwoven in their development that they are like two chapters of a single story. In 1863, while Governor John Evans was experiencing little but frustration in his attempts to arrange peace with Eastern Slope tribes, he managed a major success with the Ute Indians. At Conejos, in the San Luis Valley, the Utes agreed to cede that valley to the whites, promising to move to a reserved area on the Western Slope.

Within five years, however, the white settlers were ready for more land. Agents then escorted a delegation of Ute leaders to Washington to see the Great White Father and to be duly impressed (it was hoped) by the extent and wealth of the white man's country. During these pleasantries, the Utes were encouraged to negotiate a new treaty. That document, signed in 1868, provided that the Indians would move onto a newly designated reservation, west of the 107th meridian (a little west of the present site of Gunnison), comprising about one-third of the total area of Colorado. The federal authorities agreed to establish two agencies on this reservation. One post would be located at the White River, for the use of the northern Ute bands. The other, in the south, would serve the Southern and Uncompahgre Utes. In return for the cession of lands involved, the agencies would disburse to the Utes annual gifts of clothing, food, and supplies.

The new plans to establish reservations had hardly been completed when a mining rush forced alterations. The San Juans were (and still are) one of Colorado's rich and varied mineral areas, and it was only a matter of time before the prospector came to stay. Earlier, in 1860 and 1861, interest in the area had been aroused primarily because Charles Baker claimed to have found valuable gold placers. A small rush developed, but the golden rewards proved small and the isolation and dangers great. Despite this failure, interest did not die and in the early 1870s prospectors returned to find gold and silver mines. This time settlers came to stay.

As the whites moved in, treaties were violated, tension increased, and demands mounted to modify previous agreements. A classic example of white-Indian confrontation unfolded and within a decade the Utes would be gone, not only from the mountains but from much of the Western Slope. Although they were trespassing on Ute land, the miners would not be stopped and the government pressured the Indians into ceding a large quadrangular area which included the entire mining region. Known as the Brunot Treaty, this 1873 agreement temporarily calmed matters but provided no permanent solution.

The San Juans held great promise but grew slowly in the 1870s, partly because of their isolation and lack of rail transportation, and also because Leadville attracted more attention and capital. But by the end of the decade, mining camps were spread throughout the mountains. Some, like Silverton, Ouray, and Lake City, were supply points for a district; others, like Mineral Point, Capitol City, and Sherman, served only the nearby mines.

Unlike smaller mining areas, the San Juans gave birth to numerous rushes in such districts as Red Mountain, Rico, Telluride, and La Plata Canyon. Here in microcosm was the mining history of Colorado: discoveries were made, people flocked in, and camps rushed through a period of prosperity and then declined. Until well past the turn of the century, mining flourished, gold coming to replace silver as the foremost metal, as the miners dug deep into the mineral treasure house of the San Juans.

Ouray, Colorado, one of Colorado's prime mining camps. (Denver Public Library Western Collection)

Isolated as they were, the camps and districts offered a bountiful opportunity for anyone adventurous enough to tie them together with a road system. Del Norte and Saguache were early supply points, and out of the latter came Otto Mears, who met the challenge by building both toll roads and railroads and emerged as the "king" of southwestern Colorado road builders. One of the early Mears roads crossed Poncha Pass; another connected Saguache and Lake City; a third was built between Ouray and Silverton. These toll roads, traversing 300 miles total at their zenith, brought the first freighting by wagon into many of the new mining camps as well as considerable income to their builder. Later Mears would build short railroad lines out of Silverton to tap nearby mining areas and the longer Rio Grande Southern from Durango to Rico, Ophir, and Telluride, before tying into the Denver and Rio Grande system at Ridgway.

Besides opening this new world of mining to the white man, the Brunot Treaty had also designated Ouray as spokesman for the entire Ute nation. Federal agents disliked the uncertainties inherent in a situation where no one chief represented the entire Ute tribe and by government fiat ended this confusion. Ouray, who was part Apache, became the most famous Indian in Colorado history and until his death worked hard to maintain peace between his people and the onrushing intruders.

Ouray had been a prominent Ute leader since 1863, but not sole chief; he spoke Spanish and English, which helped him in dealing with the government. Recipient of a thousand-dollar-a-year salary plus a house, Ouray, in the eyes of the government, spoke for his people. Unfortunately, no chief could do that for all tribes and, especially among the northern bands, other leaders were more persuasive than Ouray.

Trouble was sure to come as the whites crowded into the San Juans. It culminated in the Meeker Massacre. However, even before this the *Ouray Times*, December 22, 1877, was asking why "non-producing, semi-barbarous" people occupied land which "intelligent and industrious citizens" could use. Feelings such as these were echoed by many on the Western Slope and soon the "Utes Must Go" slogan threatened to force the issue over who would control the agricultural lands north of Ouray. It was interesting that the mining camp named after the chief bore no ill-feeling against him personally, just his tribe.

The events leading to the Ute removal began not in the mining areas but to the north at the White River Agency, where Nathan Meeker, of Union Colony fame, had been appointed agent in 1878. A sincere, dedicated man, who was also naive and somewhat imprac-tical, Meeker took zealously to his task of turning the wandering Utes to a settled life. His utopian fancies, which had inspired him to organize the colony, were not as successful with the Indians.

With great energy, but little patience, Meeker moved to the task before him. Step by step his plans for civilizing the Utes moved him closer to ultimate and tragic defeat. To end the nomadic habits of the Utes, Meeker planned an agricultural society; to educate the young in white man's ways, the agency provided a school. All around them, the Utes began to see hated symbols of oppression: fences, classrooms, farm implements, including a "monster" threshing machine. The Indians protested; the agent planned new methods of "reform." Something of the proverbial "last straw" was provided when Meeker ordered the plows to work on the Indians' race-track, the scene of wild pony contests, accompanied by even wilder betting.

During the summer months of 1879 many northern Utes left the reservation, despite Agent Meeker's express orders against such wandering. Some of these Utes committed minor depredations and, more seriously, burned houses and fired forests. Others, free from

"Father Meeker's" control, spent their time more constructively. Captain Jack and others journeyed to Denver to complain to Governor Pitkin about the agent and his policies.

Meeker's orders were disobeyed. Then Johnson, one of the Ute leaders, physically attacked the agent. Fortunately, other employees protected Meeker, but by then a general breakdown in all of the fine, utopian planning was obvious. Meeker decided that army troops were necessary for the "civilizing" process, and in response to his requests for aid the army sent a contingent of cavalry from Fort Garland to round up wandering Utes and bring them back to the reservation. And on September 21, 1879, from Fort Steele in Wyoming, Major Thomas T. Thornburgh led another force of soldiers toward White River to protect the agency itself.

After five days of marching, when Thornburgh's unit had reached the Yampa River, a parley took place with Captain Jack and other tribesmen. The Indians alternated their remarks between denunciations of Agent Meeker and questions about why the soldiers were coming to the agency.

Meanwhile, Meeker had kept Thornburgh informed about affairs at White River; through this correspondence it became quite clear that it would be folly to try to move the entire contingent of soldiers onto the reservation. The Indians were extremely alarmed and the situation was too volatile to risk a full-scale threat against them. So Thornburgh agreed to halt most of his force some distance from the agency and to proceed himself with an escort of only five men.

These plans, unfortunately, were never realized. When the soldiers reached Milk Creek, near the reservation boundary, they were ambushed by the Utes. Major Thornburgh and thirteen of his men were killed in the skirmish. The rest of the force was pinned down and could not move. Finally the guide of the expedition, Joe Rankin, slipped away to the north. From Rawlins, in Wyoming, he summoned the aid of Colonel Wesley Merritt. The army also ordered the Fort Garland cavalry, already on the Western Slope, to hurry to the siege. They arrived first, but were too exhausted to accomplish much. Merritt and his men appeared three days later, and immediately began the battle to rescue the troops.

As soon as the white soldiers began the battle, the Utes raised the surrender flag. Ouray had managed to accomplish the difficult task of convincing the Utes that further fighting was futile.

Colonel Merritt and his men then moved on to the agency where they found a pathetic scene. Meeker and eleven other men had been killed, some of their bodies stripped of clothing and mutilated. Meeker's wife, his daughter Josephine, Mrs. Shadrack Price and her two children, had all been carried away by the Utes. Under the circumstances, no pursuit or revenge was possible until the captives had been located and retaken. The former Indian agent to the Uncompahgre Utes, General Charles Adams, working with Chief Ouray, finally secured the release of the hostages. The women at first stated that they had not been mistreated during their captivity; later they would tell of Ute outrages upon them. If such stories were manufactured for propaganda purposes, they were not necessary. Colorado citizens were already shouting loudly for punitive expeditions and raising the cry, "Utes Must Go!"

During the uprising, uneasy tension had descended over much of western Colorado. Rumors that the Southern Utes intended to join their northern brethren brought the state militia into the field; federal troops were sent from Texas to Fort Garland and from New Mexico to Fort Lewis. But the fighting ended before it spread. Carl Schurz, the Secretary of the Interior, now readied an official investigation of the affair. The commissioners he appointed for the task were hard put to gather testimony from witnesses. Only women had seen the massacre and were alive to tell about it, yet Ouray stood his ground in insisting that the Utes would not accept as valid the word of females testifying against males. No Utes would testify at all. Ouray also demanded that any trials take place in Washington, D. C., claiming that a fair and impartial determination of charges would be impossible to reach in Colorado. The leader known as Douglas was the only Ute ever brought to justice. He served a short sentence at Leavenworth.

For the Coloradans, the Utes had provided the necessary stimulus for a final settlement of the Western Slope. Some of the residents, Senator Henry Teller among them, demanded punishment of the offenders. But Colorado's other senator, Nathaniel Hill, thought this a "narrow and selfish view." Probably representing the majority opinion in the Centennial State, Hill believed that punishment was less important than removing the Utes so that their lands could be opened for settlement. Echoing the sentiment, the Denver *Times* put it bluntly: "Either they [the Utes] or we must go, and *we* are not going. Humanitarianism is an idea. Western Empire is an inexorable fact. He who gets in the way of it will be crushed."[1]

One of the arguments frequently used by Coloradans in their campaign to hurry the Ute removal was the high cost of maintaining the Indians on their reservation, although they never explained how the cost would be reduced by removing them to Utah: "The government might, with almost, if not equal propriety, plant a colony of Communists upon the public domain, maintaining them in idleness at public expense, as to leave the Colorado Utes in possession of their present heritage and present privileges; . . . even now . . . the Utes could be boarded at the first-class hotel in Chicago or New York, cheaper than at the present cost of their subsistence."[2]

Early in 1880, a delegation of Utes, headed by Chief Ouray, was escorted eastward to the national capital. There, in March, one final treaty was put together. The Southern Utes were now to be restricted to a reservation on the La Plata River bridging southern Colorado and northern New Mexico. The Uncompahgre Utes were to be given lands near the junction of the Gunnison and Colorado rivers—or, if land was not available there, they would be sent to the Territory of Utah. The White River Utes, too, were to be moved across the state line, to the Uintah Reservation. In return for these removals, $60,000 in back annuities would be paid, along with $50,000 in new annuities after the actual removals. But, before the treaty became binding, three-fourths of the adult males of the tribe had to sign, or mark, the document.

There was some difficulty in obtaining the necessary number of signatures, largely because the Uncompahgre Utes feared that they would be sent to Utah. But the rolls were finally completed, and the legal formalities concluded.

In Washington, critics argued that the Coloradans showed indecent haste in the proceedings. Congressman Belford answered them by asserting that in travelling to the capital from Colorado he had "crossed five states made up wholly of lands stolen from the Indians. 'And now gentlemen stand here in the name of God and humanity,' and say, while our fathers robbed and plundered the Indians, we want you to belong to the goody-goody class of people in the West."[3]

The good Chief Ouray died before the tribes had been moved to their new homes. His demise on August 20, 1880, was considered a great loss by the whites, for he had earned their respect and admiration. Even Ouray, however, probably would not have been able to help the Uncompahgre Utes in their desperate struggle to retain lands within Colorado. The whites were determined to make the removal complete, and the Uncompahgres were destined to move to the Uintah reservation. General R. S. Mackenzie, with six companies of cavalry and nine companies of infantry from Fort Garland, moved onto the Western Slope, establishing later-named Fort Crawford in the valley of the Uncompahgre River. The troops were there to help the Indian agents, if necessary, complete the removal.

On September 7, 1881, the last of the Utes passed the junction of the Colorado and Gunnison rivers. "If one had stood on Pinon Mesa, what a march of a retreating civilization he could have seen! Here was the last defeat of the red man. Here the frontiers of the white man met, crushing the Utes in its mighty embrace."4

Congress declared the Ute lands public and open for filing in June, 1882, but actually many settlers had moved in and had platted towns before the official entry day. One of the more obvious sites for planting a white settlement was the junction of the Gunnison and Colorado rivers. The protected valley, with water for irrigation constituted one of the most desirable locations on the entire Western Slope. The advantages of the place had been sized-up by a group of men from the town of Gunnison. Headed by ex-Governor George A. Crawford of Kansas, they laid out a town on the site which they first named "Ute." They changed the name to "West Denver," and, finally, when they incorporated their venture, to "Grand Junction."

Like all such new towns, it wasn't much at the beginning: a store, a saloon, a ditch company. But in 1882 the Denver and Rio Grande narrow-gauge line, from Gunnison through Sapinero and Montrose, reached the town (the railroad had secured half of the shares of stock of the town company) and the following year Mesa County was carved out of Gunnison County, with Grand Junction as the seat of the new jurisdiction. The town, with its fertile valley lands for irrigation, soon attracted enterprises sufficient to insure it the status of the urban center of the Western Slope. When the Denver and Rio Grande put the place on its standard-gauge line in 1887, the future was assured. Among other early features of the town was the Teller Institute and Indian School, built in 1886 with federal funds on lands donated by Grand Junction citizens. This institution conducted regular scholastic classes and instruction in practical trades to Ute, and later, other Indian children.

After building to Grand Junction, the Rio Grande Railroad extended its line west to the Utah border where, in 1883, it connected with the Rio Grande Western Railroad. This enterprise also had been constructed by the Rio Grande, and was soon leased to its parent; it ran westward into Salt Lake City and there, by connection with the Western Pacific Railroad, the Rio Grande reached an outlet to California. Colorado had finally achieved a circuitous but operable railroad to the west coast.

George Crawford, the "father of Grand Junction," was also the guiding spirit in the organization of the Uncompahgre Town Company. Begun in September, 1881, this company promoted the founding of a settlement which, after several name changes, became the place called Delta, the seat of the county of the same name. Montrose, on the Rio Grande narrow-gauge, was laid out in January, 1882, and like Grand Junction and Delta it housed a courthouse—for Montrose County. All three of these settlements were established originally on the basis of irrigated fields in the river bottoms, with cattle herds grazing away from the streams. Soon fruit trees had been planted, and the protected valleys and irrigation waters demonstrated the excellence of the area for orchards.

In the valley of the Colorado River, eastward from Grand Junction, was the site called Defiance. Here, in August, 1882, the later-named Glenwood Springs was located. The hot mineral waters gave the site a quality lacking in most of the other Western Slope town-sites. In 1887 the Rio Grande narrow-gauge from Leadville, on its way to Aspen, reached the town. Four years later, the standard-gauge tracks, built by the Rio Grande and Colorado Midland, connected Glenwood Springs with Grand Junction, making obsolete the toll road that had operated in the river valley between the two towns. That same year an English syndicate built an open-air swimming pool, bath houses, and a large hotel at Glenwood, antici-pating its growth as a scenic spa in the Rockies.

Above the Colorado River, the huge northwestern wilderness of the state remained largely untouched, except for ranchers with their sheep and cattle. Here and there in the valleys, towns with small populations had been platted for a variety of reasons. The region around Hahn's Peak had been propsected in 1862; again in the mid-1870s miners had engaged in extensive, but only partly rewarding, work on the placers. Hot Sulphur Springs, a pet project of *Rocky Mountain News* editor William Byers, who had homestead claims there, was named the county seat of Grand County in 1874. Farther west, Steamboat Springs dated from 1875, when the James Crawford family settled. These, and other northwestern centers like Craig and Yampa, would await the coming of the Moffat railroad, after the turn of the century, for their real development.

In the far southwestern corner of the state, Durango came into existence in 1880, thanks to the Rio Grande Railroad, which was

Opening mines in the rugged San Juans, 1875. (U.S. Geological Survey)

Frontier law: Durango's first public hanging, June 23, 1882. (Center of Southwest Studies, Fort Lewis College)

reaching out to tap the San Juan mines. Older Animas City, which had spurned the railroad's offer to build to it, found itself quickly surpassed. In 1882 the narrow gauge tracks pushed up the Animas canyon, reaching Silverton and its mines, while Durango became the area's leading supply and smelter city. Located near coal and agricultural lands, Durango quickly grew and even had its own small nearby mining rushes. A varied economy and facilities for a transportation center gave Durango a much brighter future than its mining neighbors. The Rio Grande, meanwhile, came to make the San Juan country its own and, as long as the mines held out, the venture proved to be a very profitable one.

18

Ditchdiggers and Sodbusters

In 1862, the year after Colorado Territory was created, Congress enacted the Homestead Act, culminating a struggle for ever more liberal land policies that had its origins as far in the past as the creation of the national domain itself. The new legislation provided that any United States citizen, or person with intention of becoming a citizen, who was the head of a family and over twenty-one years of age, could become possessed of 160 acres of the surveyed public domain after five years of continuous residence on his tract and the payment of a small ($26 to $34) registration fee. If the homesteader desired, the title could actually pass into his hands after six months' residence and the payment of the minimum price of $1.25 an acre.

The Homestead Act of 1862 assumed that the average family farm should comprise 160 acres. Such calculations were justified by the experience of Americans in the humid regions where older land policies had been developed. A farm of 160 acres was certainly of adequate size in the well-watered valleys of the midwestern rivers. But when the pioneers crossed the fatal demarcation line of the 100th meridian, farmers practicing traditional techniques of agriculture were doomed. Superficially the prairies might not appear different from the older regions; settlement spread over the edges of the old into the new without fanfare or publicity. But once the 100th meridian was crossed, rainfall became a major concern. The average ten to eighteen inches a year fell far short of the minimum requirements for traditional farming, and the "averages" did not reflect the seasonal variation or extremely dry years when the usual western "unusual" weather brought even less moisture. Year in and year out, agriculture such as the American farmers were accustomed to could not thrive on the high plains.

To meet the challenge of these radically different climatic conditions, the homesteaders, where possible, made radical adjustments. Some conditions seemed to be beyond control—the grasshopper invasions of the 1860s, for example. But many changes were attempted. These included the dramatic shift to irrigated farming in river valleys, the adoption of moisture-conserving techniques on the high plains, and, in both, the introduction of and experimentation with new crops. Where irrigation was possible, intensive agriculture became expedient and the standard 160 acres allowed by the federal land laws might prove to be too much land for an individual farmer, faced with the additional expenditures for irrigation equipment. Where irrigation was not possible, grazing or, later, dry farming became standard alternatives to traditional methods of agriculture. In such circumstances the old unit was much too small.

Some adjustments were attempted in the laws themselves. The Timber Culture Act of 1873, repealed in 1891, justified an increase in the size of entries by requiring tree planting on the land. Any person who kept forty acres of timber in good condition could acquire title to 160 additional acres. The Desert Land Act, four years later, allowed a homesteader the right to acquire title to a full section (640 acres) of land for a low fee, if he put the land under irrigation within three years. Neither of these adjustments gave much real relief to settlers. Before more radical departures were attempted, after the turn of the century, many homesteaders had been forced to try to work within the framework established by the existing, basic land laws.

The first Colorado farmers (excepting here the Pueblo Indians) never experienced the need to alter their techniques of cultivation. The earliest irrigators were the Spanish-Americans from New Mexico who, by moving northward into the San Luis Valley, merely exchanged farms in one arid location for farms in another equally arid place. Shortly after their arrival in the northern valley of the Rio Grande, they began to dig their ditches and to transplant the irrigation institutions they had known in New Mexico.

On April 10, 1852, the settlers on the Culebra River commenced the San Luis People's Ditch, the oldest irrigation canal in Colorado in continuous use. If the progress of ditchdigging in the valley was not spectacular, it was at least constant. Four ditches on the Conejos River date back to 1855; eleven had their beginning in 1856. In comparison with later developments in irrigation, these early systems were miniature in size. The ditches were short and narrow, providing water for only small fields of crops. The system was democratically administered, with one user each year selected to supervise the distribution of water and the maintenance of the ditch.

If language differences and geographic separation had not barred the way, the Anglo-American who began the irrigation of lands in the South Platte Valley could have learned much from the San Luis Valley farmers. But contacts between the groups were limited, and the newcomers tended to work out their systems on their own. Many of the argonauts had left their own farms in the Midwest to come to the mountains. When their enthusiasm for mining paled, with a practiced eye these typical sons of an expansive and highly mobile farming frontier surveyed the area for signs of possible agricultural pursuits. Some of them took the plunge. Within a few years they would be joined by admitted agriculturalists, like the colony farmers of Greeley and Longmont, who brought themselves and their families to Colorado specifically to engage in farming. All these men, and many who came after them, embarked on a unique experience. They had "so much to unlearn" from their earlier farming experienced in humid areas that, as one person put it, "it is better to abandon all notions and begin anew."

In the valleys of the South Platte and Arkansas rivers, and their tributaries, these first farmers, in pragmatic fashion, educated themselves to the ways of irrigation. David K. Wall is credited with the first successes in irrigation among the Fifty-niners. He had been in California and had gained some experience with artificial rainfall there. In 1859 he diverted water from Clear Creek at Golden over two acres of gardenland and cleared a promising profit from his vegetables. Soon others had copied and expanded his pattern. Within a few years, the lands accessible to the South Platte and Arkansas rivers were dotted with small farms.

A progression of sponsorship in ditchdigging ensued. The first canals—small, short, and generally confined to the "bottom lands" along the streams—resulted from individual efforts. The Greeley residents, beginning in 1870, expanded these single-farmer attempts into community or cooperative ventures, resulting in longer, larger canals that brought water to the table or "bench" land above the river beds. Similar cooperative efforts from Fountain Creek, Huerfano Creek, and the Arkansas River proper began to appear in that watershed.

By the end of the decade, 1870-1880, a further expansion of

sponsorship brought company or corporate activity. Coinciding with the increasing interest in Colorado mines and cattle herds on the part of Europeans, particularly English investors, the water systems appeared lucrative enterprises for investment. The Colorado Mortgage and Investment Company, locally known as the "English Company," completed construction of the Larimer and Weld Canal, as well as other large irrigation systems. The Travelers Insurance Company aided the financing of the North Poudre Canal. With such financial help, large canals that otherwise would have been too costly for individual or cooperative efforts were built. This was especially true in the Arkansas Valley. Almost all the larger ditches there were corporation projects: the Bessemer, Fort Lyon, Bob Creek, and Otero.

As the size and number of canals increased, the demands on the rivers and streams for irrigation water multiplied. Soon the need to supplement natural flow in the waterways was apparent. The complexities of irrigation increased as subsurface wells were sunk to provide additional water. Even more significant in portent for the future were the first searches on the western side of the ranges for water that might be brought to the Eastern Slope farms through transmontane tunnels. And, as farmers shifted crops and encountered the need for extended irrigating seasons, reservoir construction was initiated to hold the all-precious liquid for release into the canals at the time in the growing season when it was most valuable. Large reservoirs appeared in the South Platte Valley in the decade from 1880 to 1890; the Arkansas and Rio Grande valleys were developed in the same manner somewhat later.

All the techniques of farming under ditches needed to be learned by the new settlers; they also had to revise traditional Anglo-American concepts of water law to fit the new conditions. In the more humid parts of the United States, the English common law proved capable of protecting both public and private rights in the use of water. The common law doctrine—known as Riparian Rights—allowed only a limited use of river waters to the owners of the land bordering streams. Since navigation and power for mill wheels constituted the major water uses, this doctrine prohibited any use that would diminish or alter the flow of the stream and denied to the users any proprietary rights in the water.

While this system worked satisfactorily in the humid east, the arid western regions required new rules, for there all settlers came to understand that "every drop of water that runs into the sea without rendering a commercial return, is a public waste." Water for irrigation had to be diverted from the streams, and to provide security of private property—a basic doctrine of the nation's legal institutions—the man who invested capital and labor to perform the diversion needed protection in law that would insure him continued right to draw the necessary water to run his ditch and irrigate his fields. As Chief Justice Moses Hallett of the Colorado Supreme Court phrased it, in 1872, "in a dry and thirsty land it is necessary to divert the waters of the streams from the natural channels, in order to obtain the fruits of the soil, and this necessity is so universal and imperious that it claims recognition of the law."[1]

From this necessity there arose the Doctrine of Prior Appropriation, permitting the diversion of water from rivers and streams without regard to ownership of the land along the stream banks. It endowed the first users with a permanent right to water so long as they needed it and continued to use it beneficially. Priority of diversion established priority of usage rights, regardless of the geographical location on the stream where the diversion was made. Used sparingly in California earlier, the doctrine was taken up immediately by the Colorado irrigators and made official law. Congress allowed its assent to the concept in 1866; the Colorado constitution-makers of 1876 wrote it into the basic charter of the state. Both federal and state courts have upheld it ever since in most of the arid states, for the "Colorado system" was soon adopted in Utah, Wyoming, Montana, Idaho, Nevada, Arizona, and New Mexico.

The adjudication of priorities and enforcement of the rights determined by the courts became a mammoth undertaking. It would keep lawyers and judges occupied as long as the system was continued. Priorities were determined by litigation in the regular judicial establishments, with determination of suits becoming matters of record for the future. But, in time, state officials were added to the system to oversee the general operation of the water code. Colorado was the first state in the Union to provide such official supervision of water distribution. In 1879 and 1881 the legislature divided the state into three water divisions and ten water districts, both of which would be increased in number later. The divisions followed the natural drainage basins of the major rivers. After 1887 a division superintendent was appointed for each. The water districts were entrusted to commissioners who were charged with the responsibility of insuring that the water was divided according to appropriation.

As demonstrated by their acceptance of the Colorado water

institutions, western states and territories became aware of their unique problems regarding water. They began to encourage interstate sharing of knowledge and ideas. In October, 1873, a convention of delegates from Nebraska, New Mexico, Wyoming, Utah, Kansas, and Colorado met on the invitation of Governor Elbert, in Denver, to consider the possibilities of a joint appeal for federal aid in reclaiming western lands. The convention's major accomplishment was a memorial to Congress, requesting that one-half of the non-mineral public lands of the western states and territories be given to those local governments which, in turn, would use the money from their sale to reclaim arid lands for cultivation by building canals and reservoirs. Although no favorable response was given, this marked the beginnings of interstate cooperation in western water affairs.

Even earlier, Coloradans had looked to Congress for help. Representative Belford had introduced a bill seeking $50,000 for aid in reclaiming lands in the Arkansas, Platte, and Cache la Poudre valleys. The attitude of easterners had been apparent from the beginning. Belford was accused of urging Congress to "build a great series of expensive artificial lakes and ponds, and that at the next session he would go still further and demand the construction of a navy to float upon these still waters."[2] Thus began the long and still continuing dichotomy between East and West over the proper role of government in the reclamation of western lands.

Irrigation also brought the need for experimentation with new crops. Potatoes, in particular, received attention, beginning near Greeley in the mid-1880s. The crop demanded extensive storage facilities, as well as reservoir building for irrigation during the later part of the growing season. A Potato Exchange was organized which helped both in advertising the product and in initiating a marketing program. By 1890 more than 2,000 carloads of potatoes were shipped each year. Alfalfa, first grown in the territory in 1863 from seeds brought from Mexico, was studied intently at the Colorado Experiment Station and was soon planted in many irrigated areas. One flooding before each cutting sometimes produced three full cuttings of alfalfa a year.

Irrigation in the river valleys had become a well-proved technique before the agricultural settlers turned to consider the high plains that stretched between the rivers. Over the acres where the long-drive cattle had grazed and where the beginnings of the modern ranch cattle industry then were taking place, farmers now searched for a sign that would indicate possible success in plowing up the prairies.

In time the signs seemed to emerge. For one thing, the windmill had made its appearance, and perhaps enough subsurface water could be pumped by putting the prairie breezes to work to squeak through the driest months. It was largely a vain hope, but considered by many. For fencing, the barbed-wire factories of the Midwest were now turning out a successful product, at a cost low enough to afford protection for crops against the cattlemen's herds. James Oliver, by 1868, had perfected his chilled plow, and from his factory at South Bend, Indiana, and others, instruments to turn the short grass sod were now available. And there were additional signs. From the Crimea, Mennonite farmers had brought hard red winter wheat. Although difficult to mill at first, after 1881 and the introduction of chilled-iron rollers, the wheat became accepted on the grain markets.

Finally, to provide the actual catalyst in the reaction, the "rain-belt" seemed to be moving westward during the decade of the 1880s. A cycle of years of above-average rainfall led land speculators and railroad agents into claims that the "rainbelt" had marched right up to the foothills of the Rockies. "So much rain now falls in the eastern portion of the arid lands of Colorado that it is no longer fit for a winter range for cattle," pronounced the Burlington Railroad, which had completed its Chicago to Denver tracks in 1882 and was energetically planting towns along its right-of-way. 'What has brought about this great change [?] ... In our opinion, the change is due to the extensive irrigation of land lying along the eastern base of the Rocky Mountains. Great rivers, which head in perpetual snow banks, have been turned into irrigation ditches; and the water which formerly ran wastefully into the Gulf of Mexico has been turned on to the arid plains. There it soaks into the soil. The wind sweeping over the land sucks up a large portion of it. There is then moisture in the air and it is precipitated on the high lands of Eastern Colorado."[3]

With such assurances, the sodbusters came in, spilling over at first from western Nebraska and Kansas. Lured on by railroad agents who had towns to build or grants to dispose of, they settled along the Burlington Road in proximity to such towns as Akron or Yuma or Wray, all three dating from 1886. Or they followed the right-of-way of the Missouri Pacific to Eads or Arlington, or the Rock Island tracks to Burlington or Flagler, both dating from 1887. Eckley, Chivington, Springfield, Haxtun, Holyoke, Logan, and Otis—all date from the period of the late 1880s.

There were centers that had their origins earlier and now were infused with new energy, like Kit Carson, which the Kansas Pacific had moved bodily from Sheridan in western Kansas after that railroad had built across the eastern Colorado border. And there were new creations, like the Santa Fe's town of Lamar. Although blessed with some irrigable lands in the Arkansas Valley, Lamar would share some of the dry land experiences. In May, 1886, it was described: "Only five short weeks ago there was not a sign of human habitation in sight save a single log building down by the cottonwood belt that fringes the stream. From the river southward a desert-looking plain, partly covered by the short buffalo grass, extended up a gentle incline two or three miles ... Today there are five and twenty buildings completed or nearly so; many others are begun and active preparations are making to erect a large number more."[4]

Around these towns the sodbusters settled on their lands, using the federal laws to advantage by pre-empting one quarter-section of 160 acres, taking another as a "tree claim" under the terms of the Timber Culture Act, and homesteading on a third quarter-section. On the prairies they found no wood, so they set up bricks of sod to build their houses and sheds. They planted their crops and watched with a wary eye the clouds on the horizon. For a few years they anticipated success. A "boom" in land values reflected their optimism. Unimproved land soon was selling for $3 to $10 an acre, while slightly cultivated lands were bringing between $8 and $20.

And then the years of trouble began. Dry years returned to the area in 1889 and 1890. The "rainbelt" hadn't moved at all; the rainmakers' promises never came true; "the only crop was bankrupts." A general crop failure engulfed the land and the easily discouraged started to move away. The state legislature appropriated $21,250 to provide seed grain to start anew, and relief in other forms was sent eastward from Denver, to help those who decided to remain. Rainfall in 1891 and 1892 was more promising—in fact, 1892 was a good year for the dryland farmers.

But then the discouraging years came again, 1894 bringing the worst drought the region would know until the 1930s. The exodus from the plains turned into full-scale flight. While relief again was sent to those who stayed—foodstuffs and clothing and coal collected by agencies like the *Denver Republican*—the enchantment had vanished. Those who clung to their homesteads began to turn to grazing, not daring to plant more failures on their plowed fields. Most of the settlers hurried to other regions. The first assault on the high plains had failed to sustain itself. After the turn of the century, other men with new concepts of the way to wage war on the "desert" would write another chapter in the state's agricultural history.

19

New Frontiers

The year 1890 marks a convenient dividing point in Colorado's history. With the removal of the Utes and the opening of the Western Slope to white settlement, the days of the traditional frontier had come to an end. The arbitrary qualification for a frontier condition is usually considered to be an area of land with less than two residents per square mile. In 1880 the federal census had listed 1.8 persons per square mile in the Centennial State, few enough to qualify as a frontier. But by 1890 the population average had increased to 3.9 persons per square mile. The demographer's magic line had been crossed. And, if other indications were needed to demonstrate the fading of the old frontier and the emergence of new challenges, they were not difficult to discover. The economy of the state had shifted, particularly in the non-mining regions, from nomadic, grazing, pastoral pursuits to settled farms and intensive agriculture, and in the growing cities where the beginnings of industry were apparent by 1890.

The decade from 1880 to 1890 had been a time of growth and urbanization. Census statistics of every kind proved the assertion: the assessed property value of the state trebled; the number of farms quadrupled; railroad mileage almost trebled; the amount of capital invested in manufacturing increased six-fold. Denver grew from a town of 35,000 to a city of 106,000 people; Pueblo, becoming the state's "second city" increased from 3,000 to 24,000 people. In manufacturing, the number of establishments increased from 599 to 762; the number of employees from 5,000 to 9,000; the value of products from $14 million to $29 million.

Industrial growth depends on a few basic ingredients: a supply of

A coal mine, near Oak Creek.

Interior of Orendorf's store, Ouray, 1920? (Western History Collection, Norlin Library, University of Colorado)

fuel, a supply of labor, and markets in which to sell the manu-factured products. Colorado could provide two of these three essentials without difficulty. Fuel was present and plentiful; the laboring force was, or would be, ready to move to the state when opportunities for employment existed. The only real problem for Colorado's industrial advance was then, as it is now, a lack of markets. The state is a great distance from the population centers of the nation; transportation was still a problem, for the mountain barrier had never been pierced satisfactorily.

Denver, the state's major population center, was at a great disadvantage in the freight-rate structure that then existed. The Union Pacific Railroad, with heavy investments in Cheyenne, Wyoming, preferred to feed goods through that town to Georgetown and Gilpin County, because Denver was a "pool point" and Cheyenne was not. The "pooling" arrangement meant a sharing of freight profits with other railroads. Wyoming, Utah, and New Mexico cities all enjoyed more advantageous railroad rates than Denver.

Nonetheless, Colorado still boasted potentials for manufacturing greater than many other western commonwealths. Adequate iron ore and coal deposits in Colorado could support a nascent steel industry. The coal mines of the state were centered in three general areas. There was a northern field in Jefferson, Boulder, and Weld counties, the coal from which supplied Denver and other towns with fuel. A middle field in Fremont, Park, and El Paso counties had been opened. And, in the southern regions, coal deposits in Las Animas, Huerfano, La Plata, and Dolores counties had demonstrated their superiority over the other regions. Almost all this coal was bituminous or sub-bituminous. The decade from 1880 to 1890 had witnessed a phenomenal increase in production from these fields: from 437,000 to more than 3,000,000 short tons.

Coal from the Colorado mines was valuable for a variety of purposes: domestic heating, smelting ores, railroading, and fueling the emerging industrial factories. Most of the largest mines had been opened and were operated by railroad companies or their subsidiaries, like the Union Pacific's "Union Coal Company" with mines in the northern field, or the Santa Fe's "Canon City and Trinidad Coal and Coking Company" with southern field properties.

One of the biggest coal operators was the Denver and Rio Grande ally, the Colorado Coal and Iron Company, with headquarters in South Pueblo. General William Palmer, visualizing this as one of the several "supplementary" enterprises for his railroad, formed the

Colorado Coal and Iron Company in 1880 by merging three smaller companies and capitalizing the new organization at $10,000,000. The intent of the organizers was to convert Pueblo into the "Pittsburgh of the West." Blast furnaces were going by 1881 and a Bessemer converter turned out its first steel (the first west of the Missouri River), and the first rails were rolled in 1882. This was the corporation that became, in 1892, following another merger, the Colorado Fuel and Iron Company.

Another Colorado industry attractive to investors was smelting. Leadville, in its boom days, was the great smelting center of the state, but Denver and Pueblo too attracted large ore reduction plants. Several large works existed in Pueblo even before 1888 when Meyer Guggenheim built his Philadelphia Smelter there at a cost of $1,250,000. The Philadelphia operated at a loss for some time, and it was only after August Raht introduced new metallurgical processes that Guggenheim's large investment began to earn handsome profits.

Smelters and iron works were soon joined by a third "native" industry—the manufacturing of mining machinery. This was a natural outgrowth of the simple blacksmith forges and small foundries that had fabricated machines for miners since the original gold rush. Denver, in particular, emerged as a center for mining machines. Factories like those of the Mine and Smelter Supply Company, and the Hendrie and Bolthoff Company, turned out ball and stamp mills, flotation and cyanidation systems, concentrating and "bumping" tables, "roughing jigs" and a host of other highly specialized machines to treat the ores of Colorado and much of the rest of the world.

The railroads of the decade helped to bring the material to the smelters and factories and to distribute their products. In 1870 only 157 miles of railroad operated in Colorado; in 1890 there were 4,176 miles. In 1880 only two eastern trunk lines had been built into the state—the Kansas Pacific and the Sante Fe. By 1890 these had been joined by four additional roads—the Union Pacific had constructed its lines from Julesburg to La Salle; the Burlington had built through Fort Morgan to Denver; the Rock Island had entered Colorado Springs; the Missouri Pacific now reached to Pueblo. Towns and cities along the Eastern Slope were in a more competitive stituation for their freight and patronage than ever before. Three lines now connected Pueblo and Denver, for the Santa Fe had constructed its road between the two cities.

The Denver, Texas, and Gulf Railroad had acquired the trackage of

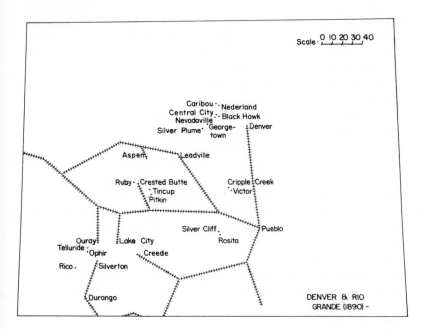

Colorado mining regions and smelter centers.

the Denver and New Orleans between Pueblo and Denver. Using the facilities of the Denver and Rio Grande from Pueblo to Trinidad, by 1888 it met the Denver, Texas, and Fort Worth there and Colorado had a rail connection running south to the Texas gulf.

Railroaders were still extending their lines on Colorado's Western Slope too. Much of this construction continued to be narrow-gauge trackage, which reached its maximum mileage in 1890. However, the disadvantages of interchanging cars between standard and narrow-gauge had already become obvious enough to lead some lines to use a third rail so that both sized cars could be accommodated.

One of the most exciting features of mountain construction these years was the Colorado Midland Railroad, a standard-gauge road that had built from Colorado Springs via Manitou, Ute Pass, South Park, Buena Vista, and the valley of the upper Arkansas River to Leadville. Begun in 1885, it tunneled a 2,064-foot passage under Hagerman Pass, at an elevation of 11,528 feet, to accommodate the traffic across the Sawatch Range to the headwaters of the Frying Pan. At the junction of that stream and the Roaring Fork of the Colorado, the road branched in two directions. One line led up the Roaring Fork to the silver mines of Aspen. The other travelled downstream to Glenwood Springs and along the Colorado River to Newcastle, which it reached in 1889. From there the Midland's trains ran west to Grand Junction over a line operated jointly with the Denver and Rio Grande.

The critical point in the system was the crossing of the Continental Divide at Hagerman Pass. The Midland began a second tunnel in 1890. The new facility—the 9,394-foot Bask-Ivanhoe Tunnel—eliminated only seven miles in total distance, but it lowered the elevation of the crossing 530 feet. By the time the new passage was finished, in 1893, the Midland had been sold to the Santa Fe road.

While Coloradans now boasted more miles of operating trackage than ever before, the state's railroad network also had come to be dominated more completely by one man than was healthful. Jay Gould controlled the Missouri Pacific, the Denver and Rio Grande, and the Union Pacific. This was a sizeable part of the Colorado rail system by itself, but, delineated further, it meant that by controlling the Union Pacific, Gould also counted as personal property the Union Pacific's old subsidiaries—the Denver South Park, the Colorado Central, and the Denver Pacific. Traffic agreements with the Santa Fe, the Rock Island, and the Denver, Texas, and Gulf spread Gould influence even further. Only the Burlington seems to have remained a free agent.

The capital city of Denver was the center of Colorado's rail network in 1890, as it had been in 1870. Despite its increase in railroad facilities, and the beginnings of an industrial complex, critics continued to complain that Denver was a city without reason for existing. It was true that services, and its role as a distribution center, rather than industry, accounted for most of Denver's growth. But the place made short work of its critics, as it had always done, refusing to believe that its destiny was not as magnificent as the mountain ranges that formed the backdrop of its location.

The Queen City now prided itself on such refinements as electric lights, electric street cars, and telephones. Denverites pointed with pleasure at the new buildings fronting the streets. British capital, organized by James Duff into the Colorado Mortgage and Investment Company, had constructed the far-famed Windsor Hotel. A second fabulous hostelry, the Brown Palace, opened in September, 1892. Horace Tabor, with his Leadville profits, put up a handsome opera house which had opened in regal style on September 5, 1881, with

Emma Abbott and the English Opera Company in "Maritana." And, in 1894, after fire destroyed an earlier structure, Denver's new Union Station was opened.

As befitting a commonwealth beginning a major chapter in its historical development, Colorado provided funds to build a new statehouse. On fifteen acres of land donated by Henry C. Brown, the cornerstone of the new Capitol was laid in July, 1890. E. E. Myers of Detroit, who had planned statehouses for Michigan and Texas, was commissioned to design the $2,800,000 edifice. Architects styled his building, completed in 1894, a "free adaptation" of the national Capitol. It is unique only in the $4,000 worth of gold leaf placed on the exterior of the dome. The rest of the building, with granite exterior and dome features, is the usual statehouse of the period.

Many newcomers—both immigrants and tourists—by-passed Denver, travelling directly to General Palmer's town of Colorado Springs. Particularly as a tourist center, the Springs rivaled the state capital. In 1890 the Manitou and Pike's Peak Railroad opened for service. The peak that Pike had been unable to climb could now be scaled in the comfort of a railroad coach. Nine miles long, with grades as high as twenty-five per cent (necessitating a rack system), the railroad proved a long-lasting magnet for the tourist industry of Colorado Springs.

But something much more exciting than cog railroads soon engulfed the Colorado Springs region. The decade of the 1890s had hardly begun when, not far from Palmer's town, the mines of a place called Cripple Creek were opened, bringing to Colorado its last big gold camp.

Gold seekers travelling the Arkansas River route in 1858-1859 had used, as had all their predecessors on the trail, the landmark of Pike's Peak to guide them to the mountains. The Peak had given its name to the gold rush and to the mining area before more official designations were made. It was natural, therefore, that the region around Pike's Peak was well prospected for placers and lodes in the early days. But from the time of the Lawrence Party in 1858 onward, many anxious argonauts had experienced the disappointment that awaited all who followed the natural instinct to search for Pike's Peak gold near Pike's Peak. Rather than the famous mountain, it was Cherry Creek and Clear Creek, and a host of other place-names, that came to identify the paying gold camps.

Not until 1874, sixteen years after the first gold seekers had guided themselves to the mountains, did the region around the Peak begin to demonstrate any mineral wealth. Even then, the first "boom" was short-lived. A few lodes were discovered, and a mining district named "Mount Pisgah" was formed about thirty-five miles from Pike's Peak. It ended almost as soon as it began, for the quantity of ore uncovered was very meager. Then a decade elapsed before, in 1884, another rush to the region occurred. This episode was even more ill-fated, for to the chagrin of the miners who hurried down from Leadville and other camps to cash in on the new field, it was soon discovered that Mount Pisgah had been liberally and unscrupulously "salted"—the claims were worthless. After this unfortunate incident, it seemed that the region had surely exhausted all possibility as a mining camp. All that remained were herds of cattle grazing on the slopes, and an evil reputation that lingered from the fraud.

Some of the grazing land in time came into the possession of two Denver real estate merchants, Horace Bennett and Julius Myers. Included in their holdings was the former ranch of Robert Womack. Womack himself remained in the area. For some years he divided his working hours between herding cattle for the ranch owners and digging in the hillsides, particularly at the site he called "Poverty Gulch." Womack had gained some experience as a miner in Gilpin County, but not enough to label him as an expert. His persistence in searching for ore thus attracted little attention, although from time to time other prospectors would appear in the vicinity to try their luck.

Most experienced mining men, however, were not interested. Everything about the region looked wrong to seasoned prospectors. There were no outcroppings of ore to indicate lodes underneath. The slopes of the mountains were free of the deep ravines that usually indicated likely sites. In the volcanic rock structure of the region, the usual quartz indicators were missing. Add all this to the already bad reputation of the place, and it is easy to explain why Womack and others who kept digging holes there were considered, in more charitable moments, "dreamers."

Yet it is Womack who is remembered as the discoverer of the riches of Cripple Creek. Late in the year 1890, he had dug his Poverty Gulch hole deep enough to take samples into Colorado Springs for assaying. While many still doubted, others listened to the fascinating yarns about those assays, reportedly indicating genuine gold. Early the following year, 1891, other fortune hunters joined the prospecting cowboy until by May considerable activity was underway.

Of necessity, chance would play a large role in the ensuing drama. Lacking the usual signs for locating lodes, the first-comers to Cripple Creek were forced into imaginative guess-work. Winfield S. Stratton's experience was not unusual, except that he was luckier than many others. Stratton was a carpenter who worked in Colorado Springs, but he had spent his vacations and free time prospecting over much of the Colorado landscape. The growing gossip about the Womack discovery soon captivated his attention. He tried several locations, without any great success. Then he constructed a theory that the granite outcroppings on the slopes of Battle Mountain might mark the end-of-the-rainbow lode of his dreams. On the Fourth of July, 1891, he pegged two claims there, naming them appropriately the "Independence" and the "Washington." History not only records that they made carpenter Stratton a millionaire, but impressively relates that eight years later he sold the "Independence" to the Venture Corporation of London for $10,000,000, believed to have been the largest mining transaction to that time.

Stratton quietly built his properties into valuable mines; Robert Womack disposed of his findings for a few hundred dollars. Both types of action would be repeated many times during the first months of the new excitement. The Cripple Creek gold fields were concentrated in an area of about ten square miles. Into this relatively tiny region poured the usual population of a mining rush—seasoned, experienced prospectors from other camps, tenderfoot amateurs up from the valley towns to try their luck, fortune hunters from far-off cities and states who began long journeys toward the 11,000-foot elevations of the new camp. With their arrival began the usual process of claims, consolidations, suits, and countersuits as everyone scrambled in pursuit of luck and the valuable patches of gold-bearing ground.

Some startling differences distinguished this last major Colorado gold field from its predecessors. Where the Fifty-niners had searched for free gold in gulch placers and mountain lodes, the Cripple Creek prospectors required re-education, for the gold of the district was largely found in combination with tellurium, in the compound tellurides called sylvanite, calaverite, and petzite. Where washing, crushing, and amalgamation with mercury had separated the earlier free gold, Cripple Creek ores required smelting, or even more complex chemical operations such as cyanidation or chlorination.

Yet much was also the same. The feverish haste to record locations still characterized the early days of the camp. The sudden influx of miners created the same necessities of goods and services and the same opportunities to supply them that the early camps had created. The same transportation difficulties of freighting over rugged mountain terrain would exist until railroads were constructed into the camp. And the same rivalries occurred between settlements aspiring for pre-eminence in the region.

Horace Bennett and Julius Myers, the Denver real estate men, surely had never planned a subdivision in their cow pasture; yet they were not slow to realize the opportunities presented, and they moved quickly to capitalize on their good fortune. Where their cattle had peacefully grazed along Cripple Creek, they soon boasted the town of Fremont, complete with hotel and bank. Residents of an earlier successful episode in town-promotion called Colorado Springs soon joined in an act of their own, laying out a rival settlement named Hayden Placer. The contest between Fremont and Hayden Placer settled into a fierce battle for the location of the United States post office. When Fremont emerged victorious, a not unusual merger took place, with the new name—Cripple Creek—adopted for the town. Incorporated in 1892, its population in the next census was 10,147. In time the mining district would include many other towns, most of them near mines and mills—Victor, Altman, Independence, Elkton, Anaconda, Arequar, Lawrence, Goldfield, Gillett. But the city with the name of the district retained its lead.

Statistics of gold production tend to be impressive; the Cripple Creek record still startles the imagination. In 1891, when the camp was first opened, perhaps some $200,000 worth of gold was mined. The following year, more than $500,000 worth was dug. By 1893 this had been increased four-fold, to a total of more than $2,000,000 worth. Then the really astronomical sums hurry along: 1896, more than $8,500,000; 1899, $19,500,000. By the last year of the century, Cripple Creek was producing two-thirds of the gold mined in Colorado, nearly one-fourth of the total production of the United States. It was a bonanza camp indeed!

The pattern of organization for both mining properties and the society of the camp developed rather quickly. Individuals had discovered the first mines; they tended to join together to gain the capital necessary to work their holdings. As outsiders, with money to invest, became interested in the mines, the opportunity for exchanging shares in the organized companies increased. One guide to the region, published in 1900, lists 496 separate mining companies with actual claims. Shares of stock in these companies were bought and sold, largely on the Colorado Springs Mining Exchange. In the last year of the century, that institution recorded 236,000,000 shares of stock exchanged, with a total value of $34,000,000.[1]

This type of mine ownership and operation led to a distinction within the district's population similar to that which Leadville had earlier introduced into the state's mining history. The mineral properties were owned by shareholders in the companies; the actual development of the properties was entrusted to managers and superintendents hired by the companies. The owners, managers, and perhaps most of the professional men in the settlements tended to form one stratum of Cripple Creek society. The other stratum was composed of miners—the laborers who offered their services in exchange for daily wages. Both groups depended for their well-being on continued successful working of the mining properties, and both were eagerly interested in the specific welfare of their own group.

This division in the Cripple Creek society was of more than casual significance. The camp had been opened only a short time when conditions outside the region conspired to make Cripple Creek a focal point of collision between the two groups. In 1893 the United States suffered a devastating financial panic that ushered in a four-year depression. The silver mines of Colorado were particularly hard-hit by the economic crisis. Laborers from closed silver mines, joined by thousands of unemployed men from over the nation, converged on the still brightly active Cripple Creek field. This influx of surplus labor, added to the uneasy apprehension of investors at the time, combined to make Cripple Creek a theater of war between capital and labor. Thus the last of the major gold fields became one of the significant elements of a turbulent decade. To understand its role, however, it is necessary to examine the political and economic conditions in the rest of Colorado.

20

Politics and Populists

The Republican Party dominated the political scene in Colorado in the years following statehood. That party was formed of various, often competing interests and factions: Denver and Leadville carried the greatest political weight and aroused envy of their position; the mountain and plains counties were jealous of each other's influence; the Western Slope felt itself too often shunted aside; and the southern part of the state demanded some rewards, even if it did not carry much power. The tightly-knit Republican leadership acted as political "broker," compromising the various demands by parceling out the "loaves and fishes." Denver usually received the largest share, followed by the mining regions. The first two U.S. senators, for example, were Jerome Chaffee from Denver and Henry Teller from Central City.

Into this situation, starting at Leadville, came the sudden influx of mining millionaires with money and political aspirations. For a decade they dominated the scene and around them swirled intrigue and quite often success. The most sought-after prizes were the United States senate seats, not the governorship. In the years 1877 to 1893, six men served as governor of Colorado—John Routt, Frederick Pitkin, James B. Grant, Alva Adams, Benjamin Eaton, and Job Cooper. Several of these men were closely connected with mining. The only two Democrats (Grant and Adams) both won primarily because the Republicans fell to fighting among themselves and were unable to heal their wounds in time to garner election victories.

The real power in the party and in the state resided in the senators, men whose names for the most part loom large, even today, in the annals of Colorado: Henry Teller, Jerome Chaffee, Nathaniel

Hill, George Chilcott, Horace Tabor, Thomas Bowen, and Edward Wolcott. All were Republicans and all either powerful political figures or men of prominence and wealth. Bowen's, Tabor's, and Hill's fortunes were based on mining; Chaffee and Teller were closely allied with mining interests. These men had money to lavish on the Republican Party and they merited political consideration when they demanded it.

Although the governorship might be allowed to go to lesser men and be used as a pawn to gain a greater end, the party leadership played the senate contests with deadly seriousness. Frank Hall, who observed the situation firsthand and from the inside, commented: "The bane of our political system is the eternal and almost frantic craze that possesses nearly every politician who assumes to be a leader, and which has governed the majority of our governors, to fill a seat in the Senate.[1]

The contests were fought in the state legislature, since United States senators then were chosen by that body, not by direct election. This procedure permitted more individual bargaining and made the money flowing from the coffers of a Tabor or Bowen that much more powerful. During a hotly contested race, Denver became a hotbed of rumor and dealings. The Republicans controlled every legislature during these years, making the Democrats, until the 1890s, a permanent minority party in Colorado. Even when the Republicans lost the governorship, as they did in 1882 and 1886, they retained legislative control. Not only did the party dominate the election of senators and governors, but after the initial single term of Democrat Thomas Patterson, it held the one congressional seat throughout the period.

Actually, the parties seldom seriously differed in outlook, nor did any permanent issues sharply divide them. Both Republicans and Democrats tended toward conservatism; both seemed more interested in offices and the resulting spoils than in any major reform issues (in this they were not much different from their counterparts on the national scene). Nominations and elections often pivoted on personalities and money, starting with the gubernatorial race in 1878. Pitkin defeated William Loveland that year, but not before the race degenerated into name-calling and personal slander. Mudslinging, bribery, betrayals, and extreme partisanship came to characterize the political races. The Republicans received more attention because they were the majority party and attracted more of the mining kings into their ranks.

The classic struggle of that period unfolded in 1882-1883 for the vacated senate seat of Henry Teller, who had been appointed Secretary of the Interior by President Chester Arthur. Tabor, Bowen, Pitkin, John Routt, and the old political pro, William Hamill, entered the race; but Tabor and Bowen had the inside track. Each had money and was willing to spend it to achieve his goal. After ninety-six ballots, consuming eleven days in January, 1883, the two killed off all opposition, Bowen finally upsetting Tabor to win the six-year term; Tabor received only a token thirty-day appointment. Del Norte's Bowen, who had made a fortune in the San Juans and would become known as "Washington's finest poker player," had come to Colorado from Arkansas and had been one of the state's district judges. Charges were flung about who betrayed whom and for months afterward it appeared to be the political crisis of the age.

This sort of contest produced the highest excitement for politicians and electorate. Indeed, legislative elections were conducted with the idea of lining up support for a senate race. When men like Tabor and Bowen faced off, real drama was produced; however, the people's will and formalities of politics might be ignored in the process. It would be a decade before political machines came to replace the individualism and the emotional following of these men who played for high stakes and backed their moves with thousands of dollars.

Occasionally a legislature would gain similar attention. Such was the case with the "Robber Seventh," which scandalously squandered appropriations in 1889 and 1890. An emotional clash of public and private interests, like the attempt to create a board of railroad commissioners in 1881, could generate heated debate and state-wide interest. To resolve the financial malfeasance problem, the voters seemed to like the idea of electing Democratic treasurers, attorneys-general, or superintendents of public instruction, hoping that they would serve in a watch-dog capacity over the Republican governor and legislature.

This state of affairs lasted until the 1890s, when the political winds changed. The decade that brought the revival of gold mining in Colorado, led by Cripple Creek, was also a decade of economic crisis and political ferment. This was true throughout the United States, but Colorado seemed particularly vulnerable to the economic dislocations and peculiarly sensitive to the shifting political rearrangements.

One of the problems of the times, as usual, was money. In 1861 the mines of the United States had produced $43,000,000 worth of gold and only $2,000,000 worth of silver. But, by law, the coinage ratio was established at 15.988 ounces of silver pegged at the same price as one ounce of gold. This arbitrary balance of approximately sixteen to one, at earlier periods, had corresponded roughly with the "supply and demand"—or commercial market—ratio of the two metals. Now, however, silver was undervalued in comparison with its commercial price, and because a producer or owner of silver could receive a higher price on the commercial market, no silver had been presented for sale to the government for many years.

As the mining industry of the West developed, the relative production of the two metals tended to even out. In 1873 the quantities of gold and silver mined both were listed as worth about $36,000,000. This rapid increase in silver production brought a corresponding slump in the price of silver in the commercial market and for the first time since 1837, silver prices fell below the old mint price established at the sixteen-to-one ratio.

That is, the price would have fallen below the mint price if there had been a mint price at the time. But, in fact, federal purchase and coinage of silver had ended. In that same year of 1873, Congress had legislated a new unit of currency which, for the first time in national history, permitted the coinage of gold dollars. More than that, the gold dollars were to be used as the basic unit of value, replacing the silver dollar. The legislation was not unique; it paralleled the action of such European countries as Germany, France, Italy, Switzerland, Belgium, and Greece—all of whom had adopted the single gold standard in the previous few years.

The Coinage Act of 1873 provided for the coinage, in small quantities, of silver dollars to be used only in foreign trade, or in the country as legal payment for debts of less than $5.00. The standard silver dollar no longer existed, and with its demise the market for silver at government mints (as well as in much of Europe almost simultaneously) vanished. For the first time since the nation's coinage operation began, free and unlimited coinage of both gold and silver was abandoned. Only gold would now be purchased by the government. The bimetallic principle under which the country had always operated was gone; there was no longer a need for a fixed ratio between the price of gold and silver; the country was on a single, gold standard.

If the supply of silver had remained short and the market price for commercial silver had remained high, there would have been little cause for complaint. But as the supply of silver increased, and the market price dropped below the old pegged price that the mint had formerly paid, there were demands for a re-establishment of silver purchases by the federal government. The demands were raised by two different groups. The most obvious of the two was composed of men directly interested in the welfare of silver mines (the owners, managers, miners) and those whose livelihood depended on the same silver mines in a less direct fashion (the smelting interests, the railroads, the suppliers—in fact, much of the population of a mining state with important silver deposits). The other group's concern in silver coinage was less direct, but became equally vocal. This was the group that opposed the deflationary policy of the government and which came to look upon silver coinage as a method of inflating an otherwise restricted currency.

The inflationists had not always been enamoured of silver. Their origins, in fact, were much more closely associated with a different sort of currency—paper dollars. During the Civil War the federal government had issued fiat notes which had been dubbed "green-backs." These notes had fluctuated in value all during the war period, reflecting both the uncertainty of the outcome of the war and the disposition the federal government might make of the notes after the conflict had ended.

There were, at war's end, some $400,000,000 worth of the greenbacks still in circulation. Two more or less inter-related questions were then asked. Since some men had exchanged greenbacks for interest-bearing government bonds (with the greenbacks accepted by the government at face value, although their market worth at the time might have been much less), some people believed that, unless otherwise specified, government bonds should be redeemed in greenbacks only. This would keep the fiat money in circulation and also limit the profit investors might be able to record from their speculation. Others, however, argued that the bonds should all be redeemed in gold; to do otherwise would be unfair to investors, and also, place the federal currency on a shaky, unsound, paper basis.

The other question involved the greenbacks more directly. Should they remain in circulation—perhaps even be increased in quantity—to inflate the currency and provide a "cheap" money policy in the post-war years of economic expansion? Or, should the government follow a "hard" money policy, deflating the currency by calling in the greenbacks and retiring them from circulation?

In 1875 the federal authorities decided the question by resuming specie payments for greenbacks, thus establishing a policy of retiring the paper currency and embarking on a deflationary path. To inflationists this seemed a gross error. What was needed, this group argued, was not less, but more money in circulation. In 1865, estimates record, there was about $31.00 per person in circulation in the United States. Ten years later this amount had decreased to only about $19.00 per person. In ordinary times this would have been a rather rapid deflation. But, the inflationists insisted, these were not ordinary times. Agriculture, commerce, and industry had all expanded immensely since the war. Despite recent setbacks like the Panic of 1873, the growth of the country was certain to proceed at a spectacular rate. As that expansion of the economy took place, the need for an increase in the circulating medium would also grow.

The inflationists gradually came to understand that their best hope of success rested on their ability to organize their own political party, since neither the Republican nor Democratic party was willing to contest the "tight" money policy. In 1876, the year of Colorado statehood, they formed the Greenback Party. Two years later, in the congressional elections, they polled more than one million votes in the national elections—a good showing for a new political group.

Although Colorado's first years of statehood were not without problems (grasshopper plagues, for example), paper money never achieved any great popularity in the region. Perhaps part of the poor showing of the Greenback Party in the state resulted from the traditional distrust of a mining community to paper currency. The Greenbackers never organized more than eight counties of Colorado and even those organizations had little connection with the national movement. In 1878 the Greenback Party polled eight per cent of the state votes; two years later they received only three per cent. In a few counties, particularly Boulder, they enjoyed local victories, but this often was the result of their alliances with temperance or prohibition groups.

The failure of the Greenbackers to achieve political success did not end the inflationists' programs. An expanded currency might be brought about in other ways. Gradually the interests of the inflationists turned to silver coinage. A re-examination of the history of silver brought into focus the legislation of 1873. The inflationists now argued that if the government would revoke that coinage law, and begin to purchase silver at the former ratio of sixteen to one, the silver money minted would expand the circulating medium. Thus silver became the inflationists' new tool to bring cheaper (that is, more) money—and prosperity—to all the people.

The silver interests—as differentiated from the inflationists—had also studied the history of silver. They had come to believe that the Coinage Act of 1873 was a ruthless action designed to ruin their properties. Soon they had applied the epithet "The Crime of 'Seventy-Three" to the legislation, as they embarked on a campaign to bring congressional revision of the act.

In response to the demands of western silver interests, and the growing voice of the inflationists, Congress offered a compromise. The Bland-Allison Act of 1878, passed over President Hayes' veto, met the silver champions half-way. A total return to the pre-1873 coinage was unacceptable to the "tight" money group, but what was now presented as an alternative was a statute which allowed the coinage of a minimum of $2,000,000 and a maximum of $4,000,000 worth of silver each month by the federal mints. The quantity of silver to be purchased would be established by the Secretary of the Treasury. The mint price would equal the current market price for silver, rather than the old standard of sixteen to one. It was believed that about one-half of the silver mined each year could be moved from the commercial to the government market by this legislation. The reduced supply, presumably, would be reflected in a rising silver price.

Coloradans were very much interested in such legislation. Mining, their chief economic activity, depended on silver. In 1874, for the first time, the value of silver mined in the state had exceeded that of gold. By 1881 Colorado was the leading silver producer in the United States, and throughout the eighties production remained on that high level. This alone was enough to create deep interest, but the citizens came to believe that their very existence rested on silver mining. Not only were Leadville and the other silver camps vitally concerned. Almost all economic pursuits in the state were tied in one way or another to the mining industry; consequently, almost every Colorado resident had a vested interest in its success.

The Bland-Allison legislation failed to live up to expectations; for one thing, it did not allow a return to the old ratio price for silver and, for another, the treasury secretaries were committed to the general concept of deflation. The minimum amount was coined, when full success demanded unlimited coinage at the sixteen-to-one ratio.

To this end Colorado spokesmen were active during the 1880s. The Boulder *News and Courier*, December 17, 1880, editorialized in support of the "free and unlimited coinage of silver," a theme repeated in most Colorado newspapers in the subsequent years. In a senate speech in January, 1886, Henry Teller, who emerged as the state's greatest silver spokesman, outlined what free coinage would do. It would, he reasoned, stimulate commerce and industry, provide more employment and better wages, and bring silver back to its old price. The appeal here was broader than just Colorado, yet each point struck a responsive chord within the state. Horace Tabor made yet another appeal for free coinage, one that became increasingly frequent: "You wipe out silver off from the face of the earth and you just double the value of gold and the gold securities and the debt securities, which have to be paid in gold."[2]

Under such conditions Coloradans soon organized to promote the free and unlimited coinage of silver. The first national Silver Convention met in Denver in January, 1885, and formed the Silver Alliance, which quickly set up branches in all parts of the state. This was followed by state conventions and a Colorado Silver Association. Four years later Colorado sent forty-three delegates to a national silver meeting in St. Louis. By 1892, when a third national convention was called in Washington, D. C., the state was represented by delegates from 220 silver clubs, numbering more than 40,000 members. The foundation had been laid; the silver banner raised.

Given this interest, silver and politics were destined to join together. Colorado congressmen and candidates, of both parties, consistently championed bimetallism—that is, a return to silver coinage. But despite their energy, and the work of their western colleagues and the enthusiasm of inflationists generally, they were denied a complete victory. In 1890, during Benjamin Harrison's administration, a "half-loaf" was achieved in the passage of the Sherman Silver Purchase Act. The measure was more or less bracketed with the McKinley Tariff Act of the same year. Westerners, without personal interest in the high rates of that tariff, supported the measure in return for enactment of their desired Silver Act.

Like the earlier Bland-Allison legislation, the Sherman Act did not meet the full expectations of the silverites. It did, however, approximately double the amount of silver stipulated to be purchased by the earlier legislation: 4,500,000 ounces of silver a month, presumably enough to absorb most of the then current production in the United States. The price, again, was to be the market level, rather than the fixed ratio.

At first it appeared that the Sherman legislation might work the magic. With increased government buying, silver prices began to climb. From the low level of $.93 per ounce in 1889, silver reached more than $1.00 per ounce in 1890. Colorado, whose silver mines were now producing fifty-eight per cent of the total silver mined in the nation each year, had reason to applaud this initial effect. But the pace did not continue. The higher prices lasted only momentarily. Soon a continuing decline set in, and by early 1892 silver had not only fallen to its old level, but kept declining even further. By 1894 it would sell for only $.63 an ounce.

Disenchantment with the Sherman legislation reflected a similar disenchantment with the national policies of the Republican and Democratic parties. Neither of the traditional groups seemingly dared to alienate its eastern supporters by championing western silver ideas. Into this vacuum came a new political grouping whose elements originated in a variety of reform and dissident factions—the People's Party, more commonly known as the Populists.

Historians often trace the rise of the Populists through the agrarian reform organizations like the Grange and its successors, the Alliances. But some Greenbackers also entered the Populist grouping, as did labor reformers and many others. The results can be seen in the variety of programs the Populists sponsored: a graduated income tax; government ownership and operation of the transportation and communication networks; the Australian secret ballot; an eight-hour day for labor; political devices like the referendum, initiative, and the direct election of United States senators; and—the most important in explaining the success of the party in western mining regions—free and unlimited coinage of silver at the legal ratio of sixteen to one. In time the silver issue became the lode-star of the party nationally as well as regionally.

The Populists organized a full ticket for the election of 1892 in Colorado, at the same time preparing to support the national ticket headed by James B. Weaver of Iowa, candidate for President. The party's candidate for governor, Davis H. Waite, who had moved to Colorado in 1879, was a man of considerable political experience. A Democrat before the Civil War, and then an ardent Republican, he had served in the legislatures of both Wisconsin and Kansas. In Aspen, he practiced law, became a justice of the peace and the first Superintendent of Schools for Pitkin County. He had also affiliated with the labor party there, serving as local secretary for the Knights of Labor.

Waite's conversion to Populism led him to newspapering. In 1891 he founded a radical weekly titled the *Aspen Union Era*. Unlike many of his followers, whose conversion to Populism extended only as far as the free silver plank, Waite was a thorough-going reformer, particularly convinced that the railroads needed curbing to provide protection for the state's consumers. He also consistently opposed all schemes of "fusion"—that is, alliances with Democrats espousing free silver, or any other such group. "The two [old] parties," he is quoted as saying, "have only seven principles, and they are 'two loaves and five small fishes.' "[3]

In the election of 1892, the Silver Democrats gained control of their party and brought it to the side of both the national and state Populist tickets, despite Waite's fear of "alien" support. The Republicans attempted to sit on the fence on the money issue. In so doing they gave a decided advantage to the Populists, for their out-and-out silver championing stood in stark contrast to the Republican attitude. The Denver *Times* might believe that "the average Colorado Populist is simply a Republican or Democrat with a grievance," but that grievance concerned silver, the state's major industry, and the election returns were indicative of its potency as a campaign issue.

Colorado, which had given its three electoral votes to Republicans Hayes, Garfield, Blaine and Harrison, in 1892 voted for Populist James B. Weaver. The margin was impressive: 53,584 votes for Weaver; 38,620 for Republican Harrison. On the basis of the 1890 census, Colorado was now entitled to two representatives in Congress, and these seats were filled by Populists John C. Bell and Lafe Pence. At home, Populist Davis H. Waite was elected governor. With the aid of Silver Democrats, his party would control the newly-elected state Senate, although the Republicans retained a one-vote majority in the state House of Representatives. Radicalism had triumphed at the polls. Time would tell how successful this new force in politics would be in promoting and legislating its reform programs.

21

The Silver Crusade

Eighteen-ninety-three proved to be an inauspicious year to test the tenets of Populism as advocated by Governor Waite. The price of silver continued to fall, threatening to carry with it the entire Colorado economy. Anxiety was evident in the Centennial State, but so was the determination to press ahead. The *Weekly Republican* (Denver) cheered its readers on January 4: "Colorado has such great resources that it cannot be crushed. The people have faith in the future and in their ability to develop its possibilities and bring about again an era of prosperity." But facts belied such rhetoric. Uneasiness appeared throughout the country, especially among eastern investors, who feared the demand for silver might force the government's hand and bring about inflation, based on the depreciated silver coin. Nor were they encouraged as the government gold reserves steadily diminished, nearing the $100,000,000 mark, then considered the magic point above which the gold dollars and the government were secure. By strenuous measures, the lame duck Harrison administration kept the amount barely above that figure until Grover Cleveland was inaugurated.

Other indications, meanwhile, pointed toward imminent financial distress. Commercial failures led banks into contracting loans; speculators began to dump their holdings on an already failing market. Many Colorado silver mines—some a decade or more old—were producing only lower-grade ores. Ominous news for the western silver interests arrived from abroad in June, when India ceased coining silver. The collapse of that market sent the price tumbling precipitately; in four days it dropped from eighty-three to sixty-two cents an ounce. For many Colorado mining and smelting men, this seemed the final judgment, dooming them to economic collapse. They declared that they would have to shut down their properties until a recovery in the price of silver allowed profitable operations.

Nor were the mining camps and smelters the only scene of trouble. These years brought a severe drought to the agricultural areas, making life perilous on every farm and ranch, and impossible on the Eastern Slope dry lands where homesteaders had followed the mythical "moving rainbelt," only to discover that they had settled where "normal" rainfall was practically non-existent. The ensuing exodus from the high plains added another problem to those generated in the mines and mills.

The full force of the economic crash hit the state in July. Within a few days twelve Denver banks closed, smelters stopped operating, real estate values tumbled, and every newspaper from the mining regions brought further disheartening reports of mine closures and business failures. Failures, dismissals, foreclosures—it all added up to a sad picture; even the Denver tramway suffered, as people walked to save fares. The *Rocky Mountain News*, July 20, tried to rally Coloradans, "Shoulder to Shoulder, men, while the war upon Colorado continues." And it did seem like a war to those involved, a war upon Colorado's major economic pillar—silver. The chance for more silver legislation was nil; in fact, President Cleveland was about to call a special session of Congress to repeal the Sherman Silver Purchase Act.

Governor Waite gave the state some unneeded notoriety in July, when he addressed a mass meeting of delegates from throughout Colorado who had convened to discuss the deteriorating situation. In analyzing the current conditions, he insisted that civil liberties would need defense, asserting that, "it is infinitely better that blood should flow to our horses' bridles rather than our national liberties should be destroyed." This phrase, taken out of context, received much newspaper publicity, particularly in the conservative press, and from it the governor earned the nickname "Bloody Bridles." Conservatives shuddered at the specter of such "rabid frothings" in this western commonwealth.

In Colorado, however, Waite's comments did not miss the mark by far. Blighting conditions covered the state and unemployment soared; many of those out of work drifted to Denver in the vain hope of finding work. Tensions mounted as the burden grew almost intolerable for the capital city, which provided tents and food but could not continue to support the growing numbers. Every possible effort was made to move them out of Denver; railroads reduced fares to the east and even carried the men without compensation. This relieved the immediate problems, but Denver was fully aware of the gravity of the times.

The Colorado Bureau of Labor Statistics, attempting to ascertain the depth of the crisis through a statewide mailing of questionnaires, issued a discouraging report on September 1. It listed 377 business failures, 435 mines closed (895 producing mines had been operating in late 1892), and over 45,000 out of work. Terms such as "gloomy, very bad, desperate, dull, depressing, blue and disheartening" were used to describe the general feelings in various towns. An unidentified person in Bent County wrote, "Low prices of farm products and scarcity of money have made the condition of our people a deplorable one." Another correspondent from Aspen bemoaned, "The situation is bad and couldn't be very much worse. If we get no favorable legislation, Aspen and vicinity is a goner."[1] Other estimates placed the number of unemployed at thirty to fifty thousand men, out of a total population of about 450,000.

The panic of 1893, of course, was not confined to Colorado; it just appeared to contemporaries that the state was the hardest hit in a nation-wide depression. Many interrelated factors had brought about the situation: the long-standing western and southern agricultural distress; overexpansion by industry, particularly the railroads; withdrawal of foreign investors; and a generally shaky international financial situation. Each of these contributed to the gold reserve drain and/or caused the panic, but a generation of eastern conservatives pointed its finger at a single scapegoat as being responsible, the Sherman Silver Purchase Act. Cleveland, who had hardly been inaugurated when the $100,000,000 barrier was broken, concurred. Repeal of the act now became the panacea, for which Cleveland called the special session of Congress in August.

No joy was generated in Colorado over such action. Although the act had never been comprehensive enough to answer the silverite demands, it was still the only positive legislation they had, and no mention had been made about altering the disliked tariff which, to gain votes, had been bracketed with the Sherman Act back in 1890. Now all the attention of the silverites was focused on one issue— prevent repeal; they were joined by other groups who favored inflation or had other interests in common. All the old arguments and slogans were resurrected to acquire new significance in the urgency of this crisis. Colorado's two Republican senators, Henry Teller and Edward Wolcott, both exerted themselves valiantly in the debate. Teller was particularly effective. Ordinarily less of an orator than many politicians of the age, he now phrased the Colorado position neatly:

> We are neither cast down nor dejected. We know what
> nature had done for us, and we know that a State with
> more than 100,000 square miles of territory, with
> more natural wealth than any State east of the
> Missouri River, will be able to take care of herself. . . .
> We do not disguise the fact that we are to go through
> the valley of the shadow of death. We know what it
> means to turn out our 200,000 silver-miners in the fall
> of the year. We know what it means when every man
> in the State who has a little money saved must put his
> hand in his pocket and draw it forth to keep from
> starving the families of the laborers of our State. While
> we are ready and willing to meet the occasion, yet if
> anybody on this floor thinks for a moment that we are
> to be destroyed, I want him to understand that the
> State of Colorado will be infinitely stronger and great-
> er than many of the States whose representatives are
> attacking us now by this infamous financial policy.
> But . . . the iron will enter our souls. We shall not
> forget that in this contest . . . the men with whom we
> have stood shoulder to shoulder in the economic battles
> heretofore have almost to a man forsaken us. We in
> the States of Nevada and Colorado have held those
> States in the Republican column for many a year. We
> have maintained a Republican majority in this
> Chamber by our votes. We have stood by our Eastern
> brethren who believed in the protective system. . . even
> when it would have been to our local interest to vote
> against certain measures.
>   But how much aid . . . have we had from them?
> How much sympathy? How much support? . . . We
> shall not abandon the faith that is in us. But when we
> shall be asked to yield our judgment to their judgment
> upon economic questions in the future, if we do not
> respond as promptly as we have in the past, I trust
> they will not be surprised.[2]

Words, however, could not stem the tide. Repeal was voted by Congress. Since the federal government had demonstrated, by Congress' action, an inability or unwillingness to rescue the state from its plight,

Governor Waite now determined to resort to "home remedies." He summoned the legislature into special session, and requested from the lawmakers a series of relief measures.

The Populist governor's program was doomed even before he presented it. Even many of his own party were unwilling to consider relief or reform measures, other than national silver legislation, the only Populist proposal that interested them. The Colorado legislators did agree to minor modifications of the state laws regarding debts and interest rates. But these measures were designed to remedy the effects and not the cause of the troubles.

Governor Waite's basic proposal was presented as an alternative to the federal silver purchases, which Congress had recently ended. He suggested that the state of Colorado use its sovereign powers to buy the silver mines in the state, sending the metal to Mexico where it would be coined into dollars. These would be returned to Colorado to be used as a local circulating medium. Waite's opponents refused to be convinced. They labelled the proposed coins "Fandango Dollars" and almost laughed the scheme out of the legislative chambers. In the process they managed to further brand the governor a radical—perhaps even an un-American—schemer. And the governor's problems had only begun.

While the legislative session had been busily disposing of Waite's relief proposals, serious news began to emanate from one prosperous area of the state. For years the repeated mining rushes had acted as a safety valve to drain off surplus population from less prosperous districts. Now this release was gone and only Cripple Creek appeared new and booming. Many men rushed there in hopes they could capture a share of the golden treasure; they found instead a surplus labor market, which favored only the mine owner. When the owners had posted notices of an extension of the daily working shift from the usual eight or nine hours to ten hours, sans an increase in wages, the miners responded with demands for a restoration of the former scale. This demand was augmented by one for recognition of the new union, the Western Federation of Miners, the first units of which had been organized in the district the previous year.

By the end of February, most of the mines and many of the smelters of the district were shut down. When the mine owners obtained a court injunction against strikers' interference, the union prepared for battle to keep non-union laborers from working the properties. Soon there were three armed forces in the area: the union, with armed headquarters on Bull Hill, near the town of

Altman; the sheriff and his deputies, representing El Paso county (of which Cripple Creek was a part until its separation in 1899 as Teller County), who seem to have acted largely on the part of the mine owners, and finally, the state militia, sent to the district on orders of Governor Waite.

Violence threatened from all sides; there were some beatings, and some dynamiting of mine properties. A battle between militiamen and the sheriff's posse threatened. But finally, with the governor, union officials, and responsible mine owners closeted for a conference on the Colorado College campus in Colorado Springs, cooler heads prevailed. The union and the operators signed a settlement, returning the workers' scale to what it had been, with promises of no discrimination against workers. The Western Federation of Miners had won its first Colorado strike.

Although the Cripple Creek strike was settled in June, 1894, it would become a major ingredient in the election campaign that fall. Waite and his Populist friends would receive the blame for the troubles in the gold camp, and all the rest of the miseries of that unhappy time. Besides the Cripple Creek affair, the "third party" would have to attempt to explain its role in the railroad strike of that summer, when Colorado had felt the effects of Eugene Debs' American Railway Union's battle against the Pullman Company, as well as the continuing economic depression, the unrelieved unemployment problem, and the affair of the previous spring known as "City Hall War."

Shortly after the legislative session had ended, early in March, 1894, Waite had become embroiled in a conflict with the Denver Fire and Police Board. In the years before reformers gained "home rule" for Colorado cities, the administration of the city of Denver had been made an integral element of state government. Governor Waite dismissed two members of the Denver Board, but they refused to be fired and locked themselves in City Hall, daring the Governor to physically remove them.

Sides quickly formed. Supporting the Board members were the police and fire departments, and the notorious Denver "bunco king"—Soapy Smith—and his friends. They armed themselves and prepared to defend the bastion of City Hall. Waite summoned militia units, which drew up on Fourteenth Street with cannon loaded and small arms ready to storm the citadel. Federal troops arrived on the scene, along with thousands of Denverites who moved downtown to watch the battle. They waited all day, while Waite hesitated to give the attack order. In the evening, the Governor commanded the militia to return to its barracks, having decided to take the issue to the courts. In time the courts would answer: a governor had the right to remove and replace officers, but not to use force to do so.

Besides the burdens of "City Hall War," labor troubles, and economic depression, the Populists had a further political liability in the campaign of 1894. The Democrats parted company with them, to run a separate slate of their own. The Republicans campaigned on promises to redeem the state from the odium and evil consequences of Populist "misrule." In the canvass that fall they won most of the state offices. They elected Albert McIntire governor and sent John Shafroth to Congress. The election was notable as the first in the history of the state in which women were eligible to vote. The year before, woman suffrage had been approved, making Colorado the second state (after Wyoming) to provide this equality between the sexes. The entrance of the ladies into the polling places, however, probably had not been a decisive element. Disenchantment with Populist Waite had become widespread enough to defeat the reformers without the women.

Ironically, the Republicans soon had an opportunity to demonstrate their ability to cope with a strike situation not unlike the Cripple Creek disturbances which had contributed so heavily to the Populist defeat in the election. In June, 1896, the Western Federation of Miners, enjoying an enviable reputation among workers after its Cripple Creek success, struck the silver mines of Leadville for a $3.00 wage scale. Leadville was in trouble enough, because of the falling silver price, and the strike soon turned the camp into a potentially explosive arena. As the miners left their jobs, they abandoned the pumps, and the mines immediately flooded.

The patterns of Cripple Creek were soon repeated. The owners concentrated their attentions on importing strikebreakers; the union struggled to seal off the roads and mines of the district to keep the "scabs" from coming in. When the union assaulted and fired ground-buildings of several mines that had managed to open with non-union workers, the owners hastened appeals to Governor McIntire for help. Soon the militia was on its way to the Cloud City. But this time there was a difference, for the troops' presence allowed the owners to reopen most of their mines with imported laborers. The strike dragged to a close. Not even Eugene Debs' extended Leadville visit during the struggle could revive support for the union. What the Federation of Miners had gained in Cripple Creek in 1894 during

Waite's administration, they partly lost in Leadville in 1896, under McIntire's regime.

During the summer of 1896, while the strike in the silver camp continued, national politics commanded almost equal attention among most Coloradans. The nation was rousing itself for the campaigns of a presidential election. The Republicans met in national convention in June in St. Louis. There the western silver interests in the party were completely submerged. When William McKinley won the nomination, on a platform espousing the single gold standard, Henry Teller led a group of western Republicans from the convention hall, pledging to continue the fight for free silver in other ways.

When the Democrats met in Chicago, it was quite another story. There the inflationists and silverites controlled a majority of the delegates' seats. They wrote a platform calling for free and unlimited coinage of silver at the sixteen-to-one ratio, and awaited the appearance of the man to lead their fight. Enthusiasm developed among Democrats to name Senator Teller to a place on the ticket, believing it would draw silver Republicans to the cause. But William Jennings Bryan masterfully swayed the convention, and it stampeded for him as its champion. To the *Rocky Mountain News*, July 11, 1896, Bryan was the very embodiment of the "new order of things, new issues, new men, new geographical groupings"; he was the man of the hour. Conservative Cleveland—Sherman Act repeal and all—was repudiated by his own party.

Normal political relationships in Colorado were immensely disrupted by such proceedings. Some Republicans, like Senator Edward Wolcott, tried to ride out the split, insisting on loyalty to the national ticket and platform *and* free silver. Their attempts were generally unsuccessful. Other Republicans could not support the national policies of the party. Led by Teller, they organized the Silver Republican Party, thereby opening the gates to a wild process of "fusions" with other groups. The scramble for alliances finally resulted in the Democrats and Silver Republicans joining in one state ticket, while the Populists and National Silver factions presented another.

Both combinations endorsed free silver and William Jennings Bryan. The McKinley Republicans tried to enlist support for the regular party's position and candidates, but with little success. The basic battle centered on the contest between the Democratic-Silver Republicans, championing Alva Adams for governor, and the Populist-National Silver group, led by M. S. Bailey.

The election of 1896—"The Battle of the Standards"—in both state and nation divided the country as it had not been divided since the fateful election of 1860. Silver was the token, but it represented much more than mere metal and mining. To the gold-minded Republicans who rallied around William McKinley, it was clear that "the underlying, fructifying element of this 16 to 1 movement is Socialism. It is the same old effort to get something for nothing."[3] To the ranks of the Bryan supporters, it was equally clear that nothing but victory in the election would save the country from crucifixion upon "the cross of gold." Passions mounted right up to the day of polling. Not the strangest of many strange episodes during the campaign was the action of Colorado's "Mr. Gold" himself— Cripple Creek's Winfield Stratton—who endorsed free silver and Bryan. In fact, Stratton went even further. He announced a public wager of up to $100,000 that Bryan would win, a possibility that the regular Republicans believed would immediately and substantially reduce his own personal fortune.

No one offered to take Stratton's bet. Coloradans, at least, seemed to have decided early that silver would triumph at the polls. When election day arrived, they marked their ballots in full expectation of success. The count showed that the state's voters, for the first time, had given Colorado's electoral votes to a Democrat. William Jennings Bryan had overwhelmed Republican McKinley in the state, 161,269 to 26,279. Alva Adams was chosen governor and his Democratic-Silver Republican slate captured the state offices. But, in the rest of the nation, events followed a different pattern. McKinley carried the majority of the states; Bryan and Free Silver had gone down to defeat.

In Colorado, some of the more optimistic people continued to hope for a return of free silver on into the new century that soon followed. But their hopes were destined to dwindle and, eventually, to die. Having fought a passionate contest over the issue once, the American people seemed content with their decision. Interest in the "money question" faded in the general prosperity of the United States in the years that followed. The death of silver left Colorado, however, with an inheritance of muddled political groupings and the challenge of building the state's economy on a foundation other than a government-supported market for the product of the silver mines.

22

The Good Old Days

Looking back on it now, it seems rather strange that the decade of turmoil and trouble described in the preceding chapters would later be remembered as the "Gay Nineties" and that future generations would harken back to the time when the nineteenth century ended and the twentieth century began as "the Good Old Days." The very fact, however, is useful to keep human history in perspective. The grimness of the decade and the sporadic eruption of economic and political problems into violence are likely to dim the equally important fact that men, women, and children found time to live their lives, enjoy entertainments and recreations, and even glory in the advances of their society.

The years from 1890 to 1914 and the outbreak of World War I in Europe were, in many ways, years of transition. While the economic structure of state and nation were constantly undergoing violent stresses and changes, and political battles enlisted high passions, quieter, less spectacular social shifts also were occurring. These changes eventually created patterns of social life more similar to contemporary concepts than had ever existed before.

Many elements of society, of course, remained unchanged. Many aspects of life in Colorado continued from earlier times. The process of filling up the land with people, for example, despite the closing of silver mines and other economic setbacks, continued apace. When the census counters finished their survey in 1900, a thirty per cent gain had been registered in Colorado's population, compared with a national increase of only twenty per cent. The state now counted almost 540,000 people. The vast majority of these people (eighty-one per cent) were native born whites. Only seventeen per cent of the population was foreign born.

While part of this increase in population is explained by the natural birth rate, immigration also added numbers. Neither labor difficulties, mine closings, nor ill-fated attempts to settle the dry lands of the Eastern Slope brought an end to the movement of people into Colorado. Some of these newcomers followed the old pattern of health-seekers, searching for relief from tuberculosis or other ailments. Others followed the even older trail of the treasure-hunters, finding employment in Cripple Creek, or Thomas Walsh's exciting new Camp Bird mine near Ouray, or in other mines or smelters. And during these years another old concept continued to attract immigrants—colony settlements.

Like the older colony endeavors, these group settlements varied greatly both in motivation and in success. A few examples will illustrate how various they were. In 1898 the Salvation Army established the enterprise known as Fort Amity in southeastern Colorado between Granada and Holly on the Arkansas River. This was one of several colonies the "Army" planted in various states. In many ways, the ghost of Carl Wulsten survived in the scheme, for the plans envisioned moving underprivileged laborers and their families from slum areas of eastern and midwestern cities onto a thousand-acre tract. Families would each be allotted ten acres of land and the necessary livestock and implements to re-establish themselves as agriculturalists. Thirty families from Chicago and Iowa, under the direction of Colonel Thomas Holland, settled the colony. Lands were plowed and planted to cantaloupes and, later, sugar beets. For a time Fort Amity prospered; the original 120 settlers were joined by others until 350 persons were resident in the colony. But exasperating problems also appeared. Particularly discouraging was the water seepage which deposited alkaline residue on the lands, making them unfit for farming. Before the end of its first decade, Fort Amity was closed.

A second experiment involved immigrants from the Netherlands. In 1892, the Holland American Land and Immigration Company of Utrecht dispatched a colony of 200 adults and children from Amsterdam to a site in the San Luis Valley. On arrival in Colorado, these immigrants were housed temporarily at Alamosa, and almost from the beginning ill-luck visited them. Diphtheria and scarlet fever broke out among the children, resulting in thirteen deaths. When it appeared that the company managers were totally neglecting them, the colonists organized their own government, but it could not reverse the ill-fortunes that beset the colony. Eventually most of the group moved from Colorado to farm lands in Iowa.

A third colony followed a different pattern. In 1893, during the midst of the economic ruin caused by the panic of that year, ten persons in Denver organized the Colorado Co-operative Company. From its inception, this was to be a utopian enterprise, where "equality and service rather than greed and competition should be the basis of conduct" and where Henry George's "single tax" concepts were to be practiced. The organizers issued 1,000 shares of stock at a par value of $100, with a maximum of one share, and one vote, allowed to each member. The company selected a site for its settlement on a mesa above the San Miguel River in western Colorado. By 1895 twenty members had established a town there, originally called Pinon, moved in 1905 and re-named Nucla.

They erected a saw mill, providing occupations for the colonists in the building of fruit boxes for the orchardists in the Uncompahgre Valley. A large irrigation ditch was later completed, making farming on a more extensive scale possible. Despite internal crises, the expulsion of dissident members, and litigation between the colony and the Denver group, the settlement survived and continued a slow growth. Nucla thus marks one of the successful colonial efforts in the state's history.

A fourth colony dated from after the turn of the century. In 1910-11, O. T. Jackson, a Negro, led seven families to a location between Greeley and Fort Morgan and established the settlement known as Dearfield. Inspired by Booker T. Washington's *Up From Slavery*, and encouraged by the then governor of the state, John F. Shafroth, the colony, like so many others, enjoyed an initial success. Sixty families moved to Dearfield during its first six years. But later discouragements brought ultimate failure. Since Colorado's Negro population had never been large—in 1900 it comprised only two per cent of the total population—no sizeable continuing migration to the colony from Denver or other towns was possible. Most of the Negro settlers lacked experience as farmers, and most of them also lacked the capital necessary to sustain themselves in years when crops failed. Gradually the families withdrew from the place, and today Dearfield is a near ghost-town, with no Negro residents remaining.

Through colony-type plantings and individual immigrants, Colorado's population grew. The state also hosted thousands of temporary visitors each year as more and more vacationers embarked on western tours to see what remained of the American frontier and to enjoy the climate and scenery of the Rocky Mountain West. Many of these tourists were introduced to Colorado through conventions of national organizations which scheduled assemblies at Denver. One of the largest of these was the 1892 conclave of the Grand Encampment of the Knights Templars. The American Federation of Labor met in Colorado's capital city in 1894; the American Library Association the following year; the first International Mining Congress convened there in the summer of 1897; the American Medical Association gathered the next year.

Tourists still arrived in Denver, or Colorado Springs, or Pueblo, by railroad and, for the most part, what they saw of the mountains was limited to the views from railroad coaches. In fact, excursion tours would continue for many years to form a major part of the tourist industry. But omens of a future change had already appeared. In the last year of the nineteenth century, the first motor car (electric) was seen on the streets of Denver. Two years later W. B. Felker entered his name in the history books by driving a steam-powered Loco-mobile to the summit of Pike's Peak, long before the famous automobile toll road had been constructed. By 1902 there were 200 vehicles in Denver alone.

Introduction of automobiles brought a new phase to an old problem of the area—transportation. The elementary components of the problem were obvious almost from the beginning. Colorado's area is not only large (eighth in size in the Union); it is also rugged in topography. Yet the same terrain that made road building expensive was what tourists in the days ahead would want to drive through to see the natural splendor of the Rocky Mountains. The relatively small population of the state would be called on to maintain long stretches of highways that were extremely costly to build and repair.

Much of the impetus for road building came from the automobile clubs which, in time, joined with the local group of the Good Roads Association. One of their major objectives was to have a highway commission developed within the state government. By 1908 this campaign had succeeded, but the battle had only begun. Appropri-ations for construction and maintenance of highways remained a continuing concern. One solution to the problem that gained favor in the early years was the old device of using convict labor to construct roads. In 1899 the state provided that all sentences (including life imprisonment) might be commuted for good behavior and work on the highways. Since the state experimented during this time with a short-lived abolition of capital punishment, there were increased numbers of convicts to be used. Under this relaxation of the penal laws a state road was constructed from Pueblo to Leadville, the Skyline Drive at Canon City was completed, and a road to the top of Royal Gorge was opened. These were actually designed as wagon roads, but the car enthusiasts welcomed their construction. Progress however, proved slow: in 1914 the state counted only 1,192 miles of improved highways, compared with 38,588 miles of unimproved roads. By that time 13,135 passenger cars had been registered under a new state licensing act.

In the years ahead automobiles would completely change the character of the industry of "tourism." New needs would revolutionize the entire enterprise of luring travellers to the state and entertaining them during their visits. But the growth of the industry did not wait for that revolution to end—in fact, during the "good old days," some innovations to encourage tourists were developed which form unique footnotes to the history of Colorado.

In the southwestern corner of the state, in 1906, a long campaign to preserve the relics of the Cliff Dwellers finally achieved its goal with the creation of Mesa Verde National Park. The crumbling edifices of the prehistoric Indians there had first been seen by white men, as far as records tell us, after the Mexican War when, in 1849-50, Lieutenant James Simpson reported seeing ruined structures in the walls of Mancos Canyon. A United States geological team surveyed in the area in the early 1860s, but not until 1874 was a scientific investigation of the ruins undertaken. Then the "Photographer of the West," William H. Jackson, led an official exploration and completed the first photographs of the dwellings.

The difficulty of access to the many areas of the mesa, and the wide expanse over which the ruins are to be found, has made discovery of new sites a never-ending process. The Jackson party, for example, missed many of the larger ruins, including Cliff Palace, which was not found until 1888. Then three cowboys, Richard and Al Wetherill and C. C. Mason, searching for stray cattle on the mesa top, viewed it from across a canyon.

By that time pot-hunters had begun searching and carrying away the artifacts they found. Amateur diggers and trained scientists, like Baron Gustav Nordenskold, the eminent Swedish archeologist, engaged in the sport. Nordenskold visited the mesa in 1891, taking with him when he left a collection of more than 600 choice artifacts that today are housed in the National Museum at Helsinki, Finland. The pot-hunters threatened to leave nothing but "ruined ruins," and various groups in Colorado began to agitate for preservation of the mesa and controlled, scientific exploration of its treasures. Particularly vigorous in this effort was the Colorado Woman's Club, and its "branch" organization, the Colorado Cliff Dwelling Association. After years of work, they and their allies persuaded the federal government to preserve the site. In 1906 Mesa Verde National Park was created.

Nine years later, in the northern part of the state, a second national park was set aside—Rocky Mountain National Park, encompassing within its 405 square miles some of the finest mountain scenery and unspoiled wilderness in the nation. Here again, vigorous Colorado sponsorship was essential to success, particularly the determined crusade of Enos A. Mills. Federal authority also created Wheeler National Monument, northeast of Creede, an area of picturesque lava and rock formations, in 1908, and Colorado National Monument, west of Grand Junction, a site filled with grotesque natural structures of red stone, in 1911. All these held great promise as tourist attractions for visitors to the Centennial State.

Tourists also were lured to Colorado cities where several of the towns seemed to have a passion to engage in "palace building." Pueblo businessmen, in the 1880s, had started the movement with the plans for what they termed the "Mineral Palace." Their idea was to call attention to Colorado's mineral resources and, of course, to provide a man-made structure for tourists to enjoy along with the natural wonders of the Rockies. This edifice was to be plated, both exterior and interior, with colored marbles, slates, mica, spar, pyrites and quartz. Statues of King Coal and Queen Silver would reside in the temple. Unfortunately, the committee ran short of funds, and changes in the blueprints were necessary. The masons and carpenters finished their labors in time for a splendid opening on July 4, 1890, as throngs flocked to see the "monstrosity" with its 25 highly ornamented domes.

Then Leadville decided to build a palace—this one of ice. In the winter of 1895 a mammoth frozen structure of Norman design, covering five acres, enclosed a ballroom, skating rink, restaurant, and carnival displays within ice walls eight feet thick. Leadville's high elevation and cold temperatures allowed tourists to flock to the Palace until the spring of 1896, making the Crystal Carnival of the Cloud City a great success.

Other towns called attention to themselves in other ways. The "festival" concept seemed well calculated to attract tourists. Each autumn the newspapers commented on one of these: "On Thursday . . . September 5, Watermelon day at Rocky Ford will be celebrated.

It is the oldest of the state's autumn festivals, and continues to hold an undiminished sway over the popular heart. The melon crop this season has been unusually large and of a fine quality, and tons of watermelon and cantaloupes will be on the ground for free distribution to the thousands of guests who are expected. The great Arkansas Valley fair will be in progress at the time, with a magnificent display of the products of that section of the state, and the big beet sugar factory will be open for the inspection of visitors. In addition to these attractions a special programme of sports has been prepared. There will be running and trotting races for large purses, a five-mile automobile race and a five-mile cowboy race."[1]

The Rocky Ford festival honored the melon; at Denver an even more grandiose festival each October from 1895 to 1912 honored silver, and the state's productivity in general, at the Festival of Mountain and Plain. This celebration lasted a week. Designed to some extent on the well-established New Orleans Mardi Gras pattern (with many of the floats for the first parades shipped from New Orleans and many artists imported from there to help in preparing them), the Festival of Mountain and Plain offered something of interest to everyone. Masquerades with street dancing, parades, the Silver Serpent Ball with a Queen of the Festival attended by the Slaves of the Silver Serpent, provided romantic illusions for escape from the grim realities of everyday life. During the week sporting events added thrills of participation and plenty of chances for "speculation." The holiday week in Denver provided a natural climax for a variety of contests—bicycle racing, fire runs, rock-drilling, and—for a time—rodeo riding.

The bicycle races were reminders of that short-lived era before the advent of the motor car, when the craze for bicycle riding had generated bicycle clubs throughout the state and the thrills of novelties like the "century rides"—that is, rides of a hundred miles a day—or the actual construction of the first part of a projected cycle path from Denver to Palmer Lake. The "fire runs," sometimes conducted at night as illuminated events, brought back to Denver the thrills of contests among volunteer fire companies racing as hook and ladder crews or hose companies to test their skill in laying hose or setting and climbing ladders. Denver itself by this time had "gone modern" by organizing a paid fire department. But throughout the rest of the state, the volunteer brigades still flourished, complete with handsome uniforms and a desire to capture the coveted prizes at state tournaments.

It was the rock-drilling contests, in many ways, which furnished the most exciting of the Festival's offerings. Competitive rock-drilling was a natural outgrowth of the state's most important industry. Local matches were held in the mining camps; counties then selected champions, often at Fourth of July celebrations; the county champions were sent to Denver to compete in the state finals at the Festival of Mountain and Plain. The rules governing the contests were rigidly drawn. Because the purses were large (as much as $5,000) and even larger sums were wagered on the contests, the judges administered the regulations carefully.

The contests lasted fifteen minutes. In "single-jack" competition a driller used a four-pound hammer and a three-quarter-inch drill; in double-jack performances one man handled a hammer weighing six to eight pounds and the other worked a seven-eighth-inch drill. The passing minutes were called out by a timer. Several elements contributed to victory: speed of blows (with incredible records sometimes attained; as many as seventy-five blows per minute recorded); care with turning the drill, for the hole had to be smoothly rounded; the sharpness of the drill; the type of stone used. Silver Plume granite, because of its hardness and uniformity, was usually employed. Given the right combination, a double-jack team could drill a hole thirty-two to thirty-five inches deep in a fifteen-minute contest.

The rodeo events of the Denver festivals were natural reflections of another state industry. These years, however, they were not as universally popular as the rock-drilling contests. The Colorado Humane Society, in particular, viewed the rodeo events with disgust, and often intervened to eliminate the more brutal aspects of the contests between men and beasts.

Generally, though, not only at festival time but all through the year, spectator sports were becoming more popular—and more highly organized. Horse racing, the favorite diversion of the area, dating back to the days of Indian pony races, took a more "eastern tone" after the organization of the Overland Racing Association in Denver in 1887. Buying and developing a track, the association attempted to "put Denver on the racing map." Baseball, too, began to generate some of the enthusiasm on the part of spectators that would make it the "great American pastime." On Memorial Day, 1902, nearly 11,000 persons attended games of the Western League, to watch the Denver team play the Milwaukee nine. And the athletic contests between teams of the state colleges brought out partisan spectators.

The sports pages of the newspapers give something of the flavor of the times—for example, this headline from 1901:

RAN FROM FIELD
BOULDER FOOTBALL PLAYERS ALMOST MOBBED
BY STUDENTS AT FORT COLLINS
CHARGED AGRICULTURAL TEAM WITH EMPLOYING A
PROFESSIONAL
AND THE TROUBLE FOLLOWED
GAME ORDERED FORFEITED AFTER AN EXCITING
CONFERENCE[2]

Forfeiting football games was by no means the only problem the colleges encountered during the "good old days." Some of the institutions were "growing up," but financial difficulties impeded their progress. In 1900 the University of Colorado reported a total of 433 students in the collegiate program and another 356 in attendance at the preparatory school. Eighty professors, instructors, and lecturers taught these students and tried to convince the legislature of the need for larger appropriations. "If the state would direct more revenue its way," sympathetic editors explained, "such as the universities of Kansas and Nebraska enjoy," the University would be an even better school than it was.[3]

The oldest Colorado institution for higher education—the University of Denver—was reportedly in debt some $165,000 in 1900, with some $15,000 due on back salaries of the faculty. In 1892 the first building at the college's new University Park campus was finished. But there were threatened foreclosures and rumors that the building would be turned into a glue factory. Only the valiant efforts of Chancellor Henry Buchtel and William G. Evans kept the school from such an inglorious fate. At Golden, where the School of Mines was building an international reputation among mining colleges, student discipline seemed to be a problem. In 1900 the students went on strike because a professor of descriptive geometry flunked all but twelve members of a class of seventy.[4]

In spite of the difficulties experienced by the established colleges, several new institutions were hopefully launched during these decades. The state-supported colleges—the University at Boulder, the Agricultural College at Fort Collins, and the School of Mines at Golden—were joined by two publicly-supported teacher training schools. In 1890 the residents of Greeley finally realized success in their campaign to house a college. They had lost to Fort Collins in a bid for the Agricultural College, and to Colorado Springs when the Congregationalists decided to locate their college. Now the state decided to establish its first normal school in Greeley. By 1911 the school's program had been expanded to a four-year, degree-bestowing curriculum and the name had been changed to Colorado State Teachers College. In answer to demands from Western Slope residents for similar privileges, the legislature established a second normal school at Gunnison.

In Denver, Colorado Woman's College was initiated in these years. Patterning it after such schools as Vassar and Wellesley, its founders hoped that the new school might be supported in an interdenominational fashion, with Baptists, Presbyterians, Episcopalians and Methodists all represented on the board of directors. The scheme for a "union" women's college failed to materialize, but the blueprints for a building had been completed and the structure itself erected. After some years of leasing to an Oddfellows Lodge, in September, 1909, the college enrolled its first students. The year before, the Presbyterians opened Westminster University north of Denver, a coeducational college which shifted to a boys' school in 1915 and, two years later, suspended operations.

The last in the list of new collegiate institutions had its origins considerably earlier. In 1883, at Morrison, near Denver, the Catholics had established the College of the Sacred Heart. Five years later it was joined with Las Vegas College, moved from New Mexico, on a new campus nearer the city. The first graduating class of three gained their diplomas and the institution that in 1921 would change its name to Regis College had sent its first graduates into the world.

Nor was education confined to ivy-covered halls. What today would be termed "adult education" had begun its tentative origins in a variety of fashions. The Chautauqua, with its lectures and moralistic entertainment, thrived with particular vigor at Palmer Lake and Boulder. State funds, in 1903, established a Colorado Traveling Library, so that books on wheels could find their way to the more remote areas of the state. The State Historical and Natural History Society, organized in 1879, successfully petitioned the general assembly for money to construct a museum building in 1909. Six years later residents and tourists could view the artifacts and souvenirs of Coloradans who, just a half-century earlier, had rushed to Pike's Peak to dig gold.

Finally there were the daily newspapers—the "poor man's college." Crusading editors still existed; Dave Day, for example, who moved his

Solid Muldoon from Ouray to Durango in 1892, or Colonel L. C. Paddock, who edited the *Boulder Camera* from 1892 to 1940. But personal journalism was fading from the scene. The invention of high-speed presses and linotype machines brought enormous expenses and necessary attention to both advertising and circulation statistics. This revolution of the "fourth estate" was dramatically apparent in the Denver newspaper scene.

Thomas M. Patterson owned the oldest paper in the state, the *Rocky Mountain News*. He had made the journal the best known daily paper in the region. But this pre-eminent position was threatened by the *Denver Post*, begun in 1892, purchased by Frederick G. Bonfils and Harry H. Tammen three years later. Bonfils and Tammen turned Denver newspapering into a three-ringed circus, or something worse. The *Post* owners intended to make money, if not set journalistic standards, and a wild long-lived era of "yellow" journalism descended upon the city as the rival newspapers jostled for supremacy. Luridness, sensationalism, and gallons of red ink were believed capable of augmenting circulation statistics. If journalistic standards—or even good taste—were the test, the "good old days" already belonged to the past.

23

The Era of Industrial Welfare

Despite the gloom broadcast over the Centennial State by the defeat of Bryan and Free Silver in 1896, new challenges in the opening decade of the new century were met with vigorous responses. The silver campaign had been predicated on economic intervention by the federal government; Coloradans had hoped that such outside aid would restore prosperity to the silver mines directly, and all of the state's economy indirectly. When the American voters rejected the silverites' scheme, they ended the hopes of many who had looked to Washington for help. Attention shifted to the local, internal scene. In the years that opened the new century, most Coloradans attempted to find their own solutions to their problems.

Yet paradoxically, it was largely forces reaching Colorado from far outside its boundaries that generated the major problems of the times. The new era of corporate organization had begun to invade the Rocky Mountain West, somewhat belatedly in comparison with its growth in more mature sections of the country. These new industrial organizations were designed to accomplish nothing less than nation-wide control within their specific spheres. Mergers and consolidations of companies into "trusts" continued unabated, despite state and national legislation designed to eliminate their more dangerous or obnoxious practices. The East and Midwest had been engaged in debate over these economic "states within states" for some years; in Colorado the problem only now began to take shape.

A natural accompaniment of the "trust" was the corresponding growth of labor organizations. As business enterprises grew in size, the old-type relationship between employer and employee vanished, leaving the individual worker shorn of his stature and even his importance to the employer. No longer owning the tools necessary for the creation of the product, finding their skills less important as the labor market expanded, the individual workers hesitantly began to join together to form unions that, like their business counterparts, swelled in size and in power.

The economic dislocations of the years from 1890 to 1900 undoubtedly helped to accelerate the growth of both trusts and unions. In the depression years, solvent corporations were able to amalgamate themselves with less fortunate enterprises, and to seek strength against future panics by tightening their control through larger, and perhaps more efficient, organization. Laboring men, desperate for work during the depression, often joined unions as the last resort to protect their wages, or even their jobs.

No more obvious omen of these changes was afforded Colorado residents than the reports that they read in their newspapers in the last year of the nineteenth century concerning the formation of what came to be called the Smelter Trust. Ore reduction in Colorado was big business; the smelters that handled the telluride gold ores of Cripple Creek alone comprised a major segment of the state's industry. The early Colorado smelters had been relatively small affairs, centered near the mining camps. Then, as coke replaced wood as the fuel for the reduction operations, many plants had been relocated, and others had been built, in cities where railroad transportation eased the problem of fuel supply. Denver and Pueblo both had become important smelting centers, although cities closer to the ore sources, such as Leadville and Durango, also were famous for their reduction works.

In the year 1899, on April 4th, Coloradans learned that this scene had been radically altered. On that day the largest smelting concerns, not just in the state, but across the country, had joined together to form the American Smelting and Refining Company. Capitalized at $65,000,000, incorporated in New Jersey, this gigantic combination encompassed the Colorado Smelting Company and the Pueblo Smelting Company plants at Pueblo, the Durango Smelter at Durango, the Omaha and Grant and the Globe smelters at Denver, and the Arkansas Valley and Bi-metallic smelters at Leadville, in addition to eleven companies located in other states. Coloradans also soon learned that one of the leading spirits behind the combination was H. H. Rogers, representing the interests of the Standard Oil Company, notorious in anti-trust circles as the first American trust.

Such a huge combination, with control of so many of the

country's smelters and reduction mills, presumably would be able to completely monopolize the smelting industry, arranging prices and wages at will. But, at the beginning, there was one important segment of the industry not included in the merger. The Guggenheims had not joined; their Pueblo smelter, the Philadelphia Smelting and Refining Company, along with their Mexican and Perth Amboy works, remained outside. Rumors suggested, that the Guggenheims had refused $11,000,000 for their properties. Financial experts guessed that the family decided that too many of the merged concerns were not particularly profitable. The thing to do was to wait until these had been reorganized or eliminated.

Meanwhile, with the Guggenheims aloof, competition might remain a feature of the industry. Actually, however, negotiations between the trust and the family continued. Within two years the monopoly was complete. In 1901 the Guggenheim brothers agreed to exchange their properties for one-third of the American Smelting and Refining Company's stock. They had also managed to purchase more than one-sixth of the trust's stock on the open market. They now controlled the trust.

Miners, mine owners, laborers in smelters and refineries, and consumers generally, found much to fear in the new trust. And if the American Smelting and Refining Company was the largest and most dramatic illustration of the new industrial concept, it was still only one of several examples of modern business enterprises. In the eyes of many, an even greater problem than size was the constant interjection of "outside" control and manipulation of domestic enterprises. As a frontier region, Colorado traditionally had looked to the East for investment capital; in fact, it still did and would continue to do so for many years. But a growing recognition that loss of control naturally followed outside investment alarmed many people, particularly the laboring men.

Anyone who had watched the dramatic battles for control of the Colorado Fuel and Iron Company at Pueblo, with its ore and coal mine properties in many areas, should have been aware of the trends of the time. John C. Osgood, who had headed the company since its formation in 1892, first engaged in a titanic struggle to retain control against the assaults led by financier John W. Gates. That battle had hardly been won when a second engagement pitted Osgood against E. W. Harriman. This time Osgood needed help, and found it in the financial strength of John D. Rockefeller and George J. Gould. But, "like the Briton of old, these two men . . . proved to be his Hengest and Horsa, for although he succeeded with their assistance in defeating his antagonist, he no sooner threw himself free from his grip than he found himself overshadowed by his allies, to whose influence he was obliged to succumb."[2] With Osgood's retirement a short time later, Colorado's largest single industrial enterprise fell to "alien" control.

The industrial empire of the Colorado Fuel and Iron Company extended into ore mines and coal fields, particularly the southern fields around Trinidad where the best coking coals in the state were found. Thus corporate, and often eastern, control of the coal fields accompanied the changes in ownership of the parent corporation. Much the same sort of consolidation occurred in other coal fields in Colorado. The railroads had been particularly responsible for opening the fields and they, too, were engaged in the game of mergers, bringing extensions of their consolidations to the coal mines.

The Panic of 1893 carried many of the region's railroads into receivership. On their emergence they took new, consolidated forms. An example was the Colorado and Southern Railway Company, incorporated in 1898. Into this new system were merged several historic Colorado roads: the old Colorado Central, the Denver Pacific, the Kansas Pacific, the South Park, the Denver and Fort Worth. Ten years after its formation, a further consolidation took place when the Burlington Railroad purchased the Colorado and Southern.

Another illustration can be seen in the history of General Palmer's Rio Grande railroad. George Gould, the eldest son of financier Jay Gould, in 1901, became president of the Denver and Rio Grande's board of directors. Gould owned the Missouri Pacific system and he now pushed consolidation of the Rio Grande and the Rio Grande Western (the Utah extension of the Colorado road) with his other properties.

Just how difficult it was for a newcomer to attempt penetration of an economic activity largely controlled by corporate groups with eastern offices was well demonstrated when David H. Moffat decided to build a new railroad in the state. Moffat's credit rating, seemingly, should have insured him success, for his interests in the First National Bank of Denver, and other banks, and his investments in the Denver Tramway Corporation, provided a large reservoir of proven financial strength. Added to that was the profit from his sale of the Florence and Cripple Creek Railroad, which he had owned. But there was immense hostility to his new scheme of driving a road—the Denver, Northwestern and Pacific—across Rollins Pass toward Salt Lake City.

Capitalized in 1902, at $20,000,000, Moffat's road reached Gore Canyon across the Continental Divide by 1907. Four years later Moffat died, his entire fortune invested in the endeavor and the railroad still not constructed to the coal fields of Routt County. Financial distress sent the road into receivership in 1912, leading to reorganization as the Denver and Salt Lake Railroad Company. Moffat had built the road over passes with extremely high grades, making operating costs almost prohibitive. This arrangement, however, he had always considered a temporary necessity. Some day a tunnel through the Continental Divide would be built to accommodate the trains. From 1913 onward, after it became apparent that the revenue from the railroad alone would never be adequate to finance a tunnel, state aid for the construction was sought.

Paralleling the concentration of economic activity on the part of corporations was the gathering strength of organized labor. In this, the Colorado scene again resembled the general development in the rest of the nation, except perhaps for the fact that the Colorado unions displaying the most "muscle" during the early years of the twentieth century did not include the American Federation of Labor. This union, under the leadership of Samuel Gompers, had become the foremost organization of skilled workers in other parts of the country. In Denver, and other towns, craftsmen had federated with the A.F.L. But other unions had organized the mining camps and smelters, where skilled workers formed only a small minority of the total labor force.

In the hard rock mining camps, the Western Federation of Miners had followed its early victory at Cripple Creek with rapid growth. In 1902, of the 165 local units of the Western Federation, forty-two were to be found in Colorado, and the headquarters of the union were located in Denver. The coal fields of the state, on the other hand, were considered the province of the United Mine Workers of America, a national, industrial union that encompassed eastern, as well as western, coal miners.

Certain conditions, more or less peculiar to the Colorado scene, contributed to the explosiveness of the contests between capital and labor during these years. One element was the quantity of unskilled labor demanded in the coal fields, gold mines, and smelting works. Newly-arrived immigrants and unemployed workers could always be found to recruit into the ranks of non-union workers during times of crisis. Thus, in many instances, the struggle between mine owners and labor unions focused on the question of hiring non-union labor—a struggle on the part of the mine owners to import such men and an equally desperate struggle on the part of the unions to intimidate, or drive off by physical force, the non-union workers.

Another contributing feature of the Colorado economy was the relatively large degree of "paternalism" inherent in the mining industries which the unions came to resist and which the mine owners hoped to continue. Mines had often been opened in remote, inaccessible areas, where companies had found it necessary to build boarding houses, company houses, and company stores in order to attract to these out-of-the-way places the laborers needed to fully develop their mines. Often, however, what began as a convenience developed into a method of control which mine operators enjoyed. The limitations of freedom for the worker who lived in company housing, bought his groceries at the company store, perhaps was paid in company "scrip" (that is, paper currency valid only at the company store) came to be resented, and one of the objectives of the unions was to help the individual worker untie the strings binding him to the company facilities.

An additional cause of stress in the Colorado industrial scene was the aftermath of the economic depression of the 1890s. While most of the rest of the nation bounced back into vigorous prosperity, the Colorado mining picture remained troubled. Cripple Creek gold found ready markets, but silver prices never recovered. Between 1900 and 1910 silver sold for prices ranging from fifty-two to sixty-eight cents an ounce, far below the nineteenth century levels.

Both capital and labor viewed the battle as occurring simultaneously on two fronts: legislative and direct action. Both sides engaged in attempts to persuade the General Assembly to enact statutes providing substantive gains, or defenses against their opponent's actions. Labor, for example, was able to succeed in its campaigns for the establishment of a Bureau of Labor Statistics (charged primarily with enforcing labor legislation) in 1887; an anti-blacklist law, in the same year; two statutes (1897 and 1899) allowing combinations of laborers to exist outside the conspiracy statutes, but *not* including the "right" of collective bargaining; a semi-monthly pay act, in 1901; and an eight-hour-day constitutional amendment, in 1902. Capital, on the other hand, convinced the legislature in 1899 that combinations of laboring men should not be allowed to deter, in any way, employees from continuing work if they wished, or to boycott or intimidate employers. In 1905 the legislature also met demands of employers in providing that picketing,

Playing tennis at 11,500 feet at the Tomboy Mine above Telluride.

or any method of obstructing or interfering with any worker's job, was illegal.

The legislative battles often did not end in the chambers of the General Assembly. Laws on statute books and laws litigated might be, and often were, two different things. Both capital and labor defended their legislation in the courts; one of labor's constant refrains these years was that the judiciary was composed of conservative, business-allied judges who constantly interpreted statutes for the benefit of employers and to the detriment of the unions.

The other arena in which the two antagonistic groups battled each other involved more direct action. The union, once established in an industry or mine, sought to convince the owners that, since its voice represented the will of the workers, it should be allowed to bargain collectively for the work contract. To gain such recognition from the owners became the primary objective of most of the unions during these years; once that was achieved, the substantive details of labor contracts—hours, wages, conditions of work—could be negotiated. The strength of the union, and in its eyes, the welfare of the worker, thus depended on the ability of the union leaders to force recognition and the process of collective bargaining.

Employers were equally intent in their refusal to recognize the legitimacy of the unions' demands for recognition. Denying completely the concept of collective bargaining, employers insisted that their relationship with each worker was an individual contract, and on that basis only would the workers' rights exist. The strike was the ultimate weapon (excepting here, the resort to violence which all too often characterized the ultimate method on both sides) in the hands of the union; by calling the men out on strike, it was hoped that the economic damage to the property owner would force him into negotiation. Owners tended to look upon strikebreakers, or non-union workers, as an equally valid weapon. Let the men leave their jobs; other workers would be glad to replace them, and the union would disintegrate.

An example of the fact that the underlying contest in many labor disputes of the era was the question of union recognition is the Telluride strike of 1901. The owners of the Smuggler-Union Mines refused to negotiate with the Western Federation of Miners in a dispute concerning the "contract system" of pay which the union wanted abolished. The operators hired strikebreakers on exactly the same terms denied to the union. Finally, Federation members literally drove the non-union workers from the district. While the violent methods employed captured newspaper headlines, the historical significance of the event rests on the fact that the question of working conditions or wages was less an issue than union recognition.

In between, or perhaps above, the interests of labor and capital stood the general public's concern. Theoretically, this interest could be represented best by the duly elected officials of the community and state. All too often, however, the local authorities proved impotent to deal with the violence engendered, and state officials tended to be prejudiced in their action. Sometimes the prejudice, suspected or real, was directed to the side of the union, as many citizens believed the situation to be in the Cripple Creek difficulties of 1894 during Governor Waite's administration. The unions believed, however, that more often the pattern of the company's call for protection and the penetration of the strike zone by the state militia (with an accompanying declaration of martial law) worked to labor's disadvantage.

While industrial warfare erupted in many incidents during the years from 1894 to 1914, a common pattern seemed to develop in most of the episodes. The specific complaint that led to the strike might vary; wages, hours, working conditions, or any combination of them (with the desire for union recognition usually involved as well), might be the spark which set off the clash. The outcome might also vary considerably, depending on the strength of the union, its ability to control its members, the determination of the mine or mill owners and their ability to keep their properties operating with non-union labor, and—often to a large extent—the climate of public opinion and the attitude and actions of the governor and the militia leaders. Notwithstanding these variables, the general patterns can be seen by examining, as illustrations, the strikes of 1903-1904 at Cripple Creek and the coal field disturbances of 1910-1914.

The years 1903 and 1904 were punctuated by outbreaks of labor difficulties. Denver smelters, Idaho Springs and San Miguel County mines were struck for eight-hour-day contracts; coal diggers in both northern and southern fields engaged in strikes. But it was at Cripple Creek that the bitterest and most violent of the crises occurred, and it was there that the Western Federation of Miners suffered one of its worse defeats. The Cripple Creek fields were still prosperous; millionaires continued to be made from the ores and their refinement. The field was also to become highly organized, on both sides. Under the dynamic leadership of Charles H. Moyer and "Big Bill" Haywood, the Western Federation had managed to enlist the majority of the fields' miners. The owners of the properties had organized a Mine Owners' Association. And in the governor's chair was James H. Peabody, a Canon City businessman destined to become a central figure in the conflict.

It was in the reduction works at Colorado City, where Cripple Creek ore was processed, rather than in the gold fields themselves, that the battle originated. The Western Federation of Miners, eager to complete its membership rolls among the mill workers, called out 3,500 Cripple Creek miners in a sympathetic strike to force union recognition in the mills. While these preliminary difficulties in the summer of 1903, on the surface, seemed settled, the trouble had only begun. Soon the mill workers were out again, this time to secure a reduction from twelve to eight hours of work a day. By the end of October the gold miners were also on strike again.

As the mine operators imported non-union labor from outside the district, the union formed armed camps to barricade the roads and railroads leading into the fields. After appeal to Governor Peabody, the Mine Owners soon welcomed an investigatory committee and, immediately afterwards, on its recommendation, the governor dispatched the militia to Cripple Creek. In his inaugural address in

1903, Peabody had pledged to protect lives and property. Those sympathetic to labor, however, felt that he shared the hostility of the business community toward the WFM and tended to direct the power of his office against the union.

Both sides recognized the value of propaganda in enlisting favorable public support, and soon more direct techniques appeared. The Western Federation published "scab lists" with pictures and descriptions of non-union workers in a clear attempt to intimidate the strikebreakers by inviting retaliatory measures against them. The mine owners instituted a card system, blacklisting members of the union from further employment in the district. Thus did the hard-won legislative victories, on both sides, fare in a direct-action contest.

As the strike continued it became warfare for unconditional surrender. Terror reigned in Cripple Creek as both miners and mine operators moved from intimidation and threatened violence to violence itself—raw and brutal. The climax was reached on June 6, 1904, when Harry Orchard, a professional terrorist in the employ of the union, dynamited the railroad station at Independence. Orchard had timed his foul deed to occur when a maximum number of strikebreakers would be present; his handiwork resulted in thirteen deaths and many more wounded among the non-union workers. While Orchard's identity as the perpetrator of the crime was unknown, each side blamed the other for the murders. The mine operators' strongmen now moved in, wrecking the office and plant of the *Victor Record*, a newspaper that had remained friendly to the union, rounding up strikers in wholesale lots, confining them in the infamous "bull pens" of the district, and driving many of them out of the camp. Seventy-three men were dispatched, under guard, to the Kansas border and there abandoned on the prairie.

Revulsion over the violence (for which the public blamed the union more than the owners), the continued support of the militia and the drastic employment of martial law, along with the help of the Citizens' Alliance, all led to an operators' victory. By midsummer, 1904, the strike was over, although the Western Federation of Miners never did terminate it officially. But the union had lost. The mine owners reopened their mines with non-union labor, and although the Federation would later attempt to re-establish its locals in the area, it never again assumed its former significance in Cripple Creek.

In the years that followed this terror-filled strike, Colorado would experience continuing industrial warfare. But not until 1914, a full decade later, did violence again reach such heights. Then the scene shifted, from the gold fields of Cripple Creek to the coal mines of the state. The miners' voice had also shifted, for the coal fields had become the organizing province of the United Mine Workers of America. For some years the U.M.W. had engaged in sporadic strikes in both northern and southern coal fields. These were now climaxed, in September, 1913, by an all-out effort. When the southern miners voted their strike, they listed as demands the recognition of their union, a ten per cent increase in wages, stricter enforcement of the Colorado eight-hour law, health and safety regulations, and the right to select their own living quarters, eating houses, and doctors.

John Lawson assumed the leadership of the Colorado units of the United Mine Workers. He was aided during the strike by the best talents among the union's national organizers, including the spectacular Mary Harris, the miners' "Mother Jones"—an eighty-two-year-old Socialist.

The usual pattern of events began to unfold. The mine operators, with the Colorado Fuel and Iron Company acting as spokesman for the group, attempted to open their properties with non-union labor; the miners bent every effort to keep the strikebreakers out of the fields. The owners hurried appeals to the statehouse; the governor sent the militia to the region. As the striking miners withdrew from the underground works, they formed tent colonies near the mines where they and their families were sustained by union funds.

Tension in the fields mounted and violence seemed inevitable as the soldiers sent to guard the properties, and the miners living nearby, scuffled with each other. The climax came on April 20, 1914, at Ludlow Station, eighteen miles north of Trinidad. When miners and militiamen tangled, the soldiers began to drive the miners from their tent colony which housed some 900 men, women, and children. Five miners and one militiaman were killed; but even worse, fire burned through the colony and it was later discovered that two women and eleven children had been burned to death, or suffocated, in what the United Mine Workers immediately labelled the "Ludlow Massacre."

Nor was this the end, for a ten-day war broke out up and down the coal fields, with "burnings, dynamitings, and murders" making up the pattern of the hour. Governor Elias Ammons now decided that the situation was beyond control of state officials and appealed to President Woodrow Wilson for intervention by the United States Army. By April 30 a contingent had reached Trinidad, ready to replace the militiamen.

With uneasy quiet enforced by the army, negotiations seemed possible. Arrangements were finally completed, ending the strike officially, in December, 1914. The United Mine Workers had to settle for something less than complete victory. The union was refused bargaining rights and withdrew from the Colorado coal fields, leaving the miners still unorganized. But the substantive goals of the miners were realized in large measure in protected conditions of work, better hours, and higher pay.

To replace the organization the miners were denied, the Colorado Fuel and Iron Company proceeded to establish a "company union" which purported to give a vehicle for voicing workers' grievances. Hailed by many at the time as a sensible compromise to the labor disturbances that had rocked the state for more than two decades, the "Rockefeller Plan" in time demonstrated the flaws that trade union men had always objected to in company union devices. Despite the generous welcome that greeted the plan at its inception, it proved in many ways a weak friend to the laboring man.

24

Water and Sugar

The gold mines and coal fields were not the only Colorado arenas of change during the first years of the new century; agricultural techniques were also being transformed. More quiet than their counterparts in industry and mining, the agricultural changes were no less important. Both in the irrigable river valleys and on the dry-farming regions of the high plains, innovations wrought an evolution in crops and methods of cultivation that made farming in the Centennial State quite different from what it had been before.

The most apparent change on the arid plains during the first years of the twentieth century was the renewed interest of homesteaders in conquering the challenges of the "Great American Desert." The new assault on the drylands was a much more sober, rational process than that which had transpired in the 1880s. Then enthusiasms had been buoyed by false hopes about shifting "rainbelts" and other impossible ideas. Now, as deserted homesteads that had been forsaken during early discouragements were taken up again, there was more understanding of the problems faced. Not all of the original settlers had moved out, of course. Some sturdy souls had managed to sustain themselves through the years of drought. But many of the farms had been left to revert to open range; many of the sodhouses and shanties had begun to tumble and decay. Now the exodus had halted and the land began to fill up again.

Pioneering on the high plains would always be hard work. There were no short-cuts to success. But to a people who had grown up with a seemingly inexhaustible supply of free land, and a nation that still supported a major part of its population by direct participation in agriculture, what was left of the frontier remained a place of promise to aspiring men, despite all the handicaps to success. American society still applauded the initiative and energy of the self-made, small farmer. From time to time the newspapers of the day would demonstrate that, although it was fading fast, the American dream of an agrarian yeomanry still existed. For example, readers of a Denver newspaper undoubtedly applauded one Henry Engle ". . . who lives near Kiowa . . . an example of what a man can accomplish on a homestead in a short time. Mr. Engle took up a homestead about six years ago, with a capital of one dollar and a half, and a family of eight children to support. He now owns his home, is out of debt, and has the following stock: Eighteen head of cattle, five horses, eleven hogs, and a lot of chickens and ducks."[1]

To help homesteaders like Henry Engle, the resources of several public agencies were available. Both the state Agricultural College and the federal government, through its Department of Agriculture, experimented with seeds, soils, and methods of cultivation. From these experiments certain drought-resisting crops were propagated; new strains of seeds were evolved; tillage methods were studied until those best suited to the arid plains were recognized and encouraged. Thus the techniques of scientific dry farming spread. The farmers plowed their land deeply after each harvest, and after each rainfall they pulverized the top soil by disking to keep it free from weeds and, at the same time, to prevent evaporation of precious moisture into the sponge-like atmosphere. Some farmers left half their soil uncropped, but tilled throughout the summer months, each year. Through the publications of the Department of Agriculture, the work of the state dry-land experiment station at Cheyenne Wells (dating from 1893) and the federal station at Akron (begun in 1907), and agencies like the International Dry Farming Congress (organized in Denver in 1907 and meeting in yearly sessions), the new approaches were publicized.

Since some farmers planted only half of their acreage each year, the dry-farming techniques emphasized anew the inadequacies of the national land laws. Larger expanses of land were an absolute necessity in the arid plains region. In 1909 the federal government, recognizing the situation belatedly, enacted the "Enlarged Homestead Act" which revised the basic homestead unit from 160 to 320 acres. In 1916 a further modification allowed a full section of land (640 acres) under the "Stockraising Homestead Act." This was intended to offer grazers an opportunity to obtain ranch lands in desirable quantity. Here again, however, the action was "too little, too late." More than a section was necessary to run even small size herds.

Nonetheless, the importance of homestead legislation in the development of Colorado should not be minimized. In the years from 1868 to 1961, the total final homestead entries in the state totalled 107,618, involving 22,146,400 acres of land. Only Montana and North Dakota totalled more entries; only Montana and Nebraska recorded more acres of land taken up.[2]

An indication of the effect of the land laws and the development of dry farming and ranch cattle industries can be seen by comparing population statistics from the 1900 and 1910 censuses. Kiowa, Kit Carson, Washington, Yuma, Lincoln, and Cheyenne counties all showed remarkable increases in population, ranging from 313 per cent increase in Kiowa County to a startling 635 per cent in Cheyenne County.

Significant changes also were taking place in the irrigable valleys of Colorado. The legal structure of the doctrine of prior appropriation had already been gained. Now irrigators called upon the state to allow the creation of "district" irrigation projects. Individual, or even community, efforts, in many cases, no longer were sufficient to construct and maintain the larger projects desired. At the same time, investors of risk capital, and corporations, which had been interested in financing such projects at an earlier time, had discovered that the dividends, if any, were slow in accumulating from such investments. Many of the privately capitalized irrigation projects built in the 1880s had gone into bankruptcy during the depression of the 1890s. The owners of the lands served by the canals and ditches took over the physical assets of the defunct corporations. Those farmers now desired legislation that would allow them to maintain and expand the systems.

The General Assembly responded in 1901 with the District Irrigation Law. It allowed land owners to organize irrigation districts capable of purchasing or constructing canals and reservoirs. These districts could issue bonds to raise capital and could levy taxes on the land served in order to pay off the indebtedness. The legislature also created the position of State Engineer, an official whose duties entailed ascertaining equitable and regular water distribution.

Increasingly, irrigators looked to the state as a partner, an arbitrator, and a patron of their institutions. And the state seemed ready to accept that relationship. This became very apparent in 1901 when Kansas, on behalf of some of its citizens, brought suit against Colorado and sixteen large users of water from the Arkansas River. In the legal proceedings that followed, the state of Colorado took the initiative in preparing the defense of both the state and the private defendants against the Kansas charges. The *Kansas* v. *Colorado* litigation over the distribution of water flowing in the Arkansas River also demonstrated the fact that water was becoming scarcer in the West. Where once individual towns or men would argue about the equitable division of stream waters, now states were engaging in similar controversy. The importance of the litigation was apparently understood from the beginning; the *Rocky Mountain News* called it "the most important case ... that ever reached the supreme court from a state west of the Mississippi."

The justices of the Supreme Court of the United States undoubtedly learned a lot about western agriculture before they had finished considering the Kansas-Colorado case. Kansas had been settled from its eastern edges inward, and its earliest settlers had enjoyed natural rainfall sufficient for cultivating their crops. As a result, the state had followed the common law rules of riparian rights. Colorado had rejected the older law and had adopted the doctrine of prior appropriation. Thus two different systems of state water law collided.

Kansas claimed that its western lands were deprived of their natural waters from the Arkansas River because Colorado farmers and industries were diverting the entire flow of the river. Colorado argued that, under its prior appropriation code, the earliest users of water had preference and that "thousands of cubic feet of water were used from the Arkansas ... by farmers in Colorado ... before there were settlers enough in western ... Kansas to build an irrigation ditch, and when their people within the line of sufficient rainfall were boasting that they did not need to irrigate to grow crops ... the water they rejected was appropriated by the farmers along the base of the Rocky Mountains."³

The national government also became interested in the case. In fact, because the value of federal lands in the two states might be affected by the Supreme Court's decision, the federal government intervened in the suit. The question of national power, expressed through either the executive or legislative branches, as a possible regulator or mediator in dividing interstate river waters, was considered in the arguments. But the Supreme Court rejected the suggestion. In their opinion, handed down in 1907, the justices specifically asserted that each state had complete control of the waters within its boundaries. This not only denied federal control of interstate stream waters; it seemed to give an advantage to Colorado, for Kansas was denied relief on the basis of the evidence presented at that time. In the future, should new evidence arise, Kansas could reopen the suit.

But the opinion of the court reached much further than the single case then under consideration. The court, in effect, announced itself to be the only agency of the United States government that could become an active agent in deciding such contests. In order to provide justice in quarrels between states, the court would undertake to determine similar controversies in the future, thus originating what came to be called the "doctrine of equitable apportionment." The Supreme Court seemed to say that, regardless of the water law practiced in different states, each state had a right to some of the water in the rivers within its boundaries. In essence, the tribunal struck a severe blow at the concept of a state disposing of all the water within its borders, no matter how old the appropriations from the stream might be. Warning flags were now up; the Supreme Court would umpire future quarrels between states over irrigation water.

Colorado irrigators discovered in time what the new doctrine could mean in actual practice. The Laramie River flows north from Colorado into Wyoming. When Colorado irrigators in the Poudre Valley, on the Eastern Slope, began to construct a new tunnel to divert water from the Laramie River, Wyoming residents claimed that the additional diversion would interfere with their appropriations. The argument terminated in a law suit, *State of Wyoming* v. *State of Colorado*, instituted before the Supreme Court in 1911, with a decision delayed until 1922. There was no quarrel here between two different systems of water law; both states recognized the doctrine of prior appropriation. Rather, the argument concerned the quantity of water used by residents of the two states.

In the Kansas litigation, the Supreme Court had announced its "equitable apportionment doctrine," implying that the substantive decision as to which state got what water might fall within the jurisdiction of the court later. The justices now proceeded, in the Wyoming case, to act on their former suggestion. After considering the evidence, they awarded the quantity of water they determined had been appropriated by Wyoming users to farmers there, allowing the new Colorado irrigators the remainder of the unappropriated flow, or not more than 15,500 acre-feet a year.

The handwriting was now plainly visible. Colorado might enjoy the fact that a host of major rivers—the Colorado, Rio Grande, Arkansas,

North and South Platte, and many of their tributaries—originated within the state, but in apportionment of water between Colorado and its sister states through which the rivers flowed, the Supreme Court would determine equity. More than that, the costly process of defending the state's rights in litigation before the court would continue to drain its finances and energy. No wonder these decisions provided great impetus for the negotiation of interstate compacts or "treaties," by which the states themselves, with approval from the federal government, divided the flow of the interstate streams.

But while Colorado, and other western states, soon indicated that they preferred to bargain around the conference table for their share of interstate waters, casting off judicial arrangements, those same states eagerly invited the help of the federal government in other aspects of reclamation and irrigation development. The quarrels between states over water were only another indication of the growing scarceness of the precious resource. The shorter the supply of available water, the more complex and costly became its proper management and use. By the turn of the century many westerners had come to anticipate a partnership with the national Department of the Interior in water affairs.

By that time it was obvious that large projects, especially those involving transmontane carriage of water, would need more financial stability than either private capital or state funds could offer. The era of huge dams and reservoirs would never appear if left to private investors, who shunned such projects because of the long period of waiting for dividends. State efforts at reclamation had also been less than successful. There had long been hope that the federal government would, in some fashion, encourage reclamation of desert lands. When Congress legislated the Desert Land Act in 1877, something of a beginning had been made. Purchasers of arid land from the public domain, under the terms of that act, were allowed advantages in their contracts denied to ordinary homesteaders. Specifically, larger areas could be engrossed by an individual. But the legislation had not furthered reclamation greatly.

Seven years later Congress again responded to pleas for a comprehensive program of reclamation. The Carey Act of 1894 attempted a policy of federal-state partnerships. Up to 1,000,000 acres of arid land in each western state was to be separated from the public domain and given to the states as a reward for their causing irrigation and occupation of the land. No federal funds were involved; the initiative was left to each state. But the states proved reluctant to join the partnership. Out of a total possible 7,000,000 acres, only about 300,000 acres were actually withdrawn, demonstrating that something more tempting in the way of federal aid would have to be arranged to generate a vigorous policy of reclamation.

Thus far the record was discouraging, but those who believed that western deserts were as legitimately a congressional concern as sand-filled eastern harbors or tariff-begging midwestern manufacturers, continued to press for federal aid. When, in 1901, Theodore Roosevelt became president of the United States, they recognized in the new chief executive a friend of the West, of conservation, and of reclamation, too. They were not disappointed in their anticipations. Congress now enacted, and the president signed, the epoch-opening statute of 1902–the Newlands Act.

This legislation provided that from a Reclamation Fund, to be amassed from the proceeds of the sale of public lands in sixteen western states, surveys, construction, and maintenance of irrigation works for storage, diversion, or transmission of water were to be constructed. The projects approved by the Department of the Interior were to be repaid by assessments on the reclaimed land in the form of use fees for water delivered. The payments would create a revolving fund from which the initial costs of other projects could be financed. Later, other legislation would bring more dollars to the fund from oil and mineral royalties. And, in 1911, the Warren Act expanded the concept by allowing surplus waters from federal projects to be sold for use on land already irrigated, but suffering from insufficient water. This legislation was extremely significant for many parts of Colorado where irrigation had been instituted early, but enough water for full agricultural development had never been available.

As soon as the Department of the Interior, under the terms of the Newlands Act, established the Reclamation Bureau, one group of Colorado enthusiasts was immediately ready to present plans for a project. On the Western Slope, in the valley of the Uncompahgre River, there existed a situation ready-made for a pilot undertaking. The original settlers in the valley had anticipated that the waters of the river would be sufficient to bring some 175,000 acres under irrigation, but they had been sorely disappointed. By 1902 only 30,000 acres were actually being watered and often there was insufficient river flow to adequately irrigate those acres.

The Gunnison River flows parallel to the Uncompahgre River, just across the Vernal Mesa; the two streams join at Delta. But the lands

to be irrigated were above rather than below Delta. Unlike the
Uncompahgre Valley above Delta, the Gunnison Valley has little land
suitable for irrigation. From these circumstances arose the scheme of
tunneling through Vernal Mesa to bring Gunnison water to the
Uncompahgre Valley.

The scheme was no novelty in 1902. The Colorado legislature had
been convinced of the practicability of the idea and had appropriated
$25,000 to build a tunnel, but that sum had proved hopelessly small.
By 1900 it was fairly well agreed that the engineering and financial
resources of the state were inadequate for the task. Thus it was
natural to turn to the new Reclamation Bureau for aid. That agency
also was convinced of the feasibility of the plan and agreed to
undertake the construction and maintenance of the diversion project,
if the present and future residents on the irrigated lands paid for its
costs through water use fees.

Under Bureau approval, construction began in 1904. A decade and
a half were required to fully complete the 5.8 mile tunnel and the
extensive network of canals. But diversion of water did not wait for
completion of the entire system. By 1910 water from the Gunnison
River reached the Uncompahgre Valley. Problems would plague the
residents there for years to come—construction costs had far
exceeded estimates; use fees for water required several adjustments;
lands included in the original plans proved too alkaline, or otherwise
unfit for irrigation. But despite all the problems, the project was, and
is, memorable as the earliest of the federally-sponsored reclamation
endeavors in Colorado.

Northwest of the Uncompahgre Valley, in the vicinity of Grand
Junction, the Reclamation Bureau pioneered a second Colorado
project. Here again, private enterprise had begun reclaiming arid lands
as far back in time as the original white settlement of the valley in
the early 1880s. In fact, the irrigation facilities were quite highly
developed, with almost all the bottom lands of the Colorado River
already under ditches and initial endeavors at pumping water to the
higher lands underway. In 1902 surveys were made for the possible
expansion of the system, but local interests then were adverse to
seeking federal aid, preferring continuation of development through
private investment. Within the decade, however, the slow progress
reversed sentiments, and the residents requested the Bureau to
intervene. After completing additional surveys, the Bureau constructed a dam and canal system on the river which brought water to
otherwise inaccessible lands. The major canal stretched sixty-two

miles along the valley; by 1917 the project became operable for water deliveries.

One of the many reasons for excitement over the expansion of established irrigation systems, and the building of new facilities, was the interest of Coloradans in the prospects of sugar beet culture. Probably no other single agricultural advance in the state, during the first part of the twentieth century, generated more enthusiasm. Yet the story of Colorado sugar beet dreams was far from new. Antiquarians take pleasure in pointing out that decades earlier, at the time when petitioners requested land grants from Mexico, the men who were first given the Maxwell Grant had suggested that one of the advantages arising from their patent would be the cultivation of sugar beets on the land. They received the grant, but evidently made no effort to grow the beets.

Then, shortly after the gold rush of 1859, pioneer farmers in the valley of Clear Creek grew some beets which were analyzed as of high quality and high sugar content. What was needed to develop a full-scale sugar industry was a factory to process the beets. The *Greeley Tribune* predicted that "a fortune awaits the man, or men, who will erect a sugar factory."[4] For a time it was hoped that the state would play patron; in 1872 a bill granting a subsidy of $10,000 to the first beet factory in the territory failed in the assembly by one vote.

The faculty of the agricultural college at Fort Collins continued to encourage the industry. In 1892 a Sugar Convention in Denver aroused interest in that city's chamber of commerce. Together with the college and the federal Department of Agriculture, the Denver Chamber distributed beet seed to farmers, with promised prizes for the best results. The fact that at both Grand Island, Nebraska, and Lehi, Utah, successful beet plants were operating undoubtedly stimulated interest. In fact, Western Slope farmers raised beet crops and sent them to Lehi for processing before a Colorado factory had been built. But if a fully developed sugar enterprise was to succeed, factories nearer the fields were essential in order to keep transportation costs from devouring all the profits.

A number of individuals merit special attention as originators of the Colorado sugar beet industry. Charles E. Mitchell and Charles N. Cox were particularly influential as promoters of a factory in the Grand Junction area. They succeeded in gaining a grant of funds from Mesa County to encourage the enterprise. John Campion, who had been fortunate in his mining activities in Leadville, supported the

Grand Junction and other factories. Charles Boettcher became interested in beet sugar on a trip to Germany. He brought seed back to Colorado for distribution to farmers, finding excellent results in the irrigated regions of the South Platte Valley. He and Campion would work together in factory-building there. In the Arkansas Valley, George W. Swink of Rocky Ford, better known in Colorado agriculture as "the Father of the Cantaloupe," was a major exponent of the new industry.

The first sugar beet factory was erected in Grand Junction in 1899 by the Colorado Sugar Manufacturing Company. The returns were not as exciting as expected, and the plant continued somewhat disappointing after 1913 when the Western Sugar and Land Company purchased it. Results more closely matched expectations in the Eastern Slope installations, beginning with the American Beet Sugar Company's plant at Rocky Ford in 1900 and the National Beet Sugar Company's factory at Sugar City the same year. In 1901 the originators of the Grand Junction plant opened the first South Platte Valley factory at Loveland. The Greeley and Eaton facilities opened in 1902 and those at Fort Collins, Longmont, and Windsor the following year. Not all the towns were open-armed in welcome; some Greeley residents, for example, protested against the factory there because they feared that it would turn their town into an "industrial center."

In 1905 most of the South Platte Valley factories were consolidated in ownership and management into the Great Western Sugar Company. The leaders of this New Jersey chartered corporation, capitalized at $20,000,000, included pioneers in the state's sugar industry like Charles Boettcher and Chester Morey, and others like H. O. Havemeyer of the American Sugar Refining Company. Other Colorado men, that same year, organized the Holly Sugar Corporation. Its Colorado properties were centered, at first, in the Arkansas Valley at Swink (1906) and Holly (later moved to Wyoming). Later incorporated under a New York charter, the Holly Company bought and built factories in California, Wyoming, and Montana, as well as a plant at Delta which opened in 1920.

The "sugar vision" was so exciting those years that hardly a Colorado community escaped the infection of planting or building a processing factory. In 1911-1913 the "virus" spread to the San Luis Valley. Factories at Center, Del Norte, and Monte Vista all proved short-lived ventures. But despite these and other failures, many of the plants continued their early successes. The rapidity of the industry's growth can be seen in the production values, which rose from a mere $100,000 in 1899 to $3,600,000 in 1901. By 1909, with 79,000 acres devoted to beet cultivation, Colorado became the leading producer among the states. The high altitude, cool weather, and controlled irrigation of the state's fields gave the industry elements that would continue the Colorado sugar industry among the first ranks in the nation. Beets gave Colorado farmers a fine cash crop, even though the continued prosperity of the industry would always rest upon tariff makers in the national capital and their willingness to protect the industry from foreign competition.

25

The Progressive Era

The history of almost any state in the American Union during any decade or generation reflects, in miniature, the history of the nation itself. While local conditions and traditions distort the national image somewhat, it is only in unusual cases that the development within one of the American commonwealths fails to mirror rather accurately the larger scene of national development. Certainly this is true of Colorado during the years from 1900 to 1920. While Ludlow massacres fortunately did not occur in repetitious fashion in the sister states, and while transmontane reclamation projects or sugar beet factories could be counted as tokens of regional, local concern, the general pattern of events—and particularly the general aspirations of the population—paralleled those of the rest of the country.

The two decades that ushered in the twentieth century marked the high tide of reform sentiment throughout the United States. Many generations of Americans have been concerned with reforming squalid, corrupt, or evil conditions around them, but few generations have conducted such a vigorous battle on so many fronts at the same time. Few aspects of American life escaped the attention of the reformers; social injustices, economic discriminations, political corruption were all within the compass of their attention. Often these areas were merged, for one of the most immediate concerns of the reformers was the alliance (unholy in their eyes) between entrenched economic interests and the political machinery of government. But to many, this was only the first plateau on which to wage the battle. Once the political institutions had been cleansed and returned to the people for their own use, then social and economic injustices could be legislated away.

As in many other states at the time, the reformers in Colorado waged their first campaign against corruption in local government. From this opening battle emerged leaders for the larger campaigns to reform the state and, eventually, the nation. This was more than a mere contest between entrenched holders of city hall vs. disgruntled "outs" in local politics. The major fight in Colorado centered in the only large city in the state—Denver—where almost everyone admitted public affairs were far from pure.

The reformers in Denver did not give their allegiance to either or any political party. They had long since grown disillusioned with promises by professional partisans that clean, democratic government would result from their being placed in office. For too many years Denverites had witnessed alliances between the franchised utility companies that provided tramway, electric, gas, and other services to the city, and the men who inhabited the city hall offices. For too many years elections in Denver had been degrading scenes of corruption, vote-buying, and small armed conflicts between active political partisans. Above all, for too many years Denverites had experienced the unhealthful situation in which state governors and legislators controlled directly the bureaus and boards of the municipality, thereby compounding the evils existing in state and local political life. "City Hall War" was continuous, with dramatic episodes like the battle of Waite's regime in 1894 merely emphasizing the difficulties.

Denver reformers concocted a scheme for action, beginning with a constitutional amendment to allow Denver the right to establish "home rule." This would divorce local politics from the vortex of state affairs. Then, in order to eliminate unnecessary expense, and to simplify the government of the municipality, they proposed that the City of Denver and the County of Denver be merged into one body politic, with provision for annexation of other areas in the future. In 1904 they presented their plan to the voters, who approved the constitutional amendment in the first major victory for the reformers, or as they soon called themselves, the "progressives."

This first progressive victory led to varied results. For some of the reformers, it was only the first step in a high ladder that would eventually lead through state reforms to national and even international goals. To others, home rule for Denver was the ultimate goal itself. It is easy to smile at the utopian dreams of those who believed that once the *procedures* of government had been changed, all would be well. We now know that these same men would soon discover that the battle never ended; that when reformers grow negligent, corruptors again appear. Nonetheless, some notable achievements seemed to result from the successes of the Denver progressives. Robert W. Speer became the first mayor of the newly-organized City and County of Denver. His administration would greatly change the city's physical appearance. Denver's park system was expanded, with new boulevards and parkways laid out, viaducts built and storm and sanitary sewers constructed. The old city dump along the streambed of Cherry Creek was cleaned up; the gulch was walled and parked. Construction of the city auditorium was begun, to be near enough completion in time to host the only national political nominating convention that ever gathered in Denver—the Democratic convention of 1908. In addition, the basic plan of Denver's Civic Center was blueprinted, aided greatly in design by Henry Read, the president of the newly-formed Denver Art Commission. And to the west the city began to acquire the areas of mountain lands that would form the nucleus for the future municipal mountain park system.

Despite the accomplishments of the Speer administration, his opponents asserted that the mayor and his followers manipulated elections and were too closely allied with the corporations—that Speer was, however civic-minded, still a "boss." Moreover, Assessor Henry J. Arnold, who had come into office in 1910 as a Speer Democrat, charged that Denver's assessing system was discriminatory and riddled with inequities. Opposition to Speer crystallized late in 1911 when he summarily removed Arnold from his position. In the election of 1912, Arnold, running on the Citizens' ticket for mayor, defeated the Democratic candidate (Speer had chosen not to run) in a seeming repudiation of the mayor's policies. Regardless of the fact that many of Speer's methods were protested by reformers, however, the physical improvements of his administration were impressive. Other changes, less apparent, were also inaugurated. Two of these, in particular, would win the city praise and provide untold benefits for the citizens of Denver. Neither was so much a part of the reformers' plans as the result of the climate of the times which allowed for experimentation in human welfare. Both were largely the work of single individuals who came to personify their institutions. The earlier Denver reformers had operated as a group; men like Thomas S. McMurray, who was elected mayor of the city in 1895 on a reform ticket and re-elected in 1897, and John A. Rush, and J. Warner Mills, and many others, had shared the work and the praise for the governmental reforms. Now, in the years that followed, Judge Ben Lindsey and his Juvenile Court and Emily Griffith and her Opportunity School both translated progressive ideals into actuality.

The fame of Judge Ben Lindsey's experiment in social justice for young offenders spread far beyond the boundaries of Denver and Colorado. Convinced that juvenile offenders would respond to reformation more quickly if treated separately from adult criminals, Lindsey, in 1907, succeeded in gaining the establishment of a special court for young people. Within a short time, he had made his Juvenile Court a shining example of corrective institutions. His own deep interest in the problems of young wrong-doers in the increasingly complex industrial society helped to sustain the experiment during numerous attacks on it by those who feared that the "misty-eyed" reformers had gone too far.

Equally impressive was the early success of Emily Griffith's Opportunity School. Emily Griffith, a public school teacher in Denver, enlisted the aid of school board members, newspapers, and reformers generally, in her campaign to establish an educational institution designed to meet the needs of all persons—children and adults alike—who for one reason or another did not fit the scheduled routine of ordinary classrooms. Opened in 1914, the Opportunity School combined many different functions: there were classes for adults who desired to learn such rudimentary subjects as the English language or simple arithmetic; there were shops and training rooms for those who wished to learn trades; night classes and day classes in both academic and vocational studies provided an all-inclusive opportunity for self-improvement. Like Lindsey's Juvenile Court, Emily Griffith's pioneer effort in "continuing education" remains in Denver today, a living monument to the humanitarian and idealistic dreams of its originator.   .

Denver, of course, was not the only scene of reform. Other Colorado cities also caught the pervading spirit of "progressivism," responding with experiments in new forms of local government and new campaigns for civic improvement. In fact, it became increasingly apparent during the first decade of the twentieth century that reform ideas were looked upon with favor by many of the Colorado voters. This being the case, partisan politicians began to seriously consider the feasibility of converting their organizations to vehicles for progressive action.

Not all of the reformers' ideas were that easily handled, however. One, in particular, instilled fear rather than hope among practicing politicians. That was the concept of legislating a prohibition of the manufacture or sale of intoxicating liquor—a concept that gained many adherents during these years. Prohibition was fitted, in many ways, to the pattern of progressive thought. After the prohibitionists changed their emphasis from voluntary action to legislation, they tended to follow the same pattern as did many reformers, who planned to use the public power to enact social legislation.

The anti-liquor forces took a long time to unite their various programs. Groups like the Anti-Saloon League and the Women's Christian Temperance Union had always believed in gaining voluntary adherents to their cause. The Prohibition Party, on the other hand, had pursued a policy of direct legislation. Although the Colorado General Assembly had enacted a "local option" law, the Prohibition Party's efforts—continuous since the 1880s—to achieve statewide proscription of liquor had never met success. Finally the party came to believe that only a constitutional amendment, initiated by petition under new procedures allowed in Colorado, would bring victory.

In 1912 an amendment to prohibit the manufacture and sale of liquor was submitted to the electorate. The voters defeated the proposal, but that defeat stirred the various groups to common action. Submerging their differences, they sponsored another amendment two years later. This time the voters answered the question of ratification affirmatively, approving the experiment in social engineering, despite a two-to-one rejection of the amendment in Denver. The "wet" forces in the capital city threatened to use the new "Home Rule" prerogatives of the city to escape the effect of the law, but on January 1, 1916, prohibition became the rule in Denver and all of Colorado.

The liquor question had frightened partisan politicians, partly because the emotionalism on both sides of the issue was difficult to gauge, and partly because it tended to blur other issues and confuse the voters' allegiances. But there were other reform concepts of less danger, and in time many progressive issues became major ingredients of the campaigners' trade. The general atmosphere surrounding partisan politics in Colorado at the turn of the century probably contributed to the willingness of politicians to embrace progressive ideas. Since the last decade of the nineteenth century, when the silver question had burned brightly and fusions of factions had created a variety of temporary alliances, Colorado politics remained unstable and confused. While silver continued a political interest in the Centennial State, it brought victories to the Democratic Party in

elections, for the Democrats continued to speak hopefully of resur-
recting bimetallism from the deep grave the McKinley Republicans
had placed it in. But "liberalism" on the silver issue did not make the
Democratic Party a vehicle for liberal policies generally. In fact, the
men they placed in the statehouse often were the older-type,
conservative, professional party leaders.

The twentieth century began with a series of Democratic governors: Alva Adams served his second term (1897 to 1899), after which
the combined silver and Democratic forces successfully wooed the
voters for a two-year term for Charles S. Thomas, who was followed
by a third Democrat, James B. Orman. This sequence ended in 1902
when the Republicans won the governorship. James H. Peabody, the
new executive, inhabited the governor's office during two years filled
with labor difficulties. Governor Peabody's actions, particularly in
dispatching the militia to strike areas, set the scene for a bitter
political struggle in the fall of 1904. The Democrats, who returned
for a third time to their proven popular leader, Alva Adams,
caustically criticized Peabody's handling of the Cripple Creek and
other strikes. Adams and the Democrats seemingly convinced the
majority of Colorado's voters that they would do a better job of
ending the industrial warfare than Peabody and the Republicans
could do.

The election of 1904 was not that simply ended. Despite Adams'
apparent victory, the Republicans, in control of the legislature,
insisted that fraud and corruption had dominated the balloting in
certain counties, as it probably had in those, and others as well. In
fact, it seems clear that both parties used methods that prevented a
free and open election. Since the legislature was charged with
deciding contested seats, the Republicans declared enough vacancies
to vote an unseating of Governor Adams. Peabody was then pronounced the victor, but on condition that he resign immediately after
taking the oath of office, turning the governor's chair over to his
Republican lieutenant-governor, Jesse F. McDonald. Thus, on one
day, Colorado had the questionable pleasure of seeing three different
men in the governor's office.

The revulsion of many voters at the circus-like atmosphere of the
election of 1904 seemed to make something of an impression on the
parties two years later. The Democrats then were split into two
factions, with one wing of the state party devoted to United States
Senator Thomas Patterson and the other following Denver Mayor
Robert Speer. The Republicans decided to nominate a political novice

for governor—a man who, they hoped, would appeal to the voters as uncontaminated by former corruption, or even the suggestion of it—the Reverend Henry A. Buchtel, the Chancellor of Denver University. The split in the Democratic ranks, and the expected relief from professional partisans, gave the election to the Republicans, who also captured control of the three congressional seats and the state legislature.

Those who had looked upon Buchtel's election as the beginning of a cleaner, more progressive era in the state's politics had some cause for disappointment in the early days of the new assembly's session. One of the first duties of the new legislature was to select a United States senator. The Republican majority had little difficulty deciding to retire Democrat Thomas Patterson, replacing him with Simon Guggenheim. But many voters, of both parties, considered the election proof that the politicians had not reformed their older ways, for the Guggenheim selection seemed to follow the pattern of nineteenth century senator-making when senate seats had often rewarded men of great wealth, but little or no experience in government. Guggenheim's election brought vocal protests from Democrats, union leaders, and reformers generally. Undoubtedly the incident furthered the growing sentiment in favor of removing senator selection from the legislative chambers and placing it directly into the hands of the voters. (This was accomplished by the seventeenth amendment to the federal Constitution, proposed in 1909, declared ratified in 1913.)

Yet despite this beginning, reformers found Buchtel's term promising before it had ended. Two statutes, especially, pleased the progressives: civil service legislation and a law creating a railroad commission. Although the federal government, since the 1880s, had engaged in a gradual transformation of the old "spoils system" of political appointments to a classified, competitive civil service, many of the states continued the older ways. As a result, the appointment and tenure of public employment remained completely a weapon in the hands of the dominant political party, providing a ceaseless arena for intimidation, corruption, and "unclean" government. The reformers had early championed changes, but without success. In 1907, the Colorado General Assembly enacted the state's first civil service statute. While it would be much amended and modified, and completely revised in 1915, it marked an encouraging, if belated, beginning at cleansing one of the more notorious facets of state government.

The other epoch-making statute of the same session created Colorado's first effective railroad commission, a three-member board empowered to represent the public's interest in railroad service and rate matters. The action was really the mark of final success for the concepts of Grangers and Populists from an earlier generation. Like much of the legislation sponsored by progressives, the railroad commission act was subjected to litigation, and its effectiveness, in large measure, turned on judicial determinations. In this case, the act emerged from the courts mostly intact, dignified by a pronouncement of constitutionality. Seven years after its creation, the railroad commission was merged with the state Public Utilities Commission, also composed of three members, with powers to supervise rates and service of all utilities.

While the two-year tenure of Governor Buchtel can be seen now as of more than casual significance in the development of reformed governmental policies, the governor and his Republican Party were to be denied the historic role of innovators. When the election of 1908 approached, a new reform group appeared to seize the opportunities for translating progressive idealism into action. John F. Shafroth was a man who had demonstrated popular appeal with Colorado voters at an earlier time. Born in Missouri, a graduate of the University of Michigan, Shafroth practiced law in Denver from 1879 onward. He had entered the political scene as a Republican. Then, like many others in Colorado, he had split with the national party on the silver question in the 1890s. A fusion group of Silver Republicans, Democrats, and Populists sent him to Washington as congressman in 1894 and again in 1896. Like Teller, Shafroth had moved to the Democratic Party where he constantly championed William Jennings Bryan, anti-imperialism, and what was left of the silver issue.

As the Democratic candidate for governor in 1908 Shafroth campaigned strenuously on a platform calling for a variety of reforms. He led his party to victory and two years later he would win a second term. The four years during which Shafroth was governor produced a fruitful harvest of progressive legislation.

Merely to list all of the statutes enacted would require many pages; many of the laws were complex and their administrative history confusing. Generally, Governor Shafroth enjoyed greater success in sponsoring reforms of political devices than in the facets of his program concerned with social or economic problems. Among the major accomplishments, the constitutional amendment providing for initiative and referendum invoked enthusiastic expectations. A favorite of progressive concepts, it was believed that allowing more direct popular participation in legislating would result in a more direct representation of the citizens' interests. The legislature submitted the amendments to popular vote in 1910, and Coloradans approved the amendments allowing citizens, by petition, to initiate both amendments to the constitution or statutes, and to approve or reject by plebiscite (at their option or the General Assembly's) statutes endorsed by the legislature.

Other progressive victories included a primary election law, a campaign expenses law, an election registration law, and the creation of a tax commission. Shafroth's administration also sponsored such milestone legislation as statutes providing for regulation of child labor, woman labor, an eight-hour day for hazardous or dangerous occupations, and a labor disputes act, the creation of a state conservation commission, a factory inspection act, and a coal mine inspection law.

Shafroth's four years in office resulted in a general identification of his wing of the Colorado Democratic Party with progressive legislation. But there were many Republicans as committed to reform; in fact, one of the complicating factors of the progressive movement, throughout the United States, was the fact that no one political party held a monopoly of the movement. There were many liberal, or "insurgent" Republicans, who were certain that reform could best be worked through their organization. They had generally supported the Shafroth program, but they continued to work to make the state Republican Party the major vehicle for progressivism.

These men had national heroes to emulate, including Wisconsin's Robert M. LaFollette and former President Theodore Roosevelt. Looking forward to the election of 1912, they expected to see the national party provide a progressive candidate and platform on which they could model their reformation of the Colorado organization. Representing, generally, the small city or "outstate" interests, those progressive Republicans who favored working for reform within the party were led by Philip B. Stewart, a wealthy Colorado Springs businessman. Their hopes were dampened, however, when the regular Republicans gained control of the national nominating convention and selected William Howard Taft as candidate for a second time. But, after Roosevelt had bolted the national organization and formed his "Bull Moose" Progressive Party, the Colorado reformers followed his lead and organized a State Progressive Party.

The leader of this new faction, which was principally urban

oriented, was Edward P. Costigan. A Virginian by birth, Costigan had grown up in Colorado. He had graduated from Harvard and practiced law in Utah before he began his legal career in Denver in 1899. A Republican, he entered the ranks of the Denver reformers, working with Ben Lindsey, Irving Hale, and others in organizations like the Denver Voters' League to contest the power of the Democratic "bosses" of the city and to further "home rule," civil service, and other progressive programs.

If the reformers were divided in their allegiance to political groupings, the same was true of their opponents. The Democrats might claim with pride the accomplishments of Governor Shafroth, but there were many in the party who clung to older ways. In fact, in the eyes of most reformers, the Democratic "City Hall Machine" of Denver was a "hydra of corruption," conducting in ruthless fashion the patronage and spoils of the state's largest city. If anyone doubted the division within the Democratic ranks, he had only to remember the bitter, prolonged controversy in the party in 1911. United States Senator Charles J. Hughes had died, and the General Assembly, controlled by the Democrats, spent 123 days and 102 ballots in a futile effort to select his replacement. The factions of the party were unable to compromise, and for two years the state counted only one representative in the United States Senate.

Among conservative Democrats and regular Republicans there was common agreement that the reformers were potentially dangerous people. The conservatives viewed with alarm or horror the suggestion that the state power be extended into so many aspects of man's activities. Such regulation and regimentation, they believed, would ultimately sap the individual's initiative; it was perilously close to, if not identical with, the plans and programs of Socialists. These men agreed with Henry Wolcott, who had warned that continued progressive action would leave nothing in Colorado but the climate and the scenery by the time the progressive law-makers had finished their work. There was particular fear that progressivism would drive away "eastern investors."[1]

There was virtue in viewing the struggle, as Ben Lindsey and other reformers did, not as a struggle between parties, but rather as a contest between "people" and "privilege." Yet political contests are waged through party organizations, and the election of 1912 demonstrated the application of the rule. That year Coloradans witnessed a spirited campaign for governor among four candidates: a Republican, a Democrat, a Progressive, and a Socialist. The Progressives, in their

first campaign, nominated Costigan for governor. They hoped that
the six speeches Theodore Roosevelt delivered in the state that year
would unite the majority of the reformers with them. But, following
the national pattern, where the division in Republican ranks between
Roosevelt and Taft opened the way for victory to Democrat Woodrow Wilson, when the votes were counted the Democratic Party had
also triumphed in Colorado, electing Elias Ammons governor. In this
election, too, voters approved a state constitutional amendment
providing for judicial recall, one of the most unusual experiments in
progressivism.

Two years later the Progressives returned to the arena, again
with Costigan as their candidate. For a time they anticipated
success, for the Democrats labored under the real handicap of
explaining away the uproar resulting from the Ludlow incident and
the violence in the coal fields. The fact that controversial episodes
had occurred during a supposedly "liberal" Democratic regime perhaps hurt the cause of all reformers. But, in addition, the prohibition issue confused other distinctions. This year, it appeared, the
voters who elected to stay with the reformers divided their votes
between the Progressives and Democrats. As a result, the regular
Republicans returned to office, with George A. Carlson the new
governor.

An indication of the momentum the Progressives had attained
can be seen in the major legislative accomplishment of Carlson's
term as governor. It was inevitable that industrial relations would
concern the lawmakers, yet it is significant that the Republicans
turned to a governmental device in seeking a solution to the
problems which had generated the coal field turmoil. The *form* was
one reformers had often championed—an industrial commission,
empowered to investigate labor conditions, arbitrate labor disputes,
prevent (when possible) strikes and lockouts. The new commission
assumed many of the functions of the older Bureau of Labor
Statistics, as well as the task of administering the new workmen's
compensation program.

In such ways did progressivism permeate Colorado politics and
law. But by this time the reformers had also broadened their
objectives, and had entered the realm of national affairs.

26

State and Nation

Throughout the period of reform, Colorado progressives, regardless of party, viewed the local and state activities as only a part of an era of national reform. For that reason, they kept constant watch on other states where progressive experimentation developed, and also on pattern-producing events in Washington, D. C. Both Congress and the presidents—Roosevelt, Taft, Wilson—provided focus for the national reform movement. Generally, the federally-sponsored reforms struck responsive chords among the Colorado progressives.

Vigorous national action by either the President or Congress, however, always carried with it the threat of penetration by the national government into the state's affairs. Out of this circumstance, Colorado, like all its sister states, grew to develop a policy of discrimination in viewing the effects of national progressivism. Some legislation was very welcome. Perhaps no state in the Union was more in accord than Colorado was with Theodore Roosevelt's progressive reclamation policies. A "beneficial" tariff regarding sugar was considered essential to the welfare of the irrigation farmers. The direct election of senators and a federal income tax, both subjects of amendments to the federal Constitution, were warmly supported by Colorado reformers.

But there were other innovations that were not so welcome, and none probably excited more anxiety in Colorado than the progressive ideas concerning conservation of the country's natural resources, particularly federal forest policies. Actually, the problems of forest control, and western anxieties about the problems, antedated the surging progressive movement by several decades.

Ever since the advent of white settlement in Colorado, the residents had consumed the timber of mountain and plateau areas for a variety of purposes. Lumber for cabins and houses, fuel for smelting, timber for railroad ties, wood for domestic fuel and general commercial use—all combined to deplete the timber resources. Man's raids were joined by the forces of nature that frequently destroyed by fire, flood, and insects, the timbered slopes. For years most men had been unconcerned; if asked, they undoubtedly would have echoed General William Larimer's declaration in his Christmas celebration speech at Cherry Creek, back in 1858: "Our pineries are convenient, and will last for generations to come."[1]

But there were a few individuals, as early as the 1870s, who were concerned about the eventual depletion of the forest resources, and none was more significant than Frederick J. Ebert. He had come to Colorado, professionally trained in forestry in a German university; it was he who was largely responsible for the formation of a committee on Forest Culture at the constitutional convention, and he served as its chairman. Ebert proposed a state bureau of forestry, complete with authority to regulate timber cuttings and establish nurseries for reforestation. While he failed in his attempts to gain approval for the bureau, his committee was responsible for the insertion of these clauses in the finished constitution:

> The general assembly shall enact laws in order to prevent the destruction of, and to keep in good preservation, the forests upon the lands of the state, or upon lands of the public domain, the control of which shall be conferred by congress upon the state.
> The general assembly may provide that the increase in the value of private lands caused by the planting of hedges, orchards, and forests thereon, shall not, for a limited time to be fixed by law, be taken into account in assessing such lands for taxation.

These sections of the Colorado Constitution of 1876 marked the first recognition of forest conservation ever included in a state's basic charter.[2]

The legislature proved to be in no hurry to act on these instructions. An early effort to extend tax rebates for tree planting achieved no great success. But by the mid-1880s sentiment arose

for more vigorous policies. The immediate concern was the possibility of inducing the federal government to turn control of the
forests on the public domain over to the states. This led to the
organization of the Colorado Forestry Association, the major spon-
sor of the legislation creating a state forest commissioner in 1885.
Edgar T. Ensign, who had campaigned for forest control in
speeches and writing for some time, was appointed to the post,
although no salary, staff, or budget was assigned to him.

Of particular concern to Commissioner Ensign, and to the
Forestry Association, were the headlands out of which the major
rivers of the state flowed. If these areas were to be disposed of for
agricultural purposes, a denuding of the hillsides would undoubtedly
destroy the river flow, with untold harm to the irrigation systems
and flood safeguards. Thus, memorials and petitions to Congress
were prepared and dispatched, first requesting state control of the
watershed areas and, when that seemed impossible to obtain,
demanding federal controls.

The national government's answer was the establishment of federal forest reserves. Beginning in 1891, forested lands were withdrawn from the public domain, halting private entries and exploitation of them. Some criticisms greeted the new policy. Public
lands, to that time, had been traditionally viewed as eventually
coming under private ownership via increasingly liberal laws. The
withdrawal policy seemed to reverse long-tenured traditions,
bringing cries of "socialism" against the federal program. But
others, including Coloradans, hailed the law as a wise measure and
when the then President, Benjamin Harrison, set aside the White
River Plateau Reserve of more than one million acres in northwestern Colorado (the first in the state and the second in the
nation), his action was applauded. Harrison, during 1891 and 1892,
created four other forest reserves in Colorado—Plateau, Pike's Peak,
South Platte, and Battlement Mesa. Since neither Presidents Cleveland nor McKinley established any additional reserves in the state,
many Coloradans came to believe that the federal government was
moving too slowly in the matter. By 1903, only three million
acres, out of more than thirteen million potential acres, had been
withdrawn.

One reason for the lack of organized opposition to the federal
policy during the first decade of withdrawals was the almost complete lack of enforcement. Not until 1897 did officers begin to
patrol the reserves and bring to punishment individuals who vio-

lated the forest laws. When that began, immediate protests arose. Much of local citizens' indignation resulted from the seemingly arbitrary action of untrained, under-paid federal officials. But the grievances soon were elevated to terms of an unconstitutional demolition of states rights by the federal government.

Undoubtedly mistakes were made. Not only were the administrative personnel poorly equipped for their assigned duties; some of the federal procedures needed correction. For a time persons who owned timbered lands within the reserves were allowed to exchange those areas for agricultural lands outside. All too often the lands were stripped of timber before the exchange was completed, presenting a spectacle of extremely poor administration which could be, and was, constantly used in argument against continuing or enlarging the reserve policy.

But if sloppy administration was a cause of complaint, efficient administration created even more hostility. Theodore Roosevelt's personal interest in conservation and his decision to extend the forest policy brought the first real application of the program. During his administration the reserves were transferred from the Interior to the Agricultural department and the enthusiastic conservationist Gifford Pinchot became chief forester. A fee system for grazers in the forest boundaries was inaugurated. Illegal enclosures within the reserves were eliminated, even to physically destroying fencing, when necessary. The Forest Service personnel was upgraded, placed on civil service, and the laws were rigorously administered. Finally, President Roosevelt established fourteen new reserves in Colorado between 1902 and 1907. Older reserves were enlarged and by 1908 a total of 15,756,000 acres of Colorado lands had been withdrawn.

The hostility to this sort of "progressivism" in Colorado now reached new heights. Many felt personally injured by the new regime: newspaper publishers whose revenue from land office advertising declined; men engaged in land-location or lumbering enterprises; politicians who missed the patronage of the forest service; those who feared the fortified policy because it was new and untried; ranchers who had enjoyed free use of the reserve grazing lands; men philosophically opposed to the extension of national power into such local activities. Champions of older ways undoubtedly echoed the sentiments of the Coloradan who informed President Roosevelt: "My home is in the Reserve (the proposed Medicine Bow Forest Reserve, now the Roosevelt National Forest) and I earn my bread with a little 10-horse power sawmill, running the saw myself. If you wonder why I object to the Reserve, it is because I love liberty, hate red tape, and believe in progress. I like self government, but to be placed under a bureau and in a Reserve is too much like going back to the kind of government you impose upon your Indians."[3]

A climax in the controversy was reached in June, 1907, when a Public Lands Convention assembled in Denver. Most of the western states were represented by delegations, with the majority of the spokesmen, including Colorado's Teller and Shafroth, antagonistic to the federal policy. From Washington, D.C., came the Interior Secretary, James Garfield, Chief Forester Pinchot, and the head of the Reclamation Service, Frederick Newell, to defend the President's conservation program. The bitter debates afforded western opponents a chance to be heard, but there the matter ended. The policies were not to be reversed, if for no other reason than that the federal government controlled the land and could do with it as it wished. But it would be wrong to suggest that the federal policies were arbitrarily imposed and lacked popular support. Outside the West, most progressives applauded the efforts to conserve what remained of the nation's natural resources.

The federal authorities did adjust minor matters. Congress forbade further withdrawals by the President without its specific approval. The reserves were soon combined and consolidated, and their names were changed to "national forests." This name change was an indication of the more sophisticated concepts of conservation currently accepted in the Washington bureaus. Instead of merely setting aside "reserves" of forest lands, the national "forests" were to be *used* in a new fashion. Anticipating modern multiple-use concepts, the timber would be scientifically grown and harvested, fires and destructive diseases would be controlled, the proper use for irrigation and grazing could be arranged in the watershed areas. In time these new ideas, through education and practical experience, would gain the support and loyalty of most westerners.

After the arguments over forest policy, if any doubt remained that the great crusades of the progressives had resulted in increased exercise of authority by the national government, that doubt surely was dispelled by the last of the great crusades—the world war against the Central European powers. Of course, the impact of that struggle was felt by all people of all nations, and its effects were so far reaching that they penetrated almost all aspects of every-body's life. But the war years brought specific, and sometimes unique, changes to Colorado.

The general pattern of the times was unstinting cooperation and sacrifice on the part of the vast majority of Colorado citizens, even though many residents demonstrated reluctance to enter the war in 1917. In the fall elections the year before, Julius Gunter, a Demo-crat, had been chosen governor; the success of his party at the polls might have indicated general cooperation with Woodrow Wilson's administration. But, when the vote in the House of Repre-sentatives on the war resolution was recorded in April, only one Colorado congressman favored passage.

This is probably explained as a reflection of an older anti-imperialistic, isolationist attitude, hardly surprising when it is remembered that, at the turn of the century, when Congress debated the resolution for declaring war on Spain, it was Colo-rado's Senator Henry Teller who sponsored the amendment guaran-teeing a non-annexation promise to the Cubans whose independence from Spain was a major objective of the war. This had not then resulted, however, in any lack of enthusiasm for the "little war with Spain." Coloradans had been as stirred as the citizens of other states by the events, and the general American rush to volunteer for service had not found Coloradans hesitant. The famed Rough Riders included many Colorado volunteers; Colorado troops under Colonel Irving Hale had distinguished themselves in the assault on Manila and in later guerrilla campaigns in the Philippine Islands.

In much the same way, once war was declared against Germany and her allies, in 1917, the all-out effort to fight it rapidly and successfully engaged the energies of almost all Colorado citizens. Governor Gunter established a council of defense; the legislature, in special session, provided emergency appropriations for the war effort; citizens generally busied themselves with some form of patriotic sacrifice. One area of special concern, particularly during the anxious early months, was the exposed condition of the state's reservoirs and tunnels. Sabotage committed against them would result in extensive destruction of the state's industrial and agricul-tural facilities. When the Colorado National Guard was federalized in August, 1917, one of its first assignments was to guard those essential works.

Like all the other states of the Union, Colorado was called upon to give young men to the drafted "citizen" army. In all, counting both volunteers and draftees, the state contributed some 43,000 men to the armed forces. Of these, 1,009 died in the service; 1,759 were wounded. Battle casualties, however, totalled only 326.[4] The mustering into service of these men always provided an occasion for civilians to demonstrate their loyalty to the war effort. Gifts of tobacco, wristwatches, and mementos accompanied the soldiers and sailors on their way to the training camps. Once on their way, the "boys" would continue objects of concern for organizations like the Red Cross, YMCA, Salvation Army and, of course, their own families and friends.

Meanwhile, those left at home bought war bounds, paid increased taxes, grew war gardens in vacant lots, and cheerfully complied with the homefront campaigns of meatless, wheatless, lightless, gasless days or nights. By May, 1918, it was reported that women's councils of defense had been formed in all but four counties of the state, and Colorado women sent clothing and supplies to war-torn Europe, helped organize Red Cross work, and provided information on food conservation. The La Plata County women's council, for example, established a community kitchen in Durango to instruct housewives in the preparation of war menus and the canning of fruits and vegetables. The younger generation also helped in the war effort; in June, 1918, eleven thousand boys and girls from areas outside of Denver were enrolled in agricultural and garden clubs under trained supervision.[5]

Coloradans young and old also watched the development in the state of some innovations in both agriculture and mining. Even before America's entrance into the war, the increasing demands for food in wartime Europe had led Colorado's farmers to increase their production. Consequently, by 1917, the state's wheat, sugar, and other farmers already were rapidly extending their efforts. With demands seemingly insatiable, it was inevitable that high prices would spiral even higher; wheat rose dramatically during the war years, reaching an average of $2.02 a bushel in 1919. With this sort of market, it is not surprising to find that enormous increases in planting resulted. In Washington County alone, for example, wheat acreage increased from 31,000 acres in 1917 to 175,000 acres in 1920.[6] In Colorado as a whole, the 465,000 acres planted to wheat in 1913 had been increased by 1919 to 1,329,000 acres. Looking back at the feverish activity after the war had ended, critics found the source of much of the agricultural distress of the post-war decades in the careless fashion in which eager farmers converted the dry lands to plowed fields. But at the time it was both patriotic and profitable to engage in such bonanza farming.

Some problems accompanied the speeded-up tempo. Because of the wartime strains on the nation's transportation system and a shortage of freight cars, farmers sometimes found it difficult to get their produce to market, and at one time potato growers around Monte Vista were advised to build storage pits for crops that could not be shipped.[7] Sugar beet farmers also faced a very real difficulty after the war began because they had always relied on German production of beet seed. With that source cut off completely, the Colorado sugar producers, especially encouraged by the success of the Great Western Sugar Company's endeavors, participated in a "crash" program of propagating beet seed. Generally, the war-years were filled with optimistic agricultural expansion, and although the "mobilization" of the farms for the "Great Crusade" might have left a bitter heritage for the future, Americans were proud of the productions they achieved.

In the mountains and plateaus of central and western Colorado, the war brought several significant changes to the state's mining industry. For one thing, although metals generally experienced a price rise similar to that of agricultural products, with silver, for example, reaching as much as $1.00 an ounce, the production of most metals declined during the war years. Labor costs increased, as factories, farms, and the government all placed drains on the man-power pool. But, conversely, some metals were especially demanded for war production, and in three areas genuine "booms" occurred. One of these metals was molybdenum, used in hardening high-grade steel. On Fremont Pass, near Leadville, practically astride the Continental Divide, the Climax company opened what proved to be the largest molybdenum mine in the world. Only the great demand for this metal, resulting from the greatly increased need for steel, could have led to such a rapid development of the molybdenum properties in the very shadow of what was once Colorado's greatest silver camp.

Another metal in great demand during the war years was vanadium, also used in the manufacture of steel. Vanadium was mined as a by-product of uranium, in the far western part of the state, particularly in the Paradox Valley region. The metallurgy of uranium was still in its infancy; it had been identified as present in Colorado as recently as 1898. At that time the ores, called Carnotite, were of greatest interest for their radium content, but with the advent of the war, and the need for vanadium for steel alloy, the interest shifted. In the isolated valley where the Colorado Co-operative Society had planted its utopia only a few years earlier, reduction plants were constructed and a new dimension to the Western Slope economy emerged.

Finally, a third rare metal, tungsten, enjoyed a brief flurry of attention. Like molybdenum and vanadium, the tungsten industry resulted from the use of the metal in hardening steel. Like so many other mining stories, the Colorado tungsten saga had its beginning in earlier days, when the tungsten ore hampered miners in Boulder County who were searching for gold and silver. In this case, years elapsed both before the element was identified and before any sizeable demand for it existed, for although its use in the steel industry originated in 1859, it was not until near the close of the century that any great market for tungsten developed. The war increased demands rapidly, and a bonanza of short duration resulted, with the price leaping from $9.00 a unit ("one per cent of a ton of tungsten trioxide . . . which was about twenty pounds" [8]) in 1914 to $93.90 per unit in 1916. Again, the area of an old silver camp—Nederland—enjoyed renewed activity from the excitement of supplying the war needs with one of the earth's rarer metals.

Neither tungsten, nor vanadium, nor even molybdenum ever attained the significance in Colorado's economy that gold and silver had reached at an earlier time. And after the end of the war, as in the wheat areas of the Eastern Slope, less exciting, if not actually discouraging conditions set in. But, for the brief time of the war months, Colorado's farms and mines, mobilized for the "Great Crusade," contributed sensational harvests to the national effort.

27

The Twenties

Crusading in Colorado, as in the rest of the nation, abruptly ended with the close of the first World War. The "fall from enthusiasm" for high ideals and expectations set the stage for the decade of the 1920s–a decade in which both state and nation reverted to wishful thinking about "normalcy" and actions attempting to restore all the older virtues and none of the older evils of society. The emphasis of the age was derived from attention to material gain, personal well-being, and a return to Republican rule.

Indications of what was to come were apparent even before the war ended. Disillusionment in Colorado with Wilsonian concepts of international morality and domestic reform resulted in a Republican victory in the mid-war elections in the autumn of 1918. John Shafroth was not returned to the Senate; rather, Republican Lawrence C. Phipps replaced him. Democratic Congressmen Edward Keating and B. C. Hilliard were retired to make room for Republicans William N. Vaile and Guy U. Hardy. In the state house in Denver, Oliver H. Shoup, a Republican, succeeded Democrat Julius C. Gunter.

The Republican restoration in Colorado proved somewhat less complete and of shorter duration than the victories of the party in national elections. Shoup won a second term as governor in 1920, but the rest of the decade resembled a tennis match of politics in the contests for the governor's office, with Republicans and Democrats succeeding each other. Democrat William E. Sweet inherited the office from Shoup. Sweet's victory over Republican Benjamin Griffith returned the Democrats to a single term of power, ending with a Republican resurgence and the inauguration of Governor Clarence J. Morley in 1925. Then the Democrats returned to hold the chair with an Alamosa rancher, William H. Adams, who would three times be elected governor.

The party affiliation of the governor, however, is not the best indication of party strength. During most of the decade, the Republicans controlled the state legislature. They also dominated the representative and senatorial offices from Colorado.

In many ways, politics from 1920 to 1930 were less confused than they had been for many decades in Colorado. All though the eras of Populism and Progressivism, fusions and party divisions had conspired to complicate alignments and allegiances. Now most of that maneuvering had ended. The older leaders of the progressive movement had either returned to the Republican fold or had sought refuge in the Democratic ranks. There was, however, a series of brief flurries that threatened again to entangle party divisions.

When the decade opened, there was a possibility that the Dakota-based Nonpartisan League's invasion of the state might be successful. But the League's program of "socialistic" aid to agriculture frightened many conservatives. In 1920, when the League endorsed James Collins, the Democratic candidate for governor, many Democrats crossed over to support Republican Oliver Shoup. It should be noted, however, that despite its failure as a political force, the League's concepts of agricultural aid remained of interest to many Coloradans.

The new Ku Klux Klan was another disruptive force in the early part of the decade's politics. This anti-foreign, anti-Catholic, anti-Jewish, anti-Negro organization recruited members in Colorado so rapidly that it threatened to become a dominant force in state politics. Under the leadership of its "Grand Dragon," Dr. John Galen Locke of Denver, the Klan began its rapid rise at the precinct level in the capital city in 1924. By controlling the state Republican Assembly that year, it exerted influence in the nomination of Clarence J. Morley for governor. When the fall elections were finished, the Klan controlled not only the new governor, but the new House of Representatives as well. Its legislative programs were less successful. For a time it appeared two measures might bring Klan victories: an anti-Catholic bill that would have prohibited the use of wine in the church sacraments, and a proposal to compel all students to attend public schools. Six Republican non-Klan senators joined Democrats to keep the bills from becoming law.

While the Klan was a state-wide organization, with local units spread from Julesburg to Montrose, its greatest strength was focused in the Denver area. There it counted as its ally the mayor, Ben Stapleton, and exerted its maximum oppressions against Catholic and Jewish businessmen by proclaiming boycotts. And there, in its Monday night, hooded, cross-burning sessions atop Lookout Mountain near Golden, it provided its greatest excitement for its members.

The decline of the Colorado Klan came almost as quickly as its sudden emergence as a political force. The Denver and other state newspapers contributed to its demise with a constant barrage of ridicule and opposition. Grand Dragon Locke also contributed to his organization's fall from power. Locke had always been a strange "Grand Dragon," using only those parts of the Klan program that pleased him and rejecting the rest. Pressed finally both by federal treasury officials and national leaders of the Klan for information about his income, Locke resigned his post in the summer of 1925. Without his leadership, the Colorado Klan quickly dwindled in size and power.

While the entire Klan episode remains an ugly stain on the history of the state, a more specific indictment against the organization, and those who used it for personal advantage, can be made. Genuine problems of considerable magnitude confronted the citizens of Colorado during those years that should have received the attention of citizens and politicians alike. The two major economic interests of the state—mining and agriculture—were left in a disarranged condition as a heritage of the recent war years. If the efforts and enthusiasms that Locke and his cohorts had enlisted to combat minority groups had been directed to these areas, the state's welfare might have been greatly improved.

The Colorado mining camps emerged from the war years as greatly altered enterprises. The "ordinary" Colorado mines—silver, gold, and lead—had all declined in production. At Cripple Creek, for example, gold production, which as late as 1915 and 1916 had totalled $10,000,000 to $12,000,000 annually, had fallen to little more than $4,000,000 a year in the early 1920s. During the war there had been hopes that the new metals—tungsten, molybdenum, uranium—would continue in demand and would take the place of the old. But the booms in the rare metals had ended. Cheap Chinese ores replaced domestic tungsten ores; Belgian Congo uranium replaced Colorado ores; no mining at all was done at the Climax molybdenum mines from 1920 to 1924. In addition, as the war-inflated prices of copper and zinc tumbled downward, mining operations for those products were suspended. Laborers from the mines, and from closed smelters at Denver, Salida, and Pueblo, joined discharged soldiers and sailors to glut the labor market in the post-war years.

An economic problem of equal magnitude descended on the dry lands of eastern Colorado during the same years. Less than a decade earlier, from 1914 to 1919, the spiraling wheat prices had brought great optimism for the future. Feverish haste to put land to the plow seemed only common sense when wheat prices reached as high as $2.02 a bushel. But now the situation had changed. By 1921 wheat had fallen to 76c a bushel, and genuine distress became visible in the dry lands. One indication of this is apparent in the growing percentage of farm tenants in the state, compared with farm operators who owned their own land. In 1920, only 23 per cent had been tenants; in 1925 the percentage had risen to 30.9 and by 1930 it would reach 34.5 per cent.

One concept of relief for the farming communities found expression in the program of the Nonpartisan League, imported through the work of organizers sent into the state from the grainbelts of the Dakotas. Reflecting some of the ideas of the older Grangers, the League proposed to use state agencies to process, store, and transport agricultural products. In this way the "middle-man"—the traditional foe of the farmers—would be by-passed. While the Colorado League failed to gain control of the state government as the North Dakota farmers had done, they did anticipate success in 1923 when Democrat William Sweet, a vigorous advocate of some of their concepts, became governor. Sweet failed to convince the legislature to sanction state-operated warehouses, but legislation was enacted to provide privileges for cooperative marketing associations.

During the following years, the expansion of cooperative associations brought some stability to specialized agricultural pursuits. The potato industry of the San Luis Valley is an example. When war-time demands for food brought higher prices for potatoes, a great increase in production had resulted. Then, in 1919, prices began to decline and the individual producers felt particularly aggrieved with the facets of their industry over which they had little or no control. For example, they blamed part of their difficulty on the railroads' failure to supply freight cars at the right places at the right times. The individual farmers came to believe that through organization they might provide better transportation services, as well as more economical warehousing and more profitable sales.

In 1920 and 1921 unsuccessful attempts to create marketing cooperatives occurred. Then, in 1923, both the Del Norte Potato Growers' Cooperative Association and the Monte Vista Potato Growers' Cooperative Association were formed. Within five years these marketing groups had joined a state-wide organization, the Colorado Potato Growers Exchange. While the original emphasis was on warehousing, grading and marketing of the potatoes soon became equally important aspects of the program. Something of the same development was seen in the Western Slope fruit industry, where organizations like the United Fruit Growers' Association of Palisade were strengthened by the Cooperative Marketing Act of 1923.

The post-war depression in agricultural prices emphasized anew a growing realization that, even in the irrigated farming regions, efficient management of land and water are essential for profitable farming; that merely spreading water over planted fields will not insure good harvests. As farmers' income fell, the repayment on projects financed through the federal Bureau of Reclamation began to fall behind schedule, and the Bureau was actually faced with potential bankruptcy on some projects. A Coloradan, Dr. Hubert Work of Greeley, was responsible for some of the attempts to rectify the situation. Appointed Secretary of the Interior by President Coolidge in 1923, Dr. Work directed endeavors to train farmers settled on irrigated lands in techniques of cultivation and marketing. Specialization of crops—whether potatoes or peaches, melons or lettuce—seemed to offer the best chances for success. But even then, not all intensively-grown crops thrived. In 1929, for example, the state's first sugar beet factory, at Grand Junction, was closed down by the Holly Sugar Company which had operated it since 1916.

Probably the most significant change of the decade, however, was the inauguration of "treaties" with other states to insure an equitable division of river water for irrigation and other purposes. By the 1920s, Colorado, and other states, had arrived at the conclusion that the cost of defending their rights in contests with other commonwealths before federal tribunals—to say nothing of the danger of losing such contests—could be partly eliminated by entering into agreements with other states. By negotiating compacts for dividing river waters with competing states, the people of

Colorado could secure their property interests, and provide stability for future planning and growth, in a less expensive and hazardous fashion than through litigation.

Many men and events contributed to the change. Some of the men who had argued the state's defense of its rights in cases already litigated had looked for less complex methods of securing the state's interests. Others, who looked forward to federal help in future reclamation projects, recognized the inevitability of compromise among the competing states. Delph Carpenter of Greeley is an excellent example of those who championed the concept of river compacts. He served as Colorado's negotiator on the first three "treaties" to which the state was a party. Spurring interest in the compact idea was the long-delayed decision by the United States Supreme Court in the Wyoming-Colorado litigation over diversion of the Laramie River. That decision, announced in 1922, provided specific warning for Colorado that the older method could prove dangerous.

That year—1922—became a milestone year in water development, for it marked success in negotiating a Colorado River Compact. The Colorado River, and its tributaries, flow through seven western states. The upper basin commonwealths (Colorado, Wyoming, Utah, and New Mexico) are divided from the lower basin states (Nevada, California, and Arizona) by the great canyon of the river. Representatives of the seven states had met in January, 1919, at the invitation of the governor of Utah and had formed the "League of the Southwest" to explore common problems concerning the river's waters. Subsequent meetings at Los Angeles and Denver both pointed to the desirability of a negotiated compact, for the federal government was interested in initiating ambitious reclamation projects on the river, and state and local interests needed definition and protection.

The Constitution of the United States forbids treaties between states without special congressional sanction, but by this time Congress had enacted permissive legislation, formally extending to states the right to enter into agreements with each other concerning water or forests. Upon the authority of those statutes, representatives of the seven states met in Santa Fe, along with the Secretary of Commerce, Herbert Hoover, who represented the national interests.

The negotiators assumed that the average annual flow of the Colorado River totalled more than 20,000,000 acre-feet. By the document agreed to, this water was to be divided between the upper basin and the lower basin states in two ways. First, each group of states was guaranteed 7,500,000 acre-feet of water a year, to be divided among themselves. Practically, this meant that the upper states guaranteed they would allow 7,500,000 acre-feet of water to flow each year past Lee Ferry, the division point between basins. From the surplus water, the amount necessary to supply Mexico (presumably to be determined later by treaty between the United States and that country) would be drawn. If events proved no surplus existed, both upper and lower basins would provide the necessary quantity to satisfy international agreements, in equal portions. The remaining surplus waters, for the next forty years, would remain undivided. After that time, if the upper basin states had used their 7,500,000 acre-feet, or the lower basin states had developed use for 8,500,000 acre-feet, a further apportionment might take place.

The Colorado River Compact was scheduled to take effect after ratification by the legislatures of all of the signatory states and by the federal Congress. Six states and Congress approved; Arizona refused to ratify. Since the federal government was then proceeding with plans for the project known as Hoover Dam, and thus was more than casually interested in the compact, in 1928 the Arizona objections were by-passed by a congressional decision that ratification by six of the seven states would suffice. In 1929 the compact was declared in force.

Three years after the Santa Fe meeting to negotiate the Colorado River "treaty," Nebraska and Colorado agreed to divide the waters of the South Platte River. The year 1897 was selected as a dividing date, with all Colorado appropriators of South Platte water prior to that year guaranteed their priorities. Even earlier, in 1923, New Mexico and Colorado representatives had sat at conference and agreed upon an equitable division of the waters of the La Plata River.

Perhaps the most significant result of these compacts was the plainly visible warning for the future. Colorado, Utah, and other relatively under-developed western states began to realize that unless they fully utilized their water resources, they faced the prospect of losing their rights to other states in negotiating sessions. To insure adequate water resources for future growth, methods were needed to put surplus waters to beneficial use. It was this knowledge that caused Coloradans to begin seriously planning large-scale diversions from the thinly populated Western Slope, where the greatest amount of surplus water was to be found, to the more heavily populated, water-poor, Eastern Slope.

All the talk concerning division of river waters was based on the assumption that man is endowed with capabilities to make beneficial use of available water. And in those days, when waters were moved under mountains and across long stretches of desert, who could doubt man's ability? On June 3, 1921, however, a few moments of doubt may have occurred. On that fateful day, rivers and nature conspired to demonstrate convincingly that water and mountains might be combined to devastate rather than benefit mankind. After three days of rain in the mountains, the Arkansas River became a wrecking flood, driving into and through the city of Pueblo and down the valley, carrying with it 600 houses and an estimated $19,000,000 worth of property. More than 100 lives were lost in the calamity.

The Pueblo flood was so destructive that Governor Shoup summoned the legislature to special session. Out of the lawmakers' deliberations, rather unusual statutes emerged. All Coloradans were sympathetic to the Arkansas Valley, and recognized the legitimacy of its claims for help. But, in matters concerning public aid, the northern part of Colorado had indulged in ill-feeling toward the southern section of the state for some time. The issue that had generated the hostility was the question of state aid in completing a railroad tunnel under the Continental Divide. As recently as 1920 the northern tunnel interests had sponsored a plan that included a "middle area" tunnel at Marshall Pass to serve the Gunnison region and a southern tunnel at Cumbres Pass to pierce the San Juan Mountains, along with the long-talked-of northern tunnel. When a bond issue to finance the three tunnels was presented to the voters of the state, they rejected the suggestion, with the majority of the adverse votes registered in the southern counties of Pueblo, El Paso, and Las Animas. These areas recognized that favorable reception of the plan would mean both higher taxes and the eventual replacement of the Arkansas canyon by a northern tunnel as the main railroad gateway through the Rockies.

Now, however, the situation had changed. The northern interests intended to take advantage of the exposed condition of the southern counties. By joining the two issues—construction of flood control installations at Pueblo and a northern railroad tunnel—the special legislative session made history. In the south, a Pueblo

Railroads faced difficult winter problems in the Colorado Rockies. (Center of Southwest Studies, Fort Lewis College)

Flood Conservancy District was created, through which taxation on property could be used to raise revenue for building safeguards against future calamities. Expert engineering advice was sought, particularly from Dayton, Ohio, where flood control methods had proved successful. Plans were soon drawn to build barriers and divert the channel of the Arkansas River. Within a few years, construction was completed and the city of Pueblo was believed safe from any future major flooding.

The companion feature for the north was the Moffat Tunnel Improvement District. It also was allowed the authority to issue bonds and levy taxes to finance a piercing of the Continental Divide for a railroad tunnel. The district encompassed the towns and counties on both sides of the Divide that would benefit most directly from the tunnel: Adams, Boulder, Jefferson, Grand, Routt, Gilpin, Eagle, and Denver counties. Revenue was also anticipated from rentals to railroads for their use of the tunnel.

In many ways the building of the Moffat Tunnel was a heroic effort, even though the hoped-for completion date of 1926—the 50th anniversary of statehood—could not be met. The plans called for a pioneer bore, eight feet high and nine feet wide, driven ahead of the main tunnel to provide advance information about conditions and access to the main tunnel as it was advanced. The conditions discovered by the first bore were often discouraging. A greater amount of soft ground was found than had been anticipated, necessitating costly reinforcements. Water seepage far exceeded expectations; at one point all of Lower Crater Lake drained through a fissure. In February, 1927, the pioneer bore was completed when the two crews—one working from the east and the other from the west—met deep in the mountain. A year later, after an expenditure of nearly $18,000,000 (some $11,000,000 more than the original estimate) and a cost of twenty-nine fatalities to work crews, the main tunnel was opened. Twenty-four feet high, sixteen feet wide, six and two-tenths miles long, the Moffat Tunnel was now an operating reality.

The tunnel eliminated the greatest operating problems of the Denver and Salt Lake Railroad (Moffat Road). Each year, more than forty per cent of the road's operating costs had been devoted to moving trains over the Continental Divide. Grades up to four per cent had been costly to climb in good weather; in wintertime the snow had brought increased expenses and hazards. While the tunnel eliminated only twenty-three miles of trackage, it had reduced the roadbed grades to two per cent maximum, and the snow problems had been largely eliminated.

One feature of the tunnel's operation, however, caused constant complaint: the only railroad that could then use the costly hole was the Moffat Road, and its tracks ran only to Craig, for the original destination of the Utah capital had never been reached. Revenue from the railroad's use of the tunnel fell far below the optimistic expectations of the pre-construction days, bringing higher tax levies to the people of the improvement district. Even more discouraging, Denver still had not attained a direct western rail route, for the Denver and Rio Grande's mainline still used the Arkansas Canyon. But attention now began to center on the short forty-mile stretch between the Moffat line and the Rio Grande's tracks at Dotsero. In time, a "cut-off" would bridge the gap, and the Rio Grande's mainline between Denver and Grand Junction would be reduced by a total of 175 miles.

In many ways, the Moffat Tunnel's completion marked a dramatic end to the long and glorious struggle of Coloradans to build ever finer railroad facilities. A new day was fast approaching that would reduce the significance of the region's rail lines. In fact, the peak period of railroading had already been attained; in 1914, when the state counted 5,739 operating miles of railroad, the zenith had been crossed. Automotive advances had begun to siphon interurban passenger traffic from the short-line electrics; many sight-seers now toured the state in cars and busses, rather than railroad coaches. Truck freighting was cutting deeply into railroad revenues. All these elements, added to the decline of mining in many parts of the state, brought death to historic Colorado railroads and contraction of service on others. The Colorado Midland died in 1918. Five years later the Colorado and Southern began to abandon the old Denver and South Park road.

Even more dramatic as an omen of future transportation was the introduction of regular airline mail service in Colorado in 1926. As in the quest for transcontinental railroad service three-quarters of a century earlier, Coloradans were disappointed in their first expectations of inclusion in the direct airmail service instituted between New York and San Francisco in 1920. Cheyenne, to the north, again became the closest stop. But in 1926 a branch service was initiated between the Wyoming city and Pueblo, with stops in Denver and Colorado Springs. "Celebrations marked the start of airmail from all three Colorado cities. Ten thousand people crowded onto the Colorado Airways Field in east Denver on May 31, to watch the departure of the afternoon mail for Cheyenne. Two Curtiss-Standard J-1 biplanes, war surplus craft, transported 13,000 letters (325 pounds), the first forwarded from Denver by air to cities throughout the United States."[1] Within a short time the flights from Colorado cities were carrying passengers and freight as well as mail. By 1931, only two years after it had been opened for service, Denver Municipal Airport (renamed Stapleton Field in 1944) counted 3,600 passenger arrivals and departures.

Airplanes and automobiles not only brought changes to the state's transportation pattern; they revolutionized the fuel industry. Colorado railroads had depended on the local coal fields for their power; the new transportation consumed the products of oil fields. Colorado recorded its first producing petroleum well in 1862, when oil was discovered six miles north of Canon City. This was only three years after the Oil City, Pennsylvania, field had ushered in the "Age of Petroleum," making a Colorado well the second in the nation in point of time, if not significance. Later, in 1876, the Florence field had been opened, and Boulder County wells began production in the early 1890s. All these wells, however, were of limited significance, for most of their production was consumed in the local area. The year 1925 marked a turning point. Then the Wellington Dome, near Fort Collins, and the oil fields near Craig, were brought into production. Where, in the decade from 1910 to 1920, only 1,746,000 barrels of crude oil had been produced in the state, from 1920 to 1930 the total would stand at 12,498,000 barrels. For the first time, the last years of the decade would see production reach more than 1,000,000 barrels of crude oil annually.

The railroads' dwindling use of coal coincided with an equally devastating reduction in the consumption of coal for industrial and domestic use, brought about by the introduction of natural gas. In 1928 a pipeline from the Texas gas fields to Denver was completed, and soon the convenience of the new fuel wrecked another large market of the Colorado coal fields. While natural gas fields had been discovered in many western states before 1928, it was not until seamless, electrically-welded pipe was developed (in 1925), that it was possible to transmit natural gas over long distances.

Hard-hit from all sides during the decade, the coal fields were to undergo one additional crisis. In 1927-28, the coal miners struck the operators for wage increases (to compensate for two wage cuts in 1925) and improved working conditions. The Industrial Workers of the World, who had recently organized the northern fields, claimed that its members could not obtain a redress of grievances through the legal machinery of the State Industrial Commission. The most violent of a series of clashes between miners and mine guards occurred on November 21, 1927, at the Rocky Mountain Fuel Company's Columbine Mine near Lafayette. The coal miners there insisted on their right to enter the post office which was located on mine property; the guards refused entrance because of the proximity of the post office to shafthouses and surface installations. Six deaths and many injuries resulted from the incident. In addition, the "battle" brought a declaration of martial law to the area and, eventually, the breaking of the strike.

Out of the difficulties, however, a notable experiment in Colorado's industrial relations was born. John J. Roche, one of the owners of the Rocky Mountain Fuel Company, died in 1927 and his daughter, Josephine, inherited his holdings. Josephine Roche already had made some Colorado history as Denver's first policewoman (1912), an officer with Edward P. Costigan in the Colorado Progressive Society, and in various capacities with the Denver Juvenile Court. Her experiences in social work led her to conclusions that horrified other owners of the company: she decided that many of the miners' grievances were legitimate complaints. When other stockholders threatened to dispose of their holdings rather than invite the United Mine Workers to organize the miners, and to enter into contract with the union, Josephine bought their shares and became the owner of a $10,000,000 laboratory in which to experiment with her ideas.

In 1928 the Rocky Mountain Fuel Company signed a historic labor contract. Its stated purpose was "to establish industrial justice, substitute reason for violence, integrity and good faith for dishonest practices, and a union of effort for the chaos of present economic warfare." The road ahead proved rather rocky; in addition to the competition of gas and oil, the relatively high wage contract placed a financial burden on the company at the same time that rival companies were conducting a price-cutting campaign against Josephine's experiment. But, in the spirit of the "new age," the miners lent the company funds to meet interest payments on its bonds. The miners also sold coal, with the slogan "Buy from Josephine" effectively used as a union label. Within a few years the production rate per miner, the days of labor per year, and the working wages of the Rocky Mountain Fuel Company had all outstripped other coal mines in the state. Many observers concluded that the experiment of the second largest coal operator in Colorado had been remarkably successful.

28

Depression Decades

The decade from 1929 to 1939 conveniently marks itself for historians as the Age of the Great Depression. From the crash of the stock market in October, 1929, until the outbreak of World War II in Europe in late summer, 1939, the people of Colorado, the nation, and much of the world experienced the devastating dislocations of the most severe depression in their history. The economic collapse, and the efforts to overcome its effects, permeated almost every aspect of life.

No account of events in Colorado during the depression decade would be completely meaningful if the reader forgets the problems that some segments of the state's economy faced during the preceding years. The "Coolidge Prosperity" of the "Golden Twenties," which had promised to banish poverty permanently from the land, had never been distributed evenly across the nation. Colorado's two major enterprises—mining and agriculture—had experienced their own depressions long before the stock market crash. Gold and silver mining had never recovered their prosperity of pre-war years; the state's coal mines staggered throughout the twenties under the impact of a constantly decreasing market. And, despite recent harvests that were promising, the farmers of Colorado had endured equally troubled times.

The advent of the great depression witnessed agricultural distress compounded of several ingredients. The drastic drop in the market price of agricultural products, plummeting even faster and further than the most pessimistic observer of the troubled Twenties would have predicted, affected both irrigated and dry farmlands. A few examples illustrate the problem: hogs that sold for $12.10 in 1929 brought not more than $3.10 in 1933; potatoes that found markets in 1929 at $1.40 a bushel were down to 24c a bushel in 1932; wheat prices during the same period slid from 96c to 37c a bushel. The harvests of ranch, farm, and orchard brought less at market than it cost to gather and transport them, and were often left on fields and trees to rot.[1]

Another ingredient, adding to the distress, was the unfortunate antics of Mother Nature, who chose the worst of all possible years to withhold precious rainfall, substituting dry, swirling winds instead. The combination brought the infamous dust storms of the early 1930s. The dry years seemed unending; huge billowing clouds of stifling dust lifted precious topsoil and carried it for miles. It did little good to think back to the bonanza years of $2.00-a-bushel wheat, and realize that dust was the final harvest from lands which might better have remained grazing lands. In fact, there seemed nothing to do except watch the land being carried away. A few valiant individuals tried to pump subsurface water, but the results were as limited as the attempt was desperate. The answer, for many, was flight, as once again this farmers' last frontier witnessed an exodus of major proportions.

The flight from the farmlands became one of the familiar scenes of the decade. With falling income, and no savings left to tide them over the long, lean years, farmers found their acres foreclosed on—many at tax sales. In some dry farming areas, more than forty per cent of the farms went through forced sales. As the inhabitants moved out, their deserted acres fell prey to absentee owners who had no intention of farming, but leased the farms to tenants. All too often the tenants were "suitcase" farmers who stayed only long enough to try a crop or two, with no ambition or intention of improving the farm. Tenantry among farm operators continued to increase as it had since the end of World War I. The 34.5 per cent level of the year 1930 had risen to 39 per cent by 1935.

Many farmers, leaving the agricultural areas, moved to cities and towns, hoping to find relief from their economic troubles there. (Many others migrated to California and the Pacific Northwest; others headed west, but got no farther than the state's Western Slope.) A far from welcome sight greeted those who hoped to begin a new life in the city. Here an equally familiar scene of the decade was daily repeated: sustained by soup kitchens and bread lines, contingents of men from the army of unemployed looked for work; desperation was visible on every face. In fact, in some ways, the fury of the depression was more apparent in the urban areas, for the contrast with what had come before was greater than in the farming regions. The agricultural areas had faced difficulties throughout most of the previous decade, but the "Prosperous Twenties" had really existed in the cities and the towns. Then with a swiftness almost too cruel to be recounted, the blows had begun to fall.

The state's lack of large-scale industrial plants had kept too great an army of unemployed from appearing at first, even though large producers of manufactured goods, like the Colorado Fuel and Iron Company at Pueblo, faced with growing inventories and few orders, discharged workers as production levels dropped. By 1933, Colorado Fuel and Iron was in receivership; in 1936 it emerged as the Colorado Fuel and Iron Corporation. Enterprises, both large and small, soon were being swept downward with the same dismaying results. Banks began to tumble—nearly one-third of the operating banks in the state closed their doors. The Denver and Rio Grande Railroad entered receivership again in 1935. It was ironic that the previous year had been a climactic moment in the railroad's history. The Dotsero Cutoff had been finished, linking Denver and Salt Lake via the Moffat Tunnel, giving Colorado its direct, mainline "transcontinental" route and fulfilling, at long last, the dreams of the pioneers of the 1850s and 1860s.

Just as Colorado's experiences during the onslaught of the depression were replicas of the national scene, so the groping attempts to redeem the economic system resembled those of the rest of the nation. Observers had pointed out that although the full impact of the stock market crash and the depression was delayed in Colorado, in comparison with other states (largely because of the lack of industrialism), recovery from the depression would be equally delayed. The first thought was of local relief, where welfare agencies might extend the necessary help to take care of the destitute, while those with employment or savings conservatively managed their affairs until the storm had passed. But despite heroic efforts, private charity agencies could not keep pace with the worsening conditions.

Another response was the organization of self-help groups, such as the Unemployed Citizens' League of Denver formed in June of 1932 by a group of unemployed professional men. During the year of its operation this cooperative venture provided food for members and engaged in a wide variety of activities; members worked a prescribed number of days to receive benefits.

It became increasingly apparent, however, that neither volunteer relief nor self-help projects were sufficient to meet the emergency, and demands for state action began to be heard. To entertain those demands, the voters placed a series of Democratic governors in the statehouse. William H. Adams, chosen governor in 1928, succeeded himself in 1930. Then for three consecutive elections, Edwin S. Johnson won the governor's chair. It was upon this long-time favorite of Colorado voters that most of the demands for state help fell. Johnson had come to Colorado in 1909 for his health. He had worked for the Midland Railroad, homesteaded in Moffat County, taught school, and managed a cooperative elevator at Craig. When, in 1937, he exchanged the governor's chair for a seat in the United States Senate, his party continued to hold the governorship, electing Teller Ammons, son of former governor Elias Ammons. Not until 1938 did the Republicans return to victory with the election of Ralph L. Carr as governor.

At the time the depression began, the state had neither an income tax nor a sales tax to provide revenue. This fact played a significant part in the reluctance of state officials to commit the commonwealth to a large spending program. Moreover, Colorado's outmoded administrative procedures were ill-suited to handle fiscal matters effectively, and the state also was facing a deficit from the 1931-32 biennium. In its regular session in January, 1933, the legislature side-stepped the question of direct appropriations for relief. Rather, the legislators took the position that it was the responsibility of county governments and municipal authorities to provide relief, supplemented with whatever they could obtain from federal emergency funds. But the federal authorities soon made it clear that they did not intend to continue participation in programs for which they contributed (in the first half of 1933) eighty-five per cent of the funds through the Federal Emergency Relief Administration, while local communities provided the remaining fifteen per cent and the state contributed nothing. Thus, whether the legislature desired to engage in relief activities or not, it was obvious that without state participation in the cooperative programs, federal withdrawal was inevitable.

At a special session of the legislature in August, 1933, Governor Johnson proposed, and the legislature accepted, a plan to tax motor vehicles, earmarking the revenue for relief. The Supreme Court of Colorado soon declared this special levy unconstitutional, and while relief rolls mounted, the state remained a non-contributor. Governor Johnson called a second special session to meet in December. The legislators then attempted to demonstrate the good intentions of the state by appropriating funds to buy cattle to feed the destitute and imposing an excise tax on gasoline, with a fraction of the proceeds specifically designated for relief.

In this way, federal contributions could be continued. By the end of 1935, when federal grants to states were discontinued, and federal agencies shifted to direct work programs, Colorado had received almost $48,500,000 in relief funds from the federal government. In fact, recent statistical analyses indicate that during the period 1933-39 the western states benefited more than other sections from the New Deal on a per capita basis; Colorado ranked tenth of the forty-eight states in per capita expenditures of selected New Deal agencies.[2] No wonder that it was to Washington, rather than Denver, that those searching for personal salvation had turned their eyes.

By the end of 1935, President Franklin Roosevelt's New Deal war against the depression was already a seasoned conflict. Beginning with the specially-called session of Congress in the spring of 1933, and continuing in the months and years that followed, the nation was waging a full-scale campaign against economic havoc, using state and local agencies whenever possible to achieve cooperative success.

One of the earliest and most widely applauded programs of the New Deal was the Civilian Conservation Corps—the CCC. Young men between the ages of seventeen and twenty-three were withdrawn from the lists of the unemployed and put to work building roads and bridges, fire lanes and parks, and generally improving the national forests and lands. Colorado, with a large part of its total land encompassed within boundaries of national forests, became the scene of much CCC activity. Working out of more than forty camps, more than 30,000 men during the years from 1933 to 1942 created needed and welcome improvements in the federally-controlled areas.

Another New Deal action producing particular effects in Colorado was the 1934 abandonment of the gold standard, with the federal government calling for custody of all gold in the country and raising the price to $35.00 a fine ounce. Colorado mines that had been dormant since World War I now stirred to activity. At the time the mines had been closed, increasing labor and material costs, and the decreasing richness of ores, combined with a legally fixed and rigid gold price, had forced the closing. Now, with more efficient reduction methods, and a price rise from $20.67 to $35.00 an ounce, the Camp Bird, Cripple Creek properties and other mines resumed operations on a modest scale. The effect of the price rise in Cripple Creek is apparent in the increase from the 1933 production value of

$2,273,000 to the 1934 record of $4,479,000. Despite the increased activity in gold mining, however, production was far below pre-World War I levels.[3] Silver producers were helped temporarily by the passage of the Silver Purchase Act of 1934. Supported by agricultural as well as western mining interests, the act provided for the government purchase of silver in such amounts as to balance the nation's monetary stocks at a ratio of one-fourth silver to three-fourths gold, thus assuring a market for the white metal.

New Deal legislation brought changes for miners—and other Colorado workers—whether they were members of labor unions or not. The depression, with its armies of unemployed, had concentrated attention on the status of labor; with those then employed seeking protection for their jobs, labor unions experienced heavy increases in membership. The national administration was convinced that unfair labor practices, in which working men often had been weak bargainers against the concentration of power in capital's hands, had played a part in bringing on the economic distress. The New Deal planners now moved to provide legal safeguards for labor's bargaining and working positions. In the Wagner Act of 1935, particularly, procedures for collective bargaining were legalized, along with other guarantees to labor. In Colorado immediate adjustments were necessitated by this legislation. For one thing, the "Rockefeller Plan" that had been instituted in the southern coal fields before World War I was examined by the National Labor Relations Board on the charge that the plan actually established company unions. The Board agreed with the charge and outlawed the plan. So also, state laws prohibiting the use of boycotts and peaceful picketing by unions were declared void by the Colorado Supreme Court.

Agriculture was another area where the existing crisis offered a challenge to New Deal planners. Here the federal government acted on a variety of fronts in attempting to bring order to a confused, chaotic situation. The most massive, and most debated, of the programs were those designed to reduce the acreages planted to crops in order to produce a scarcity of marketable products. In one form or another, this concept has remained the basic foundation of federal farm legislation since that time.

A dramatic answer to the "dusted" Eastern Slope farmers' demands for help came with the offer to resettle those who were living on "submarginal" land. In 1938-39, a group of families from eastern Colorado was resettled in the San Luis Valley near Alamosa. The Farm Security Administration built houses, farm structures, and a community center for use as a school and offices. The new-style "colony" began the task of building new lives, raising potatoes on irrigated lands instead of wheat on arid acres. Other resettlement communities were "planted" near Grand Junction and near Delta.

Those who stayed on the dry lands began the slow reconstruction of both soils and personal fortunes. Federal and state programs to encourage soil conservation were initiated; dry farming techniques were adopted by almost all farmers on the high plains. Terracing, strip farming, contour listing, summer fallowing became universal practices. New crops—Kanred and, later, Tenmarq wheat, sorghums, new oats and barleys—were tested at federal and state experiment stations, and gradually replaced older strains.

In 1934 Congress enacted the first comprehensive legislation to regulate grazing on public lands. The Taylor Grazing Act of that year provided that all unappropriated and unreserved public lands in western states be withdrawn from entry until their usefulness as range lands was determined. A Division of Grazing was organized within the Department of the Interior. This agency then established and controlled (by licenses and fees) "grazing districts." Six Colorado districts regulated 6,500,000 acres of land. It was hoped that the new provisions would contribute satisfactory procedures for both sheep and cattle interests. The antagonisms between the two groups had been volatile since early days; as recently as 1917 the hostilities had exploded in the episode known as the "Gunnison National Forest War." Cowboys had tied up a sheepherder and "rim-rocked" his flock—that is, they drove the sheep over a high cliff to their deaths below.

This brief, selected catalogue illustrating New Deal agencies designed to remedy the depressed and dislocated economy should include the Works Progress Administration—WPA. Probably no other facet of the Roosevelt program more radically changed the lives of Coloradans or the landscape around them. The most visibly apparent results of the program (designed to provide jobs for the unemployed, at the same time creating worthwhile public improvements or opportunities) were the new high school auditoriums, gymnasiums, and stadiums, the bandshells and bridges and playgrounds, the town halls and courthouses scattered over the state. Unlike other relief agencies, the WPA imaginatively encompassed all kinds of unemployed—white collar as well as blue collar; skilled, unskilled, and professional people. Artists and musicians, writers and teachers were helped, along with the manual laborers.

Among the many popular projects pursued under WPA auspices were some especially welcomed by those interested in local and regional history. Old Fort Vasquez was rebuilt; local records were collected and inventoried; dioramas and other displays were constructed at the State Historical Museum in Denver. There was also something quaintly and picturesquely historical in the sight of unemployed men being taught the rudiments of gold panning in Cherry Creek, where victims of an earlier panic, almost a century before, had tried to find their fortunes in the bed of the mountain stream.

Thousands of otherwise destitute persons found work and hope through WPA employment. Early in 1936, almost 43,000 Coloradans (the peak enrollment) were WPA employees. When its activities ended in the state, in 1943, the WPA records demonstrated that the federal government had expended nearly $111,000,000 in funds; local sponsors had added more than $33,000,000 expenditures in material and labor.

Public works, used as depression-lifting devices, seemed to set a theme for the era, and none captivated the imagination more than the intricate schemes to bring West Slope water to East Slope users. Transmontane diversion of water under the Continental Divide had its origins much earlier, but the depression decade saw the first large-scale projects undertaken. Earliest of these was the completion of Denver's lining of the pioneer bore of the Moffat Tunnel, bringing water from the Fraser River on the West Slope through the tunnel and a pipe-line to the capital city in 1936. Three years later, Denver finished a diversion project for additional waters (for sewage treatment) from the Williams Fork of the Colorado River, through Jones Pass Tunnel.

In the Arkansas Valley, a new diversion project was begun, to bring Roaring Fork water to the beet and melon fields of Rocky Ford and Ordway. The Twin Lakes Tunnel, under the Divide at Independence Pass, was built to carry water into the Twin Lakes near Leadville. From there it could be sent down the Arkansas River to the lower valley. A loan of $1,200,000 from the federal Reconstruction Finance Corporation helped the project along. There were ill-fated expectations that the tunnelling through the hills near Leadville might uncover mineral veins of richness sufficient to reduce the costs of the project. No such fortune appeared, but water diversion began in 1935, with 50,000 acre-feet of new water available for the fields.

Of all the projects initiated during the decade, none quite matched the ingenious, gigantic plans for the Colorado-Big Thompson project. The scheme for bringing Western Slope water to the Big Thompson and South Platte valleys was complex both in engineering detail and in the maneuvering necessary to gain congressional approval and appropriations. Some 600,000 acres of land in the Eastern Slope valleys, to be served by the project, were already under cultivation. The federal government, with one hand, was engaged in paying farmers to grow less; to use the other hand to build projects that would increase farm surpluses seemed to many people idiotic. Thus, from the beginning, the planners promised that the new irrigation water would be used only to supplement existing supplies for land already under irrigation; no new fields would be opened. It was a fact that the cultivation of sugar beets and vegetables was increasing in proportion to the quantities of wheat and corn, and that the newer crops demanded more water per acre. On this basis, the need for additional water for old lands was explained. This quieted some opponents, although it was never possible for the advocates of the project to completely deny the charges that more water, wherever or however used, would probably grow larger harvests.

The new water for irrigation—some 310,000 acre-feet a year— would be tumbled through generators on the eastern side of the mountains as it dropped down into the valleys. When completed, the project would produce more electric power than was then used in all of Colorado. The estimates of cost were set at $44,000,000. Of this, the water users would pay back $25,000,000; the electric power sales would repay the balance.

Initially introduced in Congress in 1936, the scheme encountered a barrage of opposition. Since the proposed diversion tunnel was to run under Rocky Mountain National Park from Grand Lake to the vicinity of Estes Park, opponents argued that ugly surface installations at both ends, and a constant fluctuation of the level of Grand Lake, would mar the beauty of the reserved park area. They also insisted that the project would set an evil precedent leading to exploitation of other park lands. Reclamation Bureau promises to clear all debris, and to maintain a minimum fluctuation in Grand Lake water levels, partly silenced the opponents.

Others predicted that the farmers of the Eastern Slope would never be able to pay their cost of the project. This was a particularly cogent argument among non-western tax payers, who saw little personal benefit from the suggested project. In answering these critics, the defenders of the scheme argued that four decades would be allowed for repayment. Since the price of water in the South Platte Valley then exceeded $2.00 an acre-foot, the annual payment of more than $600,000 would satisfy the contract for debt reduction.

The most serious obstacle, however, was the fact that the Colorado congressional delegation was not united. Colorado River water from the West Slope was to be used in eastern Colorado, and Western Slope interests feared that such a mammoth diversion might dry up the river during drought years. Before they would support the project, they demanded an expansion of the plans to include reservoirs to hold the spring waters for late summer use on the Western Slope. The Platte Valley advocates hesitated to meet these demands, for total costs would obviously increase. However, without a unified state delegation, victory could not be achieved. Other states, such as Oklahoma, were busily voicing opinons that Colorado had already received far more than its fair share of reclamation funds. Thus, with reluctance, the Eastern Slope spokesmen committed their constituents to pay the cost of Western Slope reservoirs in order to achieve victory.

Re-introduced in Congress in 1937, the Colorado-Big Thompson bill gained the approval of both houses. President Roosevelt signed the measure on December 28 of that year. The system as outlined (in its basic elements) would consist of two dams on the Colorado River west of the Divide. These dams would store the waters of Granby Reservoir and Shadow Mountain Lake. The water collected at Granby Reservoir would be pumped 186 feet into Shadow Mountain Lake above. From there it would flow by gravity into Grand Lake through a thirteen-mile, nine-foot tunnel under the Continental Divide, through a power plant at Estes Park, into the Big Thompson River, and then through a system of siphons, canals, and reservoirs into the farm ditches of the valley. Ultimately four power plants would be built in addition to the generating installation at Estes Park. Only the latter plant was essential for the operation of the system, however. Power produced there was to be sent back through the tunnel to operate the Granby pumping station on the Western Slope.

Construction got underway in 1938. Almost immediately, two elements conspired to wreck the schedule. Inflation pushed the project's price tag constantly upward, and war-time priorities slowed the work. It was not until 1947 that the system was brought into partial operation, when the first water flowed through the Alva B. Adams Tunnel to the East Slope farms.

29

Life in Colorado Between Two Wars

Probably no twenty-year period in the history of Colorado witnessed as little change in the social scene as did the two decades from 1920 to 1940. Compared with previous eras, or with the years that followed the Second World War, these decades were a time of very slow growth and relatively little change. The great days of metal mining in the state had ended, and coal production was declining. The state's ranches and farms labored under economic handicaps. New or expanding older industries that might have lured laborers to the state did not exist. There was, in fact, little except the climate and scenery to induce people to settle in Colorado. The decades were a transition time; a time for quietly dropping off older aspects of a still quite isolated community and a time for unspectacular foundation-laying for modern-day Colorado.

The population characteristics alone demonstrate this. From the end of World War I until the outbreak of the second global conflict, the population of Colorado increased very slowly. Not since the decade of the 1860s—with its unique hazards of Indian wars, Civil War, refractory ores, and transportation difficulties—had the state failed to record a population increase of at least 100,000 persons. But in the years from 1920 to 1930, only 96,000 additional people were counted, a reflection of both decreased birthrate and the decreased opportunity for employment. The next decade—1930 to 1940—registered an even smaller total gain of 87,500.

Not only had the population increase slowed down; the residents of the Centennial State seemed to maintain an unusual stability in their distribution. Unlike much of the rest of the nation, which continued to experience radical declines in rural population and corresponding increases in the number of urban dwellers, Coloradans remained fairly constant in their location. In 1910, of the state's residents 50.7 per cent were classified as urban; in 1920 this had declined slightly to 48.2 per cent; in 1930 it hovered near the half-way mark at 50.2 per cent. Thus what population increases occurred were rather equally divided between farm and city. Colorado towns were no more lively than its ranches when it came to growth. Compared with earlier records, or with the startling increases that would occur after World War II, Denver's increase from 256,491 persons in 1920 to 322,412 residents in 1940 could only be described as "ordinary." Only three Colorado cities—Pueblo and Colorado Springs, in addition to the capital city—counted more than 25,000 residents in 1930.

Finally it might be pointed out that during the same decades the population of Colorado seemed to grow more homogenous. Smaller numbers of foreign-born persons found their way to the state than ever before. This was partly the result of the new, restrictive "quota" system that had been written into the national immigration laws. But it can also be somewhat attributed to the decline of mining and smelting operations, which ended labor opportunities for large numbers of unskilled workers. The foreign-born residents of the state had accounted for 15.9 per cent of the total population in 1910; by 1930 this percentage had been reduced to 8.2.

There was one exception to this general trend. In the sugar beet fields where the work of planting, thinning, and harvesting required enormous amounts of hand labor, families of migrant workers from Mexico were employed. During the 1920s this seemed to be a desirable situation, for they performed the labor cheaply and no other group was willing to work the long, back-breaking hours in the beet fields, except some Japanese-Americans from West Coast areas who had moved to the state. From time to time a few voices of protest were heard, directed against the state for its failure to regulate the working or living conditions of the migrants, or to provide educational facilities for the migrants' children. But it was not until the 1930s that a major protest was raised.

Then, when relief rolls were expanding and many men were unable to find jobs, anti-migrant sentiment appeared. To bring additional laborers into the state to compete with "native" laborers seemed to many an unjust policy. Reflecting this viewpoint, Governor Ed Johnson announced, in the spring of 1936, a prohibition against importing migrant workers. He proclaimed martial law in the areas along the southern state boundary, stationed National Guardsmen at the highways entering the state, and attempted to turn back all incoming laborers. Such actions raised serious constitutional—to say nothing of humanitarian—questions. After a few days, the governor lifted the restrictions and the migrants again appeared to labor in the beet fields.

The fact that it was the economic question, rather than humanitarian or social considerations, that finally attracted attention to the migrant labor policy is indicative of the change that had come to the social scene in the years since the reforming Progressives had administered public affairs. In the 1920s there was little need to be concerned with the cost of public welfare—or the tax rate for relief—for no programs existed in Colorado outside the county level. Until 1933, for example, the only provision made for elderly indigents in the state was the institution known as the "poorhouse." These care-taker facilities existed, if at all, at the direction of individual counties, without supervision or aid from the state government. Not until late in the decade was any change in the structure contemplated.

In 1927, in a belated beginning at welfare for older persons, the legislature awkwardly attempted to institute a state-wide policy of assistance. This first program was based upon continuing action by individual counties, with no state funds involved. Each county, if its commissioners desired, could provide a levy to raise revenue to financially assist (in their homes) needy persons seventy years or older. The attempt was doomed from the beginning. Not only was a system of state financing withheld; opponents immediately raised the constitutional question of whether it was legal for county commissioners to act in a "judicial capacity." When the courts agreed with the opponents, the act became a dead statute.

Six years later, in 1933, a new approach was made. By this time the effects of the depression had so dramatically illustrated the need for old age assistance that the long-prevailing barrier against the use of state funds for relief vanished. The General Assembly now instituted a mandatory program, under the control of county judges (to escape the unconstitutionality charges of the earlier enactment), with state funds to be augmented through county levies. Maximum payments were set at one dollar a day for subsistence. The one grave defect in the legislation, aside from allowing the counties the option of adding to state allocations, was the decision to distribute available monies on the basis of population, rather than "need." Since only one county imposed a tax to increase its revenues for the program, the state funds were distributed in such a way that the amount available to qualified pensioners might vary from $5.00 a month in one county to $27.00 a month in another county.

Meanwhile, plans for a federal social security act were progressing, and in 1936, after the enactment of the national legislation, it was necessary to change the Colorado policies to allow participation in the federal program. Some of the more restrictive eligibility requirements of the state law were eliminated, maximum pensions were set at $30.00 a month, and a finished program for old age assistance seemed established. But, as events soon proved, this was only a beginning.

The Great Depression had spawned a variety of schemes designed to bring "social justice" to every conceivable group and stratum of American society. In the case of older citizens, the needs were drastic and the suggestions offered were radical. When payrolls had to be trimmed, employers often eliminated older workers unprotected by union rules of seniority; investment failures and dwindling income from savings had created especially bleak conditions for senior citizens. Among those who turned their attention to the plight of these "oldsters" was Californian Dr. Francis Townsend, author of the plan that called for payments of $200 a month to every citizen over sixty years of age. The only basic requirement stipulated that the pensioner must retire from work and must spend his allotment during the month it was paid to him. Townsend's ideas, and those of many other "social engineers," spread across the nation during the dark depression days.

In Colorado, the National Annuity League was the agency responsible for initiating a revolutionary scheme of old age pensions. In the November elections of 1936, the voters accepted a version of the League's plan. It provided that payments of $45.00 a month would be made to pensioners sixty years of age or older. The customary liens on property of pensioners were wiped away, allowing retention of both personal property and inhabited real estate. Townsend's basic ideas appeared in the "jack pot" provision of the amendment, stipulating that the balance in the state fund designated for pensions, at the end of each year, was to be evenly divided among all the pensioners on the rolls. This not only ignored the concept of "need"; in the future, as revenues increased, it created the spectacle of part of the state's total revenue being split each January among the senior citizens.

To fund the new program, the amendment designated the state sales and use tax (which the legislature had recently adopted) a permanent tax, earmarking eighty-five per cent of the two per cent levy for the pension fund. By freezing the pension program into the constitution, the pension advocates insured maximum protection against any changes in their plan. Not until the 1950s, and then only after a strenuous campaign of education to gain acceptance of another constitutional amendment, was the state allowed to recapture some of the sales tax revenue for other purposes, at the same time providing adequately for the pensioners' welfare.

Old people were not the only group whose plight during the depression years called for new considerations of welfare. Children were equally a concern. Dependent minors, who for any of a variety of reasons could not be cared for by their mothers or guardians, earlier had come under the sympathetic eye of the Progressives. In 1913, a Mothers' Compensation Law had provided optional county welfare payments for the care of dependent children. The optional element had been retained, and, although some counties had assisted these children, as late as 1934 only thirty-three of Colorado's sixty-three counties had made any provision for administering such a program. In 1936 this was changed. The legislature passed the Dependent Children Act, making county participation in the program mandatory, insuring, in this manner, continued benefits from federal legislation.

In this, as in so many other areas, the need to meet minimum federal regulations in order to qualify for federal aid for programs was a major element motivating state action. If federal funds were available, the state intended to arrange its programs to meet the requirements to receive the assistance offered. In the early years of the New Deal, particularly, it was not always easy to ascertain precisely where the role of the state and the role of the federal agencies met. A good indication of this difficulty can be seen in Colorado's attempt to match its administrative agencies charged with welfare programs to the expanded nature of the programs themselves.

Late in the nineteenth century, a recognition of the advantages of state supervision of welfare agencies had generated a statute (in 1891) creating a State Board of Charities and Corrections. This board was given the authority to investigate public charities and to examine the conditions of correctional institutions. However, it had no control functions. Throughout its lifetime, the board remained an advisory agency only.

In 1923 the General Assembly abolished this board and created, in its place, a Department of Charities and Corrections, with a secretary directly responsible to the governor. An appropriation for two years enabled the secretary to expand the work of the department, but then, for the next eight years, no further funds were allocated. A part-time secretary continued to work in the state executive offices, taking care of the clerical chores concerning the penitentiary and other correctional institutions. By 1933, it had become obvious that, without reorganization and sufficient funds, the state's welfare agencies could not be adequately or efficiently administered. The result was the creation of a new agency—the Division of Public Welfare—which absorbed the duties and powers of the older board. Three years later the new agency's name was changed to the state Department of Public Welfare; it supervised and administered all welfare activities, including child services, outdoor and indoor care of needy persons, assistance to the aged, the blind, and would, in the years ahead, have other responsibilities assigned to its care.

In 1936, when the Colorado voters approved the pension amendment, they also gave their sanction to a constitutional amendment providing the first state tax on individual and corporation income. The proceeds of this tax, for the first years, were designated for use as a public school fund. Until that time, the only source of state aid for school districts had been the income from the state school lands; all other financing had come from levies within each district. Consequently, little uniformity existed among the public schools, even though an earlier "minimum teachers' salary law" had been enacted. The cost per student in public schools might vary all the way from the $43.14 per student enrolled in Costilla County in 1932 to the $165.34 per student in Summit County the same year.

Once the state had embarked on revenue-gathering through income taxes, the concept of "equalization" of educational facilities throughout the state began to be debated. Many of the mining areas of the state, particularly, were losing population; their assessments on real property had fallen drastically during the depression years. More and more citizens began to believe that it was in the best interests of the state to offer equal educational opportunities to all children, regardless of the county's or the town's financial condition. Not until 1943, however, was the actual legislative action forthcoming that allowed a beginning of such "equalization" through school funds to be made.

Competing with the public schools for a slice of state revenue each year were the publicly-supported colleges and universities. In the early 1920s, the state's second teachers college, at Gunnison, initiated a four-year course leading to the baccalaureate degree, and to fit its elevated status, the name of the school was changed to Western State College. In 1925 the first classes were enrolled in a third teacher-training institution—Adams State College, at Alamosa.

In addition, it was during these decades that the first modern junior colleges in Colorado were established. Designed to provide both beginning college courses and vocational training, the first such schools opened in 1925, at Trinidad and Grand Junction. Pueblo Junior College began classes in 1933. That year also marked the opening of Fort Lewis Agricultural and Mechanical College at Hesperus, where the buildings that had housed Fort Lewis in the previous century, and had then been used as an Indian school, and then as an agricultural and vocational high school, now formed the campus of a publicly-supported junior college. The General Assembly, in 1936, enacted legislation that allowed a county, or group of counties, to create a taxing district for the support of such institutions. The first new school formed under this law was the junior college at Lamar in the Arkansas Valley.

The instruments that brought the greatest change in the lives of most Coloradans, however, were not junior colleges, nor teachers colleges, nor old age pensions. Rather, the overall impact of the new mechanical triumphs—the radio, the airplane, and the automobile— probably affected the lives of more people in a more dramatic manner than any other change, except for the Great Depression itself. The state suddenly dwindled in size with the new transportation and communication techniques; mountain ranges no longer isolated the state as they had in the past.

The beginnings of scheduled commercial air flights challenged the remoteness of the Rocky Mountain West from the rest of the United States. But in communication, much of the same effect was achieved with the inauguration of regularly scheduled radio broadcasts. The year 1920 marked the origination of broadcasting in Colorado, when W. D. Reynolds started a station in Colorado Springs. The next year he moved the station to Denver where it became KLZ. Three years later General Electric started broadcasts from its Denver station, KOA. By 1940, the fifteen stations in Colorado were so located that almost every area of the state was served by one or more stations.

Even more dramatically than either the radio or the airplane, the automobile changed the daily lives of Coloradans. The mass-produced cars of the 1920s and 1930s afforded those who lived on farms, ranches, and heretofore isolated towns the opportunity to travel to urban centers at pleasure and in comfort. Mass ownership and operation of automobiles brought a continuation of earlier demands for better highway construction and maintenance. The mileage of improved roads in Colorado increased in the 1920s, largely because dollar-matching funds for construction were now available from the federal government. But a major assault upon the problem awaited the year 1935. Then Governor Ed Johnson proposed, and the legislature accepted, a state bond issue of $15,000,000 to initiate a major paving program for the state highways.

While none of these problems or changes was distinctively peculiar to the Colorado scene (for all other areas of the nation were undergoing the same changes and problems), there were unique features in the Colorado situation. The combination of unusual climate and spectacular mountain scenery had long marked Colorado as a mecca for tourists. As the shift from railroad travel to automobile touring took place, it became incumbent on Coloradans to maintain the best possible highways in order to continue to attract tourists. Not only did these visitors want adequate highways to drive over; accommodations and entertainments became part of the growing industry. The city of Denver, for example, purchased Overland Park and, in 1921, converted it to a motor camp for the use of the "gypsy motorists." The tourists provided their own cooking and living equipment and settled down for long stays at such camp grounds. Denver remodeled the Exposition Building at the park for a grocery store, soda fountain, and public laundry. City organizations scheduled concerts and lectures to entertain the tourists during their residence at the park. By 1925 this camp, and two others operated by the city, had housed an estimated 76,000 tourists.

Of course, many tourists wanted to see more of Colorado than its capital city. Among attractions, the two national parks in the state ranked high. An indication of the change that the automobile had brought to tourism can be seen in the ambitious program initiated in 1929 when the federal government began the construction of Trail Ridge Road through Rocky Mountain National Park. Because of the high altitudes, construction was restricted to the summer months; it took four seasons to build the road from Estes Park to Grand Lake. When it was finished, tourists could drive on a highway running for more than ten miles above timberline, and almost half of those miles at altitudes above 12,000 feet. The highway enhanced the popularity of the park immensely. Records indicate that in 1933 a total of

291,000 visitors, in some 83,000 automobiles, entered the mountain park gates.

Although it is more remotely situated, Colorado's other national park, Mesa Verde, also registered increases in visitors during these decades. In 1921, only 3,000 tourists (651 automobiles) were recorded at Mesa Verde. By 1933, these statistics had increased to 16,000 visitors (4,000 automobiles). Perhaps the most exciting innovation at this park was the completion of the first instrument to scientifically date the ruins of the cliff dwellers. Dr. Andrew E. Douglass of the University of Arizona, in 1929, finished his tree-ring calendar. This archeological tool, based on the natural growth of trees—with thick rings in wet years and thin rings in dry years—provided a master time-chart for timber. By comparing cross-sections from the poles used in the cliff dwellings with the new calendar, the specific dating of ruins, back to the eighth century, was possible. The veil hiding these mysterious, prehistoric Indians from modern man's knowledge had been drawn back a little further.

In addition to the national parks, tourists also were lured to the national monuments. In 1932, some 46,000 acres of land on the west slopes of the Sangre de Cristo range were designated a national monument to preserve the great sand dunes. Three years earlier, the natural "Mount of the Holy Cross" in White River National Forest, had been set aside as a monument, although in 1950, because of the difficulty of maintenance, the designation would be withdrawn. President Hoover, in 1933, proclaimed the creation of a monument in the Black Canyon of the Gunnison River.

The continuing expansion of federally-controlled lands in the state—either by the creation of monuments, or the expansion of earlier designated areas—met some local protest. Not only did this expansion remove lands from potential taxation rolls of the local and state governments; unlike the national forests, where grazing was conducted under a license and fee system, the national parks and monuments were closed to sheep and cattle. Only in times of emergency—such as war or extreme drought—and then only under limited conditions, was the general prohibition lifted. Consequently, both cattle and sheep interests felt threatened by the encroachments of federal action. Probably, however, the majority of Coloradans favored the new designations, both because they preserved the scenic wonders of a fast-fading frontier, and also because they added to the growing tourist attractions.

Not all of these attractions were federally created. In fact, one of the noteworthy endeavors to provide first-class recreation and entertainment for summer visitors resulted from the work of a dedicated group of Colorado women and their male allies. Ida Kruse McFarlane and Anne Evans (daughter of Colorado's second territorial governor) originated the concept of the Central City Festival, destined to become an outstanding example of a new type of tourist attraction. By the 1920s, the days of Central City's glory had long since passed. The town was "falling to pieces"; the famed Opera House—often termed the finest west of the Mississippi—had suffered neglect and ruin. The concept of a festival was centered around a renovation of the Opera House and the importation of quality entertainment during the summer season.

The McFarlanes inaugurated the program of rehabilitation by donating the theater to the University of Denver, thereby ensuring a tax-free status for the enterprise. The women then initiated a series of teas and functions to nourish interest in their project. They used the funds they raised to rebuild the roof of the Opera House, to restore the frescoes that had been ruined in the years when the building had housed a movie theater, and generally to rebuild and refurnish the structure. "Memorial chairs" were sold to increase the funds for the project. By July, 1932, a transfigured Opera House was ready for the opening of the first Central City Festival. Lillian Gish opened the house in a production of "Camille." One of the nation's most successful festivals had its birth that night, for in the years that followed, the charm of seeing and hearing first-rate operas and plays in a unique nineteenth century mining-town theater has proved irresistible to tourists and Coloradans alike.

30

The 1940s: A Colorado Watershed

For twenty years—from 1919 to 1939—Colorado had been a quiet place. Population growth was very slow; mining and agriculture both had suffered sicknesses that even the radical prescriptions of those years had failed to remedy. Observers might understandably predict that the glorious days of the Centennial State had passed; that never again would excitement like that generated by a Leadville or a Cripple Creek spur the fortune-seekers and fortune-makers into the state. The past was now exploitable in Central City Festivals and tourist attractions; the future lacked even the excitement that a dressed-up ghost-town could evoke.

And then, with the advent of the global conflict called World War II, everything suddenly was different. No other single event in its history and no other national crisis—not the Civil War, nor World War I, nor the Great Depression—brought to Colorado such great change as did the Second World War. Much of what contemporary Colorado is, and what the state will become in the future, results from the events of the years from 1940 to 1950.

The story of the impact of the war on Colorado is really two stories. One of these was reminiscent of Colorado's role in the earlier World War, with volunteers and draftees climbing aboard trains to be carried to training camps; with heavy demands on fields and factories to mobilize their economic resources for war; with bond quotas and servicemen's gifts and daily sacrifices for the ultimate victory over the enemies. At the same time, in a pattern quite different from that of the first war, another aspect of the more recent conflict saw military installations and scientific developments in Colorado that laid the basis for much of the complexion and character of the state after the war had ended.

The first of these stories can be told rather simply, although it is never possible to completely recapture the dedication and desire for personal sacrifice such an effort produces. It is, for example, fairly simple to record that, during the war, 138,832 men and women either enlisted or were drafted into the service of the country. This number represented approximately one eighth of the state's population. There was scarcely a family in Colorado—as in all of the nation—that, in some measure, was not affected by the seemingly insatiable, continuing call for manpower for the armed services. Of those who left the state for training, approximately 2,700 gave their lives for their country during the conflict.

These statistics are simply related. What is not so easy to recapture is the heartache of broken homes; the waiting and working for the momentous events termed VE and VJ days; the increasing demand for news from the fronts as the war progressed; the ration books and limited consumer goods—all the daily fears and frustrations that accompany modern warfare.

Again, as in the period of the First World War, the demands on farm and factory brought radical expansion of planting and fabricating to the already existing installations, at the same time spawning a host of new enterprises. The farmers' abrupt turn from the policies of recent years was almost paradoxical. Throughout the depression decade, the farmers had been directing their efforts toward reduction of acreages planted in order to induce price increases. Now they were encouraged to expand their operations, in order to meet the demand for foodstuffs. "The new bonanza had old results. The plainsmen became intoxicated by high prices and good crops. Once again they played agricultural poker with the same reckless abandon they had known in World War I. With the appearance of better times and an unprecedented demand, land values shot upward. Land that Colorado farmers had abandoned during dustbowl days sold for forty dollars an acre."[1] The climbing land values only reflected the spiraling prices that wheat and corn and sugar and beef commanded during the war years.

Of course the hazards of such rapid expansion still loomed large. "During the war any soil that would germinate seed was put to use. And after the war, in the day of the Marshall Plan and of economic aid to less fortunate parts of the world, the demand for grain stayed high. So the Westerners kept at their task of ripping up sod, searching for more soil in which to plant. A conservation writer, visiting near Cheyenne Wells, Colorado, in the spring of 1946, watched them at work and remarked: 'They were plowing again the land reclaimed from the dust by Government help and sowed back to grass in the 1930s. They were also turning over native sod on shallow soils never before plowed. This was but a sample of the mischief going on in a dozen other localities along a 600-mile front.' "[2]

Fortunately, all that had been learned in the previous two decades was not forgotten. The lessons of deep plowing and contouring, terracing and strip-farming were remembered. These techniques, along with the shelter belts of New Deal years, kept the damage from reaching the depths of the earlier era.

Agriculture responded to the wartime needs with the greatest production in Colorado's history and continued to do well in the immediate post-war years. Seldom had the farmer been in a more favorable position; not until 1949 did farm income start to slip. While the farmer and rancher prospered, their numbers persisted in declining; correspondingly, the average size of individual holdings jumped. This reflected, in part, increased mechanization of operations through the use of power-driven machinery, but it also showed the age-old attraction of the cities and the failure of the small operator to meet the changing conditions.

The factories, like the farms, found more than ready markets for their products. And, like the farmers, manufacturers not only converted their existing facilities to war production, but soon found cause to expand their capacities or construct new installations as a result of the crisis. Hardly an industrial plant in the state was untouched by the effort, whether it was a massive enterprise like the Colorado Fuel and Iron Corporation at Pueblo or a small establishment like the little Heckethorn Company at Littleton, only a few years old when the war began but soon engaged in ordnance work. The variety of war goods turned out was impressive. Even ships were built in land-locked Denver. The hull sections for escort vehicles were put together in Denver steel yards, beginning with the U.S.S. *Mountain Maid*, "launched" in the spring of 1942. Army barges also were fabricated in Denver factories before the war ended.

The Denver Arms Plant, which the federal government built in 1941, was one of the largest of the new installations. The Remington Company and, later, Henry J. Kaiser, operated it as an arsenal and ammunition works. At its height of operation, almost 20,000 workers were employed there in manufacturing cartridges, shells, and fuses. In 1942, north of Aurora, the federal government constructed the Rocky Mountain Arsenal—a chemical warfare plant which soon employed as many as 15,000 persons. Other federal facilities included a Medical Depot in northeast Denver and an Ordnance Depot at Pueblo.

These plants and depots constructed in Colorado during World War II form part of the pattern that differed radically from the experience of the earlier conflict when almost no such expenditures were designated for the state. But these installations were only a part of the vast expenditure of federal funds on wartime installations in Colorado. A cluster of major service camps and training facilities was created within the state, bringing thousands of servicemen to Colorado for training, and contributing to the tone for the development of the state after the war was ended. Two far-reaching effects resulted, in addition to the obvious contemporary changes in employment opportunities and the interjection of thousands of temporary personnel into the population of the state. For one thing, thousands of servicemen stationed in the state during the war literally "fell in love" with the mountain scenery and Colorado climate. No small part of the impressive population growth of Colorado in the post-war years, which contrasted so remarkably with the small increases in the years from 1920 to 1940, resulted from the decision of many of these wartime visitors to move to Colorado and make their home in the state after the war had ended.

During the 1940s the state's population increased by over 200,000, a greater jump than any of the other mountain states except Arizona. This was due primarily to the growth of the urban areas, especially those located on the Eastern Slope. The population increase in Denver and the three adjacent counties—Adams, Arapahoe, and Jefferson—represented seventy-eight per cent of the state's increase for the decade. In the census of 1950 these four counties had 42.5 per cent of the total population. All the mountain counties, which depended chiefly on mining, lost people during the forties. Nor were these the only ones to decline; the census revealed that thirty-five out of the state's sixty-three counties had decreased in numbers.

The other effect is more difficult to define precisely. The scientific aspects of some of the wartime installations left a "residue" at war's end. This, combined with several other features, including the determined effort of Colorado leaders to attract new industries, a climate attractive to personnel, and major efforts by existing institutions and industries to cooperate, collectively resulted in the centering along the mountain base from Pueblo on the south to Fort Collins on the north, of a complex series of scientific-research-military installations that gives to contemporary Colorado one of its unique features.

At the time, however, this was all in the future. During the war years, the object was to train young men and women to the specialties demanded by a modern armed conflict. One of the major sites for such training had its beginning before Pearl Harbor. In 1938, on a site near Aurora, the Army Air Force established an instruction center named Lowry Air Base. The headquarters of the base were housed in the buildings of the former Agnes Memorial Sanatorium that Lawrence C. Phipps built in memory of his mother. Negotiations for the installation had started in 1934, when the army began seeking a site. Denver bought the Sanatorium and another 960 acres, added 64,000 acres to the southeast for a bombing range, and presented them all to the federal government. On this land, a school for aircraft armorers and aerial photographers was authorized in 1937 and opened the following year. Also near Denver, the Navy began constructing Buckley Field in April, 1942, for use as an armament school.

Other air installations in the state included Peterson Air Field near Colorado Springs, built on the site of the city airport to train heavy bombardment groups; La Junta Army Air Field, originally planned to train British Royal Air Force personnel, but later shifted to American students who used the 521,000-acre bombing range south of the city; and the Pueblo Army Air Base, with a tract in Otero County for air-to-ground gunnery practice.

World War II was a global conflict, in every sense of the term, and the variety of battlefronts on which campaigns were envisioned placed unique demands on American forces. In anticipation of mountain campaigning, the army equipped and trained special forces at Camp Hale, located on 2,000 acres within Holy Cross National Forest. This camp was constructed in the summer of 1942 and was occupied by troops the following winter. The proximity to good ski slopes made the camp's location extremely desirable.

The largest of the military bases in Colorado was Camp Carson, an army post built on 60,000 acres of land near Colorado Springs. This new camp, named for the famed explorer-scout, Kit Carson, provided training facilities for the 89th, 71st, and 104th divisions before their departure overseas, as well as many other units of engineers, tank battalions, decontamination teams, airborne engineers, and mountain troops. More than 150,000 men were trained at Camp Carson before VJ Day. Late in the war years, as the numbers of American soldiers based at the camp declined, the facilities were used to house German prisoners of war.

"Prisoners" of a different sort were temporarily housed in another area of Colorado during the war years. In the Arkansas Valley, near Granada, on a tract of 11,000 acres, the federal government established a camp for Japanese-Americans who were interned and moved from their homes on the West Coast. Facilities to house between 8,000 and 10,000 persons were soon erected. The first of the camp's occupants arrived at Amachi in August, 1942. Most of the men and some of the women worked in the agricultural fields in the area, harvesting sugar beets and potatoes. At least two-thirds of the residents of the camp were United States citizens, and while their neighbors outside the camp argued the moral and constitutional aspects of this internment policy, many of the young men enlisted in the nation's armed services, demonstrating on the battlefields their loyalty to the United States. In Amachi, a city in itself, an internal government for the camp was soon established, as were school facilities, a newspaper for the residents, and life—in admittedly barren and restricted form—continued for the Japanese-Americans.

The Granada Relocation Camp was closed in July, 1945, even before VJ Day; other installations were shut down after the war. But Lowry Field continued to operate as a permanent training school for the Air Force; Camp Carson served as a mountain troop summer home for Camp Hale ski troops. Then, during the Korean conflict, thousands of basic trainees were schooled at Carson. In 1954 the Defense Department designated the camp a permanent installation, changing its name to Fort Carson.

The end of the war saw little change in the population of wounded and recuperating veterans in Colorado military hospitals. Fitzsimons General Hospital, which the army had first located in Aurora during World War I, absorbed many service personnel for treatment. The Navy had used Hotel Colorado at Glenwood Springs for a convalescent hospital. Since 1922, the Veterans Administration had operated a hospital at Fort Lyons on the Arkansas River. Now, as the thousands of ex-GIs needed care, the Veterans Administration selected two additional sites for hospitals in Colorado. Major medical centers were created at Grand Junction, opened in April, 1949, and at Denver, completed in 1951.

The state's colleges and universities also absorbed many ex-GIs in the years that followed the end of the war. Most of the educational institutions in Colorado had themselves "gone to war" during the

Snow-capped Pikes Peak in the distance, and the U.S. Air Force Academy in the foreground.

conflict, housing special training units. The University of Colorado had hosted a language school for the Navy; Denver University had trained air corps, language, and engineering students; a naval unit had operated at Colorado College; the state college at Greeley and Colorado A&M had housed quartermaster units; the School of Mines had trained engineers. At war's end, the colleges prepared to return to civilian pursuits, but soon they were engaged in a desperate struggle to take care of the crowds of returning veterans. Their facilities were taxed to the limits—and sometimes beyond—by the flood of students. New buildings, additional faculties, and expanded requirements of all kinds were necessitated by this unique experiment in mass collegiate education that Congress had authorized by the G.I. Bill.

All told, some 117,000 Colorado veterans took advantage of the opportunities the nation offered them (both World War II returnees and, later, those from the Korean conflict) to study at a college or university. But this was only a part of the story. Another 9,400 veterans received vocational rehabilitation training; another 77,800 used the home loan benefits provided; 5,200 qualified for similar facilities for purchasing farms, and 2,200 for business loans. The impact of the legislation on the state's economy, its educational facilities, and on the returning veterans themselves, stands in marked contrast with the earlier experience in the months and years that followed the Armistice of 1918.

The military complexion of such Colorado cities as Denver and Colorado Springs, appropriated during the war years, was to some extent diminished by the reconversion process during the first years after the war. But it had not been completely erased when the Korean episode brought renewed defense activities to the state. And, since that time, it has continued to grow. Colorado Springs, particularly, has retained a military tone, partly from the Fort Carson activities, partly from the decision in 1957 to locate the North American Air Defense Command at Ent Air Base there, and partly from the decision to build the Air Force Academy on the city's doorstep.

It was in 1949 that the Secretary of Defense, James Forrestal, created a committee to recommend a general system of education for service officers. Robert L. Stearns, the president of the University of Colorado, chaired the committee. Within a year this advisory group reported that an air academy, separate from both West Point and Annapolis, alone would answer the needs of the Air Force. When Congress authorized creation of the institution in 1954, Harold Talbott, the Secretary of the Air Force began the work of selecting a site. Three "semi-finalist" sites emerged from the screenings: Alton (Illinois), Lake Geneva (Wisconsin), and Colorado Springs. It was Talbott who decided to accept the offer of the state of Colorado of $1,000,000 toward the purchase of a tract of 17,900 acres of land, eight miles north of Colorado Springs. Situated at an altitude of 7,900 feet, the land bordered Pike National Forest and encompassed such scenic attractions as the limestone formation called Cathedral Rock and Monument Creek.

The bulldozers and earth-movers soon were at work, and the glass, aluminum, steel, and white marble buildings (designed by the architectural firm of Skidmore, Owings and Merrill) began to demonstrate their startlingly rectangular silhouettes against the mountain backdrop. The Cadet Wing moved to the Academy from its temporary campus at Lowry Field in late August, 1958. The following June the first class was graduated from the permanent campus. By that time, $140,000,000 had been expended on construction of the Academy, not including such "extras" as the football stadium and the golf course which were built with private funds.

While these changes took place, state politics rolled on in its time-honored fashion. After a two-term flirtation with Franklin Roosevelt and the New Deal, Colorado returned to the Republican column in the presidential election of 1940 by giving Wendell Wilkie a 14,000 vote majority. The Democratic advantage actually had ended in 1938, with Republican candidate for governor, Ralph Carr, defeating the incumbent Democrat, Teller Ammons. The Republicans continued to be victorious until 1946, when another party change in the governor's chair presaged a switch in the next presidential election. Harry Truman's hard-fought nationwide campaign produced a Colorado victory for him and a virtual sweep for the Democratic party in the major state elections. Not since the 1932-36 honeymoon with Roosevelt had the Democrats been so successful.

Meanwhile, as the forties ended, Colorado mining suffered a blow when the Cripple Creek mines were almost completely shut down, primarily because of the closing of the Golden Cycle Mill at Colorado Springs. Teller County had been the state's leading gold producer. The mining of precious metals, which had shown an increase since 1946, dropped off as a consequence. During the war, intensive exploration had been carried on by the Bureau of Mines in Colorado's known mineral areas to uncover needed supplies of various metals; gold and silver mining, however, had declined as a result of federal restrictions. Molybdenum, under the pressure of wartime requirements, became the state's most valuable mineral, and it was estimated, at the end of the conflict, that the Climax Molybdenum Company was producing seventy-two per cent of the world's output of this metal.

Coal production reached an all-time high in 1943 but dropped off steadily after the war, when the demand lessened and the competition from oil and gas increased. Oil, long a bridesmaid in Colorado mineral development, showed an astonishing production jump from 1.7 million barrels in 1940 to 23.4 million nine years later. The demands of modern life, from home to industry, were responsible for this development and growth.

Colorado mining took an exciting turn in the late forties with a uranium rush into the Colorado plateau and off-shoots into other areas. The excitement, a by-product of the atomic age and the "Cold War," was sparked in 1948 when the Atomic Energy Commission (AEC) concluded details of a major program for uranium exploration. For the next decade uranium lured the adventuresome as gold had done ninety years before. Attention was quickly focused on Uravan and the Paradox Valley, where the ore was known to exist, having been mined earlier. Efforts were directed particularly to recovering radium and vanadium, which had commercial value. The rich Belgian Congo discoveries in the 1920s had ended an earlier period of prosperity based on radium; vanadium, used to increase the tensile strength of steel, had been mined both before and during World War II. Grand Junction, the largest community in the area, became the natural base for much of the activity; more than one hundred uranium companies established their headquarters there, and the town took on the trappings of the feverish expansion that had hit earlier Colorado mining camps.

Gone from the scene were some of the old standbys of previous days—the burro, mining pan, pick and shovel. In their place came jeeps, low-flying airplanes, Geiger counters, and other wonders of modern invention. Thousands rushed into the region, spurred on by stories of rich discoveries. Articles in popular magazines, some romanticizing, others trying to present the "true" picture, brought nationwide attention. This was not an endeavor to be undertaken by the ignorant or unprepared—the land was rugged, dry, and vast—but they came anyway. The AEC sponsored road-building programs to the isolated sites, paid bonuses for production, and tried to keep some control from its office in Grand Junction. Like the old days, however, promoters appeared; stock speculation in penny-and-up shares seemed to be an easier way to wealth than trudging through canyons and mesas. Small towns, such as Moab and Monticello in Utah, and Rifle, Uravan, Naturita, and Dove Creek in Colorado, prospered.

In other areas, like Caribou in Boulder County, uranium ores were found; companies were organized and work started, as the demands of the "Cold War" stimulated an all-out effort to find sources of the metal. Mills and reduction plants to process the ores—for war and peacetime uses—were authorized by the AEC in various Colorado locations. They were soon operating in such scattered towns as Durango, Gunnison, Canon City, Grand Junction, Rifle, and Uravan. At Rocky Flats, between Denver and Boulder, the Dow Chemical Company, under contract to the AEC, built a defense plant to utilize the production in various, still classified, secret operations.

From 1948 through 1960 Colorado produced uranium ore valued at about $133,456,000. Production in the sixties gradually declined to roughly twenty million in 1968 and seventeen million the next

Prospecting with jack hammer air drills for uranium—Montrose County. (State Historical Society of Colorado)

vear, Montrose and San Miguel counties producing over half the total. The boom had receded by then; the lonely land that had once buzzed with activity was returning to a more normal condition. Isolation, increasing cost of operation and exploration, cutback of government support, lower prices, and depletion of older deposits had helped bring this about, as had the availability of cheaper sources elsewhere. Ore still exists, however, and someday, when the need is great enough, production will probably increase.

This last Colorado mining rush left behind typical scars on the landscape: pollution, abandoned buildings, and roads that wander to nowhere. It also left behind something different: radioactive wastes, like the tailings piles that mark the site of the mill at Durango, or the fill that was used in construction at Grand Junction.

The war years and their immediate aftermath marked a division in Colorado history. As in the gold rush years of a century earlier, an abrupt transition had occurred which ushered into existence a new era for the people of the Centennial State. Problems emerged, some new, others with only a new emphasis, that would demand increasing attention in the decades to come. Fresh opportunities also surfaced in the post-war years to challenge Coloradans. The depression, with its problems, was gone; the war which had touched the state so dramatically had passed. Colorado could never turn back to what might have seemed a more romantic era.

31

Mid-Century Challenges

During the late 1950s or early 1960s Colorado passed its first centennial, the exact year depending on whether the count was based on the 1858-59 gold rush or territorial status in 1861. The state's official celebration in 1959 was called the "Rush to the Rockies Centennial." Though the event failed to generate as much enthusiasm as its sponsors predicted (proving to be a rather pale imitation of the original gold rush), Colorado could look forward to entering its second hundred years with substantial optimism. It had come of age; the frontier period had long passed, although it would still be nostalgically remembered.

If much of the nation seemed to ignore Colorado's centennial celebration, other events did command attention. The national spotlight focused on the state when President Dwight Eisenhower (whose wife had been born in Denver) chose Colorado as his summer retreat for relaxation and fishing. His enjoyment in seeking the wily trout brought fame to the Fraser region; his heart attack while on vacation in September, 1955, made necessary a temporary White House at Fitzsimons Army Hospital.

Denver had been called the "Second National Capital" even before that event because of the number of federal agencies located there. Many of those agencies were headquartered in the old Denver Arms Plant which, after World War II, was converted into the Denver Federal Center. Other Colorado cities also hosted federal agencies, including numerous national park and forest headquarters, while Boulder was selected as the site for both a branch of the National Bureau of Standards and the National Center for Atmospheric Research.

The federal government was active in the state in other ways. In 1956 Congress authorized the Upper Colorado River Project, encompassing in a 110,000 square-mile basin plans for reservoirs, dams, and power plants in Arizona, Utah, New Mexico, and Colorado. The major purpose of this sweeping agreement was to provide an equitable division and apportionment of water in the Colorado river system. It also involved water storage, flood prevention, and electric power. Each of the states involved was allotted amounts of water to be used during the year, and a river commission was established to

Blue Mesa Dam. Aerial view showing Blue Mesa Dam, powerplant, and reservoir. (Bureau of Reclamation, U.S. Department of Interior)

Morrow Point Dam. (Bureau of Reclamation, U.S. Department of Interior)

oversee the operation. Launched with great hopes, the project took years and high costs to begin operation and then only with complaints and bickering. It was hoped that the project would "promote interstate comity," but ingrained attitudes and state interests proved hard to eradicate.

An indication, however, of the financial success of the operation was the nearly $98 million in revenues for the twelve-month period ending September 30, 1970, or $25 million more than the preceding year. Project repayment was moving ahead faster than the Bureau of Reclamation had predicted. This increased revenue came from higher than estimated sales of electric power and water.

Among the "participating projects" in the Upper Colorado system were the Blue Mesa Dam on the Gunnison River, Rifle Gap Dam near Silt, and Lemon Dam on the Florida River in La Plata County. Local irrigation and recreation benefited and all were magnets for tourists. The building of one dam aroused a great deal of controversy. The Glen Canyon Dam and Lake Powell, while providing a major recreational area and storage facility, aroused conservationists nationally because of the nature of the area inundated.

Congress also approved, in 1962, the Frying Pan-Arkansas Project for transmontane storage and water diversion to aid the southeastern part of the state. This system collected water west of the Continental

Divide and used a tunnel to carry the diverted water to the Eastern Slope, where it was stored in reservoirs before being used for irrigation and municipal water supplies. Protests were again heard from residents of the Western Slope about loss of water, but the project went through.

By this time Colorado's water position, in relation to competing states, was fairly stable. It appeared that at last the way was clear to resolve the water problems which had so long proved irritating. But the amazingly rapid growth of two of the so-called "lower basin" states, California and Arizona, particularly the Phoenix area, produced new demands on old interstate compacts by the end of the sixties.

Coloradans also effected significant changes in state programs during these years. Many of these alterations were "revolutionary" in nature, bringing the state that once had been known throughout the country as immature and ill-governed into the ranks of the more progressive, better-governed commonwealths. Improvements came in stages, particularly by way of constitutional amendments, for the Colorado voters had refused to rewrite their 1876 Constitution. In 1922, and again in 1930, proposals for a constitutional convention were submitted to the electorate and both times were defeated.

In 1956 the voters approved an amendment extending from two to four years the terms of office for governor and other executive officers. By increasing the tenure of office, it was hoped that more efficient, stable administration of state affairs could be attained. By scheduling the elections during "off-year" election years, a healthful separation of state and local affairs from presidential campaigning was achieved.

Another important step was taken the same year when, after a highly emotional campaign, voters agreed to release funds that had been earmarked in the 1936 Old Age Pension Amendment. This decision unlocked a rigid system which had frozen eighty-five per cent of the income from sales and use taxes for pension purposes, creating serious problems in financing other welfare and educational programs. Large numbers of senior citizens had migrated to the state, attracted by many factors, including the pension program, then the second highest in the United States. In 1960 in Colorado, 299 out of every 1,000 persons were 65 or older, compared to neighboring Nebraska where the figure was 92, and a national average of 141.

Colorado's children also demanded attention, as the state's educational system from elementary schools to colleges steadily enrolled greater numbers, claiming increasingly larger shares of the state budget. Legislature after legislature wrestled with the financial problem while school boards tried to uncover sources for more money at the local level. Large school districts gradually replaced the chaotic system of small districts and busing was substituted for nearby rural school houses. Local autonomy was lost, but greater efficiency and wider educational experiences were gained.

Higher education also felt the crush. In 1940 fewer than 10,000 students were enrolled at state-supported senior colleges; by 1960 the count was 26,000 students and by 1970 some spokesmen advocated limiting the size of one of the institutions (the University of Colorado) to 20,000 students. Colorado State University and the University of Northern Colorado (formerly Colorado State College at Greeley) both topped 10,000 enrollments. Some citizens looked for relief from the problems inherent in large campuses to the establishment of junior colleges; but junior colleges have a way of growing up too. Fort Lewis, started at Hesperus as an Indian school, became a high school, then a junior college, and finally moved to Durango and upgraded itself with a four-year curriculum. The junior college at Pueblo travelled a similar route, becoming Southern Colorado State College.

The state lacked an integrated administration of its public colleges and universities. Numerous governing boards, selected in various ways, resulted in less efficient planning and management than might have been possible with a unified system. The Commission on Higher Education, considered to be a coordinating force, did not live up to expectations. The problems became more pressing each year, as the cost of education on all levels continued to soar. Republicans and Democrats in the legislature vied with each other in attempts to place blame for lack of solutions while worried taxpayers awaited relief.

Both major political parties could "point with pride" to election victories during the two decades from 1950 to 1970; neither held a monopoly on the voters' affections. The fall election of 1950 saw the Republicans win state control, with Dan Thornton as governor. Thornton won a second term before the "Grand Old Man" of the Democratic Party (and one of the leading Colorado politicians of the era), Edwin C. Johnson, led his party to victory and himself to the governor's chair in 1954. Johnson, who had been involved in state politics since the 1920s, served one term and was succeeded by Stephen McNichols, who was elected three times. The Democrats dominated the governorship in the fifties; that trend was reversed in the sixties.

Governor John A. Love. (State Historical Society of Colorado)

John A. Love led the Republican resurgence. He won the first four-year governorship in his own initial attempt at elective office in 1962. This Colorado Springs, Denver University-educated lawyer retained his position through the next two elections to serve as governor longer than any predecessor. Colorado voters, however, were as maverick a group during these years as they had been earlier. For example, despite victories by Democrats Johnson and McNichols, the Republican Party captured the state's six electoral votes throughout the fifties and lost them only once in the sixties (to Lyndon Johnson in the landslide of 1964). The Republicans also controlled the United States senate seats, except for the single term of John Carroll (1956-1962). Gordon Allott (since 1954) and Peter Dominick (since 1962), both conservative Republicans, successfully withstood Democratic challenges.

On the other side of Congress, the Democrats fared better, gaining no worse than a two-two division with the Republicans and controlling the delegation after 1964. This record reflected the political durability of Wayne Aspinall, who represented the Fourth (Western Slope) District starting in 1948, and the continuing successes of Byron Rogers from the First (Denver) District after 1950.

The veteran of this group of dominant Congressmen was Wayne Aspinall, who had moved with his parents to Colorado in 1904. They settled in Palisade, where Aspinall helped develop the peach orchard industry, before turning to law and politics. A long-active member of the Democratic party, he served in both the Colorado House and Senate and has served consecutively longer in Congress than any former Colorado representative. Byron Rogers migrated to Colorado from Oklahoma, graduated with a law degree from the University of Denver, and then practiced in Las Animas. He had been the state attorney general and served four years in the General Assembly prior to his election. The youngest in both age and term of service was a New Englander, Yale-educated Peter Dominick, whose rise was rapid after first being elected to the Colorado House in 1956. The only native Coloradan of the group, Gordon Allott, was born in Pueblo. Very active in the Republican party, he held two terms as lieutenant governor before his successful senate race in 1954. Like Dominick he served in the second World War and was a lawyer.

The state was split politically much as it had been in the 1880s, although the bases of party strength had shifted somewhat. The Democrats held Denver, the Republicans the suburbs, reflecting a national pattern. The Eastern Slope plains supported the G.O.P.,

while the southern counties and Western Slope generally were congen-
ial in their responses to Democrats. In his successful campaigns,
Governor Love managed to hold his districts and make crippling
inroads into Democratic areas, while the Democrats proved unable
to find either candidates or issues attractive enough to reverse Love's
fortunes.

In the presidential election of 1968, seventy-one per cent of
Colorado's eligible voters turned out to give Republican Richard
Nixon slightly over fifty per cent of the total vote, Democrat Hubert
Humphrey forty-two per cent, and George Wallace most of the rest of
the votes. On the major political question of the sixties—the
Indo-China War—Colorado, like the rest of the country, seemed
uncertain and divided. Demonstrations, parades, sit-ins, and dis-
ruptions of speeches marked the "movement" of youth and peace
groups; "hawks" and "doves" each had their own spokesmen; unrest
on some of the university and college campuses disturbed conservatives (and some moderates) while street politics and confrontations
continued to demonstrate the highly emotional context of the
complex issue.

Another issue—less volatile, but continuous throughout the era—
involved the growing centralization of power by the federal government. That "trend" was hardly new; it had been visible for decades,
although it probably had not been a significant factor in state
politics. Increasingly, however, in the Eisenhower and later years,
Republicans and conservative Democrats warned of the effects of
"encroachments" on the local scene. Much of that warning fell on
deaf or disinterested ears. One reason, undoubtedly, was because
Colorado had long been a recipient of federal largess, and both state
parties championed and applauded aid in highway construction,
relocation of federal agencies, reclamation, and the establishment of
military bases. While there might be partisan differences in defining
the "proper" end result of a reclamation project—for example, the
division of power facilities and transmission between public and
private sectors—no spokesmen in either party suggested Colorado
wanted to do without such federal "intervention."

State leadership might be united, but as the sixties ended, new
projects proved harder to come by, as the history of the Animas-La
Plata project (a water storage and irrigation plan for southwestern
Colorado) demonstrated. Local mining interests were concerned about
one proposed dam site interfering with their work; conservationists
protested the change in ecology and the impounding of water on old
mine mill dumps, as well as other side effects.

The local opposition to the Animas-La Plata project showed that potential environmental changes resulting from federal projects would thereafter generate serious and penetrating investigation; that the older, more simplistic attitudes of unquestioned values derived from rearranging nature's work no longer prevailed. The newer, more sensitive concerns would challenge other "improvements"—from highway construction to the activities of the Rocky Mountain Arsenal.

Despite this, Colorado, like its neighboring western states, still needed the federal government and its programs. The money pumped into the state, both through direct grants and indirectly from the paychecks of numerous federal workers in the state, was vital to its economy. Federal employment in Colorado had grown steadily since World War II, reaching nearly 34,000 civilian employees in 1960 and 41,740 eight years later.

Colorado's post-war population growth continued; the rate of growth in the 1950s recorded as 2.8 per cent per year and in the 1960s as 1.9 per cent. By 1969 20.2 people per square mile resided in the state, the most populous of the mountain states, ranking thirtieth (as compared with thirty-third in 1960) nationally. Some areas in southern and southwestern Colorado lost population and counties in the eastern part of the state could not show the growth of their more prosperous neighbors. Boulder County grew fifty-two per cent between 1950 and 1960; San Juan County decreased by thirty-five per cent; Kiowa County declined by twenty-one per cent. Boulder's growth in the sixties was even more spectacular (seventy-seven per cent) while San Juan dropped two per cent and Kiowa sixteen. Colorado was becoming increasingly urbanized, hearkening back to the early days of the mining rush. The total percentage of the urban population jumped from forty-eight in 1920 to seventy-four in 1960.

The threat of urban sprawl was developing between Fort Collins on the north and Pueblo on the south in the corridor containing the most populous counties and the state's major cities. The population density in Colorado ranged from 6,915 per square mile in Denver County to .2 in Hinsdale and .7 in Mineral counties. On the Western Slope only Grand Junction and Durango topped 10,000 population, reflecting the imbalance between the state's two major geographic regions. From that imbalance, direct consequences were seen in legislative representation and in participation in directing the state's destiny.

Denver was still, as it had been from the beginning, Colorado's urban "giant," its population now exceeding a half million people. It

suffered through all the problems of a modern urban community—
government, pollution, public transportation, traffic congestion,
decaying core, and minority rights. Pollution threatened to mask the
beautiful setting; there were days when smog obscured the mountains. Denverites worried over their problems, as did their counterparts in other cities; but solutions were not easily discovered. Urban
renewal produced the Skyline Urban Renewal project, but no solutions to the problems of the slum it replaced or of the people who
had lived there. Serious questions were raised about de facto segrega-
tion in the public schools, but proposed answers, such as busing,
aroused heated protests.

The rapid movement of minority groups into previously all-white
neighborhoods unfortunately generated typical reactions which, compounded with the increasing inner-city problems, drove people into
the suburbs in search of what was called the "all-American" way of
life. What developed were virtually white suburbs, which grew
astonishingly. Arvada climbed from 4,000 in 1950 to over 45,000 in
population by the end of the sixties. The "bedroom cities" around
Denver found themselves facing common problems related to their
sudden growth and new status as satellite communities. Serious
consideration of town and regional planning in all areas was called for
as the decade closed, but public attitudes and apathy still needed to
be overcome.

The problems of minority groups were not limited to the Denver
area, but spread throughout Colorado as the Hispano struggled to
advance his position. The fight was carried on to improve the lot of
the migrant worker, the permanent rural Hispano, and those crowded
into the slums of towns large and small. Both peaceful and violent
means of protest were used; gains appeared, although small and slow
to come. In Center, in the San Luis Valley, Hispanos controlled the
town council, gained representation on the school board, and were
pressing their issues in a new and forceful manner. The decades-old
division between the Anglo and Spanish cultures, long unspoken but
real, was brought into the open at Center and at many other places
in the state.

Economically, Colorado continued in patterns developed earlier.
Agriculture dominated the non-mountainous counties, with beef
cattle, wheat, sugar beets, grains, and truck garden products major
items. The state ranked high nationally in the amount of irrigated
land, having in the mid-sixties about eight per cent of the United
States' total. But small farmers and ranchers found it increasingly

difficult to continue operations in the face of rising costs and a relatively stable income. Their plight produced much soul-searching but little concrete improvement. The decline in farming was observable in the continuing flight of many rural people to the cities where what seemed to be a brighter economic future beckoned.

Manufacturing became more diversified than ever, particularly with increased activity in the aerospace program and the movement of eastern-based companies to Colorado, especially in the Denver-Boulder-Longmont triangle. Compared to a fully industrialized state, however, Colorado remained relatively underdeveloped.

Mining, the original bellwether of Colorado's economy, showed some signs of recovering from its long slump, spurred by the lifting of the federal price ceiling on silver. Early optimism over another silver boom vanished, however, when all the cost factors were weighed carefully. Still there was more hope for the mining industry generally then there had been in years. Lake County and the San Juans led in dollar total; fifty-four out of the sixty-three counties recorded some mineral production in 1969. In 1970 Lake and San Miguel ran one and two. Molybdenum, not silver, kept Leadville high on the list of producers. Now, however, gold and silver were commonly by-products of lead, zinc, and copper mining.

The situation had changed in another way, too. An old mining camp like Silverton, which still relied primarily on mining, found its fortunes tied to fewer and generally absentee companies. Their operations were small compared to the past, but they held out the only hope since the individual prospector had long ago vanished.

Colorado leaders were faced with the complicated task of developing full and complete use of the state's natural resources. To tap these resources demanded both ingenuity and money; no longer would the public tolerate the despoiling of nature for individual economic gain. The Rulison Project (1969-70) near Grand Valley, by which the government attempted to use nuclear energy to release natural gas, while exciting in concept, raised protests about radiation, pollution, and safety.

A good example of relatively untouched potential was oil; production increased sharply after World War II and reached a peak in 1956. Durango and the surrounding area went through a mild boom, which receded in the early sixties. However, even larger reserves of shale oil are known to exist in Rio Blanco and Garfield counties, although no profitable method has been found to obtain it. A federal experimental station, the Union Oil Company, and other

Denver Broncos—Floyd Little makes an end sweep. (Denver Broncos Football Club)

agencies have worked on the problem, but the cost is still prohibitive and the national need not yet great enough to spur full development.

Professional sports on a permanent major league basis arrived in Colorado, first with the Denver Broncos, of the American Football League (which became the American Football Conference) in 1960, then with the Denver Rockets basketball team later in the decade. Despite poor initial management and a losing record (the best season in the sixties: 7-7), the Broncos emerged as a strong and popular franchise. Reflecting both interest in the sport and Denver's urban situation, 40,000 and more spectators crowded Mile High Stadium for the Bronco games.

In the 1960s Colorado entered its second century as an important tourist area. For mid-twentieth as for nineteenth century Colorado, tourism was a growing, vital industry. Sightseers and pleasure seekers no longer headed for the mountains only during the warm summer months. Skiing had become a source of income for the entire mountain area, from Durango to Estes Park. In the well-known resorts, like Vail and Aspen, thousands crowded onto the slopes on brisk winter weekends. The winter stillness of the mountains was also broken by a relative newcomer—the snowmobile—which brought economic assets and potential environmental liabilities with it.

In the summer even more tourists arrived, visiting such longtime favorites as Rocky Mountain National Park and Mesa Verde. The mountains, as always, were the magnets attracting the out-of-staters. New and convenient camping vehicles and equipment added new dimensions and problems to the tourist business. Mounting pressure on available space forced the government to consider limiting the number of people who might visit Mesa Verde each day. Hot disputes were generated on how best to utilize the recreational space: should it be preserved as a protected wilderness, available only under specified conditions? Or, should it be opened expansively to accommodate as many people for as many purposes as they desired?

Almost all Colorado communities were affected by the tourist industry. A town such as Cortez prospered greatly by its proximity to Mesa Verde and its location on a main highway. It offered services—gas, food, rooms—to all who travelled through; their purchases helped not only the businessmen but the city as well, through taxation. Hinsdale County virtually depended on tourists for its existence.

Aspen is an excellent example of a community that sold itself completely to tourism. This former silver camp languished for decades until it underwent a true renaissance, beginning in 1948. Walter Peipcke, a Chicago industrialist, began the development of the new Aspen into a health, sports, and cultural center. In the wintertime it offered skiing and in the summer a music festival. Aspen boomed as it had not since the 1880s, and what Aspen achieved, other towns dreamed of duplicating.

Not the least of the fascinating elements that combined to lure visitors and residents to the ski town of Aspen—and to the summer opera and theater season at Central City, the melodrama in Cripple Creek, or the narrow-gauge train trip from Durango to Silverton—was the chance to return to an earlier and seemingly simpler environment; to relive the days when the "West was Won." The Centennial State has much to offer in this respect and has capitalized on it in the post-war years. Over-commercialization threatened to render this heritage a tawdry tourist trap and some ties with the past, like the Tabor Grand Opera House and the Windsor Hotel, went down under the wrecker. But fortunately, in the sixties, a mounting awareness preserved some of the state's best-known landmarks.

As the 1960s drew to a close, Coloradans became increasingly aware that they were in danger of losing one of their priceless assets—an unpolluted environment. With numerous national examples to reflect upon, it seemed imperative that something be done before this magnificent heritage was lost under the weight of increasing population, urbanization, tourism, and a state-wide transportation sprawl. Smog made its hideous debut in Denver and soon a daily smog report appeared in the *Denver Post* while Boulder and other cities observed increasing evidence that they, too, were destined for trouble.

The problem was not new; miners had long polluted the atmosphere, landscape, and streams of the state, and other industries, to a lesser degree, had added to the destruction. Now, however, people were becoming aware and—more importantly—concerned. For the urban areas, the automobile, one major villain, was easily pinpointed, especially since the state has one of the highest car-per-person ratios in the world. Outside the city, it was man himself and not his machines that posed the greatest threat. Litter cluttering campsites and rest stops, mountain cabin cisterns and privies polluting streams, and increasing numbers of people swarming into wilderness and commercial vacation spots eroded much of the charm that once lured settlers and visitors. Streams became too polluted for trout; mountain lakes threatened to become open cesspools; even a major river, the South Platte, was being destroyed. Well-known resorts like Aspen and Grand Lake were facing crises brought on by over-popularity.

If the internal picture was not threatening enough, airborne pollutants were filtering into the high Rockies from southern California and northern New Mexico, where large power plants were spilling pollution into the Four Corners region. The federal government contributed its share by dumping poison wastes into the soil around the Rocky Mountain Arsenal. Finally halted in 1961, this procedure was replaced by the drilling of a deep well to dispose of the poisonous wastes under pressure. The project was finished in March, 1962; within a month Denver was hit by an earthquake, an extremely rare occurrence. By the end of 1965 hundreds of additional tremors had followed and much of the blame was placed on the well project. Protests mounted, leading to a series of investigations that raised doubts about the blame and the wisdom of attempting to dispose of poisonous wastes near any human settlement.

The solutions to these and many other questions relating to the environment and pollution were not quickly or easily found, but the awareness, interest, and activity to improve the situation augured well for the future. Re-evaluation of older slogans about growth and progress being the yardsticks against which a community or state was measured was taking place on all levels. The Colorado Environmental Commission in 1970 warned that three traditional concepts—population growth, economic growth, and reliance on the car—needed to be changed if the victory was to be won. And Coloradans, like all Americans, were attempting to respond to the challenges those changes would entail.

32

Colorado Today

As the decade of the seventies dawned, Coloradans could look backward to a decade of progress and achievement and forward to the centennial of statehood in 1976. In 1970 the population stood at 2,207,259 (78.5 per cent in urban areas), and it was estimated that 2,767,716 persons would be living in the state in 1980. Colorado's continued population growth earned it another member of the United States House of Representatives, increasing the state's congressional representation from four to five. Wholesale and retail trade and government, ranked by number employed, were the top two sectors of the economy in 1970: mining, once a leader, was in last place with two per cent of the work force. The leading agricultural products, ranked by value of production, were cattle, hay, dairy products, wheat, sugar beets, and sheep.

Tourism continued to play an important role in the state's economy due to such factors as rising income among the nation's consumers, an increase in the number of paid holidays and three-day weekends per year (Colorado Day, for example, is now celebrated on the first Monday in August rather than on August 1), and the increase in leisure time due to a shorter work week and early retirement. Some firms in the United States have shifted to a 4-day, 40-hour week (Littleton's C. A. Norgren Company is among them), and if this trend continues, many workers will have three days off each week. Perhaps it is too early to tell what effect, if any, the recession of the seventies will have on tourism, but based on past experience, Coloradans can probably expect that the year-round influx of visitors will increase. People will continue to come to the state for recreation (especially skiing), for sightseeing, and for history.

Colorado is playing an important role in the space frontier. This orbiting "Solar Observatory" built by Ball Brothers Research Corporation, was launched from Cape Kennedy, September 29, 1971. (Ball Brothers)

Statistics show, in fact, that the total visits to the state's museums and historic sites was in excess of five million in 1969. Preserving the state's heritage of historical buildings and sites is of primary importance; the National Historic Preservation Act of 1966 is a significant step.

During the late 1960s, the governor, members of the Economic Development Council, and selected businessmen periodically made "Sell Colorado" trips to induce business and industry to locate permanently in Colorado. In the 1970s, however, increasing numbers of citizens were beginning to question the desirability of unrestrained growth which might result in serious damage to the state's environment. "Just a few years ago, growth and industrial development were almost as sacred as motherhood and certainly were a sound plank in any political platform," said Governor John Love, reflecting this change early in his third term. "But fairly recently, a growing number of Colorado citizens have been saying 'stop—that's enough,' recognizing that growth simply for growth's sake is not an appropriate goal."[1]

Along with the problems presented by an expanding population, in Colorado, as throughout the nation, citizens were concerned with the ecology and the environment in the 1970s. Air pollution was a major problem in Denver and in smaller metropolitan areas as well. The first national air pollution standards are scheduled to take effect in 1975 and Denver was among those cities warned of the difficulties of meeting them unless major changes were made in commuting habits to minimize the effects of carbon monoxide production. In 1969, for example, the air over Denver averaged 113 micrograms per cubic meter of suspended particulates per day; the maximum amount allowed under the new standards is 75.[2] To comply with these standards Denver and other large cities may have to close certain sections to traffic and, in any case, will almost certainly have to institute improved mass transit systems. If such changes come to pass, the face of the capital, already being altered by the Skyline Urban Renewal Project, would be further transformed.

The question of damage to the Colorado environment was brought to the forefront in the early 1970s during the debate over the Winter Olympic Games, slated to be held in the state during the 1976 centennial. Long years of campaigning by the Denver delegation had resulted in the games being awarded to Colorado in May of 1970, despite stiff competition from Vancouver, British Columbia; Sion, Switzerland; and Tampere, Finland. Jubilant at first, Coloradans soon began to wonder how Colorado would cope with the expected influx of competitors and visitors and, indeed, whether holding the Olympics in the state was desirable at all. Among the critics of the Games is the Colorado Open Space Council, which coordinates some thirty environmental groups. The COSC is urging that protection of the environment be of first priority in making all decisions and that residents approve the holding of events in their communities before final plans are made. Emphasis also is being placed on the future usefulness of the Olympic facilities.[3]

In the mid-1970s, Coloradans will become increasingly involved in planning not only for the Olympics but also for the centennial of statehood and the bicentennial of American independence. In 1971 the legislature created the 1976 Colorado Centennial-Bicentennial Commission, consisting of nine members appointed by the governor (including two from the House of Representatives and two from the Senate) whose six-year terms will end June 30, 1977. Under the terms of the act (House Bill 1092), the commission is concerned with three principal areas—heritage, hospitality, and horizons—and with the relationship of the centennial to the bicentennial. Citizens are being urged to "recall our heritage and to place it in current perspective," to create opportunities for historic activities and events with particular emphasis on hospitality," and to "demonstrate our concern for human welfare, happiness, and freedom" through projects "which manifest pride, priorities, and hope for the future." The commission is working with agencies, groups, and individuals to insure that the 1976 observance "may be carried out to the enrichment of historical knowledge and the enhancement of the people's awareness of the depth and significance of their heritage." With pride in the past, Coloradans will look forward to an even brighter future as the state approaches its second century.

Notes

Chapter 4
[1] Quoted in LeRoy R. Hafen, "Fort Jackson and the Early Fur Trade on the South Platte," *The Colorado Magazine* (February, 1928), V, 13.

Chapter 5
[1] Francis Parkman, *The Oregon Trail: Sketches of Prairie and Rocky-Mountain Life*, 8th ed. (Boston, 1891), 301.

Chapter 6
[1] From "Report of Greeley, Richardson, and Villard, June 9, 1859" in *Early Records of Gilpin County, Colorado*, Thomas Maitland Marshall, ed. (Boulder, 1920), 9-10.
[2] March 28, 1859, quoted in Richard A. Bartlett, "Reception of the Pike's Peak Fever in the Chicago Press and Tribune," *The Colorado Magazine* (January, 1948), XXV, 32.
[3] From Jackson's Diary, LeRoy R. Hafen, ed., *ibid.* (November, 1935), XXII, 201-214.

Chapter 7
[1] Mrs. Daniel Witter, "Pioneer Life," *The Colorado Magazine* (December, 1927), IV, 169.
[2] Statements from both meetings are printed in *Rocky Mountain News*, November 10, 1859.
[3] Louis L. Simonin, "Colorado in 1867 as Seen by a Frenchman," trans. by Wilson O. Clough, *The Colorado Magazine* (March, 1937), XIV, 61.

Chapter 8
[1] Details are from accounts in the *Rocky Mountain News*, July 4 and 11, 1860.

[2] Webster D. Anthony, "Journal of a Trip from Denver to Oro City in 1860," *The Colorado Magazine* (November, 1934), XI, 237.

[3] "Dornick," in the Omaha *Nebraskian*, August 24, 1860, quoted in LeRoy R. Hafen, ed., *Colorado and Its People: A Narrative and Topical History of the Centennial State* (New York, 1948), I, 238.

[4] Milo Lee Whittaker, *Pathbreakers and Pioneers of the Pueblo Region: Comprising a History of Pueblo from the Earliest Times* (Philadelphia, 1917), 70.

[5] Quoted from report of Crawford to American Home Missionary Society, July 13, 1863, in Colin B. Goodykoontz, "Colorado As Seen by a Home Missionary, 1863-1868," *The Colorado Magazine* (March, 1935), XII, 62.

[6] See A. J. Fynn and LeRoy R. Hafen, "Early Education in Colorado," *ibid.* (January, 1935), XII, 13-23.

[7] Canon City *Times*, January 12, 1861.

[8] *Rocky Mountain News*, June 6, 1860; Wilbur F. Stone, ed., *History of Colorado* (Chicago, 1918-19), I, 766-767.

[9] *Rocky Mountain News*, June 4, 1863.

[10] *Ibid.*, July 18, 1860.

[11] Records of Eureka District, July 23, 1860, in *Early Records of Gilpin County,* 84.

[12] Records of Nevada District, April 28, 1860, in *ibid.,* 125.

[13] *Rocky Mountain News*, April 23, May 7, 1863; George F. Willison, *Here They Dug the Gold* (New York, 1931), 123.

[14] K. J. Fielding, ed., "James Thomson's Colorado Diary, 1872," *The Colorado Magazine* (July, 1954), XXXI, 202.

Chapter 9

[1] Horace Greeley, *An Overland Journey from New York to San Francisco*, Charles Duncan, ed. (New York, 1964), 133.

[2] Frank Hall, *History of the State of Colorado* (Chicago, 1889-95), I, 185.

[3] Sidney B. Morrison, "Letters from Colorado, 1860-63," *The Colorado Magazine* (May, 1939), XVI, 95.

[4] *Ibid.*, 92.

[5] Hiram A. Johnson, "A Letter from a Colorado Mining Camp in 1860," *ibid.* (September, 1930), VII, 194.

Chapter 10

[1] Hafen, in *Colorado and Its People*, I, 279-280, prints the resolutions of a Denver meeting; similar gatherings were held in other Colorado communities.

[2] Hafen, in *ibid.*, I, 312, concludes that Gerry's advance information to Evans kept the Indians from attacking.

[3] George E. Hyde, *A Life of George Bent, Written from His Letters*, Savoie Lottinville, ed. (Norman, 1968), 152.

Chapter 11
[1] Oscar Osburn Winther, "The Persistence of Horse-Drawn Transportation in the Trans-Mississippi West, 1865-1900" in *Probing the American West* (Santa Fe, 1962), 46.
[2] The details are from Hafen, *Colorado and Its People*, I, 326.
[3] Quoted from A. M. Morrison, "An Excursion to Alamosa in 1878," *The Colorado Magazine* (January, 1942), XIX, 29.

Chapter 12
[1] *Colorado Chieftain* (Pueblo), February 24, 1870, quoted in James F. Willard and Colin B. Goodykoontz, eds., *Experiments in Colorado Colonization 1869-1872* (Boulder, 1926), 67.
[2] *Rocky Mountain News*, June 27, 1870, quoted in James F. Willard, *The Union Colony at Greeley, 1869-1871* (Boulder, 1918), 273.
[3] *Colorado Chieftain* (Pueblo), October 20, 1870.
[4] Nicholas G. Morgan, "Mormon Colonization in the San Luis Valley," *The Colorado Magazine* (October, 1950), XXVII, 291.
[5] Hall, *History of Colorado*, I, 518.

Chapter 13
[1] "Letters of S. Newton Pettis, Associate Justice of the Colorado Supreme Court, Written in 1861," ed. by Paul H. Giddens, *The Colorado Magazine* (March, 1936), XIII, 72-78.
[2] Quoted in Albert B. Sanford, "Organization and Development of Colorado Territory," in James H. Baker and LeRoy R. Hafen, eds., *History of Colorado* (Denver, 1927), II, 505.
[3] Charles Thomas, "The Pioneer Bar of Colorado," *The Colorado Magazine* (July, 1924), I, 201.
[4] Quoted in Sanford, "Organization of Colorado Territory," in Baker and Hafen, *History of Colorado*, II, 519.

Chapter 14
[1] Colin B. Goodykoontz, "Some Controversial Questions Before the Colorado Constitutional Convention of 1876," *The Colorado Magazine* (January, 1940), XVII, 11.
[2] Quoted in Theodore F. Van Wagener, "Views on the Admission of Colorado in 1876," *ibid.* (August, 1926), III, 86, 88.
[3] Isabella A. Bird, *A Lady's Life in the Rocky Mountains* (London, 1910), 159-160.
[4] Frank Fossett, *Colorado* (New York, 1879), 49.
[5] *Ibid.*, 104.

[6] John Codman, *The Round Trip by Way of Panama through California, Oregon, Nevada, Utah, Idaho, and Colorado* (New York, 1879), 312, quoted in John E. Baur, "The Health Seeker in the Westward Movement, 1830-1900," *Mississippi Valley Historical Review* (June, 1959), XLVI, 104.

Chapter 15
[1] Carlyle Channing Davis, *Olden Times in Colorado* (Los Angeles, 1916), 139.

Chapter 16
[1] The statement from President Hayes' message to Congress, December 3, 1877, is quoted in Alvin T. Steinel, *History of Agriculture in Colorado* (Fort Collins, 1926), 129.
[2] *Colorado Chieftain*, July 16, 1868, quoted in Edward Norris Wentworth, *America's Sheep Trails* (Ames, 1948), 334.
[3] From Frank Benton, "How I Love Sheep," quoted in *ibid.*, 522.

Chapter 17
[1] Quoted in Dudley Taylor Cornish, "The First Five Years of Colorado's Statehood," *The Colorado Magazine* (September, 1948), XXV, 221.
[2] W. B. Vickers, "History of Colorado," in *History of the Arkansas Valley* (Chicago, 1881), 35, 37.
[3] Cornish, "First Five Years," 227.
[4] Walker D. Wyman, "A Preface to the Settlement of Grand Junction: The Uncompahgre Ute 'Goes West,' " *The Colorado Magazine* (January, 1933), X, 27.

Chapter 18
[1] In opinion in *Yunker* v. *Nichols*, 1 Colo. Rep., 553.
[2] Quoted in Hall, *History of Colorado*, II, 77.
[3] *Eastern Colorado: A Brief Description of the New Lands Now Being Opened Up* (Lincoln, 1887), 4-5.
[4] Quoted in Walter Lawson Wilder, *Robert Wilbur Steele: Defender of Liberty* (Denver, 1913), 53.

Chapter 19
[1] *The Official Manual of the Cripple Creek District*, Fred Hills, Publisher (Colorado Springs, 1900).

Chapter 20
[1] Hall, *History of Colorado*, III, 37.
[2] Horace Tabor, "Autobiography," p. 15; original copy in the Bancroft Library.

[3] Quoted in Leon W. Fuller, "A Populist Newspaper of the Nineties," *The Colorado Magazine* (May, 1932), IX, 82.

Chapter 21
[1] J. W. Brentlinger, ed., *Effects of Demonetization of Silver on the Industries of Colorado, July 1 to August 31, 1893* (Denver, 1893), 30-31.
[2] *Congressional Record*, 53d Congress, 1st Session, p. 2890. The session is described, and parts of this speech are included, in Elmer Ellis, *Henry Moore Teller: Defender of the West* (Caldwell, Id., 1941), 225-226.
[3] *Speech of Judge George N. Aldredge, of Dallas, Texas, on the Free Coinage of Silver* (Washington, 1896), 14.

Chapter 22
[1] *Rocky Mountain News,* September 2, 1901.
[2] *Ibid.,* October 13, 1901.
[3] *Ibid.,* April 16, 1900.
[4] *Ibid.,* February 14, 1900.

Chapter 23
[1] This chapter, in somewhat different form, was published as Carl Ubbelohde, "The Labor Movement in Colorado—Patterns of the Era of Industrial Warfare," *The Denver Westerners Monthly Roundup* (October, 1963), XIX, 3-16.
[2] Whittaker, *Pathbreakers and Pioneers of the Pueblo Region,* 124.

Chapter 24
[1] *Denver Republican*, January 11, 1901.
[2] Statistics from a Department of Interior pamphlet, *Homesteads* (Washington, 1962), 2.
[3] *Rocky Mountain News*, April 12, 1902.
[4] *Greeley Tribune*, November 23, 1870.

Chapter 25
[1] See *Denver Times*, March 11, 1900.

Chapter 26
[1] Quoted in A. O. McGrew, "Denver's First Christmas, 1858," *Denver Westerners Monthly Roundup* (December, 1957), XIII, 20.
[2] This account of Ebert's work and the general story of forest conservation in Colorado are based on W. J. Morrill, "Forestry," in Baker and Hafen, *History of Colorado*, II, chap. 14.
[3] H. J. Mathis to Theodore Roosevelt, August 28, 1902, quoted in W. J. Morrill, "Birth of the Roosevelt National Forest," *The*

Colorado Magazine (September, 1943), XX, 180.

[4] See Percy Fritz, *Colorado: The Centennial State* (New York, 1941), 408.

[5] Colorado Council of Defense, *Weekly News Letter*, no. 31 (May, 1918); no. 36 (June, 1918); no. 37 (June, 1918).

[6] Robert G. Dunbar, "History of Agriculture," in Hafen, *Colorado and Its People*, II, 134-135.

[7] Colorado Council of Defense, *Weekly News Letter*, no. 4 (October, 1917).

[8] Fritz, *Colorado*, 412.

Chapter 27

[1] Quoted from Lee Scamehorn, "The Air Transport Industry in Colorado," in Carl Ubbelohde, ed., *A Colorado Reader* (Boulder, 1964), 311.

Chapter 28

[1] There are accounts of the tumbling price structure and general descriptions of the depression in Colorado in Fritz, *Colorado*, chap. 24, and in Hafen, ed., *Colorado and Its People*, I, chap. 29.

[2] Leonard Arrington, "The New Deal in the West: A Preliminary Statistical Inquiry," *Pacific Historical Review* (August, 1969), XXXVIII, 311-316.

[3] In his "Colorado in the Great Depression: A Study of New Deal Policies at the State Level" (unpublished Ph.D. dissertation, University of Denver, 1964), James F. Wickens states (p. 184, n. 31) that Colorado's total mining industry began recovery only in 1936 as a result of the world armament race, creating demands for molybdenum, copper, lead, and zinc.

Chapter 30

[1] Robert G. Athearn, *High Country Empire* (New York, 1960), 311.

[2] *Ibid.*, 312.

Chapter 32

[1] Testimony of Governor John A. Love before the U. S. Senate Subcommittee on Rural Development, April 29, 1971 (copy furnished by governor's office).

[2] *Rocky Mountain News*, May 1, 1971.

[3] See *ibid.*, April 4-9, 1971, for a series of articles on the Winter Olympic Games.

Suggested Reading

General Works

Multivolume histories of Colorado include Frank Hall, *History of the State of Colorado* (4 vols., Chicago, 1889-95), valuable for the author's firsthand knowledge of many of the events; Wilbur F. Stone, ed., *History of Colorado* (4 vols., Chicago, 1918-19); James H. Baker and LeRoy R. Hafen, eds., *History of Colorado* (5 vols., Denver, 1927); and LeRoy R. Hafen, ed., *Colorado and Its People: A Narrative and Topical History of the Centennial State* (4 vols., New York, 1948).

For detailed histories of various regions see Jerome Smiley, *History of Denver* (Denver, 1901), and three works published by O. L. Baskin & Co. of Chicago: *History of the Arkansas Valley, Colorado* (1881), *History of Clear Creek and Boulder Valleys, Colorado* (1880), and *History of the City of Denver, Arapahoe County, and Colorado* (1880).

Still valuable is Percy Fritz's one-volume textbook, *Colorado: The Centennial State* (New York, 1941). Widely used in the Colorado school system is LeRoy R. Hafen and Ann W. Hafen, *Our State: Colorado* (3d ed., Denver, 1966).

Guides and Bibliographies

Virginia Lee Wilcox has compiled *Colorado: A Selected Bibliography of Its Literature, 1858-1952* (Denver, 1954). A useful research and reference tool is Donald E. Oehlerts, *Guide to Colorado Newspapers, 1859-1959* (Denver, 1964). (The Western History Department of the Denver Public Library has a card-file index to the *Rocky Mountain News* for the years 1865-85.) *The Colorado Magazine* has been published by the State Historical Society of Colorado since 1923; two cumulative indexes are available covering the years 1923-1960.

Research Collections

Major collections of research material are found in the library of the State Historical Society of Colorado, the Western History Department of the Denver Public Library and, for public records, the Colorado State Archives and Records Service, all in Denver. The Western Historical Collections is headquartered at Norlin Library, University of Colorado, Boulder; the Center of

Southwest Studies is in Durango, at Fort Lewis College. In addition, the student of Colorado and western history should not overlook the resources in the National Archives, Washington, D.C.

Chapter 1   A Prehistoric Prelude: The Dwellers in the Cliffs

A good introduction to the study of early man is C. W. Ceram, *The First American: A Story of North American Archaeology* (New York, 1971). For general accounts of the Mesa Verde Indians, see Don Watson, *Indians of the Mesa Verde* (Mesa Verde National Park, 1955) and H. M. Wormington, *Prehistoric Indians of the Southwest* (Denver, 1959); also Harold Sterling Gladwin, *A History of the Ancient Southwest* (Portland, Me., 1957).

Artifacts used in studying the Mesa Verde people are described in Earl H. Morris, *Archaeological Studies in the La Plata District, Southwestern Colorado and Northwestern New Mexico* (Carnegie Institution of Washington Publication No. 519, Washington, 1939). Excavation, dating, and description of the architectural ruins are related in Jesse Walter Fewkes, "Far View House—A Pure Type of Pueblo Ruin," *Art and Archaeology* (September, 1917), VI, 133-41; the same author's *Antiquities of the Mesa Verde National Park: Cliff Palace* (Bureau of American Ethnology, Bulletin No. 51, Washington, 1911) and in Deric O'Bryan, *Excavations in Mesa Verde National Park, 1947-48* (Medallion Papers, No. 39, Globe, Arizona, 1950).

Chapter 2   A Spanish Borderland

Early Spanish experiences in the Southwest are described in Cleve Hallenbeck, *Alvar Nunez Cabeza de Vaca: The Journey and Route of the First European to Cross the Continent of North America* (Glendale, 1940) and the same author's *The Journey of Fray Marcos de Niza* (Dallas, 1949). On Coronado, see Herbert E. Bolton, *Coronado: Knight of Pueblos and Plains* (New York, 1949) and George P. Hammond, *Coronado's Seven Cities* (Albuquerque, 1940).

The New Mexican settlements are described in George P. Hammond, *Don Juan de Oñate and the Founding of New Mexico* (Santa Fe, 1927). Indian relations and excursions northward can be studied in a series of works by Alfred Barnaby Thomas, including *The Plains Indians and New Mexico* (Albuquerque, 1940); *Forgotten Frontiers: A Study of the Spanish Indian Policy of Don Juan Bautista de Anza* (Norman, 1932); and *After Coronado: Spanish Exploration Northeast of New Mexico, 1696-1727* (Norman, 1935).

French interest in the area is described in William E. Dunn, "Spanish Reaction Against the French Advance Toward New Mexico," *Mississippi Valley Historical Review* (December, 1915), II, 348-62; and in two articles in *The Colorado Magazine* by Henri Folmer, "De Bourgmont's Expedition to the Padoucas in 1724, the First French Approach to Colorado" (July, 1937), XIV, 121-28; and "The Mallet Expedition of 1739 Through Nebraska, Kansas and Colorado to Santa Fe" (September, 1939), XVI, 161-73.

Exploration and Indian relations northwest of Santa Fe may be traced in Eleanor Richie, "General Mano Mocha of the Utes and Spanish Policy in Indian Relations," *The Colorado Magazine* (July, 1932), IX, 150-57; Joseph J. Hill, "Spanish and Mexican Explorations and Trade Northwest from New Mexico into the Great Basin, 1765-1853," *Utah Historical Quarterly* (January, 1930), III, 3-7; and Alfred Barnaby Thomas, "San Carlos: A Comanche Pueblo on the Arkansas River, 1787," *The Colorado Magazine* (May, 1929), VI, 79-91. On the Escalante expedition, see Herbert E. Bolton, *Pageant in the Wilderness: The*

Story of the Escalante Expedition to the Interior Basin, 1776 (Salt Lake City, 1950). Published as Volume XVIII of the *Utah Historical Quarterly*, this contains a full historical introduction to, and translation of, Father Escalante's Diary and Itinerary.

Chapter 3   Exploring Louisiana

A fine introduction is William H. Goetzmann, *Army Exploration in the American West, 1803-1863* (New Haven, 1959). The most recent, full-length biography of Pike is W. Eugene Hollon, *The Lost Pathfinder: Zebulon Montgomery Pike* (Norman, 1949). But see also Harvey L. Carter, *Zebulon Montgomery Pike: Pathfinder and Patriot* (Colorado Springs, 1956). For Pike's own account of his expedition, see Stephen Harding Hart and Archer Butler Hulbert, eds., *Zebulon Pike's Arkansaw Journal: In Search of the Southern Louisiana Purchase Boundary Line* (Denver, 1932) and Donald Jackson, ed., *The Journals and Letters of Zebulon Montgomery Pike, with Letters and Related Documents* (2 vols., Norman, 1966).

On the Ute Indians, see Wilson Rockwell, *The Utes: A Forgotten People* (Denver, 1956); Marvin Kaufmann Opler, *The Southern Ute of Colorado*, reprinted from *Acculturation in Seven American Indian Tribes* (New York, 1940); and Helen Sloan Daniels, ed., *The Ute Indians of Southwestern Colorado* (Durango, 1941). A good research tool is Omer Stewart, *Ethnohistorical Bibliography of the Ute Indians of Colorado* (Boulder, 1971).

For the Eastern Slope tribes, see Donald J. Berthrong, *The Southern Cheyennes* (Norman, 1963); E. Adamson Hoebel, *The Cheyennes: Indians of the Great Plains* (New York, 1960); George Bird Grinnell, *The Fighting Cheyennes*, originally published in 1915, available in a new edition (Norman, 1956); and Virginia Cole Trenholm, *The Arapahoes, Our People* (Norman, 1970).

The Long expedition may be studied in Richard G. Wood, *Stephen Harriman Long, 1784-1864; Army Engineer, Explorer, Inventor* (Glendale, 1966); in vols. XIV-XVII of Reuben Gold Thwaites, *Early Western Travels* (Cleveland, 1905) containing Edwin James' Account of an Expedition . . ."; and in Harlin M. Fuller and LeRoy R. Hafen, eds., *The Journal of Captain John R. Bell, Official Journalist for the Stephen H. Long Expedition to the Rocky Mountains, 1820* (Glendale, 1957), which is vol. VI of Hafen's *Far West and Rockies Series.* In addition, see two articles in the *Mississippi Valley Historical Review:* Cardinal Goodwin, "A Larger View of the Yellowstone Expedition, 1819-1820" (December, 1917), IV, 299-313; and Ralph C. Morris, "The Notion of a Great American Desert East of the Rockies" (September, 1926), XIII, 190-200.

Chapter 4   The Fur Frontier

The literature of the Santa Fe Trail is covered in *The Santa Fe Trail: A Historical Bibliography* (Albuquerque, 1971). The classic account of the Santa Fe trade is Josiah Gregg, *Commerce of the Prairies;* see the edition by Max L. Moorhead (Norman, 1954). A modern, imaginative account is Stanley Vestal, *The Old Santa Fe Trail* (New York, 1939), reprinted in 1957. On the fur trade generally, see the standard study by Hiram M. Chittenden, *The American Fur Trade of the Far West* (3 vols., New York, 1902); Paul Chrisler Phillips, *The Fur Trade* (2 vols., Norman, 1961); and Robert Glass Cleland, *This Reckless Breed of Men: The Trappers and Fur Traders of the Southwest* (New York, 1952). For biographies of traders and trappers, see LeRoy R. Hafen, ed., *The*

Mountain Men and the Fur Trade of the Far West (8 vols. to date, Glendale, 1965-   ). Equipment used in the fur trade is described in Carl P. Russell, *Firearms, Traps & Tools of the Mountain Men* (New York, 1967). The Glenn-Fowler operations are described in the journal of one of the leaders: Elliott Coues, ed., *The Journal of Jacob Fowler, Narrating an Adventure from Arkansas Through the Indian Territory, Oklahoma, Kansas, Colorado, and New Mexico, to the Sources of the Rio Grande Del Norte, 1821-22* (New York, 1898). Other companies, furmen, and forts are described in Don Berry, *A Majority of Scoundrels: An Informal History of the Rocky Mountain Fur Company* (New York, 1961); David Lavender, *Bent's Fort* (New York, 1954); and the following articles in *The Colorado Magazine*: Joseph J. Hill, "Antoine Robidoux, Kingpin in the Colorado River Fur Trade, 1824-1844" (July, 1930), VII, 125-32; and—all by LeRoy R. Hafen—"Fort Davy Crockett, Its Fur Men and Visitors" (January, 1952), XXIX, 17-33; "Fort Vasquez" (Summer, 1964), XLI, 198-212; "Old Fort Lupton and Its Founder" (November, 1929), VI, 220-26; "Fort Jackson and the Early Fur Trade on the South Platte" (February, 1928), V, 9-17; and "Fort St. Vrain" (October, 1952), XXIX, 242-55.

Chapter 5   The Frontier in Transition

The standary biography of John Charles Frémont is by Allan Nevins, *Frémont: Pathmarker of the West* (New York, 1939). Nevins also edited the reports of Frémont's first three expeditions, *Narratives of Exploration and Adventure* (New York, 1956). See also Donald Jackson and Mary Lee Spence, eds., *The Expeditions of John Charles Frémont. Vol. I: Travels from 1838 to 1844* (Urbana, 1970). For Carson's life, see Harvey Lewis Carter, *"Dear Old Kit": The Historical Christopher Carson* (Norman, 1968); and Stanley Vestal, *Kit Carson: The Happy Warrior of the Old West* (Boston, 1928). For Fitzpatrick, see LeRoy R. Hafen and W. J. Ghent, *Broken Hand: The Life Story of Thomas Fitzpatrick* (Denver, 1931).

Descriptions of early settlements can be found in Matthew C. Field, "Sketches of Big Timber, Bent's Fort and Milk Fort in 1839," *The Colorado Magazine* (May, 1937), XIV, 102-8; LeRoy R. Hafen and Frank M. Young, "The Mormon Settlement at Pueblo, Colorado, During the Mexican War," *ibid.* (July, 1932), IX, 121-36; Janet S. Lecompte, "The Hardscrabble Settlement, 1844-1848," *ibid.* (April, 1954), XXXI, 81-98; Francis T. Cheetham, "The Early Settlements of Southern Colorado," *ibid.* (February, 1928), V, 1-8; and Morris F. Taylor, *A Sketch of Early Days on the Purgatory* (Trinidad, 1959).

Frémont's fourth expedition is described in William Brandon, *The Men and the Mountain: Frémont's Fourth Expedition* (New York, 1955); Robert V. Hine, *Edward Kern and American Expansion* (New Haven, 1962). LeRoy R. and Ann W. Hafen have edited materials concerning the expedition in Frémont's *Fourth Expedition: A Documentary Account of the Disaster of 1848-1849...* (Glendale, 1960) as vol. XI of their *Far West and Rockies Series*. In addition, see Alpheus Hoyt Favour, *Old Bill Williams: Mountain Man* (Norman, 1962) and Frank C. Spencer, "The Scene of Frémont's Disaster in the San Juan Mountains, 1848," *The Colorado Magazine* (July, 1929), VI, 141-46.

On Gunnison, see Nolie Mumey, *John Williams Gunnison: The Last of the Western Explorers* (Denver, 1955) and "John Williams Gunnison: Centenary of His Survey and Tragic Death (1853-1953)," *The Colorado Magazine* (January, 1954), XXXI, 19-32; and Leland Hargrave Creer, "The Explorations of

Gunnison and Beckwith in Colorado and Utah, 1853," *ibid.* (September, 1929), VI, 184-92.

Indian relations are described in LeRoy R. Hafen and Francis M. Young, *Fort Laramie and the Pageant of the West* (Glendale, 1938) and two articles by Hafen, "Thomas Fitzpatrick and the First Indian Agency in Colorado," *The Colorado Magazine* (March, 1929), VI, 53-62; and "The Fort Pueblo Massacre and the Punitive Expedition Against the Utes," *ibid.* (March, 1927), 49-58.

On the Mexican land grants and early settlements, see LeRoy R. Hafen "Mexican Land Grants in Colorado," *The Colorado Magazine* (May, 1927), IV, 81-93; Harold H. Dunham, "Coloradans and the Maxwell Grant," *ibid.* (April, 1955), XXXII, 131-45; and Forbes Parkhill, "Colorado's Earliest Settlements," *ibid.* (October, 1957), XXXIV, 241-53. See also Morris F. Taylor, "Fort Massachusetts," *ibid.* (Spring, 1968), XLV, 120-42; and Duane Vandenbusche, "Life at a Frontier Post: Fort Garland," *ibid.* (Spring, 1966), XLIII, 132-48.

Chapter 6   Gold Rush

General accounts of the Gold Rush include James F. Willard, "The Gold Rush and After," which is chapter 5 of *Colorado: Short Studies of Its Past and Present* (Boulder, 1927); chapters 10 and 11, vol. I, "Gold Discoveries and the Founding of Denver" and "The Pike's Peak Gold Rush of 1859" in Hafen, *Colorado and Its People*; and an article incorporating documentary material, Agnes Wright Spring, "Rush to the Rockies, 1859," *The Colorado Magazine* (April, 1959), XXXVI, 83-120. Ovando Hollister, *The Mines of Colorado* (Springfield, 1867) and S. Burt and E. Berthoud, *The Rocky Mountain Gold Regions* (reprint, Denver, 1962) provide firsthand examinations.

The Colorado mining frontier may be related to the general history of western American mining in William S. Greever, *The Bonanza West: The Story of the Western Mining Rushes, 1848-1890* (Norman, 1963) and the shorter but more suggestive study by Rodman W. Paul, *Mining Frontiers of the Far West, 1848-1880* (New York, 1963). For terminology and mining procedures see Otis Young, *Western Mining* (Norman, 1970).

Biographical studies related to the events of the Gold Rush include George C. Barns, *Denver, the Man: The Life, Letters and Public Papers Of the Lawyer, Soldier and Statesman* (Wilmington, Ohio, 1949); Marita Hayes, "D. C. Oakes, Early Colorado Booster," *The Colorado Magazine* (July, 1954), XXXI, 216-26; and Caroline Bancroft, "The Elusive Figure of John Gregory, Discoverer of the First Gold Lode in Colorado," *ibid.* (July, 1943), XX, 121-35. See also the same author's *Gulch of Gold: A History of Central City, Colorado* (Denver, 1958).

James F. Willard, "Spreading the News of the Early Discoveries of Gold in Colorado," *The Colorado Magazine* (May, 1929), VI, 98-104; and "Sidelights on the Pike's Peak Gold Rush, 1858-59," *ibid.* (January, 1935), XII, 3-13, add interesting details. In the *Southwest Historical Series* (Glendale, 1941-42) see three volumes edited by LeRoy R. Hafen: *Pike's Peak Gold Rush Guidebooks of 1859* (vol. IX), *Colorado Gold Rush: Contemporary Letters and Reports, 1858-1859* (vol. X), and *Overland Routes to the Gold Fields, 1859, from Contemporary Diaries* (vol. XI).

The three journalists who reported on the gold fields each left a personal account of his visit: Villard in *The Past and Present of the Pike's Peak Gold Regions*, ed. by LeRoy R. Hafen (Princeton, 1932); Richardson in *Beyond the Mississippi* (Hartford, 1867); and Greeley in *An Overland Journey to San Francisco*, ed. by Charles Duncan (New York, 1964).

Chapter 7   Miners and Merchants

T. A. Rickard's *The History of American Mining* (New York, 1932) and *The Romance of Mining* (Toronto, 1945) are useful general studies. The Colorado experiences are detailed in chapter 9, "Early Mining Methods," Fritz, *Colorado: The Centennial State*; Francis S. Williams, "The Influence of California Upon the Placer Mining Methods of Colorado," *The Colorado Magazine* (April, 1949), XXVI, 127-43; and "Overland to Pike's Peak with a Quartz Mill: Letters of Samuel Mallory," *ibid.* (May, 1931), VIII, 108-15. See also Rodman Paul, "Colorado as a Pioneer of Science in the Mining West," *Mississippi Valley Historical Review* (June, 1960), XLVII, 34-50.

On coinage and minting, see Nolie Mumey, *Clark, Gruber, and Company: A Pioneer Denver Mint* (Denver, 1950) and LeRoy R. Hafen, "Currency, Coinage and Banking in Pioneer Colorado," *The Colorado Magazine* (May, 1933), X, 81-90. Transportation and communication problems are described in Oscar Osburn Winther, *The Transportation Frontier: Trans-Mississippi West 1865-1890* (New York, 1964). See also Arthur Ridgway, "The Mission of Colorado Toll Roads," *The Colorado Magazine* (September, 1932), IX, 161-69; and three articles by LeRoy R. Hafen in the same journal: "Supplies and Market Prices in Pioneer Denver" (August, 1927), IV, 136-42; "Early Mail Service to Colorado, 1858-60" (January, 1925), II, 23-32; and "Pioneer Struggle for a Colorado Road Across the Rockies" (March, 1926), III, 1-10.

Chapter 8   Culture Comes to the Gold Towns

Impressions of early architecture, as well as many other facets of pioneer Colorado's social scene, are captured in the text and invaluable illustrations in Muriel Sibell Wolle's *Stampede to Timberline: The Ghost Towns and Mining Camps of Colorado* (Denver, 1963). Duane A. Smith, *Rocky Mountain Mining Camps, the Urban Frontier* (Bloomington, 1967), presents the overall view.

The early history of the various denominations is traced in Martin Rist, "History of Religion in Colorado," in Hafen, *Colorado and Its People*, II, 199-224. Bishop Machebeuf's life is briefly detailed in Thomas O'Connor, "Bishop Machebeuf," *The Colorado Magazine* (July, 1935), XIII, 130-39. An account of Presbyterianism in pioneer Colorado is Norman J. Bender, "Crusade of the Blue Banner in Colorado," *ibid.* (Spring, 1970), XLVII, 91-118.

Ann W. Hafen and LeRoy R. Hafen, "The Beginnings of Denver University," *The Colorado Magazine* (March, 1947), XXIV, 58-66, gives details on the school's early days, but for broader implications see Michael McGiffert, *The Higher Learning in Colorado: An Historical Study, 1860-1940* (Denver, 1964). The history of Denver's first newspaper, and much of the history of the city and region as well, are imaginatively related in Robert L. Perkin, *The First Hundred Years: An Informal History of Denver and the Rocky Mountain News* (New York, 1959). See also David F. Halaas, "Frontier Journalism in Colorado," *The Colorado Magazine* (Summer, 1967), XLIV, 185-203.

Activities of temperance advocates in Colorado to 1900 are described in Elliott West, "Of Lager Beer and Sonorous Songs," *The Colorado Magazine* (Spring, 1971), XLVIII, 108-28. Entertainment on the mining frontier is described in Melvin Schoberlin, *From Candles to Footlights: A Biography of the Pike's Peak Theater* (Denver, 1941). See also Lynn I. Perrigo, "The First Two Decades of Central City Theatricals," *The Colorado Magazine* (July, 1934), XI, 141-52; Alice Cochran, "Jack Langrishe and the Theater of the Mining Frontier," *ibid.* (Fall, 1969), XLVI, 324-37; and Virginia McConnell, "A

Gauge of Popular Taste in Early Colorado," *ibid.* (Fall, 1969), XLVI, 338-50. Details on the flood of 1864 are given in Albert B. Sanford, "The Big Flood in Cherry Creek, 1864," *ibid.* (May, 1927), IV, 100-5.

Chapter 9   Legal Beginnings

The mining districts have been described by many authors, but the most useful summaries are chapter 7, "The Mining Districts" and chapter 8, "The Influence of the Mining Districts" in Fritz, *Colorado: The Centennial State*; and Thomas Maitland Marshall, "The Miners' Laws of Colorado," *American Historical Review* (April, 1920), XXV, 426-39. See also Henry A. Dubbs, "The Unfolding of Law in the Rocky Mountain Region," *The Colorado Magazine* (October, 1926), III, 113-32.

Other articles in *The Colorado Magazine* describing early government and politics are: Francis S. Williams, "Trials and Judgments of the People's Courts of Denver" (October, 1950), XXVII, 294-302; two articles by George L. Anderson, "The El Paso Claim Club, 1859-1862" (March, 1936), XII, 41-53, and "The Canon City or Arkansas Valley Claim Club, 1860-1862" (November, 1939), XVI, 201-10; "The Middle Park Claim Club, 1861" (September, 1933), X, 189-93; and Milo Fellows, "The First Congressional Election in Colorado (1858)" (March, 1929), VI, 46-47. The constitution of Jefferson Territory is printed in *The Colorado Magazine* (November, 1935), XII, 215-20.

Chapter 10   Warpaths Red and White

Colorado's first two territorial governors are the subjects of modern biographies: Thomas L. Karnes, *William Gilpin, Western Nationalist* (Austin, 1970) and Harry E. Kelsey, *Frontier Capitalist: The Life of John Evans* (Denver, 1969). See also LeRoy R. Hafen, "Colorado's First Legislative Assembly," *The Colorado Magazine* (March, 1943), XX, 41-50.

Confederate activity in southern Colorado is described by Daniel Ellis Conner in *A Confederate in the Colorado Gold Fields*, ed. by Donald J. Berthrong and Odessa Davenport (Norman, 1970), especially 126-57. See also Morris F. Taylor, "Confederate Guerrillas in Southern Colorado," *The Colorado Magazine* (Fall, 1969), XLVI, 304-23; and Duane A. Smith, "The Confederate Cause in the Colorado Territory, 1861-1865," *Civil War History* (March, 1961), VII, 71-80.

Camp Weld is described in Albert B. Sanford, "Camp Weld, Colorado," *The Colorado Magazine* (March, 1934), XI, 46-50. For Colorado and the Civil War, see, generally, Ray C. Colton, *The Civil War in the Western Territories* (Norman, 1959), and more specifically on the New Mexican campaign, William Clarke Whitford, *Colorado Volunteers in the Civil War* (Denver, 1906; reprinted 1963); Ovando J. Hollister, *Boldly They Rode: History of the First Regiment of Colorado Volunteers* (Lakewood, Colo., 1949); and Robert Lee Kerby, *The Confederate Invasion of New Mexico and Arizona 1861-62* (Los Angeles, 1958).

The Fort Wise Treaty and the complex problems surrounding it are analyzed in William E. Unrau, "A Prelude to War," *The Colorado Magazine* (Fall, 1964), XLI, 299-313. Harry E. Kelsey focuses on the role of the agent in "Background to Sand Creek," *ibid.* (Fall, 1968), XLV, 279-300. See also Lillian B. Shields, "Relations with the Cheyennes and Arapahoes in Colorado to 1861," *ibid.* (August, 1927), IV, 145-54.

For a history of the military units involved in the fighting during the era see John N. Nankivell, *History of the Military Organizations of the State of Colorado* (Denver, 1935). One of these is the topic of Blanche V. Adams, "The Second Colorado Cavalry in the Civil War," *The Colorado Magazine* (May, 1931), VIII, 95-106. Raymond G. Carey details the history of the hundred-dayers in "The Bloodless Third' Regiment, Colorado Volunteer Cavalry," *ibid.* (October, 1961), XXXVIII, 275-300.

The Sand Creek affair has attracted the attention of many authors. Good introductions to the topic are Stan Hoig, *The Sand Creek Massacre* (Norman, 1961) and Janet Lecompte, "Sand Creek," *The Colorado Magazine* (Fall, 1964), XLI, 314-35. Raymond G. Carey summarizes the problems of inter-preting the conflicting evidence in "The Puzzle of Sand Creek," *ibid.* (Fall, 1964), XLI, 279-98. A contemporary account by a participant is Lynn I. Perrigo, ed., "Major Hal Sayr's Diary of the Sand Creek Campaign," *ibid.* (March, 1938), XV, 41-57. For modern evaluations of the events, see chapter 11, "Massacre at Sand Creek," in Perkin, *The First Hundred Years;* chapter 9, "Massacre at Sand Creek," in Berthrong, *The Southern Cheyennes;* chapter 14, "The Sand Creek Massacre," in Grinnell, *The Fighting Cheyennes;* and Michael Straight's historical novel, *A Very Small Remnant* (New York, 1963). These writers all condemn the whites' actions. For contrast, see Reginald S. Craig, *The Fighting Parson: The Biography of Colonel John M. Chivington* (Los Angeles, 1959).

The Battle of Beecher Island is described in Berthrong, *The Southern Cheyennes,* 310-17. See also Merrill J. Mattes, ed., "The Beecher Island Battlefield Diary of Sigmund Shlesinger," *The Colorado Magazine* (July, 1952), XXIX, 161-69, and Harry H. Anderson, "Stand at the Arikaree," *ibid.* (Fall, 1964), XLI, 337-42. The most recent account of Summit Springs is Jack D. Filipiak, "The Battle of Summit Springs," *ibid.* (Fall, 1964), XLI, 343-54; an older sketch with the same title is by Clarence Reckmeyer in *ibid.* (November, 1929), VI, 211-20. See also Don Russell, *The Lives and Legends of Buffalo Bill* (Norman, 1960), 129-48; and James T. King, *War Eagle: A Life of General Eugene A. Carr* (Lincoln, 1963), 94-119.

Chapter 11   Smelters and Railroads

Frank Fossett, *Colorado* (New York, 1879) contains much information about mining and smelting; Charles Henderson, *Mining in Colorado* (Washington, 1926) is packed with statistics and mining data. See also Jesse D. Hale, "The First Successful Smelter in Colorado," *The Colorado Magazine* (September 1936), XIII, 161-67. The story of Georgetown is related in John Willard Horner, *Silver Town* (Caldwell, Id., 1950). On Caribou, see John W. Buchanan, "The History of a Ghost Town, Caribou," *The Colorado Magazine* (November, 1944), XXI, 201-7; and David H. Stratton, "The Rise and Decline of Caribou," *ibid.* (April, 1953), XXX, 109-18.

The literature about early Colorado railroads is extensive. An introduction is Elmer Orville Davis, *The First Five Years of the Railroad Era in Colorado* (Golden, 1948). Robert M. Ormes, *Railroads and the Rockies: A Record of Lines in and Near Colorado* (Denver, 1963) is a useful guide. Two articles by ·S. D. Mock in *The Colorado Magazine* provide useful details: "Colorado and the Surveys for a Pacific Railroad" (March, 1940), XVII, 54-63; and "The Financing of Early Colorado Railroads" (November, 1941), XVIII, 201-9.

For the history of individual lines, see Clarence Poor, *Denver, South Park and Pacific* (Denver, 1949); James Marshall, *Santa Fe: The Railroad That Built an Empire* (New York, 1945); and Robert G. Athearn, *Rebel of the Rockies: A History of the Denver and Rio Grande Western Railroad* (New Haven, 1962). The Rio Grande's history may be supplemented with the history of one of its "towns," delightfully narrated by Marshall Sprague in *Newport in the Rockies: The Life and Good Times of Colorado Springs* (Denver, 1961).

Chapter 12 Utopias in the Desert

The most useful survey of colony towns in Colorado is the "Introduction" to James F. Willard and Colin B. Goodykoontz, eds., *Experiments in Colorado Colonization 1869-72* (Boulder, 1926). Willard also edited *The Union Colony at Greeley, 1869-1871* (Boulder, 1918). Additional studies include Kathryn Young, "Pioneer Days in Sterling," *The Colorado Magazine* (March, 1927), IV, 58-63; Nicholas G. Morgan, "Mormon Colonization in the San Luis Valley," *ibid.* (October, 1950), XXVII, 269-93; Dorothy Roberts, "The Jewish Colony at Cotopaxi," *ibid.* (July, 1941), XVIII, 124-31; and Ralph E. Blodgeet, "The Colorado Territorial Board of Immigration," *ibid.* (Summer, 1969), XLVI, 245-56.

Chapter 13 Carpetbaggers' Kingdom

Earl S. Pomeroy, *Territories and the United States* (Philadelphia, 1947) and Howard Lamar, *The Far Southwest 1846-1912* (New Haven, 1966) analyze the relationships between western territories and the federal government. Elmer Ellis, "Colorado's First Fight for Statehood, 1865-1868," *The Colorado Magazine* (January, 1931), VIII, 23-30, and the same author's *Henry Moore Teller: Defender of the West* (Caldwell, Id., 1941) relate the Colorado experiences. Other biographical studies that are useful include William Hanchett, " 'His Turbulent Excellency,' Alexander Cummings, Governor of Colorado Territory, 1865-1867," *The Colorado Magazine* (April, 1957), XXXIV, 81-104; Thomas F. Dawson, "Major Thompson, Chief Ouray and the Utes," *ibid.* (May, 1930), VII, 113-22; and Albert B. Sanford, "John L. Routt, First State Governor of Colorado," *ibid.* (August, 1926), III, 81-86. See also George W. Collins, "Colorado's Territorial Secretaries," *ibid.* (Summer, 1966), XLIII, 185-208; John D. W. Guice, "Colorado's Territorial Courts," *ibid.* (Summer, 1968), XLV, 204-24; Harmon Mothershead, "Negro Rights in Colorado Territory," *ibid.* (July, 1963), XL, 212-23; and Douglas C. McMurtrie, "The Public Printing of the First Territorial Legislature of Colorado," *ibid.* (March, 1936), XIII, 72-78.

Chapter 14 The Centennial State

The debates of the constitutional convention were not officially recorded or published, but the basic order of business is revealed in *Proceedings of the Constitutional Convention* (Denver, 1907). The issues are discussed in Colin B. Goodykoontz, "Some Controversial Questions Before the Colorado Constitutional Convention of 1876," *The Colorado Magazine* (January, 1940), XVII, 1-17. See also Henry J. Hersey, "The Colorado Constitution," *ibid.* (August, 1926), III, 65-76; and Elmer Herbert Meyer, "The Constitution of Colorado," *Iowa Journal of History and Politics* (April, 1904), II, 256-74.

Aspects of life in the new state are described in S. D. Mock, "Effects of the 'Boom' Decade, 1870-1880, Upon Colorado Population," *The Colorado Magazine* (January, 1934), XI, 27-34; Elmo O. Davis, "The Famous Georgetown Loop," *ibid.* (September, 1947), XXIV, 188-90; and David Shaw Duncan, "Higher Education in Colorado," *ibid.* (January, 1937) XIV, 3-14.

Chapter 15   Carbonate Camps

Don L. and Jean Harvey Griswold, *The Carbonate Camp Called Leadville* (Denver, 1951) provides a good introduction to the topic. Carlyle Channing Davis, *Olden Times in Colorado* (Los Angeles, 1916) is a personal, informative memoir by an early Leadville newspaper editor. *History of the Arkansas Valley, Colorado* and Frank Hall's multivolume history offer a varied assortment of information on the camp, its life and people.

Transportation problems are discussed in Elmer R. Burkey, "The Georgetown-Leadville Stage," *The Colorado Magazine* (September, 1937), XIV, 177-87; two articles by Robert G. Athearn, "Origins of the Royal Gorge Railroad War," *ibid.* (January, 1959), XXXVI, 37-57, and "The Captivity of the Denver and Rio Grande," *ibid.* (January, 1960), XXXVII, 1-20; Richard Caroll, "The Founding of Salida, Colorado," *ibid.* (July, 1934), XI, 121-33; and Albert B. Sanford, "The Old South Park Railroad," *ibid.* (October, 1928), V, 173-78.

Other aspects of early Leadville are detailed in Dorothy M. Degitz, "History of the Tabor Opera House at Leadville," *The Colorado Magazine* (May, 1936), XIII, 81-89; and in Donald Fremont Popham, "The Early Activities of the Guggenheims in Colorado," *ibid.* (October, 1950), XXVII, 263-69.

Other towns are described in C. E. Hagie, "Gunnison in Early Days," *The Colorado Magazine* (July, 1931), VIII, 121-29; George A. Root, "Gunnison in the Early 'Eighties," *ibid.* (November, 1932), IX, 201-13; Duane Vandenbusche, ed., "My First Year in the Gunnison Country," *ibid.* (Summer, 1969), XLVI, 220-44; S. E. Poet, "The Story of Tin Cup, Colorado," *ibid.* (January, 1932), IX, 30-38; Nolie Mumey, *Creede: The History of a Colorado Silver Mining Town* (Denver, 1949); and Don and Jean Griswold, *Colorado's Century of Cities* (Denver, 1958).

Chapter 16   Open Range Days

The basic studies of the Colorado cattle industry are Ora Brooks Peake, *The Colorado Range Cattle Industry* (Glendale, 1937); chapter 5, "The Range Livestock Industry" in Alvin T. Steinel, *History of Agriculture in Colorado* (Fort Collins, 1926); and Maurice Frink, W. Turrentine Jackson and Agnes Wright Spring, *When Grass Was King: Contributions to the Western Range Cattle Industry Study* (Boulder, 1956). These may be supplemented with the more general works by Edward Everett Dale, *The Range Cattle Industry* (Norman, 1930), and Walter Prescott Webb, *The Great Plains* (New York, 1931).

Biographical studies of men involved in the cattle enterprises include P. G. Scott, "John W. Prowers, Bent County Pioneer," *The Colorado Magazine* (September, 1930), VII, 183-87; Edgar C. McMechen, "John Hitson, Cattle King," *ibid.* (September, 1934), XI, 164-70; Rufus Phillips, "Early Cowboy Life in the Arkansas Valley," *ibid.* (September, 1930), VII, 165-79. Other studies are: Albert W. Thompson, "The Great Prairie Cattle Company, Ltd.," *ibid.* (March, 1945), XXII, 76-83; Clifford P. Westermeier, "The Legal Status of the Colorado Cattleman, 1867-1887," *ibid.* (May, July, 1948), XXV, 109-18,

157-66; Edward Hayes, "ZA Roundup," *ibid.* (Summer, 1964), XLI, 213-24; and Sue Flanagan, "Charles Goodnight in Colorado," *ibid.* (Winter, 1966), XLIII, 1-21. Range contests in northwestern Colorado are described in John Rolfe Burroughs, *Where the Old West Stayed Young* (New York, 1962).

Chapter 17   Beyond the Continental Divide

Western Slope settlements and towns are described in Harriet Backus, *Tomboy Bride* (Boulder, 1969); Fred Espinosa, "Del Norte—Its Past and Present," *The Colorado Magazine* (June, 1928), V, 95-102; James H. Rankin, "The Founding and Early Years of Grand Junction," *ibid.* (March, 1929), VI, 39-45; Olivia Spalding Ferguson, "A Sketch of Delta County History," *ibid.* (October, 1928), V, 161-64; and Robert Brown, *An Empire of Silver* (Caldwell, Id., 1965). See also LeRoy R. Hafen, "Otto Mears, 'Pathfinder of the San Juan,' " *The Colorado Magazine* (March, 1932), IX, 71-74; and Duane A. Smith, "Silver Coquette–The San Juans, 1860-1875," *Brand Book 1969* (Denver, 1970), 221-52. David Lavender's novel *Red Mountain* (Garden City, 1963) catches the spirit of a vanished age.

Western Slope Indian-white relations are detailed in Marshall Sprague, *Massacre: The Tragedy at White River* (Boston, 1957); Forbes Parkhill, "The Meeker Massacre and Thornburgh Battle: Fact and Fiction," *Brand Book 1945* (Denver, 1946), 91-110; Elmer R. Burkey, "The Thornburgh ·Battle With the Utes on Milk Creek," *The Colorado Magazine* (May, 1936), XIII, 90-110; Walker D. Wyman, "A Preface to the Settlement of Grand Junction: The Uncompahgre Ute 'Goes West'," *ibid.* (January, 1933), X, 22-27.

Chapter 18   Ditchdiggers and Sodbusters

The most useful short account of Colorado's agricultural history is Robert G. Dunbar, "History of Agriculture" in Hafen, *Colorado and Its People*, II, 120-57. See also the previously cited Steinel, *History of Agriculture in Colorado*. Early irrigation is described in Joseph O. Van Hook, "Development of Irrigation in the Arkansas Valley," *The Colorado Magazine* (January, 1933), X, 3-11; and Robert G. Dunbar, "The Origins of the Colorado System of Water-Right Control," *ibid.* (October, 1950), XXVII, 241-62. Millard Fillmore Vance, "Pioneering at Akron, Colorado,"*ibid.* (September, 1931), VIII, 173-77, describes early settlement on the Eastern Slope.

Chapter 19   New Frontiers

Railroad and industrial activities of the era are described in Morris Cafky, *The Colorado Midland* (Denver, 1965); John Burton Phillips, "A Colorado Railroad Pool," in *University of Colorado Studies* (April, 1908), V, 137-48; and the same author's "Freight Rates and Manufactures in Colorado," *ibid.* (December, 1909), VII, 5-62; William S. Jackson, "Railroad Conflicts in Colorado in the 'Eighties," *The Colorado Magazine* (January, 1946), XXIII, 7-25; Ellsworth C. Mitick, "A History of Mining Machinery Manufacture in Colorado," *ibid.* (November, 1947), XXIV, 225-41 and (March and May, 1948), XXV, 75-94, 136-42; and Albert E. Seep, "History of the Mine and Smelter Supply Company," *ibid.* (May, 1946), XXIII, 128-34.

Other developments of the times are detailed in Howard T. Vaille, "Early Years of the Telephone in Colorado," *The Colorado Magazine* (August, 1928), V, 121-33; Elmer S. Crowley, "The Opening of the Tabor Grand Opera House,

1881," *ibid.* (March, 1941), XVIII, 41-48; and John W. Buchanan, *A Story of the Windsor* (Boulder, 1944).

On Cripple Creek and its neighbors, see Marshall Sprague, *Money Mountain: The Story of Cripple Creek* (Boston, 1953); Robert Taylor, *Cripple Creek* (Bloomington, 1966); Edgar McMechen, "The Founding of Cripple Creek," *The Colorado Magazine* (January, 1935), XIII, 28-35; S. E. Poet, "Victor, Colorado—The 'City of Mines,' " *ibid.* (May, 1933), X, 106-14; Leo J. Kenna, "Cripple Creek in 1900," *ibid.* (October, 1953), XXX, 269-75; and Mabel Barbee Lee, *Cripple Creek Days (New York, 1958).* Frank Waters' *Midas of the Rockies* (Denver, 1949) is a biography of Winfield S. Stratton.

Chapter 20   Politics and Populists

The political history of the era is described in Hall, *History of Colorado*, especially vol. III; and in Ellis, *Henry Teller.* See also Richard C. Welty, "The Greenback Party in Colorado," *The Colorado Magazine* (October, 1951), XXVIII, 301-11; and many of the titles listed for the following chapter.

Chapter 21   The Silver Crusade

For the Populists and Governor Waite, see Leon W. Fuller, "Governor Waite and His Silver Panacea," *The Colorado Magazine* (March, 1933), X, 41-47; an example of anti-Populist sentiment is Charles Hartzell, *A Short and Truthful History of Colorado During the Turbulent Reign of 'Davis the First'* (Denver, 1894). Louisa Ward Arps, *Denver in Slices* (Denver, 1959), 104-6, describes relief efforts during the depression. On the Cripple Creek strike, see Stewart H. Holbrook, *The Rocky Mountain Revolution* (New York, 1956); George G. Suggs, Jr., "Catalyst for Industrial Change: The WFM, 1893-1903," *The Colorado Magazine* (Fall, 1968), XLV, 322-39; Oliver M. Dickerson, "The Labor Movement," in Hafen, *Colorado and Its People*, II, 315-17; and Emil W. Pfeiffer, "The Kingdom of Bull Hill," *The Colorado Magazine* (September, 1935), XII, 168-72. On woman suffrage see Billie Barnes Jensen, "Let the Women Vote," *ibid.* (Winter, 1964), XLI, 13-25; and John R. Morris, "The Women and Governor Waite," *ibid.* (Winter, 1967), XLIV, 11-19.

Chapter 22   The Good Old Days

On colonies, see two articles by Dorothy Roberts: "Fort Amity, The Salvation Army Colony in Colorado," *The Colorado Magazine* (September, 1940), XVII, 168-74; and "A Dutch Colony in Colorado," *ibid.* (November, 1940), XVII, 229-36; Ellen Z. Peterson, "Origin of the Town of Nucla," *ibid.* (October, 1949), XXVI, 252-58; and the same author's *The Spell of the Tabeguache* (Denver, 1957). The Dearfield experience is related in *Colorado: A Guide to the Highest State* (New York, 1941).

On travel and tourists see LeRoy R. Hafen, "The Coming of the Automobile and Improved Roads to Colorado," *The Colorado Magazine* (January, 1931), VIII, 1-16; W. H. Jackson, "First Official Visit to the Cliff Dwellings," *ibid.* (May, 1924), I, 151-59; Virginia McClurg, "The Making of Mesa Verde into a National Park," *ibid.* (November, 1930), VII, 216-19. The Mineral Palace is described in Hall, *History of Colorado*, III, 480-83; the Ice Palace in Davis, *Olden Times in Colorado*, 337-51.

Other aspects of the era are described in Levette J. Davidson, "The Festival of Mountain and Plain," *The Colorado Magazine* (July, 1948), XXV, 145-57; Andrew W. Gillette, "The Bicycle Era in Colorado," *ibid.* (November, 1933), X,

213-17; "Hard Rock Drilling Contests in Colorado: As Told by Victor I. Noxon to Forrest Crossen," *ibid.* (May, 1934), XI, 81-85; and "Overland Park," which is chapter 9 of Arps, *Denver in Slices.*

On colleges and universities see Thomas Russell Garth, *The Life of Henry Buchtel* (Denver, 1937); June E. Carothers, "Colorado Woman's College–The Colorado Vassar," *The Colorado Magazine* (October, 1951), XXVIII, 290-98; and J. Manuel Espinosa, "The Neopolitan Jesuits on the Colorado Frontier," *ibid.* (March, 1938), XV, 64-73. Gene Fowler's famous *Timberline* (New York, 1933) continues to delight readers as a study of the era's journalism.

Chapter 23   The Era of Industrial Warfare

For details on the Colorado and Southern, see Richard C. Overton, "The Colorado and Southern Railway: Its Heritage and Its History," *The Colorado Magazine* (April, July, 1949), XXVI, 81-98, 196-219. Edward T. Bollinger and Frederick Bauer, *The Moffat Road* (Denver, 1962), describe this venture in railroading; for the building of the Moffat Tunnel, see suggested readings for Chapter 27.

A book designed to aid in the understanding of the role of organized labor is Harold V. Knight, *Working in Colorado: A Brief History of the Colorado Labor Movement* (Boulder, 1971). On company towns generally see James B. Allen, *The Company Town in the American West* (Norman, 1966). One of labor's battles is described in David L. Lonsdale, "The Fight for an Eight-Hour Day," *The Colorado Magazine* (Fall, 1966)), XLIII, 339-53.

The materials for a study of the Cripple Creek strike tend toward "special pleading" and must be used with care, but see the following: Benjamin M. Rastall, *The Labor History of the Cripple Creek District* (Madison, 1908) is a contemporary publication viewing events from a close range; Emma F. Langdon, *The Cripple Creek Strike* (Denver, 1904) is a pro-union tract; Holbrook, *Rocky Mountain Revolution*, a biography of Harry Orchard, also sets the background for Orchard's acts of violence.

Recent articles on the labor disturbances of the Peabody administration, all by George G. Suggs, Jr., are: "Strike-Breaking in Colorado: Governor James H. Peabody and the Telluride Strike, 1903-1904," *Journal of the West* (October, 1966), V, 454-76; "Prelude to Industrial Warfare: The Colorado City Strike," *The Colorado Magazine* (Summer, 1967), XLIV, 241-62; "Religion and Labor in the Rocky Mountain West: Bishop Nicholas C. Matz and the Western Federation of Miners," *Labor History* (Spring, 1970), XI, 190-206.

The fullest published account of the 1913-1914 coal strike is Barron B. Beshoar, *Out of the Depths* (Denver, 1942), a work generally sympathetic to the union. A contemporary publication on the battle at Ludlow by a UMW official, Walter Fink, *The Ludlow Massacre* (Denver, 1914), indicates something of the tone of events.

Chapter 24   Water and Sugar

The early years of federal reclamation work are described in George Wharton James, *Reclaiming the Arid West: The Story of the United States Reclamation Service* New York, 1917). The story of the first federal project in Colorado is related in Burton W. Marsh, *The Uncompahgre Valley and the Gunnison Tunnel* (Lincoln, 1909); and in Richard G. Beidleman, "The Gunnison River Diversion Project," *The Colorado Magazine* (July, October, 1959), XXXVI, 187-201, 266-85.

Chapter 25   The Progressive Era

For conditions in Denver at the beginning of the twentieth century, see Roland L. DeLorme, "Turn-of-the-Century Denver: An Invitation to Reform," *The Colorado Magazine* (Winter, 1968), XLV, 1-15. On Speer and his administration, see Edgar C. McMechen, *Robert W. Speer: A City Builder* (Denver, 1919). The auditorium and Democratic Convention of 1908 are described in "Denver's Democratic Invasion," *The Colorado Magazine* (Summer, 1964), XLI, 185-97. The history of the capitol and civic center complex is given in Virginia McConnell, "For These High Purposes," *ibid.* (Summer, 1967), XLIV, 204-23. On Denver's park system, see Seth B. Bradley, "The Origin of the Denver Mountain Parks System," *ibid.* (January, 1932), IX, 26-29. For an account of the opposition to Speer and his defeat, see J. Paul Mitchell, "Municipal Reform in Denver: The Defeat of Mayor Speer," *ibid.* (Winter, 1968), XLV, 42-60.

On Judge Lindsey's work, see Ben B. Lindsey and Rube Borough, *The Dangerous Life* (New York, 1931). Elinor Bluemel describes Emily Griffith and her school in *Opportunity School and Emily Griffith, Its Founder* (Denver, 1970).

Reasons for the success of the Republicans in 1902 are discussed in Stephen J. Kneeshaw and John M. Linngren, "Republican Comeback, 1902," *The Colorado Magazine* (Winter, 1971), XLVIII, 15-29. The gubernatorial election of 1904 and its aftermath is described in Marjorie Hornbein, "Three Governors in a Day," *ibid.* (Summer, 1968), XLV, 243-60.

Biographies of two governors of the period are Sewell Thomas, *Silhouettes of Charles S. Thomas: Colorado Governor and United States Senator* (Caldwell, Id., 1959) and Thomas Russell Garth, *Life of Henry Augustus Buchtel* (Denver, 1937). Shafroth and his administration are detailed in E. K. MacColl, "John Franklin Shafroth, Reform Governor of Colorado, 1909-1913," *The Colorado Magazine* (January, 1952), XXIX, 37-52.

For details on the progressive Republican split of 1912, see Charles J. Bayard, "The Colorado Progressive Republican Split of 1912," *The Colorado Magazine* (Winter, 1968), XLV, 61-78; and C. Warren Vander Hill, "Colorado Progressives and the Bull Moose Campaign," *ibid.* (Spring, 1966), XLIII, 93-113. Philip Stewart's relationship with Roosevelt is explored in Charles J. Bayard, "Theodore Roosevelt and Colorado Politics: The Roosevelt-Stewart Alliance," *ibid.* (Fall, 1965), XLII, 311-26. For details of Costigan's life and career, see Colin B. Goodykoontz, *Papers of Edward P. Costigan Relating to the Progressive Movement in Colorado 1902-1917* (Boulder, 1941). On the national level, see Robert Earl Smith, "Colorado's Progressive Senators and Representatives," *The Colorado Magazine* (Winter, 1968), XLV, 27-41. Judicial recall is discussed in Duane A. Smith, "Colorado and Judicial Recall," *American Journal of Legal History* (July, 1963), VII, 197-209.

Chapter 26   State and Nation

For accounts of the discovery and mining of rare metals, see Lee Emerson Deets, "Paradox Valley—An Historical Interpretation of Its Structure and Changes," *The Colorado Magazine* (September, 1934), XI, 186-98; T. M. McKee, "Early Discovery of Uranium Ore in Colorado," *ibid.* (July, 1955), XXXII, 191-203; and Percy Stanley Fritz, "Tungsten and the Road to War," *University of Colorado Studies*, Series C (Boulder, 1941), 195-205. Duane Vandenbusche and Rex Meyers, *Marble, Colorado* (Denver, 1970) is an account of a different mineral.

Chapter 27   The Twenties

Articles in *The Colorado Magazine* describing events of the decade include James H. Davis, "Colorado Under the Klan" (Spring, 1965), XLII, 93-108; Irwin Thomle, "Rise of the Vegetable Industry in the San Luis Valley" (April, 1949), XXVI, 112-25; Mary Rait, "Development of the Peach Industry in the Colorado River Valley" (November, 1945), XXII, 247-58; Ralph Carr, "Delph Carpenter and River Compacts Between Western States" (January, 1944), XXI, 4-14; Guy E. Macy, "The Pueblo Flood of 1921" (November, 1940), XVII, 201-11; Ernest Morris, "A Glimpse of Moffat Tunnel History" (March, 1927), IV, 63-70. On the tunnel, see also Edgar Carlisle McMechen, *The Moffat Tunnel of Colorado* (2 vols., Denver, 1927).

Chapter 28   Depression Decade

Bernard Mergen describes the workings of the Unemployed Citizens' League of Denver in "Denver and the War on Unemployment," *The Colorado Magazine* (Fall, 1970), XLVII, 326-37. The *Pacific Historical Review*, vol. XXXVIII (August, 1969), was devoted entirely to the New Deal in the West. Among the articles are James P. Wickens, "The New Deal in Colorado," 275-91; and James T. Patterson, "The New Deal in the West," 317-27. See Wickens, "Tightening the Colorado Purse Strings," *The Colorado Magazine* (Fall, 1969), XLVI, 271-86, for an account of Colorado's fiscal "crises" during the twenties and thirties. John A. Brennan unravels the complexities of the silver issue in *Silver and the First New Deal* (Reno, 1969).

For accounts of trans-mountain diversion projects, see Oliver Knight, "Correcting Nature's Error: The Colorado-Big Thompson Project," *Agricultural History* (October, 1956), XXX, 157-69; Donald Barnard Cole, "Trans-mountain Water Diversion in Colorado," *The Colorado Magazine* (March, May, 1948), XXV, 49-63, 118-35; and Fred N. Norcross, "Genesis of the Colorado-Big Thompson Project," *ibid.* (January, 1953), XXX, 29-37.

Chapter 29   Life in Colorado Between Two Wars

The history of welfare in Colorado is best summarized in Efay Nelso Grigg, "Social Legislation and the Welfare Program," which is chapter 12, vol. II of Hafen, *Colorado and Its People*. There is also much information in the various publications of the Colorado League of Women Voters; these generally are concerned with contemporary problems, but collectively they form excellent introductions to a variety of special topics. An analysis of the pension amendment's early effects is Don C. Sowers, "Old Age Pensions in Colorado," University of Colorado *Bulletin*, vol. XXXVII (October, 1938).

The growth of tourism these years is particularly well described in Earl Pomeroy, *In Search of the Golden West: The Tourist in Western America* (New York, 1957). On national monuments, see Frank C. Spencer, "Colorado's Desert of Shifting Sand," *The Colorado Magazine* (September, 1924), I, 241-51; and Mark T. Warner, "Black Canyon of the Gunnison National Monument," *ibid.* (May, 1934), XI, 86-97. On the Central City opera, see Bancroft, *Gulch of Gold*, 334-54. For a young man's view, see David Lavender's *One Man's West* (New York, 1943).

Chapter 30   The 1940s: A Colorado Watershed

Chapter 31, "World War II," in Hafen, *Colorado and Its People*, describes changes and events in the state during the era. The regional setting is provided in Robert G. Athearn, *High Country Empire* (New York, 1960). Sprague, *Newport in the Rockies*, details the Air Force Academy story. The *Colorado Year Book*, published periodically during these years, offers a host of facts, as do numerous state and federal publications.

Chapter 31   Mid-Century Challenges

Chapter 32   Colorado Today

Recent events in Colorado need to be interpreted and analyzed. The sources available are voluminous and only await the appearance of the imaginative researcher. The newspapers provide a mine of material, as do government documents. Nor should oral history be overlooked as an invaluable resource. The computer offers the scholar new possibilities; the statistics are available in many areas.

Current information and statistics on Colorado can be obtained from the Colorado Division of Commerce and Development, Denver. On tourism, see *A Profile of the Tourist Market in Colorado, 1968.*, issued in Denver in 1969 by the Denver Research Institute, University of Denver. *The National Register of Historic Places, 1969* (Washington, c. 1970) briefly describes the workings of the National Register of Historic Places and lists sites state by state.

Index